Building English Skills

Yellow Level

Building English Skills   Purple Level

Building English Skills   Yellow Level

Building English Skills   Blue Level

Building English Skills   Orange Level

Building English Skills   Green Level

Building English Skills   Red Level

Building English Skills

Yellow Level

Prepared by the Staff of
The Writing Improvement Project

McDougal, Littell & Company
Evanston, Illinois

Staff of THE WRITING IMPROVEMENT PROJECT

Alice E. Johnson, Librarian, Evanston Township High School, Evanston, Illinois

Marilyn V. Kemp, Chairperson, English Department, New Trier Township High School East, Winnetka, Illinois

Eric Kraft, Writer and Editor, Stow, Massachusetts

Joy Littell, Editorial Director, McDougal, Littell & Company

Robert J. Lumsden, Evanston Township High School, Evanston, Illinois

William A. Seabright, Director of Design, McDougal, Littell & Company

Agnes Stein, English Department, Bloomfield College, Bloomfield, New Jersey

Marcia Baldwin Whipps, East High School, Salt Lake City, Utah

The Staff wishes to thank the more than 1500 students who contributed samples of their writing for analysis.

Acknowledgments: See page 282

ISBN: 0-88343-468-7

Chapters 1–6 and the Handbook contain, in revised form, some materials that appeared originally in *English Arts and Skills,* by Ronald J. Wilkins et al., copyright © 1965, 1961 by The Macmillan Company. Used by arrangement.

Contents

The page numbers for the Handbook (the second half of this book) appear in red.

Handbook

The page numbers for the Handbook (the second half of this book) appear in red.

8.0 Verb Usage 151

9.0 The Right Word 170

10.0 Capitalization 179

11.0 End Marks and Commas 190

12.0 The Semicolon, the Colon, the Dash, and Parentheses 204

13.0 The Apostrophe 212

14.0 Quotations 220

Building English Skills

Yellow Level

Chapter 1

Developing Your Vocabulary

How important are words? Think how little you would know without them. Think how little you could tell others without them. When you share facts, ideas, and feelings with other people, you put words to work for you. You can share your knowledge and experience only to the extent that you have words to work with, only to the extent that you can put your knowledge and experience into words. And you can understand the knowledge and experience of others only to the extent that you understand their words.

What do you do when you meet a word that you don't know in your reading? Do you stop dead in your tracks? Do you skip the section where the word appears and try to pick up at some later point? If so, you probably realize that you've missed something and that your comprehension has suffered because of what you've missed. You know that you *should* check the meaning of the word that stopped you, but it is not always possible or practical to run to a dictionary. How else can you understand the meaning of an unfamiliar word?

The purpose of this chapter and the next is to give you tools to pry loose the meanings of words that you don't know. There are ways to approach the meaning of a word besides looking it up. One method is to study the passage in which the word appears; this method will be discussed in this chapter. Another is to study the parts of the word itself to see if you can determine part of the word's meaning from them; examining word parts is the subject of Chapter 2. If you learn to use these tools and practice using them in your own reading, you will be better able to communicate with the people around you. You will be better able to understand what they say and write and better able to make yourself understood.

Part 1

Learning Word Meanings from Context

Getting the meaning of a word from its **context,** or the passage in which it occurs, is not a new practice for you. When you were learning to talk, you picked up new words and learned their meanings by hearing them in context. When you were learning to read, many words that you did not know immediately by sight became clear because of surrounding words that you did know. If in your reading now you consciously search the context when you meet a new word, you will often find some meaning revealed.

What Context Reveals

Usually the context does not actually define a word. It gives *clues* to the word's meaning. You will have to find and use these clues. You will have to make associations between words that are familiar to you and the word that is not. You will have to put together whatever suggestions of meaning you can find and construct your own definition.

> It is feared that the noise and smoke of the new factory will cause a great *exodus* of residents from the area.

You will not find the word *exodus* defined in the sentence above. You can assume, though, that noise and smoke are not desirable to residents. Then perhaps you can guess that one definition of *exodus* is "departure."

Most words have several possible meanings. Context will offer clues to only one of these meanings, but it will be the one meaning that applies to the passage you are reading. The way a word is used in a passage determines its meaning in the passage.

> Turkey grows a large quantity of the poppies from which heroin is made. The United States has put pressure on the Turkish government to control the farming of poppies. The State Department maintains that the illegal *traffic* in narcotics will never stop as long as Turkish farmers are legally prospering from it.

The word *traffic* probably is used most often to refer to the movement of vehicles. Here we have a *traffic in narcotics*, a different kind of traffic. A dictionary will tell you that another possible meaning of *traffic* is "trade." Does that meaning fit here?

Sometimes the context simply does not give enough clues for you to understand a word. In that case you have no choice. If you want to know the meaning of the word, you will have to turn to a dictionary.

> The flowers were *dessicated* and packaged.

There is not enough information in the sentence to allow you to make a good guess at the meaning of *dessicated*. A fuller context would give more clues:

> The flowers were *dessicated* on a drying rack then ground into a powder and placed in a satin pouch, where they would give off a sweet smell for years to come.

From the passage you know that the flowers were dessicated

on a drying rack, and that it was possible after that to grind them into a powder. Those clues should suggest to you that *dessicated* is related to *dried*.

Exercises
What Context Reveals

A. In each sentence below, look for clues to the meaning of the word in italics. Try to define the word or at least to describe its meaning.

1. Because of his unusual *aptitude* with numbers, Robert decided to become an accountant.
2. During the campaign, the senator had made many promises to his *constituents*.
3. Sometimes an ex-convict's *notoriety* as a criminal prevents him from getting a job even if he sincerely wants to "go straight."
4. When he finished unpacking the dishes, there was *excelsior* all over the floor.
5. The *trajectory* of the ball carried it over the outfield and into the stands.

B. The word *standard* has many meanings. What does it mean in each of the sentences below?

1. She hoped to live up to her mother's standards of honesty in her business dealings.
2. Leading each delegation in the Olympic parade was a standard-bearer carrying the colors of his or her country.
3. The first books a college library must acquire are the standard reference works in each discipline.
4. Applicants must meet the standards of the university to be considered for admission.
5. Standard pronunciation of American English is quite different from that of the various regional dialects.

C. Which of the following sentences contain context clues to the meaning of the word in italics? What are the clues?

1. Robin was usually *cantankerous*.

2. The *edifice* would be nine stories tall.

3. Marty hated to work with Robin when she was in a *cantankerous* mood.

4. Rogers was accused of *embezzling*.

5. The philanthropist hoped to gain immortality by having the college library, an imposing nine-story *edifice*, named after her.

6. Rogers was accused of *embezzling* company funds by falsifying bank statements and making unauthorized deposits in a Swiss bank account.

Part 2

How Context Reveals Meaning

Sometimes context clarifies meaning in a very deliberate manner. You can almost sense as you read that the writer knew that a word would be unfamiliar to you and took the trouble to help you understand it. A writer can do this in any of several ways.

Restatement

If a writer suspects that readers will not understand a word, he or she may restate the concept; that is, the writer may put the concept in other words. Certain phrases and words signal a restatement of a thought. These words and phrases may be used in other ways as well, but when they follow an unfamiliar word, you can consider them signals of a restatement.

in other words	this means
that is	which is to say
to put it another way	or

Gandhi revived Thoreau's technique of *civil disobedience;* **that is,** he passively refused to comply with government regulations that affected his personal life.

Notice how the words *that is* shout out that a restatement follows.

Another kind of restatement is the appositive, in which the signal is usually a pair of commas.

> Thomas Jefferson, our third president, is responsible for the decimal money system we have today.

The appositive tells you that "Thomas Jefferson" and "our third president" are one and the same.

The simplest kind of restatement uses a form of the verb *be* to connect the unfamiliar word to a restatement of it.

> A rapier **is** a straight, two-edged sword with a narrow, pointed blade.

This type of restatement you know as a definition.

Example

Sometimes it is hard to define a word simply, but giving an example makes the meaning clear. Think how often in conversation someone says, "I can't explain it to you, but let me give you an example." The words listed below, though they may be used in other ways, are often a writer's way of saying "let me give you an example."

such as	for example
such	for instance
like	other
as	this *or* these
especially	(followed by a synonym)

Notice in the following examples how the signal words and the restatements they introduce work to clarify the meanings of the words in italics.

> **Like other** mental illnesses, *paranoia* can prevent a person from living a normal life.

Here both *like* and *other* signal that paranoia is a kind of mental illness.

As an apprentice baker, Andy practiced making elaborate *confections*. Unfortunately, **these** tarts, eclairs, and cream pies were often judged inedible by the pastry chef.

Ginseng and **other** herbs are valued for the vitality they are supposed to impart.

The speaker's remarks were largely *derogatory*. **For instance,** he charged the candidate with being insensitive to the problems of unemployment, sky-rocketing property taxes, and the high cost of energy.

Comparison

Like an example, a comparison gives you information about an unfamiliar word, but does not provide a definition. Comparisons demonstrate associations between two words or concepts. These associations can suggest meanings to you. Some of the words that signal an example also signal a comparison:

like	in the same way
as	the way
similar to	

The following examples show how comparison works to provide clues to meaning.

A *jonquil* is a bulb similar to a daffodil.

You do not get a full definition of *jonquil* in the sentence, but you do get a picture of what it is like.

This change in policy could be as *cataclysmic* as the earthquake we all dread.

The word *cataclysmic* is not defined, but you are told that an earthquake is cataclysmic, which is a clue to the word's meaning.

Contrast

In a contrast, the *dissimilarity* of two things gives you a clue to the meaning of a word. In effect, you work backwards to find the meaning of the word, because a contrast tells you not what a word means, but something that it does *not* mean. Again, certain words often signal a contrast:

but	on the other hand
although	as opposed to
on the contrary	unlike

Notice how the signal words and the contrasts they introduce give you clues to the italicized words in the following examples.

> Mr. McCabe introduced the judge with words of praise, although in private his words had been quite *disparaging*.

The word *although* signals that words of praise are different from disparaging words.

> Unlike a police force, *vigilante groups* assume no responsibility for assuring suspected criminals their protection under the law.

The word *unlike* signals that the police force and vigilante groups differ in at least one respect, that of assuring legal protection to suspects. This distinction gives you some clue to the meaning of *vigilante groups*, although it does not give you the definition of the term.

Exercises
How Context Reveals Meaning

A. On a piece of paper, write the numbers 1 through 10. For each numbered sentence on the next page, choose the letter of the answer that best explains the italicized word. Following the letter, write the context clue or clues that led you to the answer you chose.

1. He had lived a life of *rectitude* in the service of the public, but his biographer uncovered some private sins.

    a. luxury   c. virtue
    b. triumph   d. difficulty

2. By studying his *genealogy*, or family tree, Mark discovered that he was a descendant of John Adams.

    a. family history   c. political documents
    b. genetics   d. biography of a famous person

3. To operate in the black, a private college must have a sizeable *endowment*; that is, it must supplement tuition income with bequests from private donors.

    a. administration building   c. private donations
    b. alumni organization   d. government grant

4. The *porgy* was much more colorful than the other fish in the aquarium.

    a. pig   c. aquatic mammal
    b. fish d. seaweed

5. The mime troupe, dramatic club, and other local *thespians* will convene Saturday for a day-long workshop.

    a. organizations   c. singers
    b. Greeks   d. actors

6. The optometrist, unlike the *ophthalmologist*, cannot prescribe drugs or perform surgery.

    a. dental technician   c. one who fits glasses
    b. M. D. eye specialist d. pharmacist

7. Within the atom are particles like the *positron* that exist for only a very short time.

    a. brief moment   c. subatomic particle
    b. atom   d. experiment

8. A cow is an *herbivore*; that is, it feeds on plants.

    a. botanist   c. cannibal
    b. mystic   d. vegetarian

9. The pears she had picked for lunch looked *succulent,* although there were many left on the tree that were still hard and not yet ripe.

    a. green   c. hard
    b. juicy   d. large

10. Modern pewter consists of a combination of copper, tin, and antimony. This *alloy* is quite soft and presents some problems to the metalsmith.

    a. mixture of metals   c. hardware
    b. bowl   d. chemical

B. Choose a magazine article on any subject that interests you. Find every instance in which the writer has made use of the context clues described in this chapter to explain a word that might be unfamiliar to a reader. For each instance, copy the sentence or sentences in which these clues appear. Underline each word for which the writer has given context clues. Write a definition for each of these words.

C. The sentences that follow are taken from an article on cell biology. Write each of the italicized words on a sheet of paper. Following each word, write a definition for it based on what you can learn from context clues. Then list the clue or clues that led you to your definition. Finally, compare your definition with a dictionary definition for the word.

1. Cells use hormones—*insulin,* for example—to order other cells to respond to such conditions as too much sugar in the bloodstream.

2. Eventually it should be technically possible to make limitless copies, or *clones,* of people considered to be desirable.

3. *Lysosomes* also serve as cell janitors, aiding in the removal of old or defective cells from the system.

4. When your antibodies win the battle with invading cold germs they make you *immune.* On the other hand, when they lose the battle, you come down with a cold.

5. Some scientists say that cancer is caused by *mutations,* alterations in a cell's DNA, that prevent key genes from working properly.

6. Pasteur destroyed the popular belief that microorganisms arise by *spontaneous generation*. On the contrary, he said, each microbe comes from an existing microbe.

Part 3

Inferring Meaning from Context

You will not always be able to pluck the meaning of a word from its context as you did in the examples you just worked. More often, getting the meaning of a word from its context will require you to probe and hunt and put many small clues together. You will have to work your way bit by bit from the known to the unknown; that is, you will have to **infer** meaning. The connections between the unknown and the known will not always be clearly marked, and they will not always be clearly stated. You will have to look for and find these connections to conquer the unknown.

Inference from Form

The form or structure of the context sometimes gives clues to the meaning of a word. A repeated sentence pattern suggests associations between words, as in this example:

> High inflation foreshadows economic slowdown. High unemployment *portends* less spending for consumer goods.

The word *portends* is linked to the word *foreshadows* by the structure of the sentences. Both sentences follow the same pattern, with *portends* and *foreshadows* fitting into identical slots in the pattern.

If an unfamiliar word appears in a list, you may sometimes be able to determine its meaning from what you know about the meanings of the other words in the list.

On one game farm you can see a herd of elephants, a *pride* of lions, and a pack of wolves in their natural habitats.

The word *pride* is structurally linked to the words *herd* and *pack*, and their meanings are linked as well.

The repetition of key words may clarify the meaning of an unfamiliar word.

The development of motor coordination in a child is *antecedent* to the development of judgment. This gap in development is a time of great trial for the child's parents, who will find the child ready to scale the heights of stairways and furniture but not yet ready to judge the dangers involved.

Here the repetition of the word *development* makes a connection between motor coordination and judgment. The repetition of key words related to time—*development, gap, time, ready, not yet ready*—should show you that the connection is one of time. From the sense of the second sentence, which uses the same time sequence as the first, you should be able to tell that *is antecedent to* means "precedes" or "comes before."

Look also for connecting words that give some clue to an unfamiliar word. Words like *besides, however, but, yet, nevertheless,* and *despite* establish positive or negative connections between two words and the thoughts they represent. These connectives tell you whether to expect similarity or dissimilarity between the thoughts and words they connect.

Besides *migraines,* Millie also suffered from arthritis.

You can see that the word *besides* makes a positive connection between migraines and arthritis. You can't conclude from the context that a migraine is a headache, but you can see that it is some sort of malady.

When Maria began to sing, she was very aware of the audience, and her voice was *tremulous.* However, as she continued she began to get involved in the music, and her voice became strong and clear.

The word *however* should suggest to you a negative connection between a tremulous voice and a strong and clear one.

Inference from Content

In attempting to understand an unfamiliar word, ask yourself questions about the content or message of the context.

1. Does the main idea of the passage shed some light on the meaning of the word?
2. Are there descriptive words, phrases, or clauses that apply to the word?
3. Is there a hidden restatement, example, comparison, or contrast—one not highlighted by a signal word?

Ask yourself each of the questions as you read the following examples and attempt to determine the meanings of the italicized words.

> There is much to be said for a *rototiller*, even for the backyard gardener. It turns out and aerates the soil, rips up roots that would steal soil nutrients from the vegetables to be planted, and mixes lime and fertilizer throughout the top layer of soil.

The entire passage reveals what a rototiller is and what it does; the function of the rototiller is the main idea of the passage.

> In his own brutal and disrespectful way, Sam took every opportunity to *desecrate* the school with contemptuous acts. He wrote graffiti on the walls, tore locker doors from their hinges, and threw a baseball through a window.

The meaning of the word *desecrate* is described by the phrases *in his own brutal and disrespectful way*, and *with contemptuous acts*. These descriptive phrases offer some clues to the meaning of the word. In addition, the second sentence gives examples—though no signal word introduces them—of acts of desecration.

> The impact of Dr. Margolin's research was *vitiated* by lack of evidence. Had he submitted statistical data in support of his theory, his work would have been more highly regarded by the medical profession.

A contrast is established in these two sentences, but there is no signal word to help you spot it. The subject is Margolin's research. Its vitiated impact is contrasted with high regard. From that contrast you must first make the decision that research with vitiated impact is not held in very high regard. From that decision you must move further: work held in high regard would be said to have a strong impact. Once you have identified the contrast and made the connection, you are in a good position to discover some meaning for the word *vitiated*.

Exercises
Inferring Meaning from Context

A. In the following passages are italicized words for you to define. Try to discover a meaning for each word from its context. Be ready to explain what clues led you to your definition.

1

There are long periods of silence where one hears only the *winnowing* of snipe, the hoot of a distant owl, or the nasal clucking of some amorous coot.—ALDO LEOPOLD

2

Zeus is represented as falling in love with one woman after another and descending to all manner of tricks to hide his *infidelity* from his wife.—EDITH HAMILTON

3

The French Revolution has given pleasure to all *subsequent* generations, because it was an outstanding event which afterwards proved never to have happened.—REBECCA WEST

4

There are, of course, people who like to draw a line between pure and applied science—and oddly, they are often the same people who find art unreal. To them, the word "useful" is a final *arbiter*, either for or against a work; and they use this word as if it can mean only what makes a man feel heavier after meals.—J. BRONOWSKI

5

Today I fought the King of Barodia, and considering that, most unfairly, he was using a Magic Sword, I think I may say that I did well. The Countess Belvane will be interested to hear that I made 4,638 strokes at my opponent and *parried* 4,637 strokes from him.—A. A. MILNE

6

A bramble caught hold of her skirt, and checked her progress. When she began to *extricate* herself it was by turning round and round, and so unwinding the prickly switch.
—THOMAS HARDY

7

And his laugh was frankly vulgar; he seemed in his *hilarity* to be recklessly trying to rip down all the illusions that one supposed him to have been at such pains to build up.
—LOUIS AUCHINCLOSS

8

Hunting is sometimes thought to represent a basic "instinct" in human nature, and certainly there is something *elemental* and primitive in the thrill of the chase.—MARSTON BATES

9

The adventures of the evening so *disconcerted* me, that I could not sleep all night.—FANNY BURNEY

10

From the weighing tanks the raw milk is pumped through a *clarifier* that whirls out fine dust particles as well as blood cells from the cow that are often present in the milk.
—CAROLYN MEYER

B. Look up each of the words in the list below. Write a sentence or two using each word in a way that will make its meaning clear to your readers.

pellucid	fulminate
penchant	eulogize
judicious	mandate

Part 4

Gaining Precision in the Use of Words

The launching of a rocket, the assembly of an automobile engine, and the service of a tennis ball must all be done with *precision* to be done well. Precision is also a mark of skill in writing and speaking.

If you say more or less what you mean, you will be more or less understood, but if you say precisely what you mean you will be precisely understood, and your words will have force and impact. To develop precision in your use of language, you must select your words carefully. To be able to select your words carefully, you must be aware of synonyms and antonyms. They hold the key to accuracy of word choice.

Using Synonyms

Synonyms are words that have similar meanings. Most synonyms do not mean exactly the same thing. Knowing the small differences in meaning between two synonyms enables you to use each word precisely.

Learning sets of synonyms through attentive listening and reading is a slow and gradual process. A more direct method is to study synonymies in a dictionary or thesaurus. A **synonymy** lists synonyms and points out slight differences in meaning among them.

To get an idea of how a synonymy works, look at the entry for the word *heavy* reproduced from *Webster's New World Dictionary, Students Edition*. Following the definitions listed for the word is a synonymy comparing the meanings of *heavy*, *weighty*, *ponderous*, *massive*, and *cumbersome*.

Dictionary Entry for Heavy

heav·y (hev′ē) **adj. heav′i·er, heav′i·est** [OE. *hefig* < base of *hebban*, to HEAVE + *-ig*, -Y²] **1.** hard to lift or move because of great weight; weighty **2.** of great weight for the size [lead is a *heavy* metal] **3.** above the usual or a defined weight **4.** larger, greater, rougher, more intense, etc. than usual [a *heavy* blow, a *heavy* vote, a *heavy* sea, *heavy* thunder, *heavy* features] **5.** going beyond the average; to a greater than usual extent [a *heavy* drinker] **6.** serious; grave [a *heavy* responsibility] **7.** oppressive; burdensome [*heavy* demands] **8.** hard to do or manage; difficult [*heavy* work] **9.** hard to bear [*heavy* sorrow] **10.** burdened with grief; sorrowful [a *heavy* heart] **11.** burdened with sleep or fatigue [*heavy* eyelids] **12.** hard to digest [a *heavy* meal] **13.** not leavened properly [a *heavy* cake] **14.** clinging; penetrating [a *heavy* odor] **15.** cloudy; gloomy [a *heavy* sky] **16.** tedious; dull [*heavy* humor] **17.** clumsy; awkward [a *heavy* gait] ☆**18.** steeply inclined [a *heavy* grade] **19.** designating any large, basic industry that uses massive machinery **20.** designating, of, or equipped with heavy weapons, armor, etc. ☆**21.** [Slang] very good or pleasing: a general term of approval ☆**22.** [Slang] important, significant, profound, etc. **23.** *Chem.* designating an isotope of greater atomic weight than the normal or most abundant isotope **24.** *Theater* serious, tragic, or villainous **—adv.** heavily [*heavy*-laden] **—n.,** *pl.* **heav′ies 1-** something heavy **2.** *Theater a)* a serious, tragic, or villainous role *b)* an actor who plays such roles **—hang heavy** to pass in a slow, boring way; drag: said of time **—heavy with child** pregnant

SYN.—heavy implies greater weight than is usual for its size [a tiny box which was surprisingly *heavy*] and is used to suggest a pressing down on the mind or spirits [*heavy* sorrow]; **weighty** implies absolute rather than relative heaviness and is used to suggest great importance [*weighty* matters of state]; **ponderous** applies to something that is very heavy because of its bulk and is used to suggest dullness and a lack of grace [a *ponderous* lecture, full of complicated sentences]; **massive** stresses great size and solidness but not necessarily great weight and suggests an impressiveness due to great scope [a *massive* study of pollution control]; **cumbersome** applies to something that is difficult to handle because it is heavy and bulky, and suggests clumsiness [*cumbersome* rules that hinder change] **—ANT. light**

If you had looked up the word *massive* instead of the word *heavy*, you would have found the note "see **SYN.** at HEAVY." This cross reference will be found at the entry for each word appearing in a synonymy. The synonymy itself is given at the entry for the word with the broadest meaning.

After studying the distinctions drawn between the meanings of the words listed as synonyms for *heavy*, you will see that you cannot assume that synonyms can be used interchangeably. You might speak of a massive building, but not a heavy one. You might talk about a cumbersome package rather than a weighty one. You might use the word *ponderous* to describe a style of writing, but the word *massive* wouldn't do. Each of these words has its own uses, even though they all share the same general meaning. Try writing a sentence for each word in which you employ the special meaning of the word. Then try substituting the others in the sentence to see how the meaning is distorted.

If you were not aware of these synonyms, you might use the word *heavy* when you meant to express the meaning specific to one of its synonyms. You would have been settling for a general meaning when a specific one was required to make your point forcefully. The force of your point would have been diminished. Learning synonyms will help you broaden your vocabulary, expanding the range of words available to you, and enabling you to express your ideas with precision.

Exercises
Using Synonyms

A. Consult a dictionary to find synonyms for the word *approve*. Rewrite each of the following sentences, substituting a synonym for the word *approved*. The synonym you choose should express more precisely the idea put forward in the sentence.

1. Water from the new reservoir cannot be used until the Department of Health has *approved* its quality.

2. Congressman McNeil has *approved* passage of the tax reform bill.

3. A person normally develops the moral standards *approved* by the community of which he or she is a part.

4. The results of the match were meaningless, because the new playing surface had not been *approved* by the Lawn Tennis Association.

5. Commissioner Daniels wanted it made clear that accepting gifts was a practice not *approved* by her office.

B. In the following sentences words have been used that do not convey a precise and appropriate meaning. Find synonyms for the italicized words in each sentence and use a more accurate and forceful word to express the idea.

1. His generosity would *get* him the reputation of having a deep concern for all in the community.

2. When Peter dropped the bowl, it *crashed* into numberless pieces.

3. When her dog died, she became *hopeless* and brooded over its death for months.

4. The warden *asked* the prisoners about the events leading to the disruption.

5. After failing to win the approval of the judges for the third time, Michael felt *sad* and resolved never to play the piano again.

C. Answer the following questions. Use a dictionary as necessary.

1. If someone told you that you were clever, would you be pleased? Would you feel the same if you were told that you were cunning?

2. How does a silent person differ from a reticent one? Would you prefer to try to converse with a reserved person or a taciturn one? Why?

3. Review the meanings of the synonyms *shock, startle, paralyze,* and *stun.* Would a diner in an expensive restaurant be startled or shocked if he were served a bowl of soup with a mouse in it? How would other diners react if he screamed? How would the cook feel if he were fired immediately without an explanation?

4. If you have offended a person, have you necessarily insulted the person? Explain.

5. Is someone who is experiencing lethargy in a stupor as well? Explain.

6. Should you assume that a faithful churchgoer is staunchly religious? Explain.

7. If Jim is always civil to Valerie, does that mean that he is courteous? What sort of behavior would lead Valerie to consider him gallant?

8. Are you more likely to get out of bed on a cold morning if you are reluctant to get up or averse to getting up? Explain.

9. Do you admire everyone you respect? Explain.

10. When the buffalo roam, do they ramble? Explain.

D. Write a sentence using each of the following words in a way that conveys a precise meaning that could not be conveyed as well by its synonyms.

1. sincere, unaffected, heartfelt
2. show, display, exhibit, expose, flaunt
3. expect, anticipate, hope, await
4. contain, hold, accommodate
5. rational, reasonable, sensible

Using Antonyms

Antonyms are words that are opposite in meaning. An antonym of *shy* is *bold*. An antonym of *cold* is *hot*. The word *warm* contrasts with *cold*, but is not an antonym for it, because it is not at the opposite pole in meaning.

You will find antonyms listed at the end of some synonymies in dictionaries. These antonyms are roughly opposite in meaning to all the words in the synonymy. Remember, however, that a rough meaning is not what you want to convey; you want to convey a precise one. You will have to take note of the differences in meaning among the antonyms and choose them carefully.

You can use an antonym to make a contrast, which can strengthen and clarify what you are saying. In this way, antonyms, like synonyms, will make your writing more precise.

Exercises
Using Antonyms

A. Answer the following questions. Use a dictionary as necessary.

1. While making your first salad dressing, you discover that oil and vinegar are immiscible. You are surprised. What had you expected the ingredients to do?

2. If your doctor tells you that your blood is deficient in iron, what does he mean? How would he describe the opposite condition?

3. Describe a person with base motives. Describe a person with the opposite characteristics. What word would you use to describe the second person's motives?

4. A pessimist expects the worst. Who takes the view that everything will work out for the best?

5. If you still can't add and subtract, you are inept with numbers. If you spend your spare time doing differential calculus, what word would describe your way with mathematics?

B. Decide which of the following pairs of words are true antonyms. Check your decisions in a dictionary.

1. belief—distrust
2. dark—white
3. rural—suburban
4. young—senile
5. tall—shallow
6. inimical—friendly
7. convivial—unsociable
8. dexterity—maladroitness
9. intermittent—continuous
10. antithetical—identical

C. Think of an antonym for each of the following words and use it in a sentence. As you discuss the sentences in class, you will notice that other students have thought of different antonyms for the same word. This happens because the antonym of one word may have several synonyms of its own.

1. antagonistic
2. tentative
3. volatile
4. verbose
5. extinct
6. predilection
7. jocose
8. mitigate
9. phlegmatic
10. trepidation

Review Exercises
Developing Your Vocabulary

A. The word *school* has many meanings. Use context clues to decide its meaning in each of the following sentences.

1. Somewhere ahead of our boat was an enormous school of tuna.
2. Elaine claimed that her paintings did not belong to any one school.
3. Dropping enrollment throughout the city may force the closing of the Forest Avenue School.
4. I suppose I'm a member of the old school.
5. There are two schools of thought on this issue.

B. On a piece of paper, write the numbers 1 through 5. For each numbered sentence below, choose the letter of the answer that best explains the italicized word. Following the letter, write the context clue or clues that led you to the answer you chose.

1. Brown edges on the leaves of your houseplants may be a sign not of *dehydration* but of over-watering.

    a. fungus   c. mealybugs
    b. dryness   d. deterioration

2. We spent all morning in the meeting, but so much time was wasted in discussing *peripheral* matters that we never considered the important questions.

    a. momentous   c. superficial
    b. essential   d. pressing

3. Much of her career has been spent in studying the shellfish *indigenous*, or native, to Brazil.

    a. originating in   c. imported
    b. damaging   d. in danger

4. Cleaning up after the rally should be a *collaborative* effort, for as they say, "many hands make light work."

    a. coaxial   c. sustained
    b. coordinated   d. cooperative

5. We had to pick our way carefully down Mount Parnel because of the extreme *declivity* of the trail we chose, which made the others seem flat in comparison.

a. rockiness

c. downward slope

b. curves

d. lack of marking

Chapter 2

Examining Word Parts

Many large English words are built from smaller word parts. Examining each part for meaning will help you piece together a meaning for the entire word. The following are three basic word parts.

Prefix—that which comes before the main part of a word

Root—the main part of a word

Suffix—that which follows the main part of a word

Consider the word *inconceivable*. The root word *conceive*, meaning "imagine," is preceded by the prefix *in-*, meaning "not." The suffix *-able* means "capable of being." If you piece these meanings together, you get "not capable of being imagined." The meanings of word parts will not always piece together into a definition, but the meanings of all word parts will always be present in the meaning of the whole word.

A word of caution is necessary. The letters forming a prefix or suffix may appear where they are not prefixes or suffixes. For instance, *mis-* is a prefix in *misdeed*, but not in *misery*.

Part 1
Prefixes

Most of the prefixes used to form English words have more than one possible meaning. If you meet an unfamiliar word with such a prefix, you will have to decide which of the possible meanings fits the context. You may have to consult a dictionary for an authoritative answer.

Each of the prefixes in the list below has just one meaning. These prefixes, therefore, are reliable clues to the meanings of the words in which they appear.

Prefixes with a Single Meaning

bene- = good (*beneficial*)
circum- = around (*circumnavigate*)
equi- = equal (*equivalent*)
extra- = outside (*extracurricular*)
intra- = within (*intramural*)
intro- = into (*introduction*)
mal- = bad (*malformation*)
mis- = wrong (*misinformed*)
non- = not (*nonconformist*)
pre- = before (*premature*)

The prefixes below are so common that you should learn them even though they have more than one possible meaning. The most frequent meanings are given for each.

Common Prefixes with Multiple Meanings

in-, ir-, il-, im- = not (*inept*) or in (*inject*)
un- = not (*unnoticed*) or the opposite of (*untie*)
dis- = the opposite of (*disqualify*) or away (*dislodge*)
sub- = under (*submerge*) or less than (*substandard*)
super- = above (*superstructure*) or more (*superfine*)
re- = back (*recall*) or again (*restart*)

Exercises
Prefixes

A. Give the meaning of the prefix in each word below.

1. irreligious
2. noncommittal
3. reupholster
4. unseat
5. discover

6. extraordinary
7. imperfection
8. subhuman
9. reaction
10. untrustworthy

B. You have seen that the prefixes *non-*, *un-*, and *in-* (and its forms *il-*, *ir-*, and *im-*) can mean "not." In most cases, only one of these can be used in a particular word. Decide which prefix can be used with each of the words below and write the new word.

1. delicate
2. opportune
3. existent
4. complete
5. lucky
6. direct
7. able
8. payment
9. dependent
10. mature

11. resident
12. secure
13. reasonable
14. combatant
15. interested
16. adequate
17. broken
18. visible
19. legible
20. happy

C. The prefixes *mal-* and *mis-* both mean "bad" or "wrong." Usually only one can be attached to a particular word. Decide which to add to each of the following words. Write the new words.

1. spell
2. guided
3. practice
4. deed
5. content
6. took

7. adventure
8. function
9. managed
10. conduct
11. adjusted
12. demeanor

D. In the sentences below are italicized words with prefixes. From the context, try to determine the meanings of both the prefix and the whole word. Describe how you arrived at your definitions.

1. The lawyer assured her client that there would be a speedy *disposition* of his case, now that the trial date was set and the jury selected.

2. The *subtotal* of her bill did not include the tax.

3. At the climax of the piece, the hall *reverberated* with the clash of cymbals, and the music paused until the last echo had died away.

4. There were no local taxes to pay or officials to elect. The settlement had so few residents that it was still *unincorporated*.

5. We did not practice on Tuesday because of the *inclement* weather.

Part 2

Suffixes

Suffixes provide better clues to word meaning than prefixes do. Most of the suffixes that are useful for determining word meaning appear in nouns and adjectives.

Noun Suffixes

Some suffixes are used only to make nouns from other parts of speech; they add little or nothing to the meaning of a word. A great many noun suffixes, however, have a single meaning that they give to every word in which they appear. Some of the most common of these are listed below. If you see one of these suffixes in a word you don't know, think of what it means in a word you do know. You will then have made a start toward learning the new word's meaning.

Noun Suffixes with Single Meanings

-ana = collected material on a certain subject (*Americana*)

-archy = form of government (*monarchy*)

-ard (-art) = one who does something to excess (*braggart*)

-cide = killer, killing (*germicide*)

-ee = receiver of an action or benefit (*employee*)

-fication = state or action of creating or causing (*ratification*)

-ics = science or skill (*athletics*)

-itis = inflammation (*appendicitis*)

The noun suffixes in the following list also have single, specific meanings. They all indicate an agent. That is, they all mean "one who is something" or "one who does something."

Noun Suffixes Indicating an Agent

-eer (*auctioneer*)

-ess (*waitress*)

-ician (*technician*)

-ist (*pianist*)

-ster (*gangster*)

The suffix *-ess* indicates that the agent is female.

The suffixes *-er*, *-or*, and *-an* or *-ian* also frequently indicate an agent, but they are also used in other ways.

Exercises
Noun Suffixes

A. Give the meaning of the suffix in each of the following words. Then give the meaning of the whole word. Use a dictionary for help as needed.

1.	genocide	8.	homicide
2.	patriarchy	9.	anarchy
3.	divorcee	10.	politics
4.	justification	11.	laryngitis
5.	mathematics	12.	Victoriana
6.	appointee	13.	drunkard
7.	arthritis	14.	unification

B. What is a person called if he or she is involved in each of the following fields? Use a suffix indicating an agent to make the new word.

1. politics
2. psychiatry
3. biology
4. geology
5. statistics
6. conducting
7. editing
8. photography
9. pamphlet writing
10. magic

C. From the context and the suffix, determine the meaning of each word in italics.

1. A half-dozen mean-looking *buccaneers* boarded the ship and proceeded to rob the crew of their possessions.
2. Some primitive societies practiced *infanticide* on first-born children who were female.
3. General Washington showed himself a superb *tactician* in the battle of Valley Forge.
4. As a student of *aesthetics*, Frank was concerned less with whether a piece of art was genuine than with why it was considered beautiful.
5. The fact that the remains of Egyptian pharaohs are still well preserved attests to the advanced state of the art of *mummification* at that time.

Adjective Suffixes

A number of adjective suffixes have specific meanings. Because they almost always have the meanings given below, the suffixes listed are good clues to the meanings of unfamiliar words.

Adjective Suffixes with Specific Meanings

-fic = causing or producing (*honorific*)

-fold = some number times as much (*twofold*)

-ward = in the direction of (*homeward*)

-less = without (*worthless*)

-able (-ible, -ble) = capable of being, or having qualities of (*comfortable*)

Four adjective suffixes mean "full of" or "having."

Adjective Suffixes Meaning "Full of" or "Having"

-acious (*audacious*)
-ful (*wonderful*)
-ose (*verbose*)
-ous (*dangerous*)

A number of adjective suffixes have the general meaning "pertaining to." They can be translated "connected with," "tending to," or "like."

Adjective Suffixes Meaning "Pertaining to"

-ive (*protective*)
-ative (*talkative*)
-ish (*impish*)
-aceous (*herbaceous*)
-ic (*caloric*)
-al (*original*)

The last two suffixes in this group, *-ic* and *-al*, are also found in nouns, where they have different meanings.

Exercises
Adjective Suffixes

A. Give the meaning of the suffix in each of the following words. Then give the meaning of the whole word. Use a dictionary for help as needed.

1.	legible	9.	invisible
2.	guileless	10.	cherubic
3.	fallacious	11.	envious
4.	prolific	12.	leeward
5.	manifold	13.	comatose
6.	treacherous	14.	arboreal
7.	authoritative	15.	formative
8.	tenacious	16.	boorish

B. From the context and the suffix, determine the meaning of each italicized word.

1. As the debate on censorship proceeded, it appeared that the main argument between the opponents was *semantic*; they could not agree on the meaning of the words "free speech."

2. On the day students were to elect a new student body president, Sarah, who was favored to win, felt *magnanimous* toward her hard-running opponent and treated him to a hamburger.

3. When the guards filled the moat and pulled up the drawbridge, the castle was all but *impenetrable*.

4. As the finishing touch to his model of the Santa Maria, Ted added a *diminutive* Christopher Columbus.

5. Senator McNally had a *soporific* way with words that put half his audience to sleep before he'd finished his opening remarks.

Part 3

Root Words

If you cut off the prefix and suffix from a long word, you pare it down to a root word of more manageable size. Sometimes identifying the root word by itself makes understanding the meaning of the longer word easier. Consider the word *irrefutable*. It may appear unfamiliar, but if you remove the prefix *ir-* and the suffix *-able,* you will reveal the root word *refute*, which may not be unfamiliar.

Some root words serve as the base for many larger words. If you compare an unfamiliar word with other words built on the same root, you can often get an idea of the meaning of the unknown word. You may know the word *remedial*, which also has the root word *remedy*. By relating *remedial* to *irremedial*, you should begin to understand the meaning of *irremedial*.

Root Words

Identify the root word in each of the words below. Give another word with the same root word. Give the meaning of both words.

1. belabor
2. continuity
3. underexposed
4. meritorious
5. disreputable
6. illogical
7. indirectness
8. humanism
9. beautician
10. irremediable

Latin and Greek Roots

Sometimes when you remove the prefix and suffix from a word you will be left with a root that is not an English word. The Latin and Greek words listed here are the roots for many English words. Use these lists for reference. The point is not to memorize the Latin and Greek words, but to see how their meanings are contained in the English words that are derived from them. If you can accomplish this, you will be able to understand other English words built from the same roots. Because the lists are long, they have been divided into groups. Following each group are questions that give you practice in recognizing the roots in English words.

Latin Roots and English Derivatives (1)

alius = other (*alienate*)

amicus = friend (*amicable*)

animus = mind, spirit (*animate*)

bellum = war (*rebellious*)

bonus = good (*bonus*)

credere, creditus = believe (*incredible*)

cor, cordis = heart (*concord*)

corpus, corporis = body (*corporation*)

crux, crucis = cross (*crucifiction*)
dicere, dictus = say, tell (*diction*)
dormire = sleep (*dormitory*)
errare, erratus = wander (*erratic*)
facere, feci, factus = make, do (*factory*)

Exercise
Latin Roots

Find the root in each of the following words. Give the meaning of the root and the meaning of the word.

1. corpulent	9. amity
2. cordial	10. credence
3. corpuscle	11. dormant
4. crux	12. inalienable
5. coronary	13. manufacturing
6. belligerent	14. dictation
7. erroneous	15. incorporate
8. unanimous	16. bellicose

Latin Roots and English Derivatives (II)

fluere = flow (*fluid*)
gratia = kindness, favor (*gratitude*)
grex, gregis = flock (*gregarious*)
jungere, junctus = join (*junction*)
jus, juris = law, right (*justice*)
juvenis = youth (*juvenile*)
lumen, luminis = light (*illuminate*)
mandare = command (*commandment*)
manus = hand (*manual*)
multus = much, many (*multiple*)
opus, operis = work (*operate*)
pendere, pensus = hang (*pendant*)

Exercise
Latin Roots

Find the root in each of the following words. Give the meaning of the root and the meaning of the word.

1. ingratiate
2. fluent
3. jury
4. congregation
5. mandatory
6. manipulate
7. luminary
8. operant
9. pendulous
10. rejuvenate
11. conjugal
12. multimillionaire

Latin Roots and English Derivatives (III)

rapere, raptus = seize (*rapacity*)

rumpere, ruptus = break (*rupture*)

sequor, secutus = follow (*sequence*)

solus = alone (*solitary*)

somnus = sleep (*somnolent*)

stringere, strictus = bind (*stringent*)

tempus = time (*temporal*)

tenere, tentus = hold (*tenure*)

terminus = end, boundary (*terminal*)

unus = one (*unity*)

videre, visus = see (*visible*)

vincere, victus = conquer (*invincible*)

Exercise
Latin Roots

Identify the root in each of the following words. Give the meaning of the root and the meaning of the word.

1. restrict
2. insomnia

3. rapture   8. video
4. victorious   9. solitude
5. consecutive   10. terminate
6. retention   11. disrupt
7. temporary   12. unifying

Greek Roots and English Derivatives (I)

anthropos = man (*anthropology*)

autos = self (*automatic*)

biblos = book (*Bible*)

bios = life (*biology*)

chronos = time (*chronological*)

cosmos = world, order (*cosmic*)

cryptos = secret, hidden (*cryptic*)

demos = people (*democracy*)

dynamis = power (*dynamic*)

ethnos = race, nation (*ethnic*)

ge, geos = earth (*geology*)

graphein = write (*graphic*)

Exercise
Greek Roots

Identify the meaning of the Greek root or roots in each of the following words. (Some words have more than one root.) Give the meaning of the root or roots and the meaning of the word.

1. autobiography   7. dynamite
2. autonomous   8. philanthropy
3. cosmopolitan   9. bibliography
4. demagogue   10. biosphere
5. chronic   11. crypt
6. ethnology   12. geography

Greek Roots and English Derivatives (II)

homos = same (*homogenized*)
iatr = heal (*psychiatry*)
logos = word, thought (*logical*)
metron = measure (*metric*)
micro = small (*microscope*)
monos = alone, single (*monotonous*)
neos = new (*neoclassical*)
neuron = nerve (*neurotic*)
onyma = name (*anonymous*)
orthos = right (*orthopedic*)
osteon = bone (*osteopath*)
pathos = suffering (*pathetic*)

Exercise
Greek Roots

Identify the Greek roots in the following words. Give their meanings and the meanings of the words. Use a dictionary for help as needed.

1. neurosurgeon
2. monogamy
3. pathological
4. pseudonym
5. orthodox
6. homonym
7. neophyte
8. podiatrist
9. microcosm
10. logistics
11. barometer
12. neurology

Greek Roots and English Derivatives (III)

phobos = fear (*phobia*)
phone = sound (*telephone*)
pneuma = air, breath (*pneumatic*)

polis = city (*police*)

polys = many (*polygamy*)

psyche = breath, soul, mind (*psychology*)

scope = seeing, watch (*telescope*)

syn, sym = with (*synchronize*)

tele = far, distant (*television*)

therme = heat (*thermal*)

techne = art (*technology*)

Exercise
Greek Roots

Give a definition for each of the following words.

1. claustrophobia
2. pneumonia
3. polyphony
4. cosmopolitan
5. phonics
6. psychopath
7. stereoscopic
8. sympathy
9. thermometer
10. telegraph
11. technical
12. symbiosis

Review Exercises
Mastering Word Parts

A. Give the meaning of the prefix in each of the following words.

1. benefactor
2. intravenous
3. nonaggression
4. illiterate
5. improper
6. equiangular
7. insufficient
8. recover
9. mismatch
10. discover
11. subordinate
12. circumlocution
13. introvert
14. predetermine
15. superabundant
16. malodorous
17. unassigned
18. extralegal
19. irreparable
20. benefit

B. Give the meaning of the suffix in each of the following words. Then give the meaning of the whole word. Use a dictionary for help as needed.

1. fratricide
2. assignee
3. polemics
4. insecticide
5. punster
6. oligarchy
7. amplification
8. bursitis
9. Dickensiana
10. physician

C. Find the Latin root in each of the following words. Give the meaning of the root and the meaning of the word.

1. credibility
2. luminous
3. grateful
4. conjunction
5. operator
6. interrupt
7. constrict
8. prediction
9. contemporary
10. pendulum

D. Find the Greek roots in each of the following words. Give the meaning of the roots and the meaning of the word.

1. autograph
2. monologue
3. chronograph
4. polygraph
5. metropolis
6. cryptography
7. demography
8. homophone
9. telemetry
10. monopoly

Chapter 3

Writing Effective Sentences

Using the right word at the right time is the secret of a fresh and vigorous style. As your vocabulary develops, the expression of your judgments and feelings will become more precise. The *effectiveness* of your expression, however, depends upon how you put words together. In English, meaning is not conveyed by words alone; it is conveyed by words working together in groups —in phrases, clauses, and sentences.

Successful writing is therefore largely a matter of effective sentences. When you have learned to write clear, straightforward sentences, your writing will do what you intend it to do.

The authors of this text have studied over 3000 samples of student writing. They have analyzed these samples to determine the kinds of sentence problems that occur most frequently. Chapters 3–6 set forth those sentence problems and show ways of dealing with them.

Many of the sentences you will revise in these chapters were written by students your age. They did not have a chance to revise the sentences. You will be doing the revising for them.

Part 1

Avoiding Empty Sentences

The function of a sentence is to convey facts, ideas, and feelings.

Writing cannot be done in haste. It cannot be done without thought. Sentences like the following result from haste and from failure to think before beginning to write.

> Schools are too crowded because there are too many students and classes are overcrowded and the schools are too small as well as the incredible population growth.

This sentence begins well: Schools are too crowded because . . ." The writer promises to explain why schools are too crowded. What is the reason given? ". . . there are too many students . . ." That is no reason. The writer is simply saying, "Schools are too crowded because they are too crowded." As an afterthought, he adds something about school size and population growth.

Lack of classroom space and population growth are good points. They are directly related to the problem. The writer's task is to think through the relationship and to express it clearly. If he had thought first, he would not have written "Schools are too crowded because there are too many students. . . ." He might have written:

> Inadequate classroom space and incredible population growth are responsible for the overcrowded conditions of our schools.

Here is another example of an empty sentence:

> Young people find rock music appealing because they really enjoy it.

This sentence says only that young people like rock music because they like rock music. Why do they like it? If the writer had reasons, he should have given them. If he did not have reasons, he should have merely expressed his opinions. By using "because" he had led the reader to expect reasons and details. He might better have written:

> Young people find rock music appealing because they like its beat, and the lyrics express their feelings.

Exercise
Avoiding Empty Sentences

Rewrite the following empty sentences. In some cases you will need to shorten the sentences. In other cases, you will need to add facts or ideas.

1. In this play you have to have imagination, for there is no scenery and you have to supply the scenery from your own mind by using your imagination.
2. I'd like to be a commercial airline pilot because that is what I've always wanted to be.
3. Bob is planning to go to agricultural school so that he will have a good background on scientific farming before he goes into it.
4. It may cost more money to go to college than we can afford, and that is one drawback that might hinder me.
5. A football player must have a quick mind as well as quick feet, and his mind must be clear as a bell as well.
6. I liked the book because it is the kind of book I enjoy reading.
7. Most of the inhabitants of India are Hindus, but not all the inhabitants are.
8. Spirituals are a popular form of music because they have a quality of rhythm and melody that makes them one of the most popular forms of American music.
9. I was glad to have a chance to see the TV program.
10. Scientists say that foods eaten as quickly as possible after picking contain more vitamins, and that prolonged cooking or canning causes foods to have fewer vitamins than if they are freshly picked and eaten.
11. Experience with many kinds of people is an important part of education, and I think that everybody should have this kind of experience.

12. I hope the Americans get an expedition to Mars before the Russians do because I think that getting there first would be a good thing for our country.

13. I'd like to be a basketball coach because I'd love to do that and get paid for it too.

14. Always put stereo speakers at least ten feet apart from each other since ten feet apart is the best distance for them to be.

15. I know I did poorly on the test because I flunked it.

Part 2
Avoiding Overloaded Sentences

The guides to writing effective sentences are few and simple:

1. Say one thing at a time.
2. Say it clearly and directly.

Everyone has the experience of writing sentences that try to say too much. They become so crowded that the writer cannot remember what he started to say, and the reader becomes fatigued from trying to follow the thought. Even professional writers make this mistake. You don't see many of their overloaded sentences because professional writers revise their work before publication. Here is one from the editorial pages of *The New York Times:*

> To execute the mandate of the New York constitution that the state budget must be balanced and at the same time to expand the state aid to political subdivisions and individuals that he feels the growing needs and rights of the people require, the Governor proposed a record rise of $575 million in state taxes.

This passage might better have been written as follows:

> (1) The New York state constitution requires that the state budget be balanced. (2) On the other hand, the Gov-

ernor feels that the growing needs and the rights of the people require an expansion of state aid. (3) To meet these conflicting requirements, he has proposed an increase of $575 million in state taxes.

When you find an overloaded sentence in your own writing, examine it carefully. Look for the main idea; look for the subject and verb that make the framework of this idea. Start over again with this subject-verb combination. Drop irrelevant details entirely. If the left-over details are important, start with a new subject-verb combination and pull the details together around it.

OVERLOADED As it would cost too much for all the renovations needed for my concept of a perfect school the only alternative is that we be allowed to go to our lockers any time and thus the time between classes would have to be lengthened.

IMPROVED The cost of renovations needed for my concept of a perfect school would be impossible to meet. The only alternative is to lengthen the time between class periods and allow us to go to our lockers whenever necessary.

Exercise
Avoiding Overloaded Sentences

Rewrite the following overloaded sentences. There is no one right way to improve them. You may need to add words and details.

1. While I am covering these various news stories, I will be able to learn many new things as well as understand things I know even better, and also help the paper's readers to be able to learn and understand different things which happen in the world better.

2. A salesman must have a number of different approaches in order to interest the customer in more than one product, in that way giving him a choice and giving the salesman an opportunity to show the customer his need for one product or the other.

3. When Charles Goodyear dropped a piece of rubber mixed with sulphur on a hot stove, he accidentally discovered a new process, which was how rubber could be vulcanized.

4. Most numerous of all the animals in the world are the arthropods, which are animals with jointed feet and which are boneless, including the insects, spiders, and crustaceans.

5. Traveling down the Skyline Drive, you cross Natural Bridge, which is a wonder of nature, and then pass various caves such as Luray, and finally you reach Lookout Mountain.

6. When the nasturtiums did not grow, the gardener used nitrogen and when that didn't work he used moss which he worked into the soil.

7. Kutztown is in the Pennsylvania Dutch country and it is the scene of a folk festival every year, which is a unique event.

8. Some of the ancestors of the Pennsylvania Dutch came from Holland but most of them came from Germany and Switzerland, which you may already know.

9. Basketball was invented in 1891 by James A. Naismith, who was a Y.M.C.A. instructor and who needed an indoor game for winter play, so he nailed peach baskets at either end of a gymnasium and used a soccer ball for play.

10. If we had had trained actors, they would have remembered their lines, and if we had had a prompter handy, he could have prompted the actors, but we didn't.

11. Through the city of Chicago run two branches of the Chicago River, which is known as "the river that flows backward" because the flow was reversed by an amazing scientific feat.

12. I read that the world's highest mountain is not Mount Everest but a mountain in the Hawaiian Islands called Mauna Kea, which is partly submerged in the Pacific and is 33,476 feet high.

Part 3

Avoiding Wordiness

A sentence that uses more words than necessary is boring. The extra words smother the meaning. The writer with a sharp eye can spot excess words and delete them during revision of his work.

One kind of wordiness arises from needless repetition of a word or from needless use of words with a similar meaning.

> Some people prefer the *modern* artists of *today* to the classicists of centuries past.
>
> Life is *not easy* but involves many *hardships*.
>
> A *true* artist and not an amateur can be *truly* creative.
>
> The *magnificence* of the scene awed me with its *grandeur*.

Another kind of wordiness arises from the repetition of *that*.

> You understood *that* if you failed *that* you could not be on the team.
>
> I promised *that* when I returned *that* I would call her.

In the last two sentences, the second *that* may be dropped.

In general, wordiness results simply from the use of too many words. The writer may use a clause when a single word would suffice. Methods of avoiding or repairing wordiness are considered in Chapter 4 under the heading *Reduction*.

Awkward Repetition

Sentences lose their effectiveness if a word or phrase is repeated carelessly. Sometimes there is no substitute for a word, and it must be repeated. Awkward repetition is the use of a word or phrase a second or third time when it need not be repeated.

Awkward repetition can be corrected by using a synonym, by using pronouns in place of nouns, or by rewriting the sentence.

> AWKWARD   Today there are more teen-age *drivers* on the highways than adult *drivers*. Some teen-agers should not be *drivers*.
>
> IMPROVED   Today teen-age drivers, some of whom should not be permitted on the highways, outnumber licensed adults.

AWKWARD   Try studying for one month without the *television and radio on* and you will see how your grades improve because you have not been distracted by having the *television and radio on.*

IMPROVED   Try studying for one month without the distractions of television and radio, and you will notice an improvement in your grades.

Exercise
Avoiding Wordiness

The following sentences are wordy or needlessly repetitive. Revise them to eliminate these faults.

1. During an ice storm, the car slipped on the ice and slid into a ditch.

2. As a general rule I'm usually at home by four P.M. in the afternoon.

3. The Senator answered all of the questions unhesitatingly and without any reservations.

4. The essential requirements necessary for employment are carefully outlined in this thorough pamphlet which tells you everything you will need to know.

5. To my way of thinking, I think it is time to discuss salaries and working conditions.

6. I saw a man who was a suspicious-looking character crossing the street.

7. The statement is almost self-explanatory itself, so I will not try to explain it.

8. The start of English literature had its beginning in the Anglo-Saxon period, which was from the year 449 to 1066.

9. Banks recommend that you save a part of your pay check regularly and that you make a habit of doing this.

10. Would you mind repeating the question again?

11. How can I ever repay you again for your help?

12. The thermostat keeps the heat at a constant temperature all the time.

13. Europeans are learning that billboards and traffic jams are no longer strictly American institutions any more.

14. The merging together of the two railroads will eliminate unnecessary duplication of facilities.

15. Washington never wore a wig. He powdered his own hair, which was actually real, and tied it in a queue.

Part 4

Avoiding Awkward Beginnings

The normal, easily readable pattern of English sentences is subject—verb—complement. A great many awkward sentences occur when this pattern is abandoned. Certain expressions used at the beginning of a sentence create awkwardness. They delay the thought, and they add nothing to it. Usually, they are not needed at all. The most common of these offending expressions are *The fact that, What I believe is, What I want is, Being that, The reason is.*

AWKWARD *What I believe is* that the honor system has worked.

BETTER I believe that the honor system has worked.

AWKWARD *Being that* Bill never sets his alarm clock, he is often late for class.

BETTER Since Bill never sets his alarm clock he is often late for class.

AWKWARD *The fact that* you want to learn should make you study.

BETTER Wanting to learn should make you study.

AWKWARD	*What the* officers object to is the lack of cooperation.
BETTER	The officers object to the lack of cooperation.
AWKWARD	*The reason* the jet crashed *was because* of a storm.
BETTER	The jet crashed because of a storm.

Exercise
Revising Sentences with Awkward Beginnings

Revise these sentences to remove their awkward beginnings.

1. The fact that I am late is because I had a flat tire.

2. Nothing looks better to me than to see a beautiful sunrise.

3. The reason he failed to run with the ball was due to the fact that he had sprained his ankle.

4. The thing I am looking forward to being is a geologist.

5. The reason our team lost the game is because the field was wet.

6. What *stalemate* is is when a player cannot move without moving into check.

7. What everyone with children should have is a playroom.

8. The fact that I had to get a check cashed is why I am late.

9. The reason some students never get an education is because they work for marks only.

10. Being that we had seen the picture, Stan and I went to another.

11. What I am looking forward to becoming is an interior designer.

12. It is an actual fact that India has over two hundred languages.

13. When the pilot began to worry was when he was getting low on fuel.

14. What you call a squeeze play is when the batter bunts to score a man from third.

15. The reason the mayor lost the election was because his record of administration had been very poor.

Chapter 4

Revising Your Sentences

Everyone is called upon at times to speak without preparation. In conversation and discussion, in class meetings, faculty meetings, or business conferences, a question will arise on which you must say something. In these situations there is little time to arrange your thoughts. You do your best, and the quality of your "best" depends upon previous experience and training.

In writing, the situation is different. There is always a point at which you can go back over what you have written and put it in order. You can reorganize, you can rearrange your paragraphs, you can revise your sentences, This chapter deals with the kinds of revisions you will find it profitable to make in your sentences.

Part 1

Omitting Unrelated Details

The function of a sentence is to state an idea, to present facts, or to describe feelings. When unrelated details appear in a sentence, they interrupt the flow of thought. They are as distracting as an orange flower on a pink dress or as tennis shoes worn with a tuxedo.

In sentence revision, keep your mind on the main idea. Delete any detail that is not closely related to this idea.

> I would like to be a pilot like my uncle, who owns a motorboat and flies from coast to coast each week.

Clearly, the motorboat has nothing to do with being a pilot. It might have something to do with "my uncle's" success as a pilot, but his success is another matter. It belongs in another sentence.

> The colorful spectacle of the opening of the Olympics, which we follow closely, still includes the Greek custom of lighting the torch.

"Our" following the Olympics closely has nothing to do with its colorful ceremonies. If it seems important to include "our" interest, do so in another sentence.

Exercise
Omitting Unrelated Details

Rewrite these sentences, omitting details that are not related to the main idea.

1. We often go to Maine, which is known as the Pine Tree State, because we enjoy sailing and fishing.

2. Because of the parking problem, it is easier to shop at the shopping center outside our town, which has a population of 10,000.

3. The service station attendant told us that Mac's Garage would repair our odometer, which registered 26,000 miles.

4. *Sherlock Holmes,* the new Broadway play, has received unfavorable comments from the critics, who get free tickets to opening night performances.

5. The book club, which has a thousand members, has chosen this novel for summer reading.

6. Our Chevette, which is metallic blue, has two advantages over larger cars: it is easy to park and economical to run.

7. We had a sneak preview of the Manet exhibit at The Art Institute of Chicago, which is a beautiful building.

8. The alumni reunion at my parents' college, which is one of the oldest institutions in the country, takes place each June.

9. The trip to Washington, which we took last year and which we are planning to take again this year, will be well worth while if you see nothing but the cherry blossoms in bloom.

10. From lookout towers, where two of my friends have jobs, rangers maintain a constant check on forest fires.

11. "Road rash," "nose wheelies," and "360's" are key words for skateboard enthusiasts, who seem to dominate our block which is near Ohio Stadium.

12. Do you realize what you could have bought for a nickel in 1915 when all nickels were the Indian-head type?

13. Ken Griffey struck out, and Johnny Bench, who stars in television commercials, hit a grounder to second.

14. Theodore Roosevelt loved boxing, Lincoln enjoyed wrestling, and Jackson, whose nickname was "Old Hickory," owned a racing stable.

15. Birds range in size from the tiny hummingbird, which weighs less than a penny, to the ostrich, which weighs up to 300 pounds and lays eggs that some people think are quite tasty.

Part 2

Keeping Related Sentence Parts Together

In the meaning of English sentences, the verb is closely tied to the subject; it is also closely tied to the complement. Similarly, the parts of a verb phrase are tied closely together. When these related sentence parts are widely separated by intervening words, the sentence is difficult to read. In general, keep closely related sentence parts together.

AWKWARD   *Sarah,* after she had watched the new TV show, *wrote* a letter of complaint to the local TV station.(Subject and verb separated)

REVISED   After she had watched the new TV show, Sarah wrote a letter of complaint to the local TV station.

AWKWARD   The visitor to Rome *was,* as she surveyed the city, *struck* by its mixture of ancient and modern. (Parts of a verb phrase separated)

REVISED   As she surveyed the city, the visitor to Rome was struck by its mixture of ancient and modern.

AWKWARD   TV *exerts,* for good or bad, an *influence* on the public. (Verb and object separated)

REVISED   For good or bad, TV exerts an influence on the public.

Exercise
Keeping Related Sentence Parts Together

Revise these sentences to bring related parts closer together.

1. He is the last person, for all we know, who saw her alive.
2. He enjoys, unfortunately, every motion picture and television program he watches.
3. The young people were, having spent the whole day mountain climbing, tired enough to go straight to bed.
4. The coach, in all his years at camp, had never seen such fine sportsmanship.
5. The car finally, after twenty years of faithful service, had to be towed to the junk yard.
6. The date, the place, and the weather, as I remember, were the reasons that the outdoor show was so poorly attended.

7. The king's treatment of the people, to put it mildly, was inconsiderate.

8. The ceiling beams had, after many years' wear, begun to show signs of dry rot.

9. The air conditioner, for some reason or other, went completely out of commission.

10. Life expectancy, according to modern surveys, has increased from 40 to 70 years since 1850.

11. The speaker presented after dinner a history of computation from finger-counting to Univac.

12. Weasels kill more animals than they can eat often.

13. You should, if you want to stay healthy, have regular medical checkups.

14. Surface lures, in my opinion, work best on Lake Buttermilk.

15. Natty Bumppo could hit a nailhead, according to the story, at a distance of one hundred yards.

Part 3

Coordinating Related Ideas

There are times when ideas are so closely related that they should be joined in a single sentence. If the ideas seem of equal importance, they can be joined by a conjunction or by a semicolon in a compound sentence.

The coordinating conjunctions used to form compound sentences are *and, but, or, for, nor.* Each of these conjunctions has a specific meaning and therefore relates the parts of a compound sentence in a specific way: *and* and *nor* mean "in addition"; *or* means "an alternative"; *but* means "an exception"; *for* means "because."

> Now we are probing outer space, *and* the sky is no longer the limit.
>
> Extra-curricular activity is important, *for* well-rounded stu-students need more than study.
>
> John did not explain, *nor* did he intend to.

Our school glee club sang last, *but* they were the best singers in the contest.

Is José really sick, *or* is he just pretending?

Conjunctive adverbs and connecting phrases are also used to tie ideas together in compound sentences.

ADDITION	ALTERNATIVE
indeed	on the other hand
in fact	at the same time
furthermore	
moreover	
also	
besides	

EXCEPTION OR CONTRAST	RESULT
yet	consequently
still	therefore
however	hence
nonetheless	then

The choice of a conjunctive adverb depends upon the meaning the writer wants to convey. The point is that each conjunctive adverb specifies a particular meaning, just as the coordinating conjunctions do.

Note: A comma is used before the coordinating conjunction in a compound sentence. A semicolon is placed before a conjunctive adverb, and a comma is usually placed after it.

Exercises
Coordinating Related Ideas

A. From the conjunctions given in parentheses, choose the one that best fits the meaning.

1. The train service will have to be improved, (or, and, but) we will have to use the bus.

2. You can save time traveling by plane, (and, but, or) a sea trip would be restful.

3. Japan, Europe, and the United States suffer from pollution problems, (but, or, for) only the United States has addressed itself to a clean-up program.

4. It is not likely he will pay this bill, (or, and, nor) will his parents pay it.

5. Her music teacher believed Rose was ready for a concert, (and, for, but) she had been practicing all year.

6. You must get a passport, (and, but, or) for some countries you must also have visas.

7. The delegates attend the convention, (and, but, for) they also have alternates.

8. The judge asks the jury for a verdict, (and, but, or) sometimes they disagree.

9. Scuba diving is fun, (and, or, but) it can be hazardous for beginners.

10. They accepted my story, (or, but, and) the editor delayed publication.

B. Supply a suitable conjunctive adverb from the list on page 58. Copy the sentences, punctuating properly.

1. The car lost speed going uphill _____ I had to shift gears.

2. The insurgents were outnumbered _____ they continued to march in protest.

3. The leader delivered a fiery speech _____ he roused the mob to violence.

4. I wouldn't try to argue with the boss _____ it wouldn't do any good.

5. The bill for the furniture was long overdue _____ the collector sent a strong letter.

6. Kim failed to send in her admissions application and fee _____ she was unable to register for the fall semester.

7. Beth had not appeared at the information desk _____ I continued to wait for her.

8. Overeating makes a person unattractively fat _____ it harms one's health.

9. Mozart sometimes had to compose music to please his patron _____ he never abandoned his high principles.

10. Maine has large pine tree forests _____ it is called the Pine Tree State.

Part 4
Avoiding Stringy Sentences

Some sentences become overloaded because the writer strings a number of ideas together, placing *and*'s between ideas. The result is that no one idea stands out; there seems to be no organization. You can revise stringy sentences in two ways:

1. Choose the conjunction that will show the real relationship between the ideas you are presenting.
2. Divide the sentence into two or more sentences.

STRINGY   The class discussed the question of moral values in a literary work and mentioned the problem of censorship that is so controversial today and offered their own opinion about the wisdom of imposing it by law.

REVISED   The class discussed the question of moral values in a literary work. The problem of censorship, so controversial today, became a point of debate as students offered opinions about imposing it by law.

STRINGY   Innsbruck is a city and lies in the valley of the Inn River in the Austrian Tyrol and is an ideal location for the Winter Olympic Games and it has numerous and fast downhill courses which are a great challenge for the skiers who go there to compete for a gold medal.

REVISED   Innsbruck, a city in the Austrian Tyrol, lies in the valley of the Inn River. It is an ideal location for the Winter Olympic Games because of its numerous and fast downhill courses. These courses are a great challenge for the skiers who go there to compete for a gold medal.

Exercise
Revising Stringy Sentences

These sentences have too many *and*'s. Revise each sentence. In each case, you will need to make two or more sentences.

1. Many people fear old age, and they think it means becoming debilitated, and they don't try to take steps to keep themselves useful members of society.

2. Most children like to draw, and they draw freely with imagination unless some adult interferes with their work, and then they become self-conscious.

3. It is better to spend less than you earn, and then you can start a bank account and save some money.

4. The northern lights, which are huge rays of bluish-green, pink, yellow, or white light in the northern sky, are a real sight to see, and they are also called the aurora borealis.

5. The northern lights are caused by electrified particles from the sun, and these particles strike rare gases in the earth's upper air and make them glow.

6. The earth's most abundant form of animal life finally has a zoo of its own, and it is located at the Smithsonian Institution in Washington and is called the Insect Zoo.

7. AmTrak now gives its train passengers an "on-train" magazine, which is like an "in-flight" magazine, and it is called Allaboard.

8. There is a new magazine for Italian-Americans and it is called *I-AM*, and it is the first magazine ever published for Italian-Americans.

9. I was calmly waiting to make a deposit and the bank was suddenly transformed into a scene of alarms, sirens, police, and alarmed employees, and it turned out that one of the employees had pushed the alarm button by mistake.

10. The early settlers in what is now Colorado wanted to call it Jefferson, and then tried to have it named Idaho, and finally settled for the original Spanish name that the conquistadors had used, which was Colorado, and that means "reddish" or "colored."

Part 5
Subordination

The main clause is the basic structure in any sentence. It states the main idea of the sentence. Modifying clauses and phrases are used to add details to or explain the conditions that define or limit the meaning of the main clause.

The writer alone knows what his main idea is in each sentence he writes. If he writes only compound sentences, or only main clauses, he gives his reader no guidance; hence, the effectiveness of what he is saying is lost.

MAIN IDEA	LIMITING, EXPLAINING, OR DEFINING DETAILS
He has a right to protest (at any time?)	if the rules were violated. (under this condition)
Jim will be sent for (why?)	to serve as a witness. (explanation)
The actor achieved his ambition (how?)	playing the role of Hamlet. (defining details)

Materials of less importance can be subordinated (put in their proper place) by use of subordinate clauses. Adverb clauses are introduced by subordinating conjunctions, which express a great variety of relationships. (See Section 1.7 in your Handbook.) Nothing improves a sentence quite so much as substituting the right subordinating conjunction for a meaningless *and* that has been dropped thoughtlessly between two clauses.

FAULTY   The visibility was poor, and all flights from the airport had to be canceled.

REVISED   *Because* the visibility was poor, all flights from the airport had to be canceled. (adverb clause)

FAULTY   I handed in my composition, and my teacher suggested revisions.

REVISED   *After* I had handed in my composition, the teacher suggested revisions.

In each of the two foregoing examples the writer has joined two clauses that are obviously not of equal importance. The *and* placed between the clauses clearly does not mean "in addition to." It should be replaced by a subordinating conjunction.

The same kind of improvement can sometimes be made by converting a clause into a participial phrase.

> WEAK   Amy knew the facts, *and* she answered all the questions clearly and completely.

> REVISED   *Knowing* the facts, Amy answered all the questions clearly and completely. (participial phrase)

> WEAK   Big Jake was pinned under the fallen tree, *and* he shouted for help.

> REVISED   *Pinned* under the fallen tree, Big Jake shouted for help. (participial phrase)

Materials of less importance can also be subordinated by the use of adjective clauses and appositives.

> FAIR   The 8-mm. film loop is a new teaching aid. It makes our science lessons exciting and profitable.

> BETTER   The 8-mm. film loop, *which is a new teaching aid*, makes our science lessons exciting and profitable. (adjective clause)

> BETTER   The 8-mm. film loop, *a new teaching aid*, makes our science lessons exciting and profitable. (appositive)

Upside-Down Subordination

Upside-down subordination is the fault of placing an important idea in a subordinate clause or phrase.

> FAULTY   Lightning struck the car, *killing the driver*. (The killing of the driver is more important.)

> REVISED   When lightning struck the car, the driver was killed.

FAULTY	The game, *which gave us the championship,* was our last of the season.
REVISED	The game, which was our last of the season, gave us the championship.
REVISED	We clinched the championship when we won the last game of the season.
FAULTY	Dick lost his grip, *hurtling to the water below.*
REVISED	Losing his grip, Dick hurtled to the water below.

Exercises
Subordinating Ideas

A. Combine these sentences, converting one into either a phrase or a clause. Be careful to avoid upside-down subordination.

1. The brakes did not hold. The car crashed into a lamppost.
2. Last night we were watching TV. Our cat rushed into the room and sprang onto the set.
3. We were parked on the wrong side of the street. A policeman gave us a ticket.
4. The judge was busy taking notes. He did not see the demonstration the witness was putting on.
5. The teacher looked into his desk. A small white mouse jumped out onto his lap.
6. The author is only twenty-three. Her book has won widespread recognition.
7. Be sure to save the weekend of June 17 and 18 for the convention. The convention will be held in Cincinnati.
8. My birthday party for Mother was a great success. I served her favorite dishes.
9. Beth is studying chemistry. She wants to become a research chemist.
10. Laura cancelled her violin lessons. She broke her wrist.

B. Change the following compound sentences by subordinating one of the clauses. You may change it to either a subordinate clause or a phrase.

1. In the Virgin Islands, the climate is temperate, and the temperature varies only ten degrees throughout the seasons.

2. The Boers were defeated by the British, but they still retain their authority in South Africa.

3. The course in creative writing is given on Wednesdays, and it is well attended.

4. The jeweler cleaned the watch thoroughly, and the watch kept better time.

5. Howard has held important positions in Turkey and Iran, and he is now working in Beirut.

6. Veterans' Day used to be called Armistice Day, and it is a legal holiday.

7. Dad lost his car key, and ever since he has kept a duplicate key under the hood.

8. The newest ocean liners are equipped with stabilizers, and these stabilizers reduce the roll to two degrees.

9. An old-fashioned delicacy is rose-petal jam, and you can still buy it in fancy food stores.

10. President McKinley was attending the Pan-American Exposition in Buffalo, and he was assassinated.

C. Correct the upside-down subordination in these sentences.

1. Debby was taking a walk in the woods when she saw a rattlesnake.

2. The next morning I went to the gardener, telling him that he had planted my shrubs in the wrong place.

3. Although he was a minibike racing champ, he was only eleven years old.

4. The plane, which made a crash landing, came from Detroit.

5. The Coast Guard plane searching for survivors of a ditched oil tanker, flew low over Atlantic waters.

6. The train, which was three hours late because of a power failure, was en route to Boston from New York.

7. The tenement, which was gutted by fire, had corridors filled with rubbish.

8. The children, who were saved, were carried down fire escapes and ladders by firemen.

9. Whenever Dad plays golf, he has a free weekend.

10. Walking onto the stage, he whistled under his breath.

Part 6

Reduction

Reduction is the means by which bulky sentences are made compact and effective. Reduction can be achieved by changing a clause to a phrase or a phrase to a single modifier.

CLAUSE   I go to a school *which has closed-circuit television.*

PHRASE   I go to a school *with closed-circuit television.*

PHRASE   One of the old programs *on radio* was revived.

WORD   One of the old *radio* programs was revived.

CLAUSE   Swift wrote *Gulliver's Travels, which is a satire.*

APPOSITIVE   Swift wrote *Gulliver's Travels, a satire.*

If the clauses of a compound sentence have the same subject, the compound sentence can be reduced by using a compound predicate. Similarly, two clauses with the same verb can be reduced by using a compound subject.

SAME SUBJECT   The freshmen followed her advice, *and they decided to take industrial arts.*

REDUCED   The freshmen *followed* her advice and *decided* to take industrial arts.

SAME SUBJECT   The box weighs too much, *and it is awkward to carry.*

REDUCED   The box *weighs* too much and *is* awkward to carry.

Exercise
Reducing Sentences To Make Them Effective

Rewrite these sentences, reducing the italicized words to a shorter construction.

1. The university, *which has a research department,* will publish its findings in a scientific report.

2. The anthropologist, *who is a specialist in Indian life,* read a paper before the historical society.

3. The O'Keefe Center for the Performing Arts, *which is a non-profit theatre located in Toronto,* cost $12,000,000.

4. Dr. Baker, *who is a psycho-analyst and is well known,* will handle this case.

5. The blunder was mine, *but the blunder was yours, too.*

6. Wordsworth is often called a poet of nature, *and he was one of the Lake poets of England.*

7. A conference on new sources of energy was held in August, and *the conference was at Sugar Loaf Mountain.*

8. Nobody knows precisely what makes rain, *and it is one of the commonest of weather phenomena.*

9. The report, *which was long and tedious,* was delivered to an audience *which was altogether bored.*

10. Fund raising, *which is a business in itself,* is handled by experts in the field.

11. The Constitution states that the census must be taken every ten years, *and the first census was taken in 1790.*

12. Golf, *which was a favorite game of James I and Charles I, who were Stuart kings,* became known as "the royal and ancient game."

13. The cliché, *which is a trite or hackneyed expression,* should be avoided whenever possible.

14. Puerto Rico, *which is a self-governing Commonwealth associated with the United States,* is a beautiful tropical island.

15. Reading, *which is a delightful pastime,* is also an important source of knowledge.

Part 7

Parallelism

The word *and* joins sentence parts of the same kind. It may join two nouns, two adjectives, two prepositional phrases, and so on. Similar sentence parts so joined are **parallel**. If the sentence parts joined by *and* are not of the same kind, **faulty parallelism** has occurred.

FAULTY	My father enjoys *reading* and *to go to the theater.* (noun joined to phrase)
REVISED	My father enjoys *reading* and *going* to the theater.
FAULTY	Tim wondered about the *car* and *whether he could repair it.* (noun joined to clause)
REVISED	Tim wondered *whether he could repair the car.* (When a parallel is impossible, change the sentence.)
FAULTY	No one warned Meg *to bring a note* and *that she had to report to the office.* (phrase joined to clause)
REVISED	No one warned Meg *to bring* a note and *to report* to the office.
FAULTY	He sings *to entertain, for relaxation,* and *earning money.*
REVISED	He sings *to entertain, to relax,* and *to earn money.*
FAULTY	Stan is *tall, fast,* and *good coordination.*
REVISED	Stan *is tall, is fast,* and *has good coordination.*

And Which; and Who

A special kind of faulty parallelism occurs with *which* and *who*. The *and* should never appear before these words unless *which* or *who* appears earlier in the sentence.

NONSTANDARD	In the park is a lovely bridle path *and which* winds through scenic woods.
STANDARD	In the park is a lovely bridle path *which* winds through scenic woods.
NONSTANDARD	We went to interview the actor *and who* answered our questions willingly.
STANDARD	We went to interview the actor, *who* answered our questions willingly.

Exercise
Making Sentence Parts Parallel

Correct the faulty parallelism in these sentences.

1. Linda is enthusiastic, ambitious, and has seemingly unlimited energy.
2. Meg thought about her clothes and if her denim skirt and jacket would be suitable.
3. On the boat were young people dancing, older people playing shuffleboard, and others who were seated and talked.
4. Every child needs good food, plenty of sleep and exercise, and to feel he or she is loved.
5. The auctioneer, a persuasive man and who knows how to arouse interest, sold many articles quickly.
6. All pedestrians crossing at the intersection and who don't obey the traffic lights will receive tickets.
7. The storm cut off the lights, stopped the pump, and the furnace stopped going.
8. I have brown hair, brown eyes, and wear reading glasses.
9. Merton Gill was an actor with a funny face but who hated comedy.
10. Captain Ahab described the whale as a big white hussy with a mouth as long as thirty feet and would hold twenty men in it.
11. Her duties were hiring personnel and sometimes to evaluate programs.
12. David tried playing football in the afternoon and his homework at night.
13. The new baby is plump, fair, and light hair.
14. Cottonseed oil is used in steel-making, palm oil in tin-plating, and linseed oil to make paint.
15. Bob has speed, height, size, and a great all-round player.

Chapter 5

Achieving Sentence Clarity

The purpose of the writer is to state his thoughts and feelings as exactly as possible. The more carefully they are stated, the greater effect they will have. If necessary words are left out, the meaning is incomplete. If modifiers are misplaced or left dangling, the writer's meaning is distorted.

All of these errors can be caught in the process of revision. This chapter will help you with this process.

Part 1
Avoiding Omissions of Necessary Words

Omission of *That*

In some sentences the *that* introducing a noun clause must be stated to avoid confusion.

CONFUSING Beth realized the scene with Jimmy, white-haired, grieving over her death, was only a day-dream.

REVISED Beth realized *that* the scene with Jimmy, white-haired, grieving over her death, was only a day-dream.

CONFUSING Lou heard the parade, scheduled for the next day, had to be postponed.

REVISED Lou heard *that* the parade, scheduled for the next day, had to be postponed.

CONFUSING The principal understood all the students were excited about the holiday.

REVISED The principal understood *that* all the students were excited about the holiday.

Omission of Part of a Compound Verb

The parts of a compound verb are often made up of verb phrases. If these parts differ in number or tense, the complete phrases must be used for clarity.

CONFUSING The chairs were stacked, and the room swept. (chairs *were*; room *was*)

REVISED The chairs *were* stacked, and the room *was* swept.

CONFUSING	The meeting was called, and the officers elected.
	(meeting *was*; officers *were*)
REVISED	The meeting *was* called, and the officers *were* elected.

Omission of Words in Idioms

An idiom is a group of words with a meaning different from the literal meanings of the words taken one by one.

The diver *put on* his helmet.
The club *put on* a big celebration.

In the first sentence above, the words *put on* have their usual meaning. In the second sentence, the same words are an idiom meaning "to stage."

Many idioms like *put on* are composed of a verb followed by an adverb. Here are some idioms:

Idioms with <u>on</u>	Idioms with <u>for</u>	Idioms with <u>in</u>
put on	desire for	interest in
turn on	admiration for	confidence in
pile on	respect for	pride in

Idioms with <u>off</u>	Idioms with <u>out</u>	Idioms with <u>up</u>
turn off	find out	pick up
hold off	carry out	hold up
take off	pull out	give up

When two idioms are used together in a compound construction, there is a temptation to drop the adverb from one of them. This omission is awkward and confusing.

FAULTY	There was no preparation or hint of a party.
IMPROVED	There was no preparation *for* or hint of a party.

FAULTY	We were listening and worrying about the news.
IMPROVED	We were listening *to* and worrying about the news.

FAULTY	I am interested and proud of your career.
IMPROVED	I am interested *in* and proud of your career.

Exercises
Avoiding Omissions of Necessary Words

A. Revise these sentences to correct the omissions.

1. We understood the committee was going to buy the prizes.
2. The bus was loaded, and the children driven to school.
3. I noticed a dozen wasps had paid me a visit.
4. The coach noticed the player had injured his ankle.
5. She had no love or pride in her housework.
6. On the way home from school I remembered the birthday of a friend of mine was the next day.
7. I have a fear and antagonism toward most insects.
8. The grounds were cleared and a picnic table set up.
9. I discovered our old house in Cicero had been painted a shocking pink.
10. The door was locked and the windows barred.

B. Revise these sentences to correct the omissions.

1. He told me before I left the job was mine.
2. The coach was given a banquet and the players taken to New York.
3. Lee discovered all his change had slipped through a hole in his pocket.
4. We knew over a hundred students would be in the cheering section.
5. A new constitution has been drawn up and new bylaws prepared.
6. I have no respect or confidence in such a man.
7. We discovered a good CB radio would cost two hundred dollars.
8. The tubes were tested and the antenna installed.
9. He has both admiration and trust in his lawyer.
10. We heard the ships would reach the harbor within a few hours.

Part 2

Placement of Modifiers

Single adjectives are usually placed just before the word they modify. Adjective phrases and clauses follow immediately after the word they modify. The only exception is the sentence in which both a phrase and a clause modify the same word. In this situation, the phrase precedes the clause.

We cheered the boy in the class who saved the child's life.

Many adverb modifiers can be moved from one place in a sentence to another without a change of meaning. Occasionally, however, moving an adverb produces unexpected effects. In general, be careful to place adverb modifiers so that they will express your meaning exactly.

CONFUSING	Jean was *attentively* trying to listen.
REVISED	Jean was trying to listen *attentively*.
CONFUSING	I *only* ate the spaghetti.
REVISED	I ate *only* the spaghetti.
CONFUSING	Everyone *cannot* expect to be invited.
REVISED	*Not* everyone can expect to be invited.
CONFUSING	The boys were warned about reckless driving *by the coach*.
REVISED	The boys were warned *by the coach* about reckless driving.

Exercises
The Placement of Modifiers

A. Revise these sentences to correct the misplaced modifiers.

1. Ronny nearly ran the 100-meter dash in twelve seconds.
2. We saw the full moon, coming home last night.

3. My parents thought that I would die of pneumonia several times when I was a child.

4. We can hear the waves, lapping on the beach in our cottage every night.

5. Vitamin C prevents scurvy, which is found in citrus fruits.

6. Everyone couldn't get into the Volvo.

7. Lincoln wrote the Gettysburg Address while traveling from Washington to Gettysburg on the back of an envelope.

8. I could only find one ripe banana in the grocery store.

9. I bought a hat for my mother with a flower on top.

10. Take the suit to the cleaner with the narrow lapels.

B. Revise these sentences to correct the misplaced modifiers.

1. The tackle was stored in the rowboat under the seat.
2. My uncle was arrested for jaywalking by the sheriff.
3. She only wanted to do it to prove that she could.
4. The shore was littered with debris along the bay.
5. For three days I almost ate nothing.
6. The player was praised by the coach who kicked the winning goal.
7. My uncle bought a house last week in the country.
8. The boat has a very heavy cargo that is gliding downstream.
9. Joe almost agreed with everything the teacher said.
10. I found a purse on the sidewalk stuffed with money.

Part 3

Avoiding Dangling Modifiers

When a phrase or clause is placed next to a word that it cannot modify sensibly, it is called a **dangling modifier.** Dangling modifiers often appear at the beginnings of sentences.

PARTICIPLE Changing the tire, the car rolled down the driveway. (This says the *car* changed the tire.)

INFINITIVE	To be healthy, vacations are necessary.
	(This says that *vacations* are trying to be healthy.)
ELLIPTICAL CLAUSE	While sketching the scene, rain poured down.
	(This says that the *rain* sketched the scene.)

To correct a dangling participle, supply a word for it to modify sensibly, or change the participle to a main verb and give it a subject. The phrase is thus turned into a clause.

FAULTY	Riding past the castle, Arthur's gaze fell upon Guinevere.
REVISED	As he was riding past the castle, Arthur's gaze fell upon Guinevere.

FAULTY	Reading the newspaper, many facts can be learned.
REVISED	Reading the newspaper, I can learn many facts.

FAULTY	Running fifty yards, a touchdown was scored.
REVISED	Jack ran fifty yards, scoring a touchdown.

To correct a dangling infinitive, supply a word for the phrase to modify sensibly.

FAULTY	To get a license, a test must be passed.
REVISED	To get a license, *you* must pass a test.

Exercises
Avoiding Dangling Modifiers

A. Revise these sentences to correct the dangling modifiers.

1. While eating lunch, the telephone rang.
2. Coming down with fever, Mother gave Larry some medicine.
3. Climbing up, the trees get smaller.
4. While setting the table, the soup can be heated.
5. When browned on one side, turn the fish over.

6. Looking out of the plane, the clouds resemble the sea.

7. To have a good time, the hotel runs weekly dances.

8. Picking her up in his arms, the child was rushed to the doctor.

9. To really fit well, you should take in the seams of this dress.

10. After analyzing the problem, the solution was simple.

B. Revise these sentences to correct the dangling modifiers.

1. While baby-sitting, the dog ate my lunch.

2. Sitting in the pilot's seat, my mind wandered.

3. After biting the postman, I sold my dog.

4. To assemble the toy rocket, the directions must be followed carefully.

5. Playing chess for three hours, my brain stopped working.

6. To rest properly, the bed must be clean and comfortable.

7. After agreeing to cut the grass, the lawn mower broke down.

8. To become a guitar player, practice is necessary.

9. Taking me out into the garage, there was a twinkle in Dad's eye.

10. After cancelling the program, I sent a strong protest to CBS.

Exercise
Misplaced and Dangling Modifiers

Revise these sentences to correct the misplaced and dangling modifiers.

1. I knocked over a plant, waltzing on the porch.

2. I spotted some wild ducks, eating my lunch in the park.

3. Swarming over the grass and climbing up the plants, I saw some strange-looking insects.

4. Letting out the clutch, the car shot forward.

5. Leaning back in a comfortable chair, the magazine on the table attracted my attention.

6. To get a television contract, considerable talent is required.

7. Being deaf when he wrote them, Beethoven's later works are all the more remarkable.

8. To get to Times Square or Lincoln Center, two subway trains must be taken.

9. A doctor should be seen twice a year in order to stay healthy.

10. Rising vertically from the earth, the rocket's upward speed was breathtaking.

Chapter 6

Achieving Sentence Variety

Good writing requires a logical movement from one idea to another, a movement that achieves a rhythm. If the pattern and length of every sentence is the same, the rhythm becomes monotonous. When the pattern and length of sentences are varied, the rhythm is pleasing.

You can achieve a variety of sentence rhythm in the following three ways:

1. by varying sentence beginnings
2. by varying sentence structure
3. by varying sentence length

Because a writer's first job is to get his ideas down on paper, the above methods of achieving sentence variety are best used in revision. The writer who sets out in his first draft to begin each sentence in a different way is likely to find that his concern with sentence structure interferes with his natural speech rhythms, producing self-conscious and awkward passages.

Part 1

Variety of Sentence Beginnings

When every sentence in a passage begins in the same way, the effect can be monotonous. A succession of sentences beginning with the same word or with the same kind of phrase or clause can irritate or bore the reader. In the first passage below, note the irritating repetition of the word *it*. In the second passage below, note how your interest lags with the sameness of each sentence.

Sentences beginning with the same word

> Then the fog came. *It* did not roll in like a wave; *it* came from nowhere. *It* was not there—then it was. *It* wove its gray veil with shocking speed. *It* surrounded our island silently. *It* smothered sunlight and sound. *It* isolated us.

Sentences beginning with the same kind of phrase

> *Stepping out of the boat,* we landed on Spirit Island. *Pulling the boat up on the beach,* we began to explore. *Picking our way along the beach,* we could feel the stillness watching us, waiting for us.

Sentence variety can be achieved by beginning a succession of sentences in different ways—with adverb modifiers, phrases, or clauses.

> The cat carefully stalked the unsuspecting robin.
>   (subject—verb)
> Carefully, the cat stalked the unsuspecting robin.
>   (adverb modifier)
> With infinite care, the cat stalked the unsuspecting robin.
>   (prepositional phrase)
> To avoid alerting the unsuspecting robin, the cat stalked it
>   carefully. (infinitive phrase)
> Moving slowly and carefully, the cat stalked the
>   unsuspecting robin. (participial phrase)

Until it was ready for a final charge, the cat carefully stalked
the unsuspecting robin. (adverb clause)

Exercises
Varying Your Sentence Beginnings

A. Rewrite the following sentences, beginning each in accordance
with the suggestion in parentheses.

1. The stock market has been very active recently.
(Begin with *recently*.)
2. Bill stopped at the library on his way home.
(Begin with *on*.)
3. The Steelers won the championship in the first minute of
a sudden-death overtime period. (Begin with *in*.)
4. The street-repair people were following their usual schedule;
they began tearing up the pavement outside my hotel room at
two A.M. (Begin with *following*.)
5. All the clouds had disappeared by midmorning.
(Begin with *by*.)
6. The chairperson continued to bang her gavel, and the
delegates gradually quieted down. (Begin with *as* or *when*.)
7. We had trouble locating our car after the game.
(Begin with *after*.)
8. Mr. Smith fell and hurt himself as he ran to catch his bus.
(Begin with *running*.)
9. Mary forgot to buy a ticket in her hurry to board the train.
(Begin with *in*.)
10. Frontenac became a well known summer resort after the
Civil War. (Begin with *after*.)

B. Follow the directions for Exercise A.

1. A foot-high limestone marker, with the initials "MD" carved
on it, stands a few paces off the road. (begin with *a few paces*.)
2. The little town nestles comfortably against the bluff, and
seems content to dream the years away. (Begin with *nestling*.)
3. He left for Los Angeles the next day. (Begin with *the*.)

4. The Pontiac Sunbird must be considered the "best buy," because it combines high performance and low cost. (Begin with *combining*.)

5. Galileo made the first practical use of the telescope in 1609. (Begin with *in*.)

6. The workers' summer output was very poor until air conditioning was installed. (Begin with *until*.)

7. The candidate accepted defeat calmly. (Begin with *calmly*.)

8. Sonia was very calm before the trial. (Begin with *before*.)

9. Stephen Crane died of tuberculosis at the age of twenty-nine. (Begin with *at*.)

10. The arctic tern is the champion migrant bird; it travels 11,000 miles from the Arctic to winter in the Antarctic. (Begin with *traveling*.)

Part 2

Variety of Sentence Structure

In student writing, a monotonous style occurs chiefly from overuse of compound sentences. The compound sentence is a good and useful tool, but overuse dulls its edge. A succession of compound sentences is boring because the rhythm is so monotonous. As you read the following passage, note the unvarying stop-and-go effect.

> We reached Trinidad, Colorado, in the evening, and in the morning we headed south through Raton Pass. We ate lunch at Eagle's Nest, New Mexico, and then we took a roundabout route through the mountains. The gravel road was better than we expected, and the mountains were strikingly beautiful.

A succession of compound sentences can be avoided by changing one of the clauses. The clause may be made into a subordinate clause or a participial phrase. Some compound sentences can be changed into simple sentences with a compound predicate.

COMPOUND SENTENCE	We visited Taos Pueblo, and we were deeply impressed by this vigorous survival of an older civilization.
PARTICIPIAL PHRASE	Visiting Taos Pueblo, we were deeply impressed by this vigorous survival of an older civilization.
SUBORDINATE CLAUSE	When we visited Taos Pueblo, we were deeply impressed by this vigorous survival of an older civilization.
COMPOUND PREDICATE	We visited Taos Pueblo and were deeply impressed by this vigorous survival of an older civilization.

Exercises
Varying Sentence Structure

A. Rewrite the following compound sentences, changing one of the clauses in each in accordance with the suggestion in parentheses.

1. Mrs. Lambert enjoys good music, and she is a generous benefactor of the local symphony orchestra. (Compound predicate)

2. The house lights dimmed, and quiet settled on the audience. (Subordinate clause beginning with *as*)

3. The hydrant was turned on, and the firemen discovered that there was not enough water pressure to fight the fire. (Subordinate clause beginning with *when*)

4. Paul worked as a drugstore delivery boy during the school year, and he was a lifeguard at the city pool during the summer. (Compound predicate)

5. The compromise offer was acceptable to the union leadership, but it was voted down by the members of the local. (Subordinate clause beginning with *although*)

6. The town lies several miles off the main highway, and it is easy to miss. (Participial phrase beginning with *lying*)

7. The speaker seemed ill at ease, and he appeared to depend entirely on his written text. (Compound predicate)

8. The crew has made no effort to reforest the stripped acres, and a useless tangle of "weed trees" chokes this cut-over land. (Subordinate clause beginning with *because*)

9. We felt starved and arm-weary, and we gratefully grounded our canoe on a small island. (Participial phrase beginning with *starved*)

10. Paul revved the motor, and the rest of us pushed hard on the front bumper and fenders. (Subordinate clause beginning with *as* or *while*)

B. Follow the directions for Exercise A.

1. The weather was hot and humid, and the coach cancelled outdoor practice. (Subordinate clause beginning with *because*)

2. The desert sun had been unbearably hot, but the night brought a biting chill. (Subordinate clause beginning with *although*)

3. Much money has been spent on the playground, but few children use the facilities. (Subordinate clause beginning with *although*)

4. He doesn't understand the importance of compromise, and he will never be a good politician. (Subordinate clause beginning with *because*)

5. The octopus has tentacles, a horny beak, and almost human eyes, but it has internal characteristics that make it remarkably like a clam. (Subordinate clause beginning with *although*)

6. The President spent the weekend at Camp David, and then he flew to Washington for talks with the new Russian ambassador. (Compound predicate)

7. The harbor pilot climbed aboard the sleek cruise ship *Margaret B. Perrin,* and he guided her into San Francisco Bay. (Participial phrase beginning with *climbing*)

8. The TV station interrupted the program, and it issued a severe weather warning. (Participial phrase beginning with *interrupting*)

9. No one claimed the $100,000 and the police added it to their pension fund. (Subordinate clause beginning with *because*)

10. Raindrops act like prisms; they refract sunlight to produce rainbows. (Participial phrase beginning with *acting*)

Part 3
Variety of Sentence Length

A passage in which all the sentences are of about the same length, whether long or short, is monotonous. An occasional sentence of different length varies the rhythm and revives the interest of the reader. In the following passage from Albert Einstein's *Out of My Later Years*, note how the short sentences are relieved by long sentences.

> I do not consider myself the father of the release of atomic energy. My part in it was quite indirect. I did not, in fact, foresee that it would be released in my time. I believed only that it was theoretically possible. It became practical through the accidental discovery of chain reaction, and this was not something I could have predicted.

Avoiding a Series of Short Sentences

Monotony is created especially by a succession of short sentences. There are times when a conscious series of short sentences is very effective, as in narrative, when it has the effect of building up suspense. The unconscious use of a succession of short sentences, however, creates an awkward effect.

Short sentences may be combined in a number of ways:

1. by using a compound sentence.

> TWO SENTENCES   Residents reported a huge flying saucer. It was only a hole in the clouds.
>
> COMBINED   Residents reported a huge flying saucer, but it was only a hole in the clouds.

2. by using a simple sentence with a compound predicate.

TWO SENTENCES   A huge meteor struck Siberia in 1906. It plunged far down into the earth's crust.

COMBINED   A huge meteor struck Siberia in 1906 and plunged far down into the earth's crust.

3. by using a subordinate clause.

TWO SENTENCES   I entered the store. A little camera caught my eye.

COMBINED   As I entered the store, a little camera caught my eye.

TWO SENTENCES   My uncle has just received a research grant. He is a chemist.

COMBINED   My uncle, who is a chemist, has just received a research grant.

4. by using a participial phrase.

TWO SENTENCES   The comedian was shaking with laughter. He could hardly speak.

COMBINED   Shaking with laughter, the comedian could hardly speak.

5. by using a prepositional phrase.

TWO SENTENCES   Howie is relaxing. He has had a hard day in the classroom.

COMBINED   Howie is relaxing after a hard day in the classroom.

The following passage is an example of how the monotony of too many short sentences can be avoided by combining sentences.

ORIGINAL   I returned to my room. There was a note under my door. It was from Bill. He said he was in town looking for a job. He hadn't found anything yet. He was sorry to have missed me.

REWRITTEN   When I returned to my room, I found a note from Bill under the door. He said he was in town looking for a job, but hadn't found anything yet. He added that he was sorry to have missed me.

Exercises
Varying Sentence Length

A. Combine the sentences following each numbered item. Make one effective sentence.

1. Front Street was flooded this morning. Water from a broken main did it.
2. A policeman reports on rush-hour traffic on the expressway. He is in a helicopter.
3. The central human character in *Moby Dick* is Captain Ahab. He is captain of the *Pequod*.
4. At the climax of the story, the *Pequod* is sunk. Moby Dick sinks her.
5. The Epilogue to *Moby Dick* begins with a quotation from the Bible. It is from the Book of Job.
6. Mr. Smith is in San Francisco. He is house-hunting. His family is staying in Connecticut.
7. The parade went past the state capitol. It looked like a river. It lasted for hours.
8. Some shippers are storing wheat on the open ground. They dump it in huge piles. There is a shortage of railroad cars.
9. Chamblis swung at the low pitch. He drove the ball out of the park.
10. We went to a drive-in restaurant. We went there after the movie. We had hamburgers, onion rings, and French fries.
11. She had grown up in Paris. She spoke French fluently.
12. Paul called Betty. He asked her to bring her camera to the party.

13. The concern for safety has resulted in seatbelts. We also have shoulder harnesses. We also have the airbag to cushion passengers against impact.

14. The pilot settled himself at the controls. He began running down his checklist.

15. The company has been testing a new electric engine for three years. It has now decided to put the engine into production.

B. Rewrite the following paragraph, making changes in sentence structure to create fluent, readable prose.

Many of the nation's new suburban housing developments are monotonous and dull. They are advertised as the ultimate in modern living. They consist of badly built houses with fancy facades and rickety carports. Front lawns are small and useless. The developments have pastoral names like Pine Acres, Buckingham Woods, and King's Forest. Trees have been bulldozed to make way for roads and parking lots. The advertisements call these developments "communities." There is no community center—a large park, green, or lake—within walking distance of the homes. Shops, theaters, bowling centers are all miles away. People cannot "rub elbows" with their neighbors. There is no sense of community.

Chapter 7

Writing the Paragraph

The teen-ager is a universal butt of ridicule. It seems clear to me that the ridicule springs largely from envy. Adult life tends to be a pretty worn round of getting and spending. By contrast, the teen-agers seem a colorful, vivacious lot, to whom life is an exciting, tangy, complicated run of events irradiated with laughter and newly discovered relationships. The adults cannot turn the clock back, but they can jeer; and the teen-agers are clumsy, sensitive and vulnerable.— HERMAN WOUK

You probably recognize this piece of writing as a paragraph, the basic building block out of which compositions are made. Let us define the paragraph and then check this example against the definition.

Part 1

Defining the Paragraph

A paragraph is a group of related sentences with a single, unified idea that has been adequately developed. The paragraph usually has a topic sentence that states the main idea, one or more sentences that develop the main idea, and sometimes a clincher sentence that concludes the paragraph by tying up the idea.

The foregoing paragraph on teen-agers is a good example of a well written paragraph. It opens with a topic sentence that informs the reader what the paragraph is going to discuss. The writer then develops the idea by giving evidence to support what he says in his topic sentence. Sentences two, three, and four do exactly that. The last sentence is the clincher sentence, which ties up the idea of the paragraph. Notice that the clincher sentence does not merely repeat the topic sentence. Rather, it *restates* the main idea in terms of the nature of the development of the paragraph.

The preceding definition is the definition of an ideal paragraph. It is a valid definition. While there are some exceptions to this definition that will be presented later in the chapter, for our present purposes we will work with the ideal paragraph.

Here are two more paragraphs for close analysis to determine how well they fit the definition of an ideal paragraph.

Analysis 1

When I hear someone talk about the happy little birds and the delightful little animals I wince. Animals do play, or seem to, at times, and there seems to be a sense of happiness in birds sometimes; but I am not sure even of that. Birds and animals are not noticeably tolerant and life in the woods and fields is a constant round of attack and competition. When I see the way the birds squabble at our feeding station, gluttonous and ill tempered, I wish some of the sentimentalists would pause and look. Life among the birds is a grim matter of survival, and those who get pushed around too much do not survive.

The topic sentence says that the paragraph is going to discuss someone's talk about happy birds and delightful animals. It also prepares you for the writer's attitude toward his subject in the word *wince*. He implies that he disagrees with this kind of talk.

He then develops his paragraph with examples of the intolerance and fighting among birds and animals. However, while he specifically develops the problems between birds, he neglects to give equal emphasis to the specific problems between animals. In fact, his clincher sentence doesn't mention animals at all. If he had added one specific example about animals and had added animals to his clincher sentence, he would have had an ideal paragraph.

Analysis 2

> Half of Mexico is under eighteen. We are young and full of *inquietudes*. But we also have long roots in the soil. Our bronze-faced ancestors were not movie Indians, hunting buffalo and sleeping in tepees, but pioneers in agriculture, mathematics, and city building. They put poems to music and danced to please both the gods and themselves. Not waiting for America to be discovered in 1492, they founded our great capital.

The topic sentence, while interesting, is not really clear in its meaning. What it actually means, of course, is that half of the people in Mexico are under eighteen years of age. The writer begins to clarify the meaning in his second sentence, but he suddenly shifts to a description of the achievements of ancestors, which has no relationship to the idea in the topic sentence. The paragraph obviously lacks unity. It is merely a series of disconnected ideas. The paragraph has no clincher sentence because the writer has strayed so far from his original idea that it is impossible to tie the ideas together either in relationship to his development or to his topic sentence.

The Elements of the Paragraph

A well written paragraph is a logical unit of thought and seemingly simple to write. However, the writer must concern himself or herself with all of the following elements:

the topic sentence	unity	emphasis
the body	coherence	tone
the clincher sentence	adequate detail	mood

These nine elements will be discussed in detail in the remainder of the chapter.

Exercise
Analyzing the Paragraph

Study the following paragraphs. Then, using the criteria in the definition, explain which of the paragraphs are well developed, unified paragraphs, and which are not.

1

There was a "special feature"—"The Only Pacing Dog in the World." Occasionally we had seen Mr. Redfield with his Irish setter on Main Street. And we knew it was no common dog. Now at last we saw Mr. Redfield come out on the track with his horse and sulky. Alongside the right wheel so the grandstand could see him was the Irish setter, handsome with his coat of brown hair gleaming, his gait that of a pacer, the legs in that peculiar continuous sidewise throw. Twice around the half-mile track went the pacing dog. He wasn't as fast as pacing horses but the crowd believed he was the only pacing dog in the world and they cheered him and Mr. Redfield.

2

There is an old story of how the cathedral of Chartres was struck by lightning and burned to the ground. Then thousands of people came from all points of the compass, like a giant procession of ants, and together they began to rebuild the cathedral on its old site. They worked until the building was completed—master builders, artists, laborers, clowns, noblemen, priests, burghers. But they all remained anonymous, and no one knows to this day who built the cathedral of Chartres.

3

Youths the world over dream of the day when they will become men. Recognition of this achievement varies among the different cultures. Among certain tribes of New Guinea, for example, a stripling becomes a man when he can venture forth alone and return to his village bearing a neighboring tribesman's head on a spear. In many lands, a youngster assumes the responsibilities of manhood as soon as he can till the soil. American lads are considered to be full-fledged men when they are old enough to cast a ballot.

4

It required more skill to hunt the deer than any other animal. We never tried to approach a deer except against the wind. Frequently we would spend hours in stealing upon grazing deer. If they were in the open we would crawl long distances on the ground, keeping a weed or brush before us, so that our approach would not be noticed. Often we could kill several out of one herd before the others would run away. Their flesh was dried and packed in vessels, and would keep in this condition for many months. The hide of the deer was soaked in water and ashes and the hair removed, and then the process of tanning continued until the buckskin was soft and pliable. Perhaps no other animal was more valuable to use than the deer.

5

As you sway through life on a wooden leg, an odd and blessed thing happens. The rest of the world becomes accustomed, and then forgets that you have one, just as it becomes accustomed to, and then forgets the color of your eyes or whether you wear a vest. And you become accustomed to the limitations of one-legged life, such as not being able to pole-vault or drive a shift car, or being limited to half as much athlete's foot as other people have. But to children a wooden leg is eternally a surprise and a delight. Strange children gape unabashed, ask questions, and fool with it to see how it works. And when the wooden leg is actually in their own family, it is a sparkling source of entertainment.

6

We sat in front of the fire and pretended we saw pictures in the dancing flames. The people next door were not home, but their dog was barking loudly. He is a huge Irish setter with a shining red coat. We got up to investigate the noise, but at that moment Mother came in with hot cocoa. We sat down again and watched the fire. It was lovely.

7

My adjustment to my new world was a very difficult one. I ran into problems with my classmates almost immediately after returning to school. Everything proceeded smoothly enough until the entire class was out on the playground during recess.

8

Flax, plain old-fashioned blue flax, comes to bloom in a corner of the flower garden, and if there is a more beautiful floral blue than that of a flax flower one hour after sunrise I have yet to see it. Forget-me-nots, bluets, even spiderwort, cannot match it. Blue-eyed grass, out in the pasture, comes closest; but the flax so outsizes the blue-eyed grass that comparison is difficult. Flax flowers are an inch and a half across and a hundred to the clump. Each flower lasts only a day, but new ones keep coming from buds that look, under my ten-power glass, amazingly like rosebuds with their tightly rolled petals. Blue roses!

Part 2

The Topic Sentence

The topic sentence states the main idea of the paragraph. The topic sentence must have a subject: it must be about something. It must also state a point of view toward that subject. The point of view must be expandable; that is, it must lend itself to being explained or discussed or proved.

Beginning writers often start writing a paragraph, only to discover that they can't go beyond a sentence or two. There is nothing more to say. Usually that happens because the topic sentence does not have a point of view to be developed. For example, consider the following topic sentence:

The Sears Tower is in Chicago.

While this sentence is about something—the Sears Tower—it has no point of view. When the writer has written that the building is in Chicago, he has little more to say. He could add a sentence stating the exact street location, but that would be all. Let's look at a restatement of the same sentence:

The Sears Tower is one of the most exciting buildings in the world.

The sentence now has a point of view, *exciting*, that can be developed. Literally hundreds of things can be written to expand the point of view. A writer can describe the sheer mass of the building, the crispness of its style, the magnificent interior decorating, the amazing speed of the elevators, and other such things. He can explain or prove or show that the building is, indeed, exciting.

Here is another example of a sentence that would serve well as a topic sentence:

The Sears Tower is a fine addition to Chicago.

Now a writer could expand upon the idea of the many people who are hired to work there. He could discuss the number of tourists it draws to Chicago. He could describe its dramatic effect on the skyline. There is an almost endless number of ways of developing that idea.

It is true that the writer could start a paragraph with "The Sears Tower is in Chicago." Then his second sentence might be "It is one of the most exciting buildings in the world." However, it is this second sentence, not the first, that would be the topic sentence in this case. This order of sentences raises the fact that a topic sentence does not have to be the first sentence in the paragraph. Although the topic sentence usually *is* the first sentence in the paragraph, it could be somewhere in the middle of the paragraph, or even the last sentence.

By placing the topic sentence last in a paragraph, or in the middle of a paragraph, the writer can achieve variety. Just as it is desirable to have sentences of various lengths and structures to avoid monotony, so is it desirable to have variety in paragraphs by placing the topic sentence in various positions.

Exercises
Placement of the Topic Sentence

A. Find the topic sentence in each of these paragraphs, and note whether it is at the beginning of the paragraph, in the middle, or at the end. Give reasons for your decision.

1

Most bakers are interested mainly in how a loaf of bread looks. They are concerned with how little stuff they can put in it—to get how much money. They are deeply interested in using chemicals that will keep bread from molding, make it seem "fresh" for the longest possible time, and so render it marketable and shippable. They have been at this monkeyshine for a generation. Today a loaf of "bread" looks deceptively real; but it is made from heaven knows what and it resembles, as food, a solidified bubble bath. Some months ago I bought a loaf of the stuff and, experimentally, began pressing it together like an accordian. With a little effort, I squeezed the whole loaf to a length of about one inch!—
PHILIP WYLIE

2

Almost every layman I have ever met exhibits a real curiosity about songs and how they are written. It is a standing joke among authors and composers that when they meet people the first question asked of them is "Which comes first, the words or the music?" Perhaps it is high time that one of us stopped laughing at the classic query and provided a sensible answer to it. There is nothing foolish about the question. A song is a wedding of two crafts, and it is a natural thing to wonder how they meet and live together.—OSCAR HAMMERSTEIN II

3

Yes, it seemed in every respect a curious gift. An appalling one, really. For I had already a sufficiency of pets: two dogs, an English bulldog and a Kerry blue terrier. Moreover, I have never been partial to birds; indeed, I've had always rather an aversion to them: when, on a beach, sea gulls swoop and dive, I am (for example) very liable to panic and run. Once when I was five or six, a sparrow, having flown through the window of my room, became trapped there: flew about till I was almost faint from an emotion in which pity figured but fear predominated. And so it was with some dismay that I received Graziella's Christmas present: an ugly young raven with wings cruelly clipped.—TRUMAN CAPOTE

4

It seems that life is virtually certain to arise wherever conditions are at all favorable. That is a lesson we might have learned from a study of our own planet. There is hardly a spot of Earth, from the highest mountains to the ultimate depths of the sea, which some creature has not been able to conquer by suitable adaptation. Life may be found frozen eleven months out of twelve in the Antarctic wastes—or flourishing a few degrees below boiling-point in sulphur springs.—ARTHUR C. CLARKE

5

She leans her head against me and looks fondly at me with her soulful brown eyes. They are limpid and deep, and I know they speak of inner love. I stroke my hand through her long, lustrous red hair and whisper into her ear. My Irish Setter loves me as much as I love her. When I speak her name she raises her head just as a human would and waits for the praise she knows I will give her. We enjoy our moments together.

6

The irony of all this was that, in spite of her, he had turned out so well. In spite of going to only a third-rate college, he had, on his own initiative, come out with a first-rate education; in spite of growing up dominated by a small mind, he had ended up with a large one; in spite of all her foolish views, he was free of prejudice and unafraid to face facts. Most miraculous of all, instead of being blinded by love for her as she was for him, he had cut himself emotionally free of her and could see her with complete objectivity. He was not dominated by his mother.—FLANNERY O'CONNOR

B. Here are ten sentences that would make good topic sentences for paragraphs. Put one line under the subject and two lines under the point of view, like this: Spring rains brighten nature.

1. The craftsmanship on that table is superb.
2. Would you be surprised if you discovered gold in your backyard?
3. Roller skating is becoming remarkably popular.
4. The hurricane did devastating damage to the whole coast of Southern Florida last year.
5. Bears eat a lot of food before they settle in for hibernation.
6. Day in and day out I follow the same tedious pattern of life.
7. Raymond's Kitchen is the best restaurant in the Midwest.
8. Do you believe in Peter Pan?
9. I learned to like books when I was very young.
10. Swimming is the best all-around exercise for your body.

C. Develop one of the above sentences, or an original one of your own, into a paragraph of about eight to ten sentences. Your topic sentence may be at the beginning of the paragraph or somewhere in the middle or at the end.

D. Write ten topic sentences of your own on any subject. Be sure that they have a subject and a point of view toward the subject. Keep your sentences for a later assignment.

E. Select three of the topic sentences you have written and develop paragraphs from them. In your first paragraph put the topic sentence at the beginning. In your second paragraph put the topic sentence in the middle. In your third paragraph put the topic sentence at the end.

Part 3

The Body

The body of the paragraph is the substance, the evidence to support the idea in the topic sentence. While the topic sentence presents the idea of the paragraph in a neat little package, the body opens the package so you can see what it contains.

Examine the following paragraph, looking for the body and determining what it tells you.

> Nothing is more difficult for the beginning librarian than to discover in what profession he is engaged. Certain professions define themselves. Others are defined by those who practice them. The librarian's profession is of neither nature. A librarian is so called not for what he does, as the farmer who farms or the lawyer who laws, but from the place in which he does it. And the definitions of the librarians, though they are eloquent in describing the librarian's perfection, are reticent in saying what the librarian's perfections are for.—ARCHIBALD MACLEISH

You probably detected that the first sentence is the topic sentence. The other sentences, up to the last one, explain why the novice librarian has trouble determining what his or her profession is. The last sentence, of course, is the clincher.

Exercise
Determining How the Body of a Paragraph Works

In each of the following paragraphs determine what the main idea in the topic sentence is, and how the body develops or explains the main idea.

1

If you were to ask me what strictly vocational courses there are in the typical college curriculum, my answer—now that the good old habit of the "theme a day" has virtually disappeared—would be the writing of poetry and the writing of short stories. Not that I expect many of you to become poets or short story writers—far from it. But these two courses offer the easiest way to obtain some skill in expression. They force one to organize thought. They demand of one that he give meaning to every word. They train the ear for language, its meaning, its precision, its overtones—and its pitfalls. Above all, they force one to write.—PETER F. DRUCKER

2

Every American businessman knows he does not earn his living in an isolated compartment somehow separated from the rest of the life of the nation. He is not just "a businessman." He is first of all a man and an American citizen. His livelihood depends upon his ability, sometimes alone but usually in association, to make a profit out of competing with others who serve the needs of his fellow men. He succeeds most when he serves best the interest of the largest number of people.—FRANK W. ABRAMS

3

The difficulty of learning about the history of women in America is that, for the most part, it is an unwritten history of millions of private lives, whose voices, those that were recorded at all, are scattered and buried in journals and letters. It isn't hard to find out what men thought of us—their ideas about women are accessible through the laws they passed and maintained, denying or restricting women's civil and property rights, through the religions they organized and practiced, through their literature. Women did write novels, essays, poems, magazine articles, but most of these are long out of print, and the task of digging up those old sources is still ahead of us.—CONNIE BROWN and JANE SEITZ

4

Laundering was not easy in those days. The old woman had no faucet where she lived but had to bring in the water from a pump. For the linens to come out so clean, they had to be scrubbed thoroughly in a washtub, rinsed with washing soda, soaked, boiled in an enormous pot, starched, then ironed. Every piece was handled ten times or more. And the drying! It could not be done outside because thieves would steal the laundry. The wrung-out wash had to be carried up to the attic and hung on clotheslines. In the winter it would become as brittle as glass and almost break when touched. And there was always a to-do with other housewives and washwomen who wanted the attic clotheslines for their own use. Only God knows all the old woman had to endure each time she did a wash!—ISAAC BASHEVIS SINGER

5

I practiced the yo-yo because it pleased me to do so, without the slightest application of will power. It wasn't ambition that drove me, but the nature of yo-yoing. The yo-yo represented my first organized attempt to control the outside world. It fascinated me because I could see my progress in clearly defined stages, and because the intimacy of it, the almost spooky closeness I began to feel with the instrument in my hand, seemed to ensure that nothing irrelevant would interfere. I was, in the language of jazz, "up tight" with my yo-yo, and finally free, in one small area at least, of the paralyzing sloppiness of life in general.—FRANK CONROY

6

I was too young to be other than awed and puzzled by Doc Marlowe when I knew him. I was only sixteen when he died. He was sixty-seven. There was that vast difference in our ages and there was a vaster difference in our backgrounds. Doc Marlowe was a medicine-show man. He had been a lot of other things, too: a circus man, the proprietor of a concession at Coney Island, a saloon-keeper; but in his fifties he had traveled around with a tent-show troupe made up of a Mexican named Chickalilli, who threw knives, and a man called

Professor Jones, who played the banjo. Doc Marlowe would come out after the entertainment and harangue the crowd and sell bottles of medicine for all kinds of ailments. I found out all this about him gradually, toward the last, and after he died. When I first knew him, he represented the Wild West to me, and there was nobody I admired so much.—JAMES THURBER

7

When I was six or seven years old, growing up in Pittsburgh, I used to take a precious penny of my own and hide it for someone else to find. For some reason I always "hid" the penny along the same stretch of sidewalk up the street. I would cradle it at the roots of a sycamore, say, or in a hole left by a chipped-off piece of sidewalk. Then I would take a piece of chalk, and, starting at either end of the block, draw huge arrows leading up to the penny from both directions. After I learned to write I labeled the arrows: SURPRISE AHEAD or MONEY THIS WAY. I was greatly excited, during all this arrow-drawing, at the thought of the first lucky passer-by who would receive in this way, regardless of merit, a free gift from the universe. But I never lurked about. I would go straight home and not give the matter another thought, until some months later, I would be gripped again by the impulse to hide another penny.—ANNIE DILLARD

8

Even as the autumn days shorten they increase in height and breadth. It is as though there were a constant ratio which keeps the days in balance. The leaves are thinning out. The eye can reach. New vistas open. The horizon is just there beyond the trees on the other side of my river, now that the leaves have fallen. The sun slants in a window where two weeks ago there was thick maple shade. The hills are no longer remote, and at night I can look up from almost anywhere and see the constellations of Andromeda and Pegasus. Even in a land of trees, we are no longer canopied from the sky or walled in from the horizon. The earth's distances invite the eye.—HAL BORLAND

Part 4
The Clincher Sentence

We have already talked about the clincher sentence, but here is a clear definition. Not all paragraphs have a clincher sentence, but in those that do, the clincher sentence comes at the end. Some writers refer to the clincher sentence as "the second topic sentence." That is a good definition, because the clincher sentence restates what the topic sentence says. A good clincher sentence does not merely repeat the exact words of the topic sentence. After all, the whole body of the paragraph comes before the clincher sentence, so the clincher sentence must strive to sum up, or tie up, the ideas. It leaves the reader with a good, clear idea of what he has just read.

Exercises
Working with Clincher Sentences

A. Identify the clincher sentence and the topic sentence in the following paragraphs. Be ready to tell how the clincher sentence restates the idea that is expressed in the topic sentence and ties up the development of the idea.

1

When I was a boy, there was but one permanent ambition among my comrades in our village on the west bank of the Mississippi River: that was to be a steamboatman. We had transient ambitions of other sorts, but they were only transient. When a circus came and went, it left us all burning to become clowns; the first Negro minstrel show that ever came to our section left us all suffering to try that kind of life; now and then we had a hope that if we lived and were good, God would permit us to be pirates. These ambitions faded out, each in its turn; but the ambition to be a steamboatman always remained.—MARK TWAIN

2

Character is not revealed when life shows its best side, but when it shows its worst. The way to tell a print from a tapestry is to look at the seamy side. An inexperienced buyer never turns the chair upside down; an expert always does. The worth of a person, in like manner, is to be judged by how he reacts to the obstacles, the limitations, and the crosses of life.

3

The father of Horace, a famous Roman poet, had ambitions for his child. He himself had begun life as a slave, and though he became free and a respectable property owner, he was never rich. But he was only the more eager that his son should have what he had lacked. He had never learned to write—well, young Horace should. The father found teachers for him at first in Venusia. Then he got the daring idea that his boy should be taught, not in rude provincial schools, but at Rome, where the best teachers in Italy could be hired.—JOSEPH AUSLANDER and FRANK ERNEST HILL

B. Here are ten sentences. Some of them would make good clincher sentences, assuming that there was a proper body before them. Mark the ones that would *not* make good clincher sentences and be ready to tell why.

1. And that reminds me of another thing.
2. As the sun rose in the east, it promised another beautiful day.
3. A new analysis of the extent of graft among politicians would show some things that would be embarrassing.
4. The moral is: Look before you leap.
5. You can see that these facts speak for themselves.
6. I'm sure that this is the way we should follow.
7. There are a number of reasons why people lie.
8. This should have awakened you from your happy dreams.
9. Let us examine a few simple facts before we go to the police.
10. So goes the news on this day, the Fourth of July.

C. You are now ready to write a paragraph that has a topic sentence, a body, and a clincher sentence. Go back to Exercise D on page 102. You have already developed three of these topic sentences. Take any three of the remaining seven topic sentences you wrote. Construct three paragraphs, each based on one of those topic sentences.

Part 5
Paragraph Unity

Paragraphs may, and do, differ in many ways—in purpose, style, and length, for example. However, there is one vital quality that every paragraph must have. A paragraph must have **unity.** Every sentence in a paragraph must work with every other sentence toward a single end. There should be no needless sentences that lead away from the purpose of the paragraph. All sentences must mesh together like the gears in a smooth-running engine.

Examine the following paragraph to see if every sentence is needed and works together with the other sentences to one purpose.

> Why were the other students so cold and unkind? Was it because her long stringy hair hung in her eyes instead of dipping in graceful curls? Was it because she wrote poetry in algebra class and got A's in Latin without really trying? Shivering, Laura remembered how they would sit at the back of English class, passing notes and whispering. She thought of their identical brown loafers, their plastic purses, their hostile stares as they passed her in the corridors. But she didn't care. They were clods, the whole lot of them.—RONA MAYNARD

If you examined this paragraph closely, you know that it does have unity. It is centered around a girl who is shunned by the other students. She is obviously hurt by their indifference to her, and eases that hurt by saying that they are clods, that she doesn't care what they think. Because this is such a well constructed paragraph, there is not a single useless sentence. Every sentence that is needed is there and works with every other sentence.

Here is a paragraph that has some unneeded sentences. Look for them as you read.

> Perhaps the only tiresome thing about being an American is that one is continually being told by foreigners what is wrong with this country. Fortunately, most Americans seem rather to enjoy this type of criticism and wisely so because, after all, criticism is a form of homage. I have a history teacher who always criticizes me, so I know what it is like to be criticized. I get B's, but she thinks I should get A's. One criticizes only that which seems potentially perfect. There is a long history of people criticizing each other.

What happens in this paragraph is an example of what frequently happens in a composition. A word or a phrase or the subject matter itself suggests a thought to the writer, and he goes off in a new direction, forgetting what his original purpose was.

What is the word in this paragraph that diverts the writer from his purpose? You can see that it is the word *criticism*. The writer of this paragraph feels he has a complaint against his history teacher, and the complaint is triggered by the word *criticism*. The following sentences should not have been included in this paragraph: "I have a history teacher who always criticizes me, so I know what it is like to be criticized"; "I get B's, but she thinks I should get A's"; and "There is a long history of people criticizing each other."

Exercises
Unity in Paragraphs

A. Here are three paragraphs. Identify the one that has good unity. Then, using your own words and ideas, supply missing words or sentences to the paragraph that needs them to achieve unity. Finally, delete the excess words or sentences from the paragraph that has these faults.

1

The reputation of the lion as a man-killer has been greatly exaggerated. By and large it is a peaceable, good-natured beast and does not attack man unless molested. Wolves have a bad reputation, too. People mistakenly believe that they run in packs and chase humans. However, a lion is dangerous when aroused or when, as sometimes happens, it has acquired a taste for human flesh. Lions once held up the building of the Uganda Railway for nine months, during which time they killed a great many laborers. There are no wolves in Uganda.

2

Between the sunlit surface waters of the open sea and the hidden hills and valleys of the ocean floor lies the least-known region of the sea. These deep, dark waters, with all their mysteries and their unsolved problems, cover a very considerable part of the earth. The whole world ocean extends over about three-fourths of the surface of the globe. If we subtract the shallow areas of the continental shelves and the scattered banks and shoals, where at least the pale ghost of sunlight moves over the underlying bottom, there still remains about half the earth that is covered by miles-deep, lightless water, that has been dark since the world began.

3

Modern archaeology began with the discovery of buried Pompeii. Before then, the digging of treasures from the ground had been a haphazard and unscholarly affair. Visiting Pompeii is like taking a stroll into the past.

B. These three paragraphs lack unity. Study them carefully. Then add sentences where they are needed and cross out sentences that are not needed. Your final paragraphs should have a topic sentence, a well developed body, and a clincher sentence.

1

Our last football game was wild. Up until the very last play in the game we were tied 0-0. On the last play Jackson, our quarterback, kept the ball and plowed right through the middle for a score. Jackson is an All-Conference choice. He has played outstanding ball for our school. Jackson is tall and can always be recognized in the corridors.

2

I'm dating two girls, and I feel trapped. Both girls are possessive. They even talk about marriage. Their names are Lola and Sherry. I like both girls, but I'm only in high school. I don't want to get married and maybe never will. They have excellent qualities. Lola is thoughtful and mature and is into science. She will undoubtedly make a fine salary some day. Her family pressures her to make straight A's. She will finish school this year.

3

My family rented a houseboat on the Mississippi for a weekend. If prizes were given for rotten weekends, that weekend would win them all. There were a few good things. One is that the scenery was beautiful despite the rain. And the mosquitoes didn't bite much in the part of the river to which we drifted after losing our anchor. The weekend cost only $30.00. My sister insists that we should go again next year.

Part 6

Coherence

A good paragraph is coherent. The ideas are presented in a logical order and are clearly linked to one another so that the train of thought is easy to follow.

The order of ideas in a paragraph is determined by the nature of the development of the paragraph. The most frequently used ways of ordering or arranging details in a paragraph are the following:

    chronological order   spatial order   order of importance

Chronological Order

Chronological order is the order of time. For example, in developing a paragraph by an incident, you would arrange the details in the order in which they happened. In developing a paragraph by explaining the steps in a process, you would arrange the steps in the order in which they should be done. The ideas in the following paragraph are the steps, in order, that one takes in writing a business letter. Note that the ideas are actually numbered to emphasize the order.

> Making a plan for a business letter involves the following steps: 1. When a reply to a letter is to be dictated, your first step is to read the letter carefully and note everything in it that requires attention. It may be wise to underscore or encircle key words. 2. Your next step is to determine and list the points to be discussed in the reply—those needed to cover the questions asked or implied in the original letter. If the letter is not a reply to another letter, you will be concerned with the points needed to present the subject adequately; they are determined by analyzing the problem. 3. Check the points to see that everything necessary has been covered but that there is nothing superfluous. This assures a complete, unified letter. 4. Number or list the points in logical sequence.—SMART, MCKELFY and GERFEN

Spatial Order

Spatial order is the position of things in space and is usually used in descriptive writing. In describing a scene, for example, you will want to arrange the details so that the reader will know where they are in relation to the narrator. In the following paragraph, note how the writer has arranged the details so that the reader can follow the activity.

> These days our back porch was piled with baskets of peaches and grapes and pears, bought in town, and onions and tomatoes and cucumbers grown at home, all waiting to

be made into jelly and jam and preserves, pickles and chili sauce. In the kitchen there was a fire in the stove all day, jars clinked in boiling water, sometimes a cheesecloth bag was strung on a pole between two chairs, straining blueblack grape pulp for jelly. I was given jobs to do and I would sit at the table peeling peaches that had been soaked in the hot water, or cutting up onions, my eyes smarting and streaming. As soon as I was done I ran out of the house, trying to get out of earshot before my mother thought of what she wanted me to do next.—ALICE MUNRO

Order of Importance

The order of importance is given to ideas in a paragraph of explanation or argument. You will usually want to begin with the least important facts or reasons and build to a climax with the most important ones, thus providing a strong conclusion. Sometimes, however, you may wish to do just the opposite— start with your strongest or most effective reason and then support it with less important ones. In either case, your reader should be able to understand the relative importance of the ideas. Note how the arrangement of ideas in the following paragraph of explanation builds up to a climax.

The greatest pleasure in yo-yoing was an abstract pleasure —watching the dramatization of simple physical laws, and realizing they would never fail if a trick was done correctly. The geometric purity of it! The string wasn't just a string, it was a tool in the enactment of theorems. It was a line, an idea. And the top was an entirely different sort of idea, a gyroscope, capable of storing energy and of interacting with the line. I remember the first time I did a particularly lovely trick, one in which the sleeping yo-yo is swung from right to left while the string is interrupted by an extended index finger. Momentum carries the yo-yo in a circular path around the finger, but instead of completing the arc the yo-yo falls on the taut string between the performer's hands, where it continues to spin in an upright position. My pleasure at the moment was as much from the beauty of the experiment as from pride.—FRANK CONROY

Not every paragraph needs a specific order of ideas. For example, a paragraph about the pleasures of skiing could probably discuss the pleasures in any order. If you wrote a paragraph describing a sunny day in June, it probably wouldn't matter if you described the singing of the birds first and the greenness of the grass second, or the other way around. A paragraph developed by facts or examples may not follow any prescribed order if the facts or examples are of equal importance. Many writers, of course, use not one, but a combination of methods to achieve an effective paragraph.

Exercise
Order of Details in a Paragraph

A. Each of the following paragraphs is developed by a different order of details: chronological order, spatial order, and order of importance. Determine the order of each paragraph and be ready to explain your choice.

1

They reached the junction some time before the train was due to arrive and stood about two feet from the first set of tracks. Mr. Head carried a paper sack with some biscuits and a can of sardines in it for their lunch. A coarse-looking orange-colored sun coming up behind the east range of mountains was making the sky a dull red behind them, but in front of them it was still gray and they faced a gray transparent moon, hardly stronger than a thumbprint and completely without light. A small tin switch box and a black fuel tank were all there was to mark the place as a junction; the tracks were double and did not converge again until they were hidden behind the bends at either end of the clearing. Trains passing appeared to emerge from a tunnel of trees and, hit for a second by the cold sky, vanish terrified into the woods again.—FLANNERY O'CONNOR

2

An old tale accounts for the origin of the cat family in a thoroughly unscientific way. Not long after Noah had loaded the Ark with animals and set sail on his memorable voyage, he found that the vessel was overrun with mice. The original pair had multiplied so rapidly that their offspring were adding greatly to the discomforts of an already overcrowded passenger list. Even more serious were the terrific inroads the hungry rodents were making in the food supply. Noah in desperation went to the lion and asked his advice. After a moment's thought, the resourceful king of beasts took a deep breath, humped his back, and brought forth a mighty sneeze. Out from his mouth popped a pair of house cats! Needing no urging, they immediately went to work. Soon all but one pair of mice had disappeared. These Noah caught and confined in a cage till the end of the voyage.—CARL BURGER

3

The Latin American prefers to live in the more temperate climate of the highland because most of his land lies within the tropical lowlands where life can be precarious and short. In Mexico, in Central America, in Brazil, and in other parts of Latin America, there are repelling areas of damp and darkened jungle and rain forest. Here there is the endless drip of rain and almost perpetual twilight, for the sun rarely shines through the massed green ceiling of the close-growing trees. The tropical rain forest is a place of rapid birth, rapid growth, and rapid decay, and there is a dramatic closeness between life and death. There is savagery here, and there is danger everywhere—in the coils of the boa constrictor and the anaconda, in the vampire bat that must have blood, in the poisonous bite of the spider, in the bite of the disease-bearing mosquito, and in the prowling jaguar and puma. In the waters are voracious piranha, fish that can strip the flesh from man and animal within seconds. There are also eels that shock with electricity, fish that bear poison in their bodies, and the toothed menace of alligator and crocodile. There is disease in these tropical jungles, and little food, and soil that cannot be tilled for long. Men do live in a few of these jungle regions, in coastal Mexico and Yucatán, for instance, but generally life is safer and healthier in the higher places.—PAUL THOMAS WELTY

B. The sentences in the following paragraphs are not in logical order. Study the paragraphs to determine the logical order; then write down the numbers of the sentences in the correct order of ideas. Indicate which order you have used: chronological, spatial, or order of importance.

1

1. Most of us overlook good letter-writing opportunities every day. 2. Unfortunately, these letters often sound as if they had been written as school assignments, instead of with warm, human feeling. 3. Friends of mine got a note from a woman who wrote that an evening spent at their home was "one of the most delightful occasions I have ever enjoyed—one which I shall remember for ever and ever." 4. The etiquette books tell us we must write thank-you notes for Christmas, birthday, and wedding gifts, and bread-and-butter letters when we visit friends. 5. As this seemed to exaggerate the importance of the occasion, they couldn't help doubting the sincerity of the writer.

2

1. Presently, however, the sun broke through, and from the top of the rim we were able to look down over the other side on to the bright green floor of the crater, 2,000 feet below. 2. Its circular rim rises 8,000 feet above the sea, and on the day we arrived heavy rain clouds were hanging about. 3. Nothing appears to move down there; it is calm and silent as a mountain lake. 4. The really spectacular thing at this eastern end of the Serengeti Plains is the Ngorongoro Crater mountain. 5. At first sight this crater floor does not seem to be very high—it is not unlike an ordinary circular football field seen from a seat high up in the grandstand—and it is difficult to believe that the actual area is 200 square miles.

3

1. By early afternoon Walter had to give up. 2. But the moose was traveling through and kept going. 3. He trudged in after dark, tired and sick with disappointment, and I felt as bad as he did. 4. Walter followed the moose all that day without catching sight of it, made a fire and camped under a spruce tree in below-zero cold that night, and took the trail again at daylight the next morning. 5. That was the only moose track we had seen, and the closest we had come to killing fresh meat, through the whole winter. 6. His homemade snowshoes were wearing out, and he was getting so far from our camp that he did not dare to keep on.

4

1. He was immediately expelled from the community, and anyone who wanted to could kill him. 2. Theft was practically unheard of. 3. But he could take no more, and if anyone showed enough disrespect for the labor of others to steal the fruit of that labor—corn or anything else—the Mayas felt that such a person was obviously not fit to live with. 4. There was little crime among the ancient Mayas. 5. In Maya society a thief was declared an outlaw. 6. The Mayas had a rule that a man who was hungry could help himself to two ears of corn from any field he passed.

Linking Words and Expressions

Arranging your ideas in logical order in a paragraph is one way to achieve coherence. Using linking words and expressions is another way to achieve coherence.

Linking words help the reader follow the line of thought from one idea to another. Pronouns such as the following are the most useful words for this purpose because they refer to words and ideas in preceding sentences.

he, him, his	they, them, their
she, her, hers	this, that
it, its	these, those

In the following paragraph, note how the words in red refer to a previously mentioned person or idea.

In 1862 I was in the region of San Andres Tuxtla, a town of the state of Veracruz, in Mexico. During my excursions, I learned that a Colossal Head had been unearthed a few years before, in the following manner. Some one-and-a-half leagues from a sugarcane hacienda, on the western slopes of the Sierra of San Martín, a laborer of this hacienda, while cutting the forest for his field, discovered on the surface of the ground what looked like the bottom of a great iron kettle turned upside down. He notified the owner of the hacienda, who ordered its excavation. And in place of the kettle was discovered the above-mentioned head. It was left in the excavation as one would not think to move it, being of granite and measuring two yards in height with corresponding proportions. On my arrival at the hacienda I asked the owner to take me to look at it. We went, and I was struck with surprise: as a work of art, it is without exaggeration a magnificent sculpture, but what astonished me was the Ethiopic type represented. I reflected that there had undoubtedly been Negroes in this country, and that this had been in the first epoch of the world.—J. M. MELGAR

The use of pronouns is one of two important ways of achieving coherence in a paragraph. The other is the use of **linking expressions,** or connectives. Linking expressions help to move the idea of the paragraph smoothly from sentence to sentence. They do so in the following ways:

TO ADD IDEAS:

and	in addition	and then	equally important
also	likewise	further	in the same fashion
too	again	furthermore	moreover
besides	nor	as a result	

TO LIMIT OR CONTRADICT:

but	however	at the same time
yet	although	on the other hand

and yet	nevertheless	on the contrary
still	otherwise	nonetheless

TO ARRANGE IN TIME OR PLACE:

first	finally	soon	here
second (etc.)	at this point	sooner or later	nearly
next	meanwhile	afterward	opposite to
presently	eventually	at length	adjacent to

TO EXEMPLIFY OR SUM UP:

for example	in short	for the most part
for instance	in brief	in any event
in fact	on the whole	in any case
in other words	to sum up	as I have said

Exercise
Using Linking Expressions

Study the following paragraph. Determine what pronouns and what linking expressions help the coherence of the paragraph. Copy them in order, numbering each with the number of the sentence in which it appears.

1. For people with offices in the towers, especially on their upper floors, working in the World Trade Center is radically different from working anywhere else. 2. In the first place, many of them admit to being nagged by a constant fear of fire—what the Port Authority casually refers to as "The Towering Inferno" syndrome. 3. For the most part, the fear is irrational, for the WTC is constructed entirely of fireproof materials. 4. On the other hand, the WTC has already had a major fire, on February 13, 1975, when a blaze set by a disgruntled cleaning person on the eleventh floor of the North Tower caused more than a million dollars' worth of damage. 5. What burned, however, wasn't the building itself but drapes, carpets, and furnishings, although the heat of the fire did blow out windows and cause some minor structural damage. 6. Luckily, no one was injured and the fire didn't spread to any other floors, but it nonetheless proved that

the towers were somewhat less fireproof than the Port Authority had been claiming. 7. And it did little to ease the minds of those plagued by the fear of being trapped in a towering inferno.—THOMAS MEEHAN

Part 7

Adequate Detail

Writers often fail to give enough details in developing their paragraphs. For that reason the reader loses interest. After all, the reader knows only what he sees on the page before him. He can't visualize or understand or agree or disagree unless he has sufficient information presented to him. Note the plentiful details that make the following paragraph full and interesting.

> Harriet Tubman was a Negro child, a slave, born to slave parents and owned by a Maryland master. She was born in 1821, the year of the great slave uprising in South Carolina led by a black man, Denmark Vesey. All through that year, and for many years to come, Vesey's name rang through the slave cabins. His exploit frightened some slaves because masters became harsher, but it excited others to hope. As a very small child, Harriet was taught to sing a song that Vesey had made popular:
> > Go down, Moses
> > Way down to Egypt land!
> > And tell old Pharaoh
> > To let my people go!
> It was a dangerous song to sing. It had to be sung under the breath even when no white man was around. But in the years to come, it became Harriet's song.—HENRIETTA BUCKMASTER

You can respond to this paragraph because of the richness of details. You learn sufficient biographical facts about Harriet Tubman and Vesey. You learn of the origin of a song that is still sung today, and you get at least an impression of what slavery was like.

Here is the same paragraph as it might have been written by an inexperienced writer who was incomplete in giving details. It is easy to see that the full and complete version is the better of the two.

> Harriet Tubman was a slave. She was born in 1821, when Denmark Vesey led a slave uprising. Harriet learned a song that Vesey made popular called "Go Down Moses." In later years it became Harriet's song.

Exercises
Supplying Adequate Details

A. Here are some "paragraphs" that lack sufficient detail. Choose three and amplify them. Stick to the subject but supply enough details to develop them into substantial paragraphs.

1. Some exams are "bad news." I have a real fear of examinations in some of my subjects.
2. I would like to travel more. I have made trips to a few places in my lifetime.
3. I love a parade. The last parade I saw had a number of floats.
4. I used to be easily embarrassed. There are several things that happened to me which embarrassed me at the time.
5. There are some jobs around the house that I detest. I try to avoid them whenever I can.

B. These "paragraphs" also lack adequate detail. Choose three, and from your own imagination, supply details that will develop them into good paragraphs.

1. The squad car, with its siren screaming, pulled up beside the battered Chevy. A scene of devastation met the eyes of the trooper.
2. The flood waters spewed through the hole in the dam, which widened even as we watched it. Then, with fury, it hurled itself down the stream bed at the town below.
3. She mounted carefully, but she rode carelessly and dangerously at the horse show this afternoon.

4. The sun beat remorselessly on the beach. Ed, who had fallen asleep an hour earlier, woke to find he was badly burned.

5. A bear lumbered ponderously toward the tent. Standing in the entryway, Sally froze.

6. The airliner hummed through the upper air. Jane was on her way to Europe at last.

7. It was hard to tell who had started the fight. Both boys refused to talk.

8. The directions with the pattern were explicit. Phyllis began to make the dress with confidence.

9. The lake was so polluted you could almost walk on it. It was unfit for swimming.

10. The train usually runs late. It is hard to have to depend upon public transportation.

Part 8

Emphasis

Many devices can be used to make a whole paragraph or certain parts of it emphatic. For instance, you can use a strong style, with short, muscular sentences and many active verbs. You can write at length about what is important and give only a little space to what you wish to slight. You can employ striking words that are brutal or beautiful. You can use colorful descriptions. You can repeat words or phrases. You are practically unlimited in the ways you can achieve emphasis.

Exercise
Achieving Emphasis

How is emphasis achieved in each of these paragraphs?

1

Always when he looked in the mirror, his eyes were different. Sometimes they peered from out of the broken glass asking an unanswerable question, sometimes they were angry and damning, sometimes they were silent and brooding—too often they were the eyes of a dead man, jellied and black. His long, fleshy nose with its countless red pinpricks would expand and contract in time to his breathing, and the gray-striped lips that refused to open over the severe outward slant of the front teeth would strain themselves into the subtlest kind of smile. Thus he could stand, sometimes for over an hour, a silent, ugly man who could no longer tell whether he was inside the mirror or inside himself.—WILLIAM DEMBY

2

Perhaps the worst squalor created by motor cars that I have ever seen is along the supposedly scenic Route 110 crossing northern Idaho. There, near a lovely lake outside Coeur d'Alene, one passes within a few hundred feet of a junkyard containing at least a thousand carcasses of motorcars, piled four and five high. As you continue east into the mountainous mining communities, the junked motorcars are no longer gathered into yards. They simply lie abandoned, often upside-down, beside the road.—VANCE PACKARD

3

It was the best of times, it was the worst of times, it was the age of wisdom, it was the age of foolishness, it was the epoch of belief, it was the epoch of incredulity, it was the season of Light, it was the season of Darkness, it was the spring of hope, it was the winter of despair, we had everything before us, we had nothing before us, we were all going direct to Heaven, we were all going direct the other way—in short, the period was so far like the present period, that some of its noisiest authorities insisted on its being received, for good or evil, in the superlative degree of comparison only.—CHARLES DICKENS

4

Paul Bunyan, the mythical hero of the lumberjacks, is the supreme figure of American folklore. Paul was a Herculean logger who combed his beard with a young pine tree; who skidded his timber with Babe, the Blue Ox, a creature so vast that he measured forty-two ax handles and a plug of chewing tobacco between the horns; who operated a camp cookhouse where the flapjack griddle was greased by twenty-four Arabs—imported from the Sahara Desert because they could stand the heat—skating to and fro with slabs of bacon strapped to their feet; who tamed the Mississippi when it was young and wild by building river corrals and driving the river through their gates (the Great Lakes remain as evidence of this feat); who ruled the American country in the period when it was only a timberland. This epoch, according to the best authorities, began with the winter of the Blue Snow and ended with the Spring the Rain Came up from China.—JAMES STEVENS

5

Talking in low excited voices we would walk rapidly back toward town under the rustle of September leaves, in cool streets just grayed now with that still, that unearthly and magical first light of day which seems suddenly to rediscover the great earth out of darkness, so that the earth emerges with an awful, a glorious sculptural stillness, and one looks out with a feeling of joy and disbelief, as the first two men on this earth must have done, for to see this happen is one of the things that men will remember out of life forever and think of as they die.—THOMAS WOLFE

Part 9
Tone

Tone is the writer's attitude toward his subject and the coloration he gives his writing as a result of it. He can, for instance, be satirical, angry, funny, disgusted, insulting, ironic, flippant, or businesslike. He achieves his tone, or coloration, by many means: by the words he chooses to employ, by sentence organization, by the rhythms of words or phrases, by figurative language, repetition, omission, and by many other devices.

Writing, however, lacks some of the devices that oral communication has. You may have played the game at some time in which you take a simple sentence and "milk" it for its possible shades of meaning by accenting the first word, then the second, and so on throughout the sentence. Take this sentence, "He is my best friend." By simply accenting various words, you can get many meanings. You can say, "*He* is my best friend," then "He *is* my best friend," then "He is *my* best friend," and so on. You have still other possibilities if you change the statement to a question. You have, "*He* is my best friend?" or "He *is* my best friend?" and so on. You can see the various possibilities of tone just by emphasizing different words in the sentence.

You can also say one of the sentences in an angry tone. You can say it with a tone of disbelief. You can say it insistently. You can say it mockingly. You can say it scornfully. In short, you have a whole range of tones available to you, and you must be careful to establish the tone you want or risk being misunderstood.

In writing, however, tone must be achieved by a careful choice of words because you don't have a speaking voice to help you. Notice how tone is achieved in the following passage:

> The hedgerow was beaded with silver. In the English November fog, the leaves dripped with a deadly intensity, as if each falling drop were a drop of acid.

The tone of these lines is malevolent and somewhat ominous. An "English November fog" is unpleasant, and the "deadly" intensity of dripping leaves, and the rain drops like "acid" create evil images in your mind. In this description it is the careful choice of words that creates the tone.

Try to determine the tone of the following paragraph and how it is created.

> What sort of man gets busted at Columbia University? I don't know. I got busted at Columbia and I, for one,

strongly support trees (and, in the larger sense, forests), flowers, mountains and hills, also valleys, the ocean, wiliness (when used for good), good little children, people, tremendous record-setting snowstorms, hurricanes, swimming under water, nice policemen, unicorns, extra-inning ball games up to twelve innings, pneumatic jackhammers (when they're not too close), the dunes in North Truro on Cape Cod, and Raggedy Ann dolls, among other things.—JAMES SIMON KUNEN

The writer of these lines displays light-heartedness about his being "busted." He says he doesn't know why he was busted, but we realize that he *does* know. His tone is sassy and bemused. He pretends to think that the list of things he "believes" in should insure that he not be busted. He knows that by mixing an incongruous list of such things as Raggedy Ann dolls and pneumatic jackhammers, he creates a tone of saucy indifference.

Exercises
Analyzing Tone

A. Determine the tone of these paragraphs and be able to explain how the tone is created.

1

It was a gloomy night, a sad night—the sort of night when one can imagine spirits abroad. When the howling of the wind abated, a sinister sound would occasionally roll through the night—a far-off boom that held within it the voice of war.—MARIE, QUEEN OF ROMANIA

2

A child was standing on a street corner. He leaned with one shoulder against a high board fence and swayed the other to and fro, the while kicking carelessly at the gravel. Sunshine beat upon the cobbles, and a lazy summer wind raised yellow dust which trailed in clouds down the avenue. Clustering trucks moved with indistinctness through it. The child stood dreamily gazing.—STEPHEN CRANE

3

Stalin's secret police were everywhere, spying, searching, arresting, finding evidence of treason even where there was none. Thousands were imprisoned and thousands were executed, among them high-ranking Party members and military men. Often the most prominent prisoners were tortured and brainwashed into reciting horrifying "confessions" of imaginary crimes in elaborate public trials. Purge followed purge as Stalin did away with everyone he felt might be a threat to him.—ALLAN GLATTHORN

4

Hunger stole upon me so slowly that at first I was not aware of what hunger really meant. Hunger had always been more or less at my elbow when I played, but now I began to wake up at night to find hunger standing at my bedside, staring at me gauntly. The hunger I had known before this had been no grim, hostile stranger; it had been a normal hunger that had made me beg constantly for bread, and when I ate a crust or two I was satisfied. But this new hunger baffled me, scared me, made me angry and insistent. —RICHARD WRIGHT

5

True!—very, very dreadfully nervous I had been and am! But why will you say that I am mad? The disease had sharpened my senses—not destroyed—not dulled them. Above all was the sense of hearing acute. I heard all things in the heaven and in the earth. I heard many things in hell. How, then, am I mad? Harken! And observe how healthily— how calmly I can tell you the whole story.—EDGAR ALLAN POE

B. Write an original paragraph in which you establish a specific tone. State what the tone is and explain how you achieved it. This is as important to the exercise as the paragraph itself. Choose one of these tones or choose one of your own: irony, anger, amusement, silliness, scholarliness, boredom, earnestness.

Part 10
Mood

Students sometimes confuse *tone* with *mood*. Tone, you remember, is the writer's attitude toward his subject. Mood, on the other hand, is the attitude that is evoked in the reader. For example, Franz Kafka's short story "The Metamorphosis" begins with this famous opening:

> As Gregor Samsa awoke one morning from uneasy dreams he found himself transformed in his bed into a gigantic insect. He was lying on his hard, as if it were armor-plated, back and when he lifted his head a little he could see his dome-like brown belly divided into stiff arched segments on top of which the bed quilt could hardly keep in position and was about to slide off completely. His numerous legs, which were pitifully thin compared to the rest of his bulk, waved helplessly before his eyes.

In this paragraph the tone is one of acceptance, of naturalness, as if turning into an insect occurred to everyone at some time. It is a tone of detachment. However, the mood (which is what the reader feels) is one of horror and revulsion. That feeling is strengthened by the very fact that the author uses understatement.

In the following paragraph, determine both the tone and the mood and try to explain how each is achieved.

> "It is not good for man to be alone," papa used to say, quoting from the Poor Man's Almanac of Rationalizations— so we slept in various sets: four in a bed (the group plan); three in a bed (semiprivate, unless one of the three had a contagious disease, in which case he was allowed to sleep with only one, preferably one who had never had the disease); two in a bed (doubleheader); and one in a bed (critical list). Hopeless cases slept in Mama's bed. Chairs and

floors also served as beds. Floors were preferred because you could not fall off.—SAM LEVENSON

Here the tone is lighthearted and amusing. The writer describes his situation with cleverness and good humor. The mood the reader feels is the sense of fun, but while he is engaged by the cleverness of the description, underneath it all he feels compassion for the poverty and the crowded conditions of these lives. He realizes that the writer is employing humor to reconstruct the poverty of his childhood, and the mood is one of sympathy.

The following paragraph is a letter from an editor of a newspaper to his boss, resigning his position for the reasons he states. Determine the tone and mood.

> I can't write with comfort when I am interrupted so much as I have been today. The experiences are novel, I grant you, and entertaining, too, after a fashion, but they are not judiciously distributed. A gentleman shoots at you through the window and cripples *me*; a bombshell comes down the stovepipe for your gratification and sends the stove door down *my* throat; a friend drops in to swap compliments with you, and freckles *me* with bullet holes till my skin won't hold my principles; you go to dinner, and Jones comes with his cowhide, Gillespie throws me out of the window, Thompson tears all my clothes off, and an entire stranger takes my scalp with the easy freedom of an old acquaintance; and in less than five minutes all the blackguards in the country arrive in their war paint, and proceed to scare the rest of me to death with their tomahawks. Take it altogether, I never had such a spirited time in all my life as I have had today.—MARK TWAIN

The tone is straightforward and businesslike. The writer lists all his grievances with accuracy and dispatch. He doesn't seem overly disturbed by the violent experiences. The reader, after the first shock of disbelief at the murderous nature of the incidents, realizes that it is all an extravagant exaggeration at his expense. The mood is one of hilarity. It is great comedy, and the more so because of its understatement.

Creating Tone and Mood

Write three paragraphs of your own, each having a different tone and mood. State for each what the tone is and what the mood is.

Part 11

Some Exceptions to Paragraph Form

Dialogue

When a writer has characters talking to each other, he is writing dialogue. In this form of writing the author starts a new paragraph each time a different character speaks. The "he said" and "she murmured softly" are included in the same paragraph as the words spoken by him or her. The "he said" and "she murmured softly" are called *tags*. The following passage is an example of how dialogue and the tags should be paragraphed:

"Will you let me play too?" he asked.

The boy turned round and stared at him rudely. "How do you get into it?" he said quickly. We're all pals playing together."

"Well," said Agostino, with shameless persistence, "let me play too."

The boy shrugged his shoulders. "It's too late now. We've almost finished the game."

"Well, in the next game."

"There won't be any more," said the boy, looking him over doubtfully, but as if struck by his persistence. "Afterwards we're going to the pine woods."—ALBERTO MORAVIA

Exercises
Paragraphing Dialogue

A. Each of the following passages is dialogue, but it has been run together. Determine where each new paragraph should be started.

1

"Are all these birds for sale?" I asked, fixing my eyes greedily on a red cardinal. "Of course," said Mr. Bellow, and then added, "But only at the right time of year." "What's all this about the right time of year?" I asked, puzzled. "Surely if you're selling birds you can sell them at any time of the year?" "Well, some people do," said Mr. Bellow. "But I have always made it a rule never to sell at the wrong time of the year."—GERALD M. DURRELL

2

A terrible scream—a prolonged yell of horror and anguish—burst out of the silence of the moor. That frightful cry turned the blood to ice in my veins. "Oh, my God!" I gasped. "What is it? What does it mean?" Holmes had sprung to his feet, and I saw his dark, athletic outline at the door of the hut, his shoulders stooping, his head thrust forward, his face peering into the darkness. "Hush!" he whispered. "Hush!"—ARTHUR CONAN DOYLE

3

"So that's his diary," Wilson said. "He was writing in it when he died—oh, nothing interesting, just the temperatures. He wasn't romantic. God knows what she saw in him to make it worthwhile." "Would you mind if I looked at it?" "If you want to," she said. "Poor Ticki, he hasn't any secrets left." "His secrets were never very secret." He turned a page and read and turned a page. He said, "Had he suffered from sleeplessness very long?"—GRAHAM GREENE

B. The following passage is also dialogue that lacks proper paragraphing. Determine where each paragraph should begin.

"Mother," said the boy Paul one day, "why don't we keep a car of our own? Why do we always use uncle's, or else a taxi?" "Because we're the poor members of the family," said the mother. "But why *are* we, Mother?" "Well—I suppose," she said slowly and bitterly, "it's because your father has no luck." The boy was silent for some time. "Is luck money, Mother?" he asked rather timidly. "No, Paul. Not quite. It's what causes you to have money." "Oh!" said Paul vaguely. "I thought when Uncle Oscar said *filthy lucker,* it meant money." "*Filthy lucre* does mean money," said the mother. "But it's lucre, not luck." "Oh!" said the boy. "Then what *is* luck, Mother?" "It's what causes you to have money. If you're lucky you have money. That's why it's better to be born lucky than rich. If you're rich, you may lose your money. But if you're lucky, you will always get more money." "Oh! Will you? And is father not lucky?" "Very unlucky, I should say," she said bitterly. The boy watched her with unsure eyes. "Why?" he asked. "I don't know. Nobody ever knows why one person is lucky and another unlucky." "Don't they? Nobody at all? Does *nobody* know?" "Perhaps God. But He never tells."—D. H. LAWRENCE

Implied Topic Sentence

Frequently a paragraph has no actual topic sentence. Instead, the paragraph may have an implied topic sentence. If you were to read a paragraph like the following one, you would probably have no trouble knowing what it is about and supplying a topic sentence of your own if you should desire to do so.

Early man kept no records of birthdays or wedding anniversaries or the hour of death. He had no idea of days or weeks or even years. But in a general way he kept track of the seasons, for he had noticed that the cold winter was invariably followed by the mild spring, that spring grew into the hot summer when fruits ripened and the wild ears of corn were ready to be eaten, and that summer ended when sudden gusts of wind swept the leaves from the trees and a number of animals were getting ready for the long hibernal sleep.—HENDRIK WILLEM VAN LOON

You can easily see that this paragraph is about early man's lack of records to keep track of the passing of time. The topic sentence that is implied is, Early man had no calendars to record time.

The following paragraph also has an implied topic sentence. Try to determine what it is.

The Greeks thought themselves quite capable of finding out how the Universe worked. As citizens of free states, the Greeks were accustomed to govern themselves by holding public meetings. They used to listen with open minds to the arguments of orators speaking for or against any proposal, and then they would decide the matter by a vote. They followed much the same method in trying to make up their minds what they should believe about nature, including human nature. The Greeks were, in fact, the first people to use arguments deliberately as an instrument for discovering truth.—ANGUS ARMITAGE

In this paragraph the writer emphasizes the Greek way of arriving at certain truths. The implied topic sentence is, The Greeks were independent thinkers.

Cosmetic Effect

Sometimes the length of a paragraph is arbitrarily determined because an editor wants white space. Lots of white space makes a page look clean and inviting to read. He might print one sentence as though it were a paragraph or perhaps settle for two or three sentences. The most common place in which you see the artificial manipulation of a paragraph is in a newspaper.

A good paragraph is the result of a mind working hard to engage another mind. Good paragraphs are important to good writing. They develop ideas that are impossible to convey in a single sentence. Good paragraphs working together are the building blocks of compositions—and books.

Chapter 8

Ways of Developing the Paragraph

Paragraphs are developed in specific, identifiable ways. The following ways of development are the most familiar and will be discussed in detail in this chapter:

use of details	explanation
description	definition
comparison and contrast	reasoning
narration	persuasion

The purpose of a paragraph determines its manner of development. For example, the writer who wants to describe something proceeds by giving descriptive details; he doesn't use reasoning. The writer wishing to tell a story uses narration; he doesn't use definition. He does this naturally. His sense of logic tells him to do so. In short, a good writer automatically chooses the proper method of developing a paragraph. Why, then, should you bother to study the different ways of developing a paragraph? The answer is simple. If a writer is consciously aware of the form he is using, he will be able to mold and control his paragraph even more successfully than if he uses only instinctive logic to order his material.

Part 1

The Paragraph of Details

Probably the most frequently used method of developing a paragraph is by the use of details to substantiate what the topic sentence says. In the following paragraph, pick out the topic sentence. What details are used to develop the main idea? Are there any sentences that are not needed? Is there a clincher sentence?

An expedition by car across the Sahara is an interesting business. There are elaborate regulations to fulfill and precautions to be taken, even on such an easy route as the one we took. Anybody crossing the desert in his own conveyance must notify the authorities of the exact route contemplated, and post a sizeable bond as a deposit toward the expenses of a rescue car that will be sent out if, after twenty-four hours, the destination is not reached. You must carry shovels, wire netting, and rope, as well as food and water. People have died of thirst on the brink of a well, because they could not get their pails down deep enough. Nowadays few Europeans ever get lost in this part of the desert, because of severe precautions imposed by the Service Saharienne. Still, an Englishman died on the road from Tamanasset to Zinder last winter. Natives die more frequently, largely because they have been somewhat careless. They think that, with the increase in travel, a car will be bound to come along sooner or later if they are lost or waterless. Sometimes rescuers do come along. And sometimes not.—JOHN GUNTHER

The topic sentence has the point of view that a trip across the Sahara is *interesting*. If the paragraph is to be any good, it must tell why or in what way it is interesting. The body does tell at satisfactory length what makes the trip interesting, using specific details to do that. There are no unnecessary sentences. Each idea is necessary to the others. While there is no clincher sentence, notice how effective the last sentence is in its grim shortness.

The writer wisely made it a sentence of its own rather than have it a part of the preceding sentence.

Developing a Paragraph by Using Details

A. Here is a paragraph that uses details. Find the topic sentence and explain how the details support or develop the main idea of the paragraph.

> Motion pictures, the phonograph, radio, and television have all radically changed the way we live and the way we encounter the world. The movies deeply affected the theater, effectively killing the "popular" stage and leaving only a "legitimate" theater that is constantly striving for survival. The phonograph, which made it possible to preserve musical performance and speech for an indefinite period, brought sounds and words into the home that previously could be heard only in large auditoriums with large audiences. The radio brought a "radio culture" of its own, constructed entirely on sound, and consisting of home-delivered music, drama, news coverage, political speeches, and much more. Most recently, television added picture to the sound, making it possible as never before to bring the entire world into the home—this in a literal sense after the launching of satellites around the earth that pick up signals from any part of the globe.

B. Here are some subjects for a paragraph developed by the use of details. Choose one of the subjects, or one of your own, and write a paragraph. You may use any one of the sentences as your topic or you may revise it into a more interesting one, but be certain that it lends itself to a paragraph developed by the use of details. Write a body of sufficient length that has unity and coherence and include a clincher sentence. You may wish to review the elements of a paragraph that you studied in Chapter 7.

1. Math is a complicated subject.

2. The attic was filled with a strange assortment of things.
3. Tuning a car is a simple task.
4. There are some good rock groups around today.
5. There's pleasure in watching a garden grow.
6. My dog (cat, gerbil) is an interesting pet.
7. I like/dislike my after-school job.
8. The supermarket is a noisy place.
9. I like cold/hot weather.
10. I like to watch people on the bus.

Part 2

The Paragraph of Description

In a paragraph developed by description, you can describe a person, a place, or a thing. Describing the external characteristics is fairly easy, but usually you want to convey an impression of the internal qualities, too. For instance, let's say you are describing your school. You might say that it is built of red brick, has two hundred windows and twenty outside doors. That's fine as far as you have gone, but mere statistics are not enough. They're usually rather dull. You want to convey an impression of the school. You might describe it as "fortress-like" or as "grim and forbidding" or as a building "smiling in the sunshine" or as a building having a "welcoming warmth." What you do for a thing (the school) you also do for a person or a place. Try to convey a quality or create an impression.

Perhaps one of the most haunting monuments in the world is the Lincoln Memorial in Washington, D.C. The statue of Lincoln is brooding and troubled. He looks like a man who has suffered. Yet, he exudes quiet dignity and determination. This kind of description conveys a feeling about the Memorial; it creates an impression. If you were merely to note the size of the statue and tell how many tons of white marble went into it, you would have more of an inventory than a description.

Describing a Person

Read the following description of a person:

> He was, morning or evening, very correct in his dress. I have no doubt that his whole existence had been correct, well ordered and conventional, undisturbed by startling events. His white hair brushed upwards off a lofty forehead gave him the air of an idealist, of an imaginative man. His white mustache, heavy but carefully trimmed and arranged, was not unpleasantly tinted a golden yellow in the middle. The faint scent of some very good perfume, and of good cigars (that last an odor quite remarkable to come upon in Italy) reached me across the table. It was in his eyes that his age showed most. They were a little weary with creased eyelids. He must have been sixty or a couple of years more. And he was communicative. I would not go so far as to call it garrulous—but distinctly communicative.
> —JOSEPH CONRAD

This word portrait of a man not only describes his physical appearance but also interprets the essence of the man. His elegant appearance tells us that he is fastidious in his dress. The good perfume and good cigars reveal his expensive tastes. He is obviously sophisticated, a man of the world with a comfortable and well ordered life. That he is communicative but not garrulous is a sign of dignity and intelligence. The weariness in his eyes is perhaps due not only to his age but also to a kind of world-weariness.

Exercise
Describing a Person

Write a paragraph describing someone you like or respect. Try to capture some of his or her inner qualities.

Describing a Place

In describing a place you also try to capture its quality. The following paragraph describes a room in the Babbitts' home in Floral Heights.

> It was a room which observed the best Floral Heights standards. The gray walls were divided into artificial paneling by strips of white-enameled pine. From the Babbitts' former house had come two much-carved rocking-chairs, but the other chairs were new, very deep and restful, upholstered in blue and gold-striped velvet. A blue velvet davenport faced the fireplace, and behind it was a cherrywood table and a tall piano-lamp with a shade of golden silk. (Two out of every three houses in Floral Heights had before the fireplace a davenport, a mahogany table or imitation, and a piano lamp or a reading lamp with a shade of yellow or rose silk.)—SINCLAIR LEWIS

While the detailed description seems quite ordinary, the essence of the room is captured by the writer's tone in the last sentence. The writer sneers at the owners' lack of taste, and the effect is heightened with the understatement of the sentence.

Exercises
Describing a Place

A. You have five senses: touch, taste, smell, hearing, and sight. Using one of these senses—sight, for instance—write a paragraph decribing a place. Then, using one of the other senses, describe that same place. You might choose to describe the kitchen of your house. First, you might describe it by writing about what you can see. Second, you might want to write about it by describing the smells you detect.

B. Write two paragraphs, each a description of a place. Make one a place that you like and one a place that you dislike (for example, your favorite lake and the dentist's office). Without telling the reader that you like one and dislike the other, carefully use words that will make that fact clear. For instance, you might want to say that the lake is like a sparkling gem, that it lies beautifully nestled between two hills. Of the dentist's office, you might want to describe the ominous drill and the impersonal, antiseptic whiteness of the room.

Describing a Thing

Describing a thing employs the same skills as describing a place. In other words, you must use vocabulary skillfully and make use of the five senses. You also will find it helpful to use comparisons. For example, if you wish to describe the aroma of a perfume (a thing), you will discover that it is difficult, if not impossible, to describe it by itself. But it is comparatively easy to say it smells *like* something; for instance, like fresh peaches.

The following paragraph is a description of a thing. Read closely so that you can discuss the writer's skills, and watch especially for comparisons. The writer uses several comparisons in this short paragraph.

> When we got the lamp lighted, Herman was sitting in triumph with his hand gripping the neck of a long, thin fish which wriggled in his hands like an eel. The fish was over three feet long, as slender as a snake, with dull black eyes and a long snout with a greedy jaw full of long, sharp teeth. The teeth were as sharp as knives and could be folded back into the roof of the mouth to make way for what was swallowed. Under Herman's grip a large-eyed white fish, about eight inches long, was suddenly thrown up from the stomach and out of the mouth of the predatory fish, and soon after up came another like it. These were clearly two deepwater fish, much torn by the snakefish's teeth. The snakefish's thin skin was bluish violet on the back and steel blue underneath, and it came loose in flakes when we took hold of it.—THOR HEYERDAHL

Did you note the comparisons? They are "wriggled like an eel," "slender as a snake," and "sharp as knives." Did the writer use enough detail to help you "see" this fish and understand the nature of it?

Exercise
Describing a Thing

Choose a particular thing that you think would lend itself to an interesting description. As you write your paragraph, try to use comparisons or the kinds of sensory appeal that will help to make your description vivid for the reader.

Mixing Your Descriptions

You remember that you can describe a person, a place, or a thing. In actuality two—or even all three—of these subjects are often mixed together. You might mix two of them together by describing a person and a place. For example, you might describe a rock musician and the auditorium in which he is playing, with the crowd jostling and screaming. You might describe both a gardener and the garden she is tending, or you might describe a bird or an animal and its surroundings.

The following paragraph is a mixed description of a place, people, and dogs. Note the careful choice of words and the strong sensory appeal that create a vivid impression for the reader.

> I remember the cold, quiet nights and the stifling hot summers, starched summer suits and the smell of talcum, sweet-smelling black people in white dresses—my "nurses," who could be adoring and gentle and then impatient and rough—tugs at my hand and a high rich voice telling me, "If you don't behave, boy, the police gonna put you under the jail." There were three big birddogs named Tony, Sam, and Jimbo, their warm licks and loud barks, the feel of their bodies against mine in front of a black stove, the way they bounded into my bed to get me out to play, the taste of gingerbread and hot corn on the cob, and my whispered words, "God bless everybody and me."—WILLIE MORRIS

Exercise
Mixing Descriptions

Write a paragraph in which you mix two or more subjects. Be sure that your subjects are compatible, that they naturally fit together to create a unified impression.

Part 3
The Paragraph of Comparison or Contrast

Comparison means showing the similarities between two or more things, people, or places.

During the past century in France, an interesting search for the identity of the painter of the *Pieta*, a fifteenth century religious painting, has consumed art historians. They have recently identified the probable painter as Enguerrand Quarton, who is known to have painted the *Coronation*. The following paragraph of comparison documents the similarities between the two paintings.

When one looks closely at the work of Quarton and compares it to details from the *Pieta*, distinct similarities appear: the drawing of the fingers, the character of the folds in the robes, the shape of a nostril, or a lip, the tracing of an eyebrow. The *Pieta* Christ and the *Coronation* Father and Son are similar types, each with a large mass of dark hair falling regularly over the forehead. The flat gold backgrounds of both paintings give to each a sense of timelessness. The mountain behind Mary Magdalene in the *Pieta* has the same rugged planes as the peaks in the *Coronation* landscape. The hands of the *Pieta* figures, so delicate and expressive, resemble the hands of the *Coronation* Virgin. The city behind the donor's head in the *Pieta*—modeled after Jerusalem or Constantinople—is realistically drawn, like the cities in the *Coronation*. Finally, the same vivid Mediterranean light, sharply illuminating and defining forms, floods both paintings. If not an absolute certainty, the attribution to Quarton seems at least, in the words of Michel Laclotte, "very probable."—PRISCILLA FLOOD

Contrast, on the other hand, shows the differences between two or more things, people, or places. In the following paragraph, what two things are being contrasted?

The position of women, in many countries of Latin America, is quite different from that which they occupy in the United States. Of course, in a number of countries there are feminist movements, and women have changed their conditions considerably from those of their traditional status. This is particularly true of the southeastern part of South America. Yet in many countries women still lead a comparatively secluded life, their chief activities outside the home being religious and charitable. Mothers, even of the wealthy classes, have a greater hand in the bringing up of their own children than is the case in the United States. Mothers occupy a place in the home that is somewhat difficult to understand for those who are not acquainted with Latin American customs.—PHILIP LEONARD GREEN

While we often think in terms of distinct comparisons or distinct contrasts, we more frequently use a combination of both, using similarities and differences to determine our choices. We use both comparison and contrast when we shop for a new stereo, when we describe places we have lived in or visited, or when we evaluate people running for office in order to vote wisely.

In the following paragraph, both comparison and contrast are used to explain the similarities and differences between English people and Americans.

To the American who dwells for a season within these stout and well-fortified coasts there are probably no such irritating people under the sun as are the English. Perhaps this fact lies in another, namely that because many of us are sprung from them, we expect them to be more like us than they are. The initial exasperation comes when we discover immediately that this is at once a complete and baffling misconception. Our common language, the physical characteristics common to us both, many other elements of our common inheritance—all would seem to afford points of similarity between us. But these things have not resulted in resemblance or even in affinity. Three hundred years of a totally different environment and development have set us apart from them, and this must be coupled by the knowledge that each decade in their tight little island only serves to make them more uncompromisingly what they are.—MARY ELLEN CHASE

Exercises
Paragraphs of Comparison and Contrast

A. Write a paragraph in which you compare or contrast two people you know well. Be sure that you have a topic sentence that clearly states your purpose.

B. Choose one of the following subjects, or an original one of your own, and develop it into a paragraph. Your topic sentence will determine whether you emphasize similarities, differences, or a combination of both.

1. Badminton and tennis are somewhat alike.
2. My brother and I are totally different.
3. Though gerbils and rats are both rodents, I like gerbils and dislike rats.
4. Road racing is different from track racing.
5. Two books I have read recently are quite similar/different.
6. Today's teen-age boys and girls wear similar clothes.
7. As pets, dogs and cats are quite different.
8. Although they are close friends, his lifestyle is totally different from hers.
9. TV police stories are alike, yet different. (Choose two specific shows.)
10. I like _____ movies but dislike _____ movies.

Part 4

The Paragraph of Narration

Narration is the telling of a story or anecdote. Many times you wish to make a point by telling a little story to achieve your end. Narration can be a short story or a novel, of course, but you are writing only a paragraph. You needn't worry about a hero and a villain or a plot line or continuing dialogue. You're not telling a formal story. Here is a paragraph of narration.

Hopping freight trains on my way west I had one bad afternoon. A shack (hobo for brakeman) had ordered me off an open coal car where I was crouched. When the train started I got on again. The train was running full speed when he climbed down from the car ahead and another shack followed him. He put his face close to mine. "I told you to stay off the train. Now you'll come through with two bits or you'll take what you get." It was my first time with a shack of that kind. I had met brakemen who were not small-time grafters, and one who spotted me in a boxcar corner said, "If you're going to ride, keep out of sight." I figured I might owe the railroad money for fare, but the shack wasn't a passenger-fare collector, so I didn't come through with the two bits. He outweighed me by about forty pounds and when his right fist landed on my left jaw and his left fist slammed into my mouth I went to the floor. As I slowly sat up, he snarled, "Stay where you are or you'll get more." Then as he and his partner turned to go he gave me a last look and laughed, "You can ride; you've earned it."—CARL SANDBURG

Exercises
Paragraphs of Narration

A. Of course, not all subjects can be made into narrative paragraphs. Below is a list of subjects. Which of these can be made into narratives? Read carefully, for some of them can be developed as narrative paragraphs and others as paragraphs using details, depending on what you plan to say. Be ready to explain what you would say.

1. I have to admit I was really scared once.
2. Hang gliding is really becoming a major sport.
3. A laser beam can do a number of things.
4. Lake _____ is thoroughly polluted.
5. I had the surprise of my life last year.
6. Because I work during the summer, I haven't had a real vacation in years.
7. To become a Scout you have to pass some tests.
8. A fisherman can get by with remarkably few pieces of equipment.
9. After what happened to me last week I have decided to do my homework early in the evening.
10. There are positive things you can do to improve your grade.
11. After what happened recently, I don't think I will ride with Dan again.
12. We have done a number of things to improve our house.
13. Vandalism is a costly crime.
14. My best friend lives in a beautiful house.
15. I do most of the dirty household chores.
16. I saw one bad accident and do not wish to see another.
17. I suppose, since I want to be a doctor, I should study Latin.
18. Penny candy isn't penny candy anymore.
19. Giveaway shows on TV show the greed of the contestants.
20. I will have to master some study skills before I go to college.

B. Choose any one of the subjects in the previous exercise or one of the subjects below, or one of your own choosing, and write a paragraph of narration.

1. A funny thing happened to me last week.
2. When I finally arrived, I realized that the party was over.
3. My last vacation was the best I have ever had.
4. I think I have ESP (extrasensory perception).
5. And that's how I got my job.

Part 5

The Paragraph of Explanation

One purpose of a paragraph of explanation is to give reasons for something that happened—why your car overheated, why you were late to a party, why the trees on your street are dying, or why many senior citizens are not getting adequate medical care. The following paragraph explains why a man, inexperienced in traveling by foot in Alaska, lost his life-sustaining fire.

> It was his own fault or, rather, his mistake. He should not have built the fire under the spruce tree. He should have built it in the open. But it had been easier to pull the twigs from the brush and drop them directly on the fire. Now the tree under which he had done this carried a weight of snow on its boughs. No wind had blown for weeks, and each bough was fully freighted. Each time he had pulled a twig he had communicated a slight agitation to the tree—an imperceptible agitation, so far as he was concerned, but an agitation sufficient to bring about the disaster. High up in the tree one bough capsized its load of snow. This fell on the boughs beneath, capsizing them. This process continued, spreading out and involving the whole tree. It grew like an avalanche, and it descended without warning upon the man and the fire, and the fire was blotted out! Where it had burned was a mantle of fresh and disordered snow.—JACK LONDON

Note how completely the writer explains the disaster, how one event leads to another from beginning to end. There are no missing details to confuse the reader. The writer has provided a vivid explanation of why the fire went out.

The following paragraph is an explanation of a different kind. It is an explanation of a process: how to repot a plant.

> Certain procedures should be followed in repotting a plant. First, select a pot only slightly larger than the one the plant is

in now, with a hole in the bottom for drainage. If using a clay pot, soak it in water for several hours before using it. Place a piece of broken pot over the drainage hole so the soil doesn't leak out, and add a small layer of new soil. Second, tap the potted plant gently on the bottom to loosen the soil. Then, holding your hand over the soil on top, turn the pot sideways and tap the pot gently as you turn it. When the soil is sufficiently loosened to remove the plant, slowly withdraw the plant, keeping the ball of soil as intact as possible. Finally, carefully set the root ball into the new pot and fill in new soil around it. Tap down the soil to remove any air pockets, water it thoroughly and allow the plant to drain.

Exercises
The Paragraph of Explanation

A. The following subjects lend themselves to paragraphs of explanation by giving reasons why something happened. Choose one of the subjects, or one of your own, and write a paragraph of explanation.

1. Christmas has become commercialized.
2. Fire trucks from three neighboring communities were called into action.
3. Recreational facilities are inadequate for the neighborhood.
4. The child fell down the bank and rolled all the way to the bottom.
5. It happened late at night on a wet, foggy road.
6. Inflation is a serious threat to people on a fixed income.
7. The role of women is changing.
8. She couldn't seem to do the work that was required of her.

B. Write a paragraph that explains a process. Explain how to baste a turkey or how we get light from a fluorescent tube or how a cake rises or how a band makes patterns on the football field at half-time. If you would rather choose a subject of your own, you may do so, but be certain that it describes a process.

Part 6
The Paragraph of Definition

People sometimes find themselves in needless argument with someone, only to find later that the argument came about because the two disputants had different interpretations of a term. Sometimes we are unable to understand the gist of a discussion simply because we don't understand a key term. For at least two reasons, then, a writer should clarify terms he uses that might not be readily understood.

For example, do you know what an astronaut means when he talks about *attitude*? It means the angle at which a capsule enters the atmosphere. If the attitude is too wide, the capsule bounces off the atmosphere and bounces out into space again. If the attitude is too narrow, the capsule burns up in its plunge through the atmosphere.

Would you understand *cloning* or *synapse* if you found these terms in an article? If not, you would welcome a definition of them in the article. If you need help with different terms, so does your reader.

The following selection is a paragraph of definition. Note that the writer does not give a definition as a dictionary would. He tries to define a term in relation to a reader's experience.

"Debriefing" is one of those service terms that give English professors the willies. What it really amounts to is a verbal account of the mission, which is taped for further study and comparison with the teletaped data, while the crew's memory is still fresh enough to encompass little details that might be overlooked or forgotten later. As they say in the detective novels, you're supposed to "spill your guts" to the debriefing interrogators, gripes and all. If John and I had any major gripes, I don't remember them. *Molly Brown* [our space capsule], had done everything we had asked of her, with a fast submarine ride thrown in for free.—VIRGIL GRISSOM

The Paragraph of Definition

A. Here is a paragraph of definition. Read it carefully and then try to write a better definition of the same word. While you may need to consult an encyclopedia for additional information, try to write your paragraph in language that is easy for the average reader to understand.

> There is a kind of scientist who studies the things that pre-historic man made and did. Such a scientist is called an *archaeologist*. It is the archaeologist's business to look for the stone and metal tools, the pottery, the graves, and the caves or huts of the men who lived before history began.

B. Defining something well and interestingly is not always easy. Take some simple object, like a chalkboard, a chair, or an umbrella and define it. You need not take one of these objects, but be sure to take something commonplace.

Part 7
The Paragraph of Reasoning

It is sometimes difficult to make a reader accept your ideas. Writing a paragraph of reasoning is helpful in such a situation. You don't merely present a conclusion to a reader. You take the reader through your reasoning process so that he or she can follow your thinking step-by-step. Here is a paragraph of reasoning. Find the topic sentence and identify the steps in reasoning that the writer goes through.

> Once when I was fighting against a very strong current deep in the sea, I had an idea. These currents are steady, strong, and may be found in thousands of places all over the world, only a short distance beneath the surface. Why not put specially designed turbines there to generate substantial amounts of

power? We produce electric current from our great rivers as they fall toward the sea. The sea itself has far more and greater rivers within it that are not being used. Ravelli told me that in Brittany there is a plant on the seashore that uses the current in this way, proof that my thought is not fantastic.
—FOLCO QUILICI

You have recognized the topic sentence as the first one in the paragraph, but it requires an explanation. You are not told what the "idea" is. The body of the paragraph explains the idea through a reasoning process.

Exercise
The Paragraph of Reasoning

Write down a non-debatable fact and construct a list of reasons why it is a fact. Then develop your reasons into a paragraph with a good topic sentence and a clincher sentence. Here is an example of what you are to do:

FACT:

Many people going to Europe by ship sail from Montreal.

REASONS:

1. For almost a third of the trip to Europe, the ship is in the St. Lawrence River. If you go this way, for part of the trip you can look about you and see more than just water.

2. People who fear seasickness better their odds against getting sick by being on land-bound river for part of the way.

3. You are more likely to have sunny days on the river than on the cold, and often foggy, Atlantic Ocean.

You may develop one of the following subjects, or one of your own.

1. Going steady in high school can be a mistake.

2. There is very little nighttime darkness in Sweden during the summer.
3. Most students want summer jobs.
4. At times it is good to be alone.
5. Traveling by plane is more efficient than traveling by rail.
6. Daily exercise is an aid to good health.
7. Money can help make life pleasant if it is not misused.
8. Television is mostly one big bore.
9. Trading stamps don't really give you free merchandise.
10. Swimming is a popular sport.

Part 8

The Paragraph of Persuasion

Most persuasive writing is on a topic that is debatable. This kind of writing usually has one of two purposes:

1. **To persuade someone to do something.** For example, you might try to persuade someone to support your program, buy your product, or vote for your candidate.

2. **To persuade someone to accept your belief or point of view.** For example, you might try to persuade someone to accept your point of view on women's rights, TV programming, or professional football.

Read the following two paragraphs. What is the purpose of each?

1

At this point, I have to pause briefly to deal with the hordes of Flying Saucer believers who have suddenly appeared on the horizon, waving affidavits and smudgy photographs. To dispose of them would need another article a good deal longer than this one, not all of it printable. I'll merely state my views on this agitated subject, without giving the reasons that have led me to them after several years of thought, reading, interviewing, and personal observations. I think there may be

"Unidentified Flying Objects" which are exactly what their name implies, and which may turn out to be quite interesting and exciting when we discover their cause. At the same time I am pretty sure that they're not—repeat *not*—spaceships. If they were, many consequences would have arisen. (The most obvious: we and the Russians would be the best of friends.)
—ARTHUR C. CLARKE

2

The cult of beauty in women, which we smile at as though it were one of the culture's harmless follies, is, in fact, an insanity, for it is posited on a false view of reality. Women are not more beautiful than men. The obligation to be beautiful is an artificial burden, imposed by men on women, that keeps both sexes clinging to childhood, the woman forced to remain a charming dependent child, the man driven by his unconscious desire to be—like an infant—loved and taken care of simply for his beautiful self. Woman's mask of beauty is the face of the child, a revelation of the tragic sexual immaturity of both sexes in our culture.—UNA STANNARD

Both of these paragraphs take one side on an issue on which people differ. The first paragraph on UFO's makes it clear that while the writer accepts the idea of UFO's, he doesn't believe there are manned spaceships flying down to Earth from other planets. He is trying to persuade you to believe him.

In the paragraph on women's beauty, the writer hopes to persuade you to her point of view. You have to decide for yourself whether you are persuaded to her viewpoint.

Exercise
The Paragraph of Persuasion

Write a paragraph of persuasion on some controversial issue on which you have a feeling. Perhaps you agree or disagree with something you have read. Perhaps you have some feeling about a social or political issue. Perhaps you have feelings about television programming. Try to be objective in your arguments so that your emotions don't get in the way of your thinking.

Ways of Developing the Paragraph

Study the following paragraphs and determine in what way each of them has been developed. Be prepared to explain your decision.

1

Seen nearer, the Thing was incredibly strange, for it was no mere insensate machine driving on its way. Machine it was, with a ringing metallic pace, and long, flexible, glittering tentacles (one of which gripped a young pine tree) swinging and rattling about its strange body. It picked its road as it went striding along, and the brazen hood that surmounted it moved to and fro with the inevitable suggestion of a head looking about. Behind the main body was a huge mass of white metal like a gigantic fisherman's basket, and puffs of green smoke squirted out from the joints of the limbs as the monster swept by me. And in an instant it was gone.—H. G. WELLS

2

For centuries, in the pursuit of beauty, Chinese women used to bind their feet, trying to compress them to the ideal three inches. To achieve this ideal beauty, no suffering was too great. At about the age of four, a girl's feet were bandaged: the toes were pulled backward so tightly that blood and pus later oozed from the bandages, a toe or two might fall off, and death from gangrene was possible. If the girl survived, she would never be able to walk freely again without a cane or the support of attendants. But the excruciating pain and the loss of freedom were worth it, for the tinier her feet, the richer the husband she might get. She might also win first prize in one of the many tiny-foot beauty contests. All ladies had bound feet; it was fashionable; natural feet were ugly; only tiny feet were beautiful.—UNA STANNARD

3

I can't help it, I'm crazy about thoroughbred horses. I've always been that way. When I was ten years old and saw I was going to be big and couldn't be a rider I was so sorry I nearly died. Harry Hellinfinger in Beckersville, whose father is Postmaster, is grown up and too lazy to work, but likes to stand around in the street and get up jokes on boys like sending them to a hardware store for a gimlet to bore square holes and other jokes like that. He played one on me. He told me that if I would eat half a cigar I would be stunted and not grow any more and maybe could be a rider. I did it. When Father wasn't looking I took a cigar out of his pocket and gagged it down some way. It made me awful sick and the doctor had to be sent for. and then it did no good. I kept right on growing. It was a joke. When I told what I had done and why, most fathers would have whipped me but mine didn't.—SHERWOOD ANDERSON

4

Moon-green and amber, a strip of fading sky glowed across the trail of the vanished sun. Far below, the opal sea paled to mother-of-pearl. Then, over sea and sky, strode the sudden dark of the tropics and in an instant the southern stars flamed and flaked through the violet night. A long, tense moment, with sea and sky waiting, and a rim of raw gold thrust itself above the horizon as the full moon of midsummer climbed toward the zenith. Rising, its light made a broad causeway across the sea clear to the dark reef which lurked in the shimmering water.—SAMUEL SCOVILLE, JR.

5

Of course there were cats. The island had cats, and the windows everywhere being open, they could leap in and out. Nobody knew whose cats they were. They came and went. The cook had one or two she fed from time to time, though the palace did not claim them, but there were more. Once when the servants were away Candida had laid out a dressed chicken to broil for supper. She went away for a moment, and when she came back there were four or five cats in the room; a huge gray tom was just leaping through the window bars with the chicken in his mouth while the others followed him into the bushes moaning and snarling. When Candida took her parakeet out of the cage to play with it and let it fly in the room, she always closed the shutters, not just because it might fly away, but because of the cats.—CHARLES G. BELL

6

Women are in less need of more work than of a more sensible class of occupations on which to wisely spend their energies. To this end, also, we need a general reconstruction in the division of labor. Let no women give all their time to household duties, but require nearly all women, and all men also, since they belong to the household, to bear some share of the common household burdens. Many hands make light work, and hearts would be lightened in proportion. I would seek to have society so readjusted, that every man and every woman could feel that from three to six hours of each day were absolutely at his or her own disposal; and that the machinery of business or of the family would go on unimpeded meantime.— ANTOINETTE BROWN BLACKWELL (1874)

7

Machines and tools have always been created in the image of man. The hammer grew from the balled fist, the rake from the hand with fingers outstretched for scratching, the shovel from the hand hollowed to scoop. As machines became more than simple tools, outstripping their creators in performance, demanding and obtaining increasing amounts of power, and acquiring superhuman speed and accuracies, their outward resemblance to the natural model disappeared; only the names of the machine's parts showed vestiges of their human origin. The highly complex machinery of the modern industrial age has arms that swing, fingers that fold, legs that support, and teeth that grind. Machines feed on material, run when things go well, and spit and cough when they don't.—JOHN H. TROLL

8

Opposite the station is a crumbling brown wall. In the shade of it lie men, children, a woman, bundles of rags that writhe feverishly. We ask someone what's the matter with them.—Nothing, they are dying. A boy almost naked, his filthy skin livid green, staggers out of the station, a bit of bread in his hand, and lurches dizzily towards the wall. There he sinks down, too weak to raise it to his mouth. An old man with a stick in his hand hobbles slowly towards the boy. He stands over the boy a minute and then, propping himself up with his stick, grabs the bread and scuttles off around the corner of the station. The boy makes a curious whining noise, but lies back silently without moving, his head resting on a stone. Above the wall, against the violet sky of afternoon, Ararat stands up white and cool and smooth like the vision of another world. —JOHN DOS PASSOS

9

The owner of the voice came backing out of the undergrowth so that twigs scratched on a greasy windbreaker. The naked crooks of his knees were plump, caught and scratched by thorns. He bent down, removed the thorns carefully, and turned round. He was shorter than the fair boy and very fat. He came forward, searching out safe lodgments for his feet, and then looked up through thick spectacles.—WILLIAM GOLDING

10

The notion that advertising can somehow "manipulate" people into buying products which they should not buy is both arrogant and naive. It has been proved false repeatedly by advertising's inability to keep an inferior product afloat, or to sell against primary trends. When an advertising campaign is highly successful, it will almost always be found that the wagon has been hooked onto a strong tendency which existed before the ads were written. It is not a difference in quality or amount of advertising that makes campaigns for filter cigarettes successful, while campaigns for non-filter cigarettes fail; lung cancer is the dominant fact here, though you would not expect to find this expression in a cigarette ad.—MARTIN MAYER

Chapter 9

Writing a Composition

A composition is a piece of writing that expands a topic or idea. The paragraphs that make up a composition relate to each other in a way that develops the main idea while maintaining unity and coherence.

In this chapter you will examine the steps involved in writing a composition. The basic steps are these:

1. Choosing and limiting your subject
2. Writing down your ideas
3. Organizing your ideas
4. Outlining
5. Writing your first draft
6. Revising
7. Writing your final draft

If you follow this step-by-step procedure when you write a composition, you will find your job easier and your composition more effective.

Part 1
Choosing Your Subject

Your first step in writing a composition is to decide on a subject. What are you interested in? Do you know enough about a subject you're interested in to write about it at some length? If not, are you sufficiently interested in it to find more information about it? Do you know where to find more information? There are an endless number of subjects to write about, of course.

If you are interested in ecology, you might want to write about the conversion of open fields to industrial sites or shopping plazas, thus depriving ground birds of nesting sites; or the importance of planned reforestation of timber land or burned-over areas; or the efforts to control water pollution.

If you play tennis, you could write about the spirit of competition, or about the role of women in tennis, or about the origins of the sport. Your interest in your topic will enliven your writing. The reverse is also true; a lack of interest in a topic will produce a composition that will fail to interest your readers.

Limiting Your Subject

In this chapter we are discussing a five-paragraph composition, which is approximately 500 words. When you limit the expansion of an idea to that length, you can easily see that subjects that are too broad or general in scope can't be adequately developed. You need to limit your subject. Consider the subject of ecology. That is an unlimited field, and many books would have to be written to cover it adequately. If you proceeded to limit a subject, the process would work as follows:

UNLIMITED:	Ecology
SLIGHTLY UNLIMITED:	Ecology in the United States
2,000-WORD LIMITATION:	Water Pollution in the United States

1,000-WORD LIMITATION:	Water Pollution in the Great Lakes
500-WORD LIMITATION:	Recent Improvements in the Pollution Level of Lake Erie

Exercise
Limiting the Subject

Here is a list of broad subjects. Within each subject, find three narrow subjects suitable for a composition of 500 words. Keep these subjects for a later exercise.

1. Mass Media	6. The Space Age
2. Politics	7. Careers
3. Unidentified Flying Objects	8. Music
4. Endangered Species	9. Health
5. Senior Citizens	10. Historical Sites

Determining the Controlling Purpose of Your Composition

Determining the controlling purpose of your composition will become clearer to you as you select and limit your subject. You may decide that your subject is best developed by a clear explanation of a situation. You may want to develop it by giving detailed information. You may want to prove a point or explain an attitude. Whatever your purpose may be, it is important to write it down so that you can keep it in front of you as you proceed to develop your material. It will help you stick to your subject and accomplish what you set out to do.

Write out your controlling purpose in a sentence such as the following:

The controlling purpose of this composition is to explain the nature of the recent improvements in the pollution level of Lake Erie.

This sentence will not, of course, appear in your composition, nor will it be your title. Your title will be only a few words. The sentence will be merely a constant reminder of what you are going to write about and the direction you're going to take.

Exercises
Determining the Controlling Purpose
of a Composition

A. In the exercise on page 165 you limited each of ten broad subjects to three possible compositions of 500 words. Choose three of these limited subjects and (1) write an appropriate title for each and (2) a statement of the controlling purpose that you would follow. Keep this work for a later assignment.

B. Choose a subject that interests you enough to write a composition on. Limit your subject sufficiently for a 500-word paper. Write a tentative title for your paper. Then write a one-sentence controlling purpose for your subject.

Part 2

Writing Down Your Ideas

Now that you have chosen your subject, limited it, and stated your controlling purpose, the next step is to write down your ideas on your subject.

Perhaps you already have all your ideas. Perhaps you need to check the accuracy of some points in reference books or other source material. Perhaps you need to do more extensive reading or research in a certain area. (See Chapter 13 on Using the Library and Reference Materials.) When you have completed all the necessary reading or research, you are ready to write down your ideas on your subject.

Because you don't want to interrupt your flow of ideas, jot down whatever ideas come to mind. Don't worry about order or phrasing or style. Just get your ideas on paper. At the top of your paper write your tentative title and the statement of your controlling purpose so that when you begin to arrange your ideas and eliminate unnecessary ones, you can do so in terms of your controlling purpose.

Your first list of ideas might look something like this (pay no attention to the asterisks):

TENTATIVE TITLE   Who Killed the Trolley?

CONTROLLING PURPOSE   The controlling purpose of this composition is to explain why the decline of the trolley car was caused by the advent of the automobile.

trolley was attractive and comfortable
shift to automobiles
trolleys become rundown
* rise of the automobile industry
cheap trolley fares
network of trolley lines
trolley was quiet and relaxing
could we use trolleys today?
automobiles compete with trolley
improvements in automobiles
* auto shows
* foreign cars
trolley was dependable
* rising cost of auto maintenance
* cost of gas and oil
automobile always available
traffic problems
automobile new and exciting
* family auto trips
* camping sites
rise in use of automobiles
automobile threatens trolley
trolleys went on excursions
trolley was popular
* jobs for motormen
* jobs in auto repair shops
trolley car disappears

You can see how some of these ideas have no relationship to the controlling purpose of the composition. These unrelated ideas, marked with asterisks, should be eliminated at this point so that your composition doesn't go off in the wrong direction. "Rise of the automobile industry," "auto shows," "foreign cars," "family auto trips," and "camping sites" are broad topics that cannot be handled adequately in a five-paragraph composition. "Rising cost of auto maintenance," "cost of gas and oil," "jobs for motormen," and "jobs in auto repair shops," also marked with asterisks, have nothing to do with the purpose of the composition.

The job of deleting inappropriate or unmanageable material is an important step in sorting out and evaluating your material. In some cases, an idea may seem important enough to retain at the moment, but you may find that it is of no value when you begin to organize your ideas. If that happens, eliminate the idea at that time.

Exercises
Writing Down the Ideas

A. In Exercise A on page 166, you wrote a title and a controlling purpose for three limited subjects. Select two of these titles and controlling purposes and list under them all the ideas that come to your mind for developing that subject. After studying your lists, cross out those ideas that would be unmanageable or irrelevant to the controlling purpose of each composition. Keep these lists for a later assignment.

B. Do the same as above for your own composition.

Part 3
Organizing Your Ideas

Now that you have tested your ideas against your controlling purpose and have eliminated those that are too broad to handle and those that are irrelevant, you are ready to organize your ideas.

For example, in the final list of ideas concerning the trolley car, you will notice that certain ideas begin to emerge as major points: "*shift to automobiles*" is an important point in developing the idea of the controlling purpose. Ideas related to this one are "automobile always available," "automobile new and exciting," and "automobile threatens trolley."

Another major point seems to be "*automobiles compete with trolley*," and related ideas are "trolleys become rundown," "improvements in automobiles," "traffic problems," "rise in use of automobiles," and "trolley car disappears."

A third major point is "*trolley was popular*," and related ideas are "trolley was attractive and comfortable," "cheap trolley fares," "network of trolley lines," "trolley was quiet and relaxing," "trolley was dependable," and "trolleys went on excursions."

That leaves only one idea not accounted for: "could we use trolleys today?" Because that seems like the germ of an idea for a conclusion, we will set it aside for the moment.

We now have three major points to develop—just the right number for the body of a five-paragraph theme:

> shift to automobiles
> automobiles compete with trolley
> trolley was popular

The final problem is to determine the order of these three main headings. When you plan a composition, you must present your ideas to the reader in some kind of logical order. Ideas that are not closely related can move from least important to most important or from simple to complex. However, ideas that depend on other ideas to be clearly understood must be presented in logical order. If point B cannot be understood without Point A, then Point A must come first in your composition.

Let's see if logical order applies to the three major points. The controlling purpose is as follows:

> The controlling purpose of this composition is to explain why the decline of the trolley car was caused by the advent of the automobile.

It seems obvious that before we can talk about automobiles, we have to discuss the trolley car because it came first. The shift from the trolley car to the automobile obviously comes next, followed by the automobile competing with the trolley. Thus, the logical order of ideas for the development of the body of the paragraph is as follows:

> trolley was popular
> shift to automobiles
> automobiles compete with trolley

The next step is to organize the related ideas under the major ideas in their logical order of development.

> trolley was popular
>
>> cheap trolley fares
>> trolley was dependable
>> trolley was attractive and comfortable
>> trolley was quiet and relaxing
>> trolley went on excursions
>> network of trolley lines
>
> shift to automobiles
>
>> automobile new and exciting
>> automobile always available
>> automobile threatens trolley
>
> automobiles compete with trolley
>
>> trolleys become rundown
>> improvements in automobiles
>> rise in use of automobiles
>> traffic problems
>> trolley car disappears
>
> leftover good idea: could we use trolleys today?

Exercises
Organizing the Ideas

A. Continuing your work with the lists in Exercise A on page 168, organize the ideas under both subjects into the major points and their related ideas in the order you would develop each of them in a composition. Save this work for a later assignment.

B. Do the same as above with the ideas for the subject for your own composition.

Part 4
Outlining

Now that you have organized the main topics and their related ideas for the development of the body of your composition, you are ready to make an outline. Your outline will show you at a glance what ideas you are going to develop, their relationship to each other, and the order in which you will develop them.

An outline can be either a **sentence outline,** in which all the ideas are expressed in complete sentences; or a **topic outline,** in which the ideas are expressed only in words or phrases. The topic outline is easier to do and will be adequate for your composition.

Outlining Procedure

1. Write the title above the outline.

2. Write the statement of your controlling purpose a few spaces below your title.

3. Use standard outline form. The following example is a sample arrangement of numerals and letters that will constitute the form of your outline.

```
I.
   A.
   B.
      1.
      2.
         a.
         b.
            (1)
            (2)
               (a)
               (b)
II. (etc.)
```

4. Number your main headings with Roman numerals. Use capital letters for subtopics under each main heading. Divide your subtopics in descending order of importance: first Arabic numerals, then small letters, then Arabic numerals in parentheses, then small letters in parentheses.

5. Indent subtopics, placing the letters or numerals directly below the first letter of the first word in your preceding topic or subtopic.

6. Do not use the words *Introduction, Body,* and *Conclusion* in your outline. These are merely organizational terms in planning a composition.

7. Use only one idea for each topic or subtopic.

8. Do not use a single subtopic. Use either two or more, or none at all. A topic cannot be divided into fewer than two parts.

9. Begin the first word of each topic and subtopic with a capital letter. Do not use periods after topics or subtopics.

10. Make all main topics parallel in form. Make each group of subtopics parallel in form. For example, if the first main topic is a noun, all the other main topics must be nouns. If the first subtopic under the main topic is a prepositional phrase, the remainder of that group of subtopics must also be prepositional phrases.

Example of an Outline

Here is the final outline of the body of the composition on the trolley. Two major organizational units, the Introduction and the Conclusion, have not been worked out at this point, so we will leave them blank.

WHO KILLED THE TROLLEY?

The controlling purpose of this composition is to explain why the decline of the trolley car was caused by the advent of the automobile.

I.

II. Early popularity of trolley
- A. Cheap fares
- B. Dependability
- C. Attractiveness
    1. Comfortable
    2. Quiet
    3. Relaxing
- D. Excursions
- E. Network of lines

III. Gradual shift to automobiles
- A. Newness
- B. Convenience
- C. Threat to trolley

IV. Resulting competition
- A. Deterioration of trolley
- B. Improvement of automobiles
- C. Increased use of automobiles
- D. Traffic congestion
- E. Disappearance of trolley

V. (leftover idea: could we use trolleys today?)

Exercises
Making an Outline

A. The following list contains all the ideas needed for a complete topic outline: a title, a group of main topics, and several groups of subtopics. Arrange all the ideas in outline form, using all the items, and numbering and lettering them properly as main topics and subtopics. Place the title at the top of the outline.

Sustains life	The history of the sun
In art	Size
Effect of the sun on the earth	In worship
Creates energy	Important facts about the sun
Mass	Heat
In music	In literature
Future study of the sun	Brightness
Movement	Affects weather
Mythology of the sun	Man and the sun

B. Correct the following topic outline, keeping the following points in mind: (1) Every topic and subtopic must relate to the controlling purpose. (2) Main topics should be parallel in form; each group of subtopics should be parallel in form. (3) Subtopics should never be fewer than two. (4) Organizational terms should never be used. (5) In a topic outline, complete sentences should not be used.

A VISIT TO CHICAGO

I. Introduction: The "Windy City" on the shore of Lake Michigan

II. Greater Chicago

    A. Downtown Chicago
       1. The Loop
       2. Michigan Avenue, called "the million-dollar mile"

    B. Moving to the near-north side

III. Who the people are

    A. Ethnic groups
    B. Economic levels: very low and very high

IV. The city has many attractions

    A. Culture

        1. The Art Institute

    B. Museums

        1. Museum of Science and Industry
        2. Field Museum of Natural History
        3. Shedd Aquarium displays fish

    C. Orchestra Hall also provides culture

    D. Sports

        1. Soldier Field, for football games
        2. Amphitheatre

    E. In conclusion, Chicago is a diverse city

C. In Exercise A on page 171, you organized the ideas under both subjects into the major points and their related ideas in the order you would develop each of them in a composition. Now put these ideas into proper outline form according to the instructions in this section.

D. Do the same as above with the order of ideas for your own composition.

Part 5
Writing Your First Draft

You now have a working title that you may wish to revise later. You have a statement of your controlling purpose, and you have an outline of the body to work from. You are now ready to write your first draft, which will include your introduction and conclusion.

With all this preliminary work behind you, it would seem that the actual writing should be easy. That is not always true, however. Sometimes you don't know how to start, especially with the introduction. If that happens, begin writing with the second paragraph, which is information that you have at hand. You can always work on the introduction later, after you have become involved in the act of writing.

The most important thing is to begin somewhere and keep writing. Don't worry at this point about sentence structure, word choice, or punctuation. You can concentrate on those aspects when you revise your composition.

Your composition will have three basic parts—a beginning, a middle, and an end; in other words, an introduction, a body, and a conclusion. That may seem like an obvious statement, but each of the parts plays a crucial role in an effective composition. The writing of each part of the composition will be considered in turn.

The Introduction

The introduction ordinarily has two functions: to *introduce* the reader to the subject and to *interest* the reader in it. A five-paragraph composition usually devotes one paragraph to an introduction. Effective introductions can be constructed around quotations, startling statistics, or interesting anecdotes.

The following introductions are three possible ways of beginning the composition on the trolley.

QUOTATION:

I want to hire out as the Skipper
(Who dodges life's stresses and strains)
Of the Trolley, the Toonerville Trolley,
The Trolley that Meets all the Trains.

—DON MARQUIS

Don Marquis would be out of luck in the city of Babbington today. The trains are barely running, and the trolley has been a long time gone. Only the automobiles are running.

STATISTIC:

In the city of Babbington in 1910 nearly a hundred trolleys were operating on 198 miles of track. Today none of the track remains, and the only trolley has been made into a diner. The automobile has taken over.

ANECDOTE: Last month, the street that I live on was torn apart for resurfacing, and I discovered, buried beneath the macadam, the remains of what was once a genial and reliable public servant—The Babbington and Hargrove Street Railway. The resurfacing was necessary, of course, because the automobiles had worn down the road.

Besides getting attention, each of these introductions tells the reader what the composition is about, namely that the trolleys that once ran in Babbington no longer operate, and that the automobile has taken over. The beginning of a composition should never be a flat statement of intent like the following:

In this paper I will describe the decline of the trolley and show how the automobile caused this decline.

Such a statement might be an appropriate statement of purpose for the writer to use as a guide, but it has little appeal for a reader.

Exercises
An Effective Introduction for a Composition

A. Rewrite and expand three of the following introductions to heighten the appeal for the reader and inform the reader of the subject of the composition. Use a quotation, a statistic or an anecdote.

1. We all use a great deal of paper every year, but most of us take it for granted.
2. I'll never forget the time I tried to learn to juggle.
3. Many people think that sightings of unidentified flying objects began in the twentieth century. They're wrong.
4. Compiling a dictionary requires a lot of work.
5. Something must be done about the cat and dog population explosion.

B. With the previous possibilities for introductions in mind, write a beginning paragraph for your composition that introduces the subject and captures your reader's interest. Be sure to test it against your controlling purpose to be sure you have included all aspects of your purpose in your introduction. For example, if the introductions for the composition on the trolley had failed to include the automobile, the reader would think you were going to discuss only the trolley car.

The Body

The middle part of the composition, or the body, is the longest section. In a five-paragraph theme it would consist of three paragraphs. It is here that the writer must accomplish his or her purpose. In writing the body of your composition, be sure to observe the following points.

1. **Use your outline as a guide.** Remember that the purpose of your outline is to establish a clear and appropriate pattern for the development of your ideas. If you abandon the outline, you are certain to lose the clarity you have worked to achieve.

2. **Keep your purpose in mind.** Work to accomplish what your controlling purpose promises you will accomplish. If you set out to explain something, be certain that you explain it as clearly as possible.

3. **Divide your writing into paragraphs.** Using your outline as a guide, devote a paragraph to each main topic. Begin each paragraph with a topic sentence. Develop each topic fully, including all subtopics.

4. **Provide clear transitions.** A transitional device at the beginning of a paragraph indicates how the idea to be dealt with relates to ideas in preceding paragraphs. There are a number of ways to establish smooth transitions between paragraphs. The use of the following transitional devices will help your reader follow your ideas.

Using Transitional Devices

Transitional Words and Phrases. In Chapter 7 you studied linking expressions, or connectives, that are used to achieve coherence within a paragraph and to help the reader move smoothly from one idea to another. Certain words and phrases are also important to help the reader move smoothly from one paragraph to another. The following transitional words and phrases are the ones most often used in the first sentence of a new paragraph.

TO INDICATE TIME RELATIONSHIPS

before	earlier	once	sooner or later
during	later	then	at this point
after	soon	in time	at the same time
afterward	first	eventually	
at last	next	finally	

TO INDICATE LOGICAL RELATIONSHIPS

since	besides	furthermore
therefore	consequently	and then
because	inevitably	as a result

TO INDICATE SIMILARITY

as	also	similarly	in the same way
like	again	another	equally important
and	likewise	moreover	
too	equally	in addition	

TO INDICATE CONTRAST

but	however	otherwise
yet	although	in contrast
nor	nevertheless	on the contrary
still	nonetheless	on the other hand

Each of the following sentences is the first sentence of a paragraph. Notice how the transitional devices serve, in each case, to link the new topic to that of the preceding paragraph. You can even guess what the preceding paragraph was about without having read it.

The graves, *however*, were all around them as a reminder of their struggles and loss.

First he would have to have the roof fixed, or they would not be able to stay there for long.

The prospect of widespread crop failure is *equally* threatening to countries that escape it, since they will be compelled to share their provisions with less fortunate nations.

Pronouns. You can use a pronoun to refer to an idea in the preceding paragraph. *This, that, these* and *those* are frequently used as transitional words, either as pronouns or as adjectives.

However, when these words are used as adjectives, they must be followed by a noun that clarifies the reference for the reader. For example, if you say, "This was open to criticism," and the reader has to ask, "This what?" you are not communicating your ideas. Say "This policy," or "This action," or whatever specifically you are referring to.

Other pronouns also operate as transitional devices. Study the sentences that follow, all of which are opening sentences of paragraphs, to see how the device works.

Brad approached *them* and tried to become one of their group, but they didn't make it easy.

This crisis was only the beginning.

Jamie had been taking *that* train for weeks without noticing who his companions were.

Repetition. Using a strategic word from one paragraph in the opening sentence of the following paragraph preserves the flow of meaning from one paragraph to the next. Note how repetition is used as a transition in the following examples.

1

Modern-day homesteaders are wondering what they can live in that will be an efficient structure for conserving energy and yet will suit their aesthetic tastes. They have put up all sorts and shapes of houses from log cabins to foam domes.

For those who choose to live in a log cabin, there is actually a log cabin kit that looks like a giant Lincoln Log set.

2

In 1972 the governor of Vermont proposed a new source of fuel for electricity. The new source was to be found just about everywhere in Vermont, and he proposed that it was more reasonable to use a cheap, plentiful source than to buy costly and vanishing foreign oil. He was talking about trees.

The trees the governor proposed to feed to the furnaces were not the virgin forests that people yearn to see in Vermont every fall, but surplus timber and deformed trees that prove worthless as lumber.

Sometimes a writer will repeat more than a single word; he will make use of a whole idea from one paragraph to start off the next. In this case the repetition refers directly and deliberately to the preceding paragraph. Note how the device works in the following examples.

3

Most meteorologists will admit to not being taken seriously by their audience. They present their visions of the upcoming weather every day, and if 10% of the time they are completely wrong, the public casts doubts on every forecast.

The weathermen's credibility problem is only one of the characteristic trials of the profession.

4

A recreational fisherman can get so hooked on his pastime that even fantastically adverse conditions cannot keep him home. In mid-February the lakes of northern New England are dotted with figures swathed in goose down, toting their gear to chosen spots where they will drill for water.

Ice fishing is a surprisingly simple undertaking, requiring no fancy equipment and only the most basic of skills.

Exercises
The Body of the Composition

A. Choose a magazine article that interests you and write down the opening sentences of ten paragraphs that employ transitional devices discussed in this section. Explain how the devices work in each example.

B. Write the body of your composition, which will consist of three paragraphs. Here are points to remember:

1. Keep your controlling purpose in front of you.
2. Use your outline as your guide.
3. Develop your three paragraphs completely.
4. Provide clear paragraph transitions.

The Conclusion

The conclusion of the composition should "wrap things up." It should bring your key points together and leave the reader with a sense of completeness. The single most effective way to achieve a sense of completeness is to return in the conclusion to the ideas you used in your introduction. This procedure gives the reader the feeling of having come full circle. If you like, you may think of the composition as something like a sightseeing tour. The writer promises the readers an interesting tour; the readers climb aboard and the writer conducts the tour; and then at the end the writer brings the readers back to the point where they started.

The composition on the trolley might have a conclusion like the following if the writer had chosen the anecdote for her introduction.

> The street I live on has been repaired and repaved, and the tracks are buried once again. Traffic struggles along as it did. But now the automobile is in trouble. Will something new come along to replace it? I don't think so. I think something old will come along to replace it. I look forward to sitting on the curb sometime soon and watching a crew install tracks on top of the macadam—trolley tracks, of course.

Notice how the writer has returned to the anecdote she chose to open her composition. She recalls the image of the tracks being dug up by having them buried again. The reader has learned why the automobile caused the decline of the trolley, and the possibility of new tracks being laid over the old gives the reader something new to think about.

Exercise
Writing an Effective Conclusion

Write the concluding paragraph of your composition, returning to the method you used for the beginning. Try to achieve a sense of completeness by including all the necessary ideas in your controlling purpose.

Part 6
Revising

It is in this stage of writing that the careful writers are separated from the careless. In revision, a merely acceptable piece of writing can become something really good. If you follow the suggestions below, you will produce a revision that is an improvement over your first draft.

1. **Read your composition aloud.** The importance of this step cannot be overemphasized. Nothing else will show you so clearly where your ideas were not fully developed or where your thinking was fuzzy or where your sentences were awkward. If possible, read your work to someone who will be critical of it. Use the criticism in your revision.

2. **Revise for content.** Is your purpose for writing clear from the outset? Have you said enough? Is your information accurate? Are your ideas laid out clearly?

3. **Revise for form.** Have you organized your composition clearly and logically? Have you given each main idea its own paragraph and introduced it with a topic sentence? Are your para-

graphs coherent? Are all your ideas clearly related to each other? Have you made connections between ideas by using transitional devices?

4. **Revise for wording.** Have you used the most precise words to express your ideas? Review the information on synonyms and antonyms in Chapter 2. Use a dictionary or thesaurus to check the meanings of key words in your composition and to locate ings closer to what you intended, revise the wording. Have you used figurative language where appropriate, to make your writing more vivid?

5. **Check for capitalization, punctuation, and spelling.** Obviously, faults of these kinds will distract your reader from what you are saying. If necessary, consult Sections 10-16 in your Handbook.

A Model Composition

Following is a revised, completed composition based on the outline that appears on page 173.

WHO KILLED THE TROLLEY?

Last month, as jackhammers split the blacktop on my street to uncover some pipes, workmen laid open the grave of a bit of local history. Beneath my street, and beneath streets all over town, lie the tracks of the Babbington and Hargrove Street Railway. The once beloved and reliable trolleys are gone, driven underground by the automobile.

The introduction offers an anecdote and asserts the purpose of the composition: to recount how the trolley, which was enjoyed in its day, has been supplanted by the automobile.

When it was in its prime, the trolley was cheap, dependable and attractive. A rider could go a long way on a few cents. The schedule was so regular that people

The first paragraph of the body of the composition corresponds to number II and its subtopics in the outline. The

sent messages and even groceries with the conductor to be picked up at the other end of the line. People rode in comfort on the upholstered seats. The cars were electric, and so were quiet and smokeless. The ride was slow, and passengers had a chance to get to know each other and to take in the sights as they rode. In the summer, open cars with wicker seats were added, and on holidays special excursion cars took families to amusement parks on the edge of town. The B & H allowed easy transfer to other lines, and it was actually possible, though certainly not efficient, to travel from New York to Boston on the network of trolley lines. People regarded the trolley as an ideal means of transportation.

first sentence is the topic sentence, and the rest of the paragraph illustrates what the topic sentence states.

Then along came the automobile. It was noisy and uncomfortable and unreliable, but it caught the public's fancy from the first. This machine would take you wherever you wanted to go whenever you felt like going there, with no waiting, no transfers, no crowds. Little by little, the trolley began to seem less attractive and the automobile more so. The loss of passengers on the B & H meant a loss of income, and this meant the equipment could not be kept in good repair. The trolleys became less dependable and less attractive, and more people abandoned the trolley for private cars.

The first word of this paragraph suggests a time relationship between this paragraph and the last. The writer is advancing chronologically. The first sentence also reminds the reader of the thesis of the composition, that the automobile was the undoing of the trolley system. The paragraph as a whole corresponds to number III in the outline.

While the trolley companies were struggling with declining revenues and ailing equipment, automobiles were becoming more reliable and more plentiful.

Again, the first word of this paragraph provides a transition between this paragraph and the one before it that indicates

Automobile traffic was competing with trolley traffic in the streets. Intersections could get pretty confusing, and cars were becoming numerous enough to create traffic jams. Eventually the cars crowded the trolleys off the streets, and the tracks were paved over to make a wider and smoother surface for traffic.

a time relationship. The paragraph corresponds to number IV in the outline.

The street I live on has been repaired and repaved, and the tracks are buried once again. Traffic struggles along as it did before, but there is talk of getting people out of their cars and into some other kind of transportation. The automobile is not quite so wonderful as people first thought. Will something new replace it? I hope not. I hope something old will replace it. I look forward to looking out to the street one day soon and watching a crew install tracks on top of the blacktop—trolley tracks, of course.

The final paragraph constitutes the conclusion of the composition, and as such brings the reader full circle—back to the street in front of the writer's house. The "tour" is complete. After reviewing the past, the writer projects her imagination into the future, which she envisions as repeating the past, and leaves the reader with something to think about.

Exercise
Revising a Composition

Revise your composition, following the suggestions in this section. Prepare a clean, final version.

Chapter 10

Using Figurative Language

Sometimes the essays we write or the articles we read use all the words correctly, obey all the rules of grammar, are organized into proper paragraphs, and yet make dull reading. The writing, although correct, lacks flavor. We find ourselves plodding from word to word, from sentence to sentence. The words pile up on the page and run across our minds, but never excite our senses. Some of the meaning may even be lost as the unstimulating words glide right past us. At this point, the writing calls for figurative language.

What is figurative language? Like language in general, it is composed of words. The difference is that these words are used in a manner that calls upon one or all of our five senses to understand the message. In our imaginations we are made to listen to sounds, to see pictures, to taste flavors, to touch textures, or to smell odors. This sensual awareness not only adds color to writing but also arouses an emotional response in the reader. The sound of a *hiss* sets our spines tingling, and we feel fear. *Sparkling seas* sets up points of light as well as the exhilaration of brisk breezes and running movement. *Cool as a cucumber* has us tasting the crisp summer vegetable. The *sweet breath of roses* in the air reaches our nose. We are made to feel the touch of the child's *velvet cheeks*.

This kind of language figures, or decorates, our writing. We sit up and take notice when words shed their literal meanings. Turns of speech in which cheeks become velvet and roses have breath make us see and feel in different ways. Concepts are clarified and insights sharpened. For example, in science, magnetic tensions are made comprehensible when we visualize "lines of force," or see wind forces concentrating around the "eye" of the hurricane.

Since the days of Homer, who wrote of "rosy-fingered dawn," literature has been in the business of using figurative language. It is from literature, going back to the days of the ancient Greeks, that we get labels and definitions for these figures:

onomatopoeia	metaphor	hyperbole
alliteration	simile	personification
assonance	symbol	

Part 1

Onomatopoeia

Onomatopoeia is a Greek word meaning the making of poetry. As a literary device used today, **onomatopoeia** means using words whose sounds mimic, or echo, their meaning. The word is a mouthful, but if you separate it into its syllables, you see how appropriate it is for naming a figurative device: o/no/ma/to/po/ei/a. With its wavy rhythm, repetition of vowel sounds and suggestive ending, its very sound echoes the meaning: poetry.

Certain words come on strong with sound. In producing an image of sound, these words define themselves:

whirr   squash   rumble   crackle   murmur   pop   bang

These and many other word sounds are used by advertising

writers, headline writers, and sports reporters, as well as writers in general, to resound in the ears of our imaginations.

In the following example, we not only hear but feel the sound:

> Casey Jones was the throttle-puller of the Illinois Central's crack Cannonball.

The words pulse and throb with the sound and rhythm of a fast train moving over steel rails. The image of another sound is added with the repetitive *t*'s of throttle. Each time Casey Jones pulls the throttle to control the flow of engine fuel, a bursting, explosive sound is released that is related to the sound of a cannonball as it is fired. Try to imagine the combined sounds in your mind's ear.

Exercises
Using Sounds That Echo Their Meaning

A. In the following examples from the sports pages, find the sound words and show how they are appropriate to the sport.

1. NETTLE CLOUT WINS AGAIN FOR YANKS
2. Stennett cracks a single into center field.
3. Ken Stabler fired two second-quarter touchdown passes yesterday to knock the San Francisco 49ers from the unbeaten ranks.

B. In the following, state what sounds echo their meaning, and what the meaning is.

1. The thunder roared overhead, then rolled and rumbled through the cave of the sky.
2. The moan of doves in immemorial elms,
    And murmuring of innumerable bees.
3. The small sticks hissed and sputtered.

C. What feelings do the sounds of the italicized words arouse?

1. The sharp *scratch* of a match on the bricks startled him.
2. The soggy leaves were *squashed* beneath her foot.
3. *Sizzling* hot dogs greeted his ears and nose.

4. The garden was alive with the *buzz* of bees.
5. The bow *twanged* and the arrow *whizzed* to the target.

D. Write a sentence describing the motion of a car, cycle, or plane, using words that mimic the sound each makes.

E. Write a sentence using onomatopoetic words to describe each of the following. Make each word sound as vivid as you can.

a fire	a storm	leaves falling
a fountain	a crowd of people	a window breaking
a whip	a ringing phone	someone crying
a bird	a whistle	inside a cave

Part 2
Alliteration and Assonance

Alliteration and assonance are related instances of sound imagery. In **alliteration,** identical or similar consonant sounds are repeated, usually at the beginning of words close to each other, such as the following:

a bend of birch trees   the rolling rumble of rocks
the silver sweep of the sea   a Monday morning message

Assonance repeats vowel sounds, usually within words close to each other, such as the following:

moaning and groaning   a red felt headdress
snap, crackle and rattle   find a rhyme for time

Alliteration and assonance may be used separately, or jointly, as in "Another Somebody Done Somebody Wrong Song" where the *s*'s and *o*'s set up a dual rhyming effect.

A pulsating effect occurs when the same sounds return to strike our ears. When the repetition is joined to the sound mimicry of onomatopoeia, it adds intensity. Listen to the "beat, bang, blow" of the hammer, or the "ding-dong" of bells.

Headline writers recognize the value of repetitive sounds. Alliteration in bold print catches the prospective reader's attention: EARTHQUAKE TREMORS TROUBLE PEKING. The repetition of sounds, whether in headline writing, sports reporting, or writing in general, is pleasing to the eye and ear. It adds flavor to writing and makes the reader more responsive.

Exercises
Using Alliteration and Assonance

A. Examine the following for alliteration and assonance. Some sentences may combine both; others contain only one. Explain how the sound effect works, whether as (1) decoration, (2) catchy attention-getter, or (3) evocation of atmosphere or action.

1. Fall foliage takes a final fling.
2. Join the Jippi Jappa Festival in Jamaica.
3. For her, the newly formed leaves were bursting buds of promise.
4. The dismal dusk of darkening days is with us now.
5. Volvo Dial-a-Deal
6. Dogged Determination Drives Winner
7. Weaving wildly down the track, the cars crashed through the barriers in a press of wrenching metal.
8. WHAT A SEASON OF SPARKLING SPECIALS
9. MAD DOG—Ruthless Bandit or Rebel Hero?
10. YANKEE HOPES AGAIN SNAGGED AS REDS COMPLETE SWEEP

B. Search the advertising pages of your newspaper, or TV commercials, for catchy sound effects. Bring them to class and discuss them.

C. Listen to the lyrics of your favorite songs for assonance. Bring in examples. Is there a mood that the assonance strengthens? What is it?

D. Write three sentences using alliteration or assonance, or both. You may choose your own subject or write about the sights and sounds, smells or tastes, wherever you may be doing your homework.

Part 3

Metaphor

Metaphor (from the Greek "transfer") is that figure of speech which superimposes one image on another. One image must be dissimilar to the other. The characteristics of one object or event are transferred to another even though literally this cannot be the case. Metaphor occurs only when the assertion is preposterous.

"Man is a wolf" is a metaphorical statement that imposes the image of a wolf on that of a man. In literal fact, man is not a wolf. *Wolf* has been given a twist in meaning so that it can serve as metaphor for man. Some of the characteristics of *wolf* have been transferred to *man*. The statement that "Man is an animal," for example, is literally true. Thus it cannot be a metaphorical statement.

Metaphor serves several functions. It may be used as above to emphasize a feeling. The writer who says that "Man is a wolf" expresses his disgust at the nonhuman and wolf-like characteristics of man. We understand that he is comparing neither the coat nor the cry of the wolf but the animal's more vicious or aggressive qualities. Perhaps this is not fair to the poor wolf, who, if he had the voice, might in turn say: Wolf is a man.

Metaphor also shows new relationships and gives new insights. Have you ever seen the moon in the way the poet E. E. Cummings calls it to our attention?

> Notice the convulsed orange inch of moon
> perching on this silver minute of evening.

We have all seen the orange silver of a new moon in the sky at dusk, but this description helps us to see it in a new way. Because "perching" is a characteristic of birds, the image of a bird has been imposed on that of the moon and serves as metaphor. Literally, there is no such thing as a "silver minute." In this case, the silver color of the sky has been combined with the concept of time to create a precise moment of observation. The skillful use of metaphor has created new relationships and deeper insights into this fleeting moment. The word *convulsed,* of course, intensifies the shape of the new moon.

With tongue in cheek, the humorist-poet Ogden Nash makes fun of metaphorical speech:

> Then they always say things like after a winter storm the snow is a white blanket. Oh it is, is it? All right then, you sleep under a six-inch blanket of snow and I'll sleep under a half-inch blanket of unpoetical blanket material and we'll see which one keeps warm.

After long and repeated usage, metaphor loses its original force, and, used literally, becomes incorporated into the language. When you "thread your way" through the crowd you no longer think of the original image. The "legs" of a table belong to it as certainly as the legs of a dog; and the "head of state" or the head of any organization brings no image of heads to mind. After repeated use in a specific field, metaphor becomes the *jargon* of that field. When Jack Nicklaus "shoots" a 69, and when Bjorn Borg "breaks" service, the images are literal in that the original *breaking* and *shooting* figures no longer come to mind. We accept and use them as part of our daily speech patterns.

Mixed Metaphor

Mixed metaphors originate in those phrases in which the original image has slipped away. Coming too quickly to the unwatchful writer's pen, a phrase mixes with others, also quickly drawn. Now we may have two or more sets of contradictory or uncongenial images combined:

> You've buttered your bread; now lie in it.
> The hand that rocked the cradle has kicked the bucket.

In some writing, mixed images may nevertheless effect a unified impression. In sports writing, for instance, hard-hitting verbs are of mixed imagery but the force of the verbs prevails. Analyze the separate images of the following underlined verbs:

At Milwaukee, George Scott, who homered in the first inning, <u>smacked</u> a bases-loaded single to left field and lifted the Brewers to a 4–3 victory over Oakland, <u>snapping</u> the A's winning streak at nine games.

Cliché

Clichés are overused metaphors. When the original image is lost, repeated phrases, emptied of meaning, strike hollowly at our ears. *Spilled milk, dogged determination, ladders of success, sands of time* are figureless phrases. When they serve as apt expressions to communicate meaning quickly, they may be regarded as a kind of shorthand. Their use should be carefully guarded; overdone, it may lead to boredom and even stranger results.

Exercises
Analyzing the Use of Metaphor

A. Explain the metaphors in the following examples. What are they, what characteristics are joined, and what new insights are given?

1. Little streams are freighted with a caravan of leaves.
—MARGARET WALKER
2. An escalator rides on dinosaur spines.—BARBARA HOWES
3. His eyes were gun barrels.—JON STALLWORTHY

B. One politician has said of the opposition that it was "rattling the dusty old skeleton of Watergate." Another said: "To sweep Watergate under the rug you need a big broom." Explain what is meant by each statement. Do the politicians differ? In what way?

C. In what way is the term "running mate" an accurate image of the vice-presidential candidate?

D. "We got to cut down our errors," said Fairbanks. "How? If I knew, I'd bottle it and sell it." What would Fairbanks bottle, and why would he sell it?

E. Explain the metaphors in the following sentences by showing how the metaphorical makes an image of the literal.

1. Everything in nature is closing up shop for the season.
2. The help he received from Mr. Cartwright proved to be a bright ray of light in a very dark night.
3. Apartments are tenanted tight as hen-houses, people roosting in every cupboard.—BARBARA HOWES

F. In the recent presidential campaign one candidate accused the other of "waffling," or doing a "flip-flop." How do these images literally describe the action? How do they differ from a "sitting on the fence" position?

G. Give examples of five metaphors from sports reports or popular songs.

H. In the following examples of mixed metaphor, take the metaphorical images literally to show how they make each other ludicrous:

1. When I realized he had a finger in every pie, it gave me food for thought.
2. He turned tail and fell into the well of despair.

Part 4
Simile

Simile is a figure of speech closely related to metaphor. Again, the characteristics of one object or event are joined to those of another in a way that is literally not true. Simile differs from metaphor in that the comparison made between two things is indicated by connectives such as *like, as,* or *than;* or by verbs such as *resemble.* "Man is a wolf" is a metaphor; "man is like a wolf" is a simile. In this case, the metaphor would be a more forceful statement than the simile. Often, however, the simile is preferred to the metaphor because it can state directly what the shared characteristic is.

When someone writes: "Mr. Smith is as crafty as a fox" or "Mr. Smith is as swift as a fox," we know exactly what qualities Mr. Smith shares with the fox. The Mr. Smith who roars like a lion is different from the Mr. Smith who is a leader, like a lion. However, when we say, "Mr. Smith acts like a harassed husband," we are no longer using figurative language because the statement may be literally true.

Attaching animal characteristics to human beings has long been a feature of figurative writing. After taking a humorous exception to figurative language, James Thurber cites a few similes of praise: "as brave as a lion, as proud as a peacock, as lively as a cricket, as graceful as a swan, as busy as a bee, as gentle as a lamb," and goes on to say:

> We sometimes observe that he [man] has the memory of an elephant and works like a beaver. (Why this should make him dog-tired instead of beaver-tired I don't know.)

Some of the similes cited above have indeed become dog-tired and as limp as a worm. Yet similes have the potential power to make for vivid writing. A newspaper article says of a character at a neighborhood meeting that "he drifted through the shaded room like ectoplasm clothed in blue jeans." How do you picture this character, both as a physical shape and the kind of importance he had in that room?

Exercises
Analyzing the Use of Simile

A. In your words, what kind of writing is "limp as a worm"?

B. In each of the following sentences, pick out the simile and explain the comparison made between the two terms:

1. A line of elms plunging and tossing like horses.
—THEODORE ROETHKE

2. Birds flickered like skipped stones across the vast inverted pond of heaven.—RAY BRADBURY

3. An automatic smile flashed across her face as if it were an electronic scoreboard.

4. My Mama moved among the days like a dreamwalker in a field.—LUCILLE CLIFTON

5. Second-hand sights, like crumpled, mud-smudged postcards.—CAROLYN M. RODGERS

6. Sails flashing to the wind like weapons.—ROBERT HAYDEN

7. Objects arranged like rows of fine teeth.—ISHMAEL REED

C. In the following examples, both metaphor and simile are used. Find each and make a literal translation.

1. The bus was trapped like a fly in the spider's web of traffic.

2. Now Luther filled his life, which had been as empty as the desert wastes. ‑

3. His life style moved up and down like a horse on life's merry-go-round.

D. Complete the following similes:

1. Prices are rising like _____ .
2. He felt as if he were a _____ .
3. The beach was as hot as _____ .
4. Our team ran over the opposition like a _____ .
5. In the blizzard the familiar landscape resembled a _____ .
6. As he read the new directions, his thoughts whirled faster than a _____ .

E. For the following similes, substitute comparisons that are both more original and more to the point:

1. busy as a bee
2. gentle as a lamb
3. crazy as a loon
4. fierce as a lion

Part 5
Extended Metaphor

When an image created by metaphor occurs repeatedly in a passage, the metaphor is said to be extended. The extended metaphor emphasizes the point being made or elaborates on it. Notice how the Poet Karl Shapiro extends the metaphor in the following passage:

> The ambulance at top speed floating down
> Past beacons and illuminated clocks
> Wings in a heavy curve, dips down,
> And brakes speed, entering the crowd.

Two entirely different images, an ambulance and a large bird, have been superimposed upon one another. The metaphor has been extended by describing the movement at different stages.

Here is another extended metaphor:

> The sea—quick pugilist—
> uses for a pun
>   ching
>   ball
> the restless little boats.
>
> With the towel of the wind,
> even rubs down the boxer's
> sweaty body.
>
> The buildings—
> ringside fans—
> crowd close to watch
> the big training.—
>
> DEMETRIO HERRERA

What are the two dissimilar images in this metaphor? What characteristics of the sea does the boxer image describe?

In the following passage, Patrick White extends an image of

"trumpeting corn" to make more vivid the immensity of field after field of corn stretching beyond the horizon.

> All through the middle of America there was a trumpeting of corn. Its full, yellow, tremendous notes pressed close to the swelling sky. There were whole acres of time in which the yellow corn blared as if for judgment.

The shape of the corn and its color make for a trumpeting image that is repeated in the "tremendous notes pressed close to the swelling sky" and in the figure of corn that "blared as if for judgment." The blaring "as if for judgment" refers to the horn waking the dead on judgment day and may be read here as emphasizing the strength of the corn's statement.

When you write an extended metaphor, you must be very sure that the characteristics of one image can be superimposed upon the other in a believable way. If you tried to create a metaphor with an ice cube and a piece of butter, for example, you would soon run into difficulty. Reread the three extended metaphors in this section and notice how believably each of the two dissimilar images work together.

Exercises
Analyzing Extended Metaphor

A. The following passages are extended metaphors. Determine what the metaphor is and how it has been extended.

1. The progress of science is strewn, like an ancient desert trail, with the bleached skeletons of discarded theories which once seemed to possess eternal life.—ARTHUR KOESTLER

The preceding may be read omitting the adjectives *ancient, bleached, eternal.* What do these adjectives add?

2. He's known as "Candy," but he doesn't melt in your mouth. And he especially doesn't melt in a pennant race. John Candelaria, at the untender age of 22, has emerged as the big rock candy mountain of the Pittsburgh Pirates' pitching staff.—DAVE ANDERSON

3. These great brown hills move in herds, humped like bison, before the traveling eye. Massive above the farms, they file and hulk daylong across every distance; and bending come as the sun sinks (orange and small) beyond their heavy shoulders, shaggy at evening, to drink among the shadowy lakes.—ROBERT WALLACE

B. In the following passage, what extends the "ice flow" simile? What is metaphor and what is simile?

His approach to tennis is as cold as winter, as methodical as an ice flow. If indeed, there are passions that churn within him, they are locked away and rumble unnoticed.—Article on Bjorn Borg in *The New York Times*

C. Here is a simple metaphor. Determine exactly what two images are being compared. Then extend the metaphor, selecting those characteristics of each that will superimpose believably on each other to reveal new relationships between them.

About an excavation
a flock of bright red lanterns
has settled.—CHARLES REZNIKOFF

Part 6

Symbol

A **symbol**, speaking literally, is anything that represents something else. In its general use, a symbol is a public convention, something that everyone agrees upon and recognizes. The flag is a symbol of our country. The cross is a symbol of Christianity. For some people a Cadillac or a Lincoln is a symbol of wealth.

We live in a world of symbols. Words are symbols. The word *chair*, for example, is not the chair itself. It is a symbol for the actual chair. Uniforms are symbols of professions, flowers are symbols of emotions, certain animals are symbols of strength. Symbols like these are easily recognized by most of us.

Literary symbols, on the other hand, are often more difficult to recognize because they usually deal with abstractions, such as wealth, power, greed, society, war.

When writers create their own symbols, as Patrick White did with the corn on page 201, they usually do so with metaphors in which the basic idea is not stated. If one thinks of the "trumpeting of corn" as the insistent blaring of corn making a statement about America's great agricultural wealth, the corn becomes a *symbol* for the large-spread richness of American soil. The reader must assume that that is what the corn is trumpeting about.

When the song by Cat Stevens asks: "Where do the children play?" it makes the playing children a symbol of innocence and joy that he fears our mechanized society may be losing.

Exercises
Analyzing Symbolism

A. Determine what the following images symbolize:

a map	a donkey
a heart	an elephant
a red cross	a dollar sign
a white flag	a wedding ring
a halo	the American eagle
a rabbit's foot	a long feathered headdress

B. Explain the symbolism in the following:

1. He sank into the great sleep that awaits us all.

2. Larry Csonka, admitting he has been acting like a "turtle," came out of his shell today. He said: "I know I've been less than cooperative. But in terms of publicity, there's a time to be a turtle and a time to be a rabbit. There's a danger in talking too much."

3. Mahalia Jackson, the gospel singer, once said, "I've been singing now for almost forty years, and most of the time I've been singing for my supper as well as for the Lord."

4. And he shall be like a tree planted by the rivers of water, that bringeth forth his fruit in season; his leaf shall not wither; and whatsoever he doeth shall prosper.—*The Bible*

Part 7

Hyperbole

Hyperbole (from the Greek, "overshooting") is a figure of speech that uses bold and obvious exaggeration:

> The sky's the limit.
> I'm the greatest of all time.

These statements are obviously figurative. Even Muhammed Ali, given his religious faith, would not take himself seriously in claiming to be the greatest of all time.

Although hyperbole is used to make something bigger than life, smallness too can be exaggerated:

> Her brain is so small it could fit the head of a pin.
> He's so thin no door is tight enough to keep him out.
> She's so tiny you'd miss her in a crowd of ants.

Hyperbole is not intended to deceive anyone, nor is it in any sense a realistic description. The writer exaggerates a quality to emphasize it, or, by enlarging the event, infect the reader with his enthusiasm. The writer of advertising copy does not expect you to believe that the circus coming to town is the greatest event in history. He is merely arousing your enthusiasm with the largeness of his claim. As propaganda, of course, hyperbole is an effective tool.

Exercises
Analyzing Hyperbole

A. In the following sentences, explain in greater detail what makes these figures hyperbole. How would you describe the effect they may have on the reader?

1. He's so crooked he has to screw his socks on in the morning.
2. In that great cavern of his mind a thought is as lost as a gull on the high seas.

3. That's as exciting as watching paint dry.

4. Let us spend one day as deliberately as Nature, and not be thrown off the track by every nutshell and mosquito's wing that falls on the rails.—HENRY DAVID THOREAU

B. What other figure of speech is used in the preceding sentences besides hyperbole?

C. Search for examples of hyperbole in newspaper advertisements and TV commercials. Select the truly infectious ones and list those whose claims are so trite, colorless or absurd that you would ignore the product.

D. Write a sentence about each of the following, using hyperbole in your statement:
1. best friend
2. worst enemy
3. action of a sports event, whether in real life or on TV
4. a TV comedy or movie
5. your pet
6. your team's record
7. a car or cycle you admire
8. your talents in a game or activity in which you excel
9. your last report card

Part 8

Personification

Personification gives to a concept, or to an inanimate object, the qualities of a living thing, either animal or human.

> The mountains rose majestically.
> Earth wears a green velvet dress.

Speaking literally, can we say of mountains or earth that they "do" anything of their own volition? Mountains (except in cases of extreme natural agitation) do not move at all, and the earth does not wear clothes. By endowing these inanimate things with life-like qualities, we are again using figurative language. Because these characteristics are often associated with persons, the figure is called *personification.*

As a way of humanizing events, personification proves useful for making abstract ideas more vivid:

> Education, that great liberator of the human spirit, cannot be overvalued.

Personification engages our attention. We are more likely to respond to the personal than to the impersonal. In ascribing personal characteristics to inanimate objects, the writer involves our feelings and our sensations. The moon "in all her glory" becomes a woman creature in whose radiance we take pleasure. When we read, "the wind blew and blew until its breath was spent," our own breathing feels the difficulty.

In its long history, language has taken many figures, such as personification, and put them into its standard lexicon. Running was once an animal and human characteristic. Today brooks run, stockings run, time runs, and thoughts run, among others. Overuse, as in other figures, has robbed many images that were once vividly pictured. Who any longer sees "time marching on"?

With proper care not to use the obvious, personification remains a rich source of figurative meaning. Try your own hand at making your writing come to life with the breath of a living body.

Exercises
Using Personification

A. "The bottom was deep, soft clay; he sank in, and the water clasped dead cold round his legs."—D. H. LAWRENCE

What is the image you feel?

B. Write sentences that give the quality of life to the following:

1. rain
2. kitchen

3. classroom
4. school
5. a sports event

C. Name several products personified in TV commercials.

D. In the following, what are the personified qualities?
1. forbidding buildings
2. moaning seas
3. lonely city streets
4. throbbing machines
5. roar of traffic
6. scarred landscapes

Review Exercises
Using Figurative Language

A. Each of the following sentences contains one or more of the literary figures discussed in this chapter. Identify the figures and be prepared to explain them. In some cases a word or phrase may be part of more than one figure.

1. I am a miner for a heart of gold.—NEIL YOUNG
2. Its mouth gaped, exposing a fence of teeth like daggers.
3. Nadia Comaneci electrified crowds and bollixed computers by compiling the first perfect gymnastic score swimming in an "ocean of air."—*Time* Magazine
4. Come to a Whale of a Sale at Macy's!
5. The leaves scattered as if the wind were the enemy.
6. The ferocious sea growled at the borders of the shore.
7. There was a sweet sadness in the air that sang of the last rose of summer.
8. The bubble popped, leaving a layer of sticky stain on his face.
9. The whiz-bang Volkswagen Society shifts into 4th gear.—LIZA COTTON
10. Her voice burst upon the audience with a cry of crazed passion.

11. By now most of the sumacs at the roadside and in the corner of the back pasture begin to look like Sioux war bonnets and are ready to lead the parade right into Indian summer.—*The New York Times*

12. Farmers heap hay in stacks and bind corn in shocks against the biting breath of frost.—MARGARET WALKER

B. The following literary passages combine several figures to create impressions, atmosphere, or the formation of an idea. Identify the figures and state the emotional effect created.

1

No man is an island, entire of itself; every man is a piece of the continent, a part of the main. If a clod be washed away by the sea, Europe is the less, as well as if a promontory were, as well as if a manor of thy friend's or of thine own were. Any man's death diminishes me because I am involved in mankind, and therefore never send to know for whom the bell tolls; it tolls for thee.—JOHN DONNE

2

Let the sea-gulls wail
For water, for the deep where the high tide
Mutters to its hurt self, mutters and ebbs.—ROBERT LOWELL

3

I feel the sun on the stone above me; it's striking, striking, like a hammer on all the stones and it's the music, the vast music of noon, air and stones vibrating.—ALBERT CAMUS

4

And neither did I like the heavy, sickening, greasy carrion-breath that poured from the mouth of the Hotela la Bantu, where the natives hunched intent at zinc-topped forms, eating steaming no-color chunks of horror that bore no relation to meat as I knew it. The down on my arms prickled in revulsion from the pulpy entrails hanging in dreadful enticement at the window, and the blood-embroidered sawdust spilling out the doorway.—NADINE GORDIMER

5

Here and there, near the glistening blackness of the water, a root of some tall tree showed amongst the tracery of small ferns, black and dull, writhing and motionless, like an arrested snake. . . . Darkness oozed out from between the trees, through the tangled maze of the creepers, from behind the great fantastic and unstirring leaves; the darkness, mysterious and invincible; the darkness scented and poisonous of impenetrable forests.—JOSEPH CONRAD

c. Write a paragraph, or short account, of a recent emotional experience, using figurative language as much as possible. You may use one of the following topics, or you may select your own.

1. a party
2. a school sport victory or defeat
3. an automobile drive in traffic
4. a movie or TV show
5. an accident in which you or someone close to you was involved
6. an important event in your family, such as a birth, death, wedding, graduation
7. a personal outdoor adventure, such as a hike or camping trip
8. the habits of your pet
9. your successful accomplishment of something done with great difficulty
10. a long-held wish finally obtained

Chapter 11

Imaginative Writing

While exact knowledge is important for survival, it is the poet who understands the value of imagination in our lives. Here is what the poet Stephen Spender says about imagination.

It is for human living that imagination is indispensable.
Exact knowledge is only a fragment of the knowledge we
   need in order to live.
We can have no exact knowledge of ourselves, far less of
   other people.
There is no exact answer to the problems
   we are perpetually troubled by and have never solved;
   yet we must have some faculty by which we can deal
   with them.
We cannot ask science to tell us whether our lives have
   a meaning,
   or why we should pursue good and avoid evil,
   or how we should live with our neighbors.
Imagination does not answer these questions;
   perhaps the only answer for them is in faith.
What imagination does is to give us a vivid sense of them.

Part 1

Expository Writing and Imaginative Writing

All writing deals with ideas, and most writing is either expository or imaginative. Sometimes, of course, the two overlap.

The word *exposition* means "a setting forth," "an explanation." When a writer wishes to convey ideas as simply and clearly as he can, he writes exposition. He can develop his ideas in any of the ways listed at the beginning of Chapter 8, but his main purpose is to explain his ideas to the reader.

The main purpose of imaginative writing, on the other hand, is to probe the reader's mind and emotions in a way that expands the nature of experience. It is more subjective, more personal writing. It consciously appeals to the senses, uses figurative language, and is more self-conscious of style than expository writing.

For example, here is a subject:

The birds of spring arrived today.

You could use exposition, writing about the date, the species of birds or the availability of food for them. You could explain their migratory habits. You could also treat the subject imaginatively, writing about the ear-catching songs of the birds, the color of their plumage, and the beauty they bring to the season.

Sensory Appeal in Imaginative Writing

In imaginative writing, the senses play an important role. Strong sensory impressions stretch the imagination and help the reader to experience the world around him in fresh, new ways. The following selection is an imaginative description of how a young boy's senses are heightened and intensified by the beauty of the world around him.

> The grass whispered under his body. He put his arm down, feeling the sheath of fuzz on it, and, far away, below, his toes creaking in his shoes. The wind sighed over his shelled ears. The world slipped bright over the glassy round of his eyeballs like images sparked in a crystal sphere. Flowers were sun and fiery spots of sky strewn through the woodland. Birds flickered like skipped stones across the vast inverted pond of heaven. His breath raked over his teeth, going in ice, coming out fire. Insects shocked the air with electric clearness. Ten thousand individual hairs grew a millionth of an inch on his head. He heard the twin hearts beating in each ear, the third heart beating in his throat, the two hearts throbbing his wrists, the real heart pounding in his chest. The million pores on his body opened.

Which of the five senses are appealed to here? Point out specific examples. Can you find and identify the figures of speech? How does this description make you feel? Can you explain why this description makes you feel as you do?

Exercises
Expository Versus Imaginative Writing

A. Here are twenty subjects that lend themselves either to expository or to imaginative writing. Study them carefully. If you think the subject lends itself to expository writing, label it *Ex*. If you think it lends itself to imaginative writing, label it *Im*. In some cases you may feel that the subject can be handled either way. In that case, use both labels. Be prepared to support your label.

1. The price of lumber has risen dramatically.
2. They don't make movies as glamorous as they used to.
3. The beauty of a rainbow fills me with awe.
4. I need special insoles in my shoes.
5. Photography is an expensive hobby.

6. Tall ships (sailing ships) are exciting to see.

7. That rocking chair could tell some fascinating stories if it could talk.

8. Reading a book is like taking a journey.

9. Happiness and pleasure are not the same thing.

10. Honesty is its own reward.

11. Have you ever watched porpoises at play?

12. Puppies are the friendliest things on earth.

13. Have you ever watched someone about to get a medical injection?

14. The way to make money is to work hard.

15. My cousin is a totally unpredictable person.

16. Music helps me live my life.

17. Attic junk can be more than just junk.

18. We took a 300-mile trip on Sunday.

19. When I get up, I always look out the window first.

20. I would like to have travel stickers all over my luggage.

B. Using one of the above subjects, or one of your own, write an expository paragraph about it. Then, using the same subject, write an imaginative paragraph.

Part 2

Style in Imaginative Writing

At the beginning of this chapter we said that expository writing explains ideas to the reader, while imaginative writing expands the nature of experience. Here are two paragraphs, one expository, one imaginative. The subject of both paragraphs is the moment of lift-off of Apollo II from the then Cape Kennedy on its way to the moon. The expository paragraph was written by a reporter at the scene. The imaginative paragraph is by a well known writer, also at the scene, who calls himself Aquarius. Study the two paragraphs and note particularly the difference in style.

At ignition, nothing that TV says or does can re-create the waves of sound that actually buffet the ears, chest and gut of the spectator. The slowness of lift-off contrasts incredibly with the acceleration into flight. The head goes back, hands are raised to block out the sun, tears of relief and perhaps pride fill the eye. The sense of brute power boring an escape hole through the atmosphere is heightened by a sudden realization that one is being left behind. The earth itself seems to be dropping away as fast as the wingless rocket is accomplishing the completely unnatural act of heaving itself upward and bursting through the sky.

IMAGINATIVE PARAGRAPH

Then it came, like a crackling of wood twigs over the ridge, came with the sharp and furious bark of a million drops of oil crackling suddenly into combustion, a cacophony of barks louder and louder as Apollo-Saturn fifteen seconds ahead of its own sound cleared the lift tower to a cheer which could have been a cry of anguish from that near-audience watching; then came the earsplitting bark of a thousand machine guns firing at once, and Aquarius shook through his feet at the fury of this combat assault, and heard the thunderous murmur of Niagaras of flame roaring conceivably louder than the loudest thunders he had ever heard and the earth began to shake and would not stop, it quivered through his feet standing on the wood of the bleachers, an apocalyptic fury of sound equal to some conception of the sound of your death in the roar of a drowning hour, a nightmare of sound, and he heard himself saying, "Oh, my God! oh, my God! oh, my God! oh, my God! oh, my God! oh, my God!" but not his voice, and the sound of the rocket beat with the true blood of fear in his ears, hot in all the intimacy of a forming heat, as if one's ear were in the caldron of a vast burning of air, heavens of oxygen being born and consumed in this ascension of the rocket, and a poor moment of vertigo at the thought that man now had something with which to speak to God—the fire was white as a torch and long as the rocket itself, a tail of fire, a face, yes now the rocket looked like a thin and pointed witch's hat, and the flames from its base were the blazing eyes of the witch. Forked like saw teeth was the base of the flame which quivered through the lens of the binoculars. Upwards. As the rocket keened over and went up and out to sea, one could no longer watch its stage, only the flame from its base. Now it seemed to rise like a ball of fire, like a new sun mounting the sky, a flame elevating itself.

In the expository paragraph, you probably noticed that the sentences are of average length, and the vocabulary is not unusual. While the senses are accounted for, there is no appeal to them, and there is only one example of figurative language. The description of the event is mainly informative, though interesting.

The imaginative paragraph is breathtaking in the length of the sentences. The rush of words seems to parallel the driving energy of the lift-off. The vocabulary is unusual and stretches the imagination far beyond the facts. The appeal to the senses is strong, and the figurative language heightens and intensifies the experience in an extraordinary way. The total effect of the experience is awesome.

Exercise
Writing an Imaginative Paragraph

The following subjects lend themselves to imaginative writing. Choose one, or one of your own, and write an imaginative paragraph of description. Develop your paragraph well, and try to use a style that is appropriate to your subject. Try to use sensory appeal and figurative language, wherever appropriate, to stretch the reader's imagination.

1. The balloon escaped from the child's hand.
2. From the air, the ground looked like a study in miniatures.
3. The snow covered everything.

4. The city sounded like a huge machine that had suddenly gone out of control.
    5. Everything she touched seemed strange and unnatural.
    6. The plants in the yard had grown ten feet overnight.
    7. He plunged into the water and groped his way along the bottom.
    8. The large containers of ice cream were every color imaginable.
    9. I had never seen anything like it.
    10. I remember the scene very well.

Sports Writing

Perhaps some of the most colorful expository writing occurs in the sport field. Even here the difference in writing styles can vary greatly. The following selections describe the final rounds of the famous Joe Frazier-Muhammed Ali heavyweight championship fight in 1971.

1

Slowly finding his rhythm, Frazier seemed to grow stronger as Ali began to weaken. In the eleventh round, the roundhouse lefts that had earlier been missing Ali by as much as a full foot began to find their mark. Rocked by two hammering hooks, the staggering Ali barely managed to hang on until the bell. Coming back, Ali won the 14th, but 21 seconds into the final round, Frazier caught him with a head-snapping left hook that dropped him flat on his back. Dazed, Ali was up at the count of three, but his game attempt to rally was too little, too late. The decision for Frazier was unanimous.

2

Frazier was the human equivalent of a war machine. He had tremendous firepower. He had a great left hook, a left hook frightening even to watch when it missed, for it seemed to whistle: he had a powerful right. He could knock a man out with either hand—not all fighters can, not even very good fighters. Usually, however, he clubbed opponents to death, took a punch, gave a punch, took three punches, gave two, took a punch, gave a punch, high speed all the way, always working, pushing his body and arms short for a heavyweight, up through the middle, bombing through on force, reminiscent of Jimmy Brown knocking down tacklers, Frazier kept on coming, hard and fast, a hang-in, hang-on, go-and-get-him, got-him, got-him, slip and punch, take a punch, wing a punch, whap a punch, never was Frazier happier than with his heart up on the line against some other man's heart, let the bullets fly—his heart was there to stand up at the last. Sooner or later, the others almost all fell down. Undefeated like Ali, winner of 23 out of 26 fights by knockout, he was a human force, certainly the greatest heavyweight force to come along since Rocky Marciano.

The first selection is a fast-moving, detailed account of the action. While it contains figures of speech such as "roundhouse lefts," and "hammering hooks," it concentrates mainly on telling what happened. In the ordinary language of factual reporting, it is certainly adequate, and we know that Frazier won the eleventh round.

The second selection also tells us that Frazier won the round, but it proceeds in a different way. The language jabs and punches like Frazier. The phrases imitate a boxer's footwork and balance. The description of Frazier's physical strength and his feelings toward fighting help us understand why he won the round. We feel we have had a ringside seat at this fight.

Exercise
Reporting a Sports Event

Using as your subject some sports event that you attended or saw on TV, write a report of that event. Try to employ a style that re-creates the quality of the event, using strong sensory appeal and appropriate figurative language. Try to make the event come alive for the reader.

Description

Now let's move to an entirely different subject, in a different time and place. Let's take a ride on a trolley car. The trolley car has given way to more modern forms of transportation, but it still exists in a few places: the cable car in San Francisco, the trolley car in New Orleans and the commuter trolley in Pittsburgh. The following selection is a piece of expository writing describing the commuter trolley.

> Visitors can enjoy one of the best real-life trolley rides in the country by visiting Pittsburgh and taking the route from downtown through the surburban South Hills section. The scenic, curvy ride is part of a daily routine for thousands of Pittsburgh commuters, but it's very much like an amusement park "thrill" ride for visitors. The car rattles, shakes, and grates violently enough to give the rider the feeling that he will be hurled onto the floor if he doesn't hang on for dear life. Forget about reading newspapers en route to work.

This description is interesting and informative. Here is another description, handled in a different way.

> The first light on the roof outside; very early morning. The leaves on all the trees tremble with a soft awakening to any breeze the dawn may offer. And then, far off, around a curve of silver track, comes the trolley, balanced on four small steel-blue wheels, and it is painted the color of tangerines. Epaulets of shimmery brass cover it, and pipings of gold; and its chrome bell bings if the ancient motorman taps it with a wrinkled shoe. The numerals on the trolley's front and sides are bright as lemons. Within, its seats prickle with cool green moss. Something like a buggy whip flings up from its roof to brush the spider thread high in the passing trees from which it takes its juice. From every window blows an incense, the all-pervasive blue and secret smell of summer storms and lightning.

Down the long elm-shadowed streets the trolley moves along, the motorman's gray-gloved hand touched gently, timelessly, to the levered controls.

Where does the writer appeal to the senses in this description? How many different colors do you see? What senses other than sight are involved? What is the writer's tone—his attitude toward his subject? What is the mood—the effect on the reader?

How does the writer evoke a childlike quality in this description? Does the writer see the world as a child might see it? Can you explain this view? Does it stir any feelings or memories of your own childhood?

Here is another description of a trolley car. What figure of speech is predominant? To what sense does it mainly appeal? Does this description have the same childlike quality as the previous one? How does the style differ?

A street car raising its iron moan; stopping, belling,
and starting; stertorous; rousing and raising again
its iron increasing moan and swimming its gold windows
and straw seats on past and past and past, the bleak spark
crackling and cursing above it like a small malignant
spirit set to dog its tracks; the iron whine rises on rising speed;
still risen, faints; halts; the faint stinging bell; rises again,
still fainter; fainting, lifting, lifts, faints foregone: forgotten.
Now is the night one blue dew.

Exercise
Writing an Imaginative Description

Using any subject that appeals to you, write an imaginative paragraph or a longer composition of description. Try to make it appeal to the reader's senses and use figurative language to stretch the reader's imagination. Be aware of vocabulary and try to let your writing style convey the impression you are trying to create.

Chapter 12

Clear Thinking

Clear thinking is important to our lives because it serves the process of communication. Our lives are constantly involved in reading, writing, speaking and listening. In order to give and receive intelligent messages, we must be able to think clearly and to reason well. We must be able to recognize and understand the often subtle techniques for distorting reason, or truth.

Part 1

Establishing Facts

Clear thinking begins by determining what is factual and what is not. *Webster's New World Dictionary* defines a fact as "a thing that has actually happened or that is really true." A fact, then, is entirely different from something you might imagine, or guess, or feel.

Statements of fact can be proven true or false. If you state that your team lost last week, you have presented a statement of fact, as it can be proven true or false. Someone can either verify the statement or refute it. Factual statements are necessities in our daily lives. The existence of newspapers is dependent upon them. Advertisers are required to be factual in their claims; they must be prepared to verify the statements they present if a competitor or customer challenges them.

There are two methods for verifying a statement of fact:

1. Observe the claim for yourself.
2. Consult a reliable source.

If a classmate states, "It's snowing," or "The lunch today is pizza," you can readily check the truth of his statement. You can verify some scientific statements in the lab and you can check math theorems.

Most statements of fact, however, must be checked indirectly, by consulting a reliable source. You can determine whether you answered a test question correctly or not by consulting your textbook. You can settle an argument regarding a sports record by consulting an almanac or similar source. Being able to establish statements of fact is a requirement for a valid research paper, and being able to find the correct source efficiently is a time-saver when you're given a lengthy assignment.

Exercise
Checking Facts

Below are fifteen statements of fact. By using all available resources, including atlases, almanacs, encyclopedias, dictionaries, etc., determine the truth of the statements. Correct the false statements.

1. The Miami Dolphins have won four division championships, but only two Super Bowls.
2. Crediting General Douglas MacArthur with the statement "I shall return," is an error.
3. The average rainfall in Death Valley is .5 inch per year.
4. The tallest man in the world is recorded at 8 feet 11 inches.
5. The Gulf of Tonkin is an arm of the South China Sea that divides Vietnam and Thailand.

6. The name Joseph is Hebrew in origin, and meant, "He shall add."

7. West Germany is an area of 41,535 square miles, while that of Texas is 162,840.

8. A rhynchocephalian is one of an order of mammals.

9. More tea is produced in China than in any other country.

10. The Olmecs are believed to have been one of the first major civilizations of the New World.

11. Jefferson Davis was imprisoned at Fort Monroe, accused of plotting Lincoln's assassination.

12. Vampire bats do not suck their victim's blood; they first numb the skin by licking it, then bite and lap the blood.

13. The country with the highest recorded murder rate is the United States.

14. The Cadillac automobile was named after the founder of Detroit.

15. The movie *The Godfather* was the biggest moneymaker in motion picture history.

Part 2

Distinguishing Between Facts and Opinions

We don't deal in factual statements too often; the major portion of our day is spent exchanging opinions. There is nothing wrong with opinions; they are necessary to our lives and they enrich our speaking and writing. A requirement to express ourselves only in statements of fact would certainly guarantee boredom. You have many valid opinions, and it's frustrating to be ignored or discounted when you offer them. However, a sound opinion is quite different from an unsound one. *A sound opinion is one that is supported by facts, or can be traced to a reliable source.* Sometimes, however, we confuse opinions and facts.

The one sure way to differentiate between facts and opinions is to administer a simple test. Statements of fact can be proven true or false. Statements of opinion cannot.

Ways To Express an Opinion

You can express an opinion in any of three ways: (1) by making a judgment, (2) by making a prediction, or (3) by making a statement of obligation. Each of these ways is described below.

Making a Judgment. To say that the sun is shining and the temperature is in the 80's is a statement of fact. However, if you say, "It's a beautiful day," you've given your opinion. The difference lies in the word *beautiful*. This is a judgment word. After all, a "beautiful" day to a skier is one in which the temperature is in the thirties. Furthermore, some people think that rain is "beautiful." Hence there is no way to prove the statement true or false because of that one judgment word, *beautiful*.

The meaning of judgment words differs between people, depending upon their backgrounds and values. For example, a $49.95 outfit may seem cheap to one person, but expensive to another. Here are examples of other judgment words:

pretty	worthless	bad
attractive	cheap	kind
unattractive	honest	mean
ugly	dishonest	moral
valuable	good	immoral

Making a Prediction. Another type of opinion is the prediction. "The sun will rise tomorrow" seems valid, yet there's always the chance that it won't. "We're going skiing," "I get my cast off next week," and "The doctor will be with you in a moment" are all predictions. Until they have actually occurred, you cannot prove these statements true or false.

Making a Statement of Obligation. A third type of opinion contains one or more words of obligation. The key words in statements of obligation are *should, ought to, must,* and other similar terms. For example, "Students should get good grades," "You ought to brush your teeth three times a day," and "You must drive within the speed limit" all contain words of obligation. When delivered in an authoritative tone, they sound like factual statements, but they're not. Like statements of judgment and predictions, they cannot be proven true or false.

Exercise
Fact or Opinion?

Below are twenty statements. Decide whether each is a verifiable fact or an opinion. If it is an opinion, is it a judgment, a prediction, or a statement of obligation?

1. R-rated movies are more popular than those rated PG.
2. The Surgeon General has determined that cigarette smoking is harmful to your health.
3. In October we will observe Conservation Week.
4. R-rated movies result in greater profits than those with a PG rating.
5. The doctor has given Mr. Olson six months to live.
6. The study of English is invaluable to a person's education.
7. The President has declared one week in October as Conservation Week.
8. Carrots contain Vitamin A, which is essential to developing night vision.
9. Cigarette smoking is harmful to your health.
10. Mr. Olson will die within six months.
11. Mr. Donahue is a better mathematics teacher than Mr. Johnson.
12. Penicillin is remarkably effective in fighting flu.
13. Speeding is illegal and unethical, and it results in fatal highway accidents.
14. Mr. Donahue's students received higher scores on the mathematics section of the SAT than Mr. Johnson's.
15. The majority of fatal highway accidents are due, directly or indirectly, to speeding.
16. Penicillin has reduced the number of deaths from pneumonia.
17. You should take a serious interest in the political system of our country.
18. Senator Stafford's victory in the election means that he has retained his seat in the Senate.
19. It also means that Senator Stafford was the best qualified of the candidates.
20. The victory means that he will hold his seat in the Senate for at least another six years.

Should you eliminate all judgments, predictions, and obligations from your speaking and writing? That isn't necessary. Most of the opinions in the exercise on page 227 could be supported by factual evidence that would result in sound opinions. It is sound opinions that are important.

Part 3

Supporting Your Opinions

Sound opinions require support. By using facts based on past experience, scientific data, and other reliable resources, you can prove that "The sun will rise tomorrow." The overwhelming number of times it has already risen every day provides strong proof for the opinion that it will do so again tomorrow. A statement of obligation such as "Students should earn A's to guarantee college scholarships" could be supported by the following facts:

> Colleges consider G.P.A.'s and test scores when awarding scholarships.
>
> Of the forty-three graduating seniors who have been awarded scholarships to college from your school, thirty-eight had G.P.A.'s in excess of 3.6.
>
> The National Merit Scholars have high school G.P.A.'s of 3.8 to 4.0.

By using statements of fact you can support your opinions so that they are valid.

The most difficult opinion to support is that based on judgment words. If you state that "*Jane Eyre* is a fascinating book," you must be prepared to support the word *fascinating* by drawing specific facts from the book to uphold your judgment. A statement such as "The characters are vivid and the plot is suspenseful and exciting" is meaningless. Describe one of the "vivid" characters. Elaborate on the "suspenseful and exciting" plot by specifically citing two or three scenes. Support your opinions and you'll find people paying more attention to them and showing more respect for your evaluation and ideas.

Exercise
Using Facts To Support Opinions

Using three of the opinions listed, write three statements of fact to support each. Be careful not to use any judgment words in your support.

1. Because of the crimes and indiscretions of a few, politicians have lost the respect of their constituents.
2. Poverty destroys ambition.
3. Poverty stimulates ambition.
4. Spanish is an easier language to learn than Latin.
5. Television is responsible for the rapid rise of nonreaders in American schools.
6. Television is a powerful educational force.
7. Professional sports are getting out of hand.
8. Tobacco is as destructive to the human body as marijuana, and should be illegal.

Part 4

Dealing with Generalizations

Politicians are crooked! Teenagers are irresponsible! Welfare recipients are lazy! These are examples of one of the most common errors in reasoning—generalizing. There is evidence that a few politicians have been proven guilty of various charges. All of you have run into some irresponsible friends. At any economic level there are going to be some lazy individuals. By attributing the faults of a few to a complete group, you have committed the error of generalizing. Generalizing destroys your argument, and justifiably so.

Generalizations are broad statements based on a number of instances. The three generalizations above dealing with politicians, teenagers, and welfare recipients would be difficult to support as stated. However, by inserting a qualifying, or limiting, word, you could attempt to support them. You'd have a difficult task, as each of the statements contains a judgment word, but you could attempt some factual evidence.

To guard against generalizing you must be aware of "absolute" words, and be prepared to qualify your statements with less sweeping words. Below is a list that should be useful.

Absolute words		Less sweeping words	
all	everyone	most	
every	everybody	many	
each	everywhere	much	
none	nobody	few	a small
no	nowhere	some	number
no one			
always		usually	occasionally
all the time		generally	at times
		frequently	tends to be
		often	is apt to be
		sometimes	
never		seldom	infrequently
		rarely	not often
		hardly ever	

Even when you have qualified your statement, you must be cautious. Did you make the statement based on a number of instances, or only one or two? Which of the following statements could be factually supported:

> Politicians are crooked.
> Some politicians are crooked.

Most politicians are crooked.
A few politicians are crooked.

Teenagers are irresponsible.
Some teenagers are irresponsible.
Most teenagers are irresponsible.
A few teenagers are irresponsible.

Some generalizations are harmless and are usually simple exaggerations. The statement, "There's never a parking place close to school," could be translated to mean "There's rarely a parking place close to school when I get here." The often-heard statements, "The phone always rings when I'm in the shower," "Every time we plan a picnic it rains," and similar statements influence no one, and are used conversationally. They emphasize our feelings and become common means of expression.

On the other hand, some generalizations are actually harmful. If you decide not to eat in a certain restaurant or not to buy a certain product because of only one unfortunate experience, that's your decision. But if you attempt to influence others by stating that the restaurant serves spoiled food, or the product falls apart, you are being unfair. While these examples seem quite simple, you'd be surprised how influential generalizations can be when carefully worded and phrased. Consider the statement, "Labor unions are responsible for the rising cost of living." This type of statement could be used in a political campaign, or to influence support for a piece of legislation. It is not only a sweeping generalization but it is also harmful in its effect.

Exercises
Dealing with Generalizations

A. Decide whether the following generalizations are harmful or harmless; then rephrase the statements by qualifying them.

1. Humankind is an endangered species.
2. American products are the world's best.
3. Juvenile delinquents come from broken homes.
4. Labor unions are controlled by gangsters.

5. Small cars are more practical than large cars.
6. Students who don't behave in school should be expelled.
7. In two years the schools in our state will be badly overcrowded.
8. People who eat balanced meals are healthy.
9. People without high school diplomas lack the minimum basic skills.
10. No other teacher gives as much homework as Mr. Treadwell.

B. Write an opinion concerning one of the following topics. Using your opinion as a topic sentence, develop a paragraph to support it. You must use a minimum of three factual statements in your support, but no additional opinions. Avoid using any generalizations.

Politics	Capital Punishment
Movies	Alcoholism
A Television Series	Drug Addiction
Divorce	Marriage

Part 5

Avoiding Stereotypes

The most harmful generalization is the stereotype. It is used for members of certain races, religions, professions, and nationalities. There are few of us who have not heard an ethnic joke, an ugly remark about policemen, a racial slur, or a remark intended to degrade women. The stereotype is not only harmful to those at whom it is aimed but also reflects the speaker's or writer's biased attitudes.

Exercise
Avoiding Stereotypes

What stereotypes have you heard expressed recently? Using one or two as examples, try to determine the purpose behind the remark. What can be done to eradicate this type of harmful generalization?

Part 6

Detecting Fallacies in Reasoning

Generalizing is one of the mistakes in reasoning that are known by the broader term **fallacies.** Fallacies result in confusion, errors, and lost arguments. In order to reason effectively, you must be aware of the common fallacies so you can avoid them in your speaking and writing.

The Limited-Choice Fallacy

This fallacy is committed when a statement is presented that offers too limited a choice of alternatives. Faced with what satisfies us as being a neat "either-or" situation, we close our minds to the possibility that there may be other alternatives.

> We're losing money at the factory; we must either raise our prices or close down.

On the surface this alternative may seem logical. It is certainly simple and straightforward. However, other possibilities should be investigated: borrowing money for new machinery that will produce more efficiently; hiring new managers; turning to new products. The above statement would be more realistic if it said, "We're losing money at the factory; we must find a way to produce at a profit again, or close down."

> The prisoner told the police, "I did't want to hold up that filling station, but I had to. My family was starving."

This emotional plea is calculated to win sympathy for the holdup man, but it is not an example of straight thinking. What the prisoner has said, in effect, is this: "I had only two choices: either commit a crime or let my family starve." There are other alternatives to a problem of this kind. In this country there are lawful ways for needy families to get help from state and private welfare organizations long before sinking to the starvation level. Besides, any kind of job he could have obtained would have been an alternative to robbery.

Exercise
Avoiding the Limited-Choice Fallacy

Find the fallacy in each of the following statements.

1. My friends, the problem is simple. If Smith is nominated we will lose the labor vote; if Jones is nominated, we will lose the farm vote. The answer is also simple. There are a lot more laborers than farmers, so Jones will be nominated.

2. Why didn't the school authorities let the team make that out-of-state trip? Are they trying to wreck our athletic program?

3. At the time of the Revolution, the American colonists had to choose between liberty and death.

4. If the city does not increase taxes, it will have to cut the size of the police force.

5. This candidate has little support, so he must be unfit.

6. If I don't pass English this term I can't go to college.

7. Capital punishment is a necessity; otherwise murderers would be paroled and turned loose on the community.

8. Without a legal right-to-die law, terminally ill patients and their relatives will endure needless suffering and expense.

9. Drug users are losers!

10. I can't go to the party without a new outfit.

11. Money is necessary for a political candidate's success.

12. Another war will destroy civilization!

13. If I don't have a car I'll never get to school on time.

14. Either you get high grades or you might as well quit school and prepare for a life of unemployment.

15. The only way to beat the high cost of gasoline is to buy a motorcycle.

The Only-Cause Fallacy

You commit the Only-Cause Fallacy when you choose only one cause as important when actually more causes are involved. Only-cause reasoning flourishes among those who "second-guess" at athletic events. Conway School has just lost a football game, 19–18:

> The fullback lost that game for us. He missed his block on the free safety when the halfback got loose on that long run in the last minute. If he hadn't, we'd have won. The coach ought to bench him until he learns how to block.

The game wasn't quite so simple to a scout in the stands. That trained observer noted the following:

1. The line was very weak, especially in the middle.

2. Pass defense was weak. The cornerback who almost got away in the last minute allowed four critical third-down passes to be completed in his territory.

3. The placekicker tried to kick points after touchdown but couldn't get them away because of the weak line.

4. The fullback was their best player in every way. On the last-minute play, which nearly won the game, he took out the right linebacker, then went downfield and almost got the free safety.

While it is much easier to blame one group or one person for an unfortunate situation, you should always look deeper than the obvious, easy answer. Can you spot the fallacies in the following statements?

> The Communists are responsible for today's international tensions.
>
> Our heavy weekend accident toll is the result of carelessness.
>
> Do you want to get rid of that tired feeling? Use Pep-Up Vitamins.
>
> Clean up the City! Elect George Bailey mayor!

These fallacious statements can be rephrased and made valid by recognizing the complicated problems involved:

> Communists are an important force behind today's international tensions. (There are others.)
>
> Carelessness is probably the leading cause of weekend accidents.
>
> Pep-Up Vitamins will help you if that tired feeling is the result of a vitamin deficiency.
>
> Vote for more efficient city government! Vote for George Bailey!

Exercise
Avoiding the Only-Cause Fallacy

Find the fallacy in each of the following statements.

1. The run-down condition of the school building proves that the janitors are not working hard.

2. The teacher is unfair. I spent more time reviewing for the test than anyone else in the class, and I got only a "C."

3. As she approaches her one-hundredth birthday, Mrs. Moffit says she owes her remarkably good health to regular hours and yogurt.

4. In explaining his party's defeat in yesterday's state election, the party chairman said, "I believe it was the result of the bad weather, which undoubtedly kept many of our voters from the polls."

5. It's no surprise that Joe won the photography contest again; his expensive camera is better than anyone else's.

6. Everyone in my family has bad teeth; naturally I have more cavities!

7. I'll never be successful here; I'm the wrong color (or religion or sex).

8. Naturally we're experiencing inflation; look at the increase in farm costs.

9. I knew he wouldn't ask me out again; he dates only the wealthy girls.

10. If we don't get a new coach we'll never take State!

11. It's too bad Jan and Sandy are so confused—but then, their parents just got divorced.

12. Adopted children are always insecure.

13. How could he pass math? He's had his mind on basketball all term.

14. We never get colds in our family because we drink orange juice daily.

15. Mrs. Gilmore died of lung cancer; I didn't even know she smoked!

The False-Cause Fallacy

You commit the False-Cause Fallacy when you reason that because B happens after A (or at the same time as A), A is the cause of B.

> A man walked up to a bus stop and noticed that the little man already there was snapping his fingers, regularly and deliberately, every few seconds.
>
> The newcomer's curiosity grew stronger as the snapping continued, and he began to stare.
>
> The little man noticed, nodded, smiled a small, wan smile, and said, "It's to keep the wild elephants away."
>
> "Wild elephants?" gasped the other. "Why, there aren't any wild elephants within five thousand miles of here!"
>
> "I know," the snapper said, brightening a little, but never breaking his rhythm. "Effective, isn't it?"

The elephants stay away during the finger-snapping; therefore, the finger-snapping is the reason the elephants stay away.

Even though the ridiculous nature of this fallacy is obvious in the case of the wild elephants, the fallacy is surprisingly common. Most of our superstitions are thought to have had their beginnings in this kind of reasoning. Black cats are held responsible for bad luck; bridesmaids wait to catch the bridal bouquet to ensure their marriage. Many superstitions are based on the False-Cause Fallacy.

The fact that B follows A is never enough reason to say that A is the cause of B. There may be good reason to investigate whether A is really the cause of B, but this may require a long, difficult procedure. However, without the investigation you have no evidence.

> Mrs. X writes, "After switching to your detergent, my clothes are definitely brighter."
>
> That mechanic must have done something to the engine while he was checking the oil and battery. The car ran a lot more smoothly before.
>
> I wish they'd close that new factory. I've had a sore throat ever since they opened because of the pollution.

Each of these statements is fallacious because there is no definite evidence that A really was the cause of B. On the other hand, you must never make the equally foolish mistake of saying that A cannot be the cause of B. You can say only that it is not certain that A is the cause of B.

Exercise
Avoiding the False-Cause Fallacy

Explain the fallacy in each of the following statements. Then rephrase the statement so that it will be true.

1. It's going to be a long, hard winter; the squirrels are growing a heavy coat of fur and are starting to pile up nuts early.

2. That new stove must be defective. It either burns the food or leaves it raw.

3. Their uncle must have left the Gormans a lot of money when he died. The will was opened on Monday, and they bought a new car on Thursday.

4. That teacher is no good; I've failed every test in that class.

5. The new family that moved into the neighborhood last week is behind all these petty thefts. We never had any trouble before they came.

6. I'm so glad we finally fluoridated our water. Our cavities have decreased considerably.

7. Without the swine flu shot, I'd probably be dead.

8. Look how inflation has leveled off—thanks to the Republicrat party being in power.

9. That speed reading course is responsible for my higher grades.

10. The counselor shouldn't have called my parents; now I'm restricted for six weeks.

11. We never would have lost that game without that referee!

12. The weirdos always come out during a full moon.

13. I study better with the stereo and TV on.

14. Poverty is a direct line to ignorance.

15. Of course Saul Bellow won the Nobel Prize. He's already written other notable best-sellers.

False Analogy

An **analogy** is a comparison of two things which, though basically different, are alike in some important way. Analogy is perhaps the commonest form of reasoning because it is an easy way to explain or persuade. Because it is easy to follow and understand, it is likely to be effective. However, if the similarity between the two things is not important to the point you are trying to make, you have made a false analogy.

Consider these two statements made by a mother.

1. Jim is doing well at college. Since Bill is his brother, Bill will probably do equally well.

2. Jim is doing well at college. Since Bill's high school grades were just as good, he will probably do equally well.

The fact that the boys are brothers is certainly important to their mother. But it is not important to the college prospects of Bill, which is the point we are considering. The first analogy, then, is false. Since high school grades are a fairly reliable means of forecasting college success, the second analogy would seem to be valid.

An analogy stands or falls on the similarity established between the two things being compared. Before making use of an analogy, test it with these two questions:

1. Are the two things I am comparing really similar?
2. Is this similarity important in the analogy?

An analogy never proves anything; it does not provide certainty. All it can do is establish probability; that is, indicate that something will probably happen or that something is probably true. It can never give certainty that something will happen, or that something is true.

Because an analogy is not proof, it should not be used in an argument. You can state that because oranges and lemons give you hives, tangerines probably will too. But you cannot assert that tangerines are unhealthy. While that may seem simple, arguments are too often based on analogies. You may hear it said that one party has been in power during two major economic recessions, so if you elect it to office again, we'll have another recession.

Exercise
Avoiding False Analogy

Explain why each of the following analogies is false.

1. Sue should be on the debating team; she's the smartest girl in class.
2. I'm sure Fred will be as good a basketball player as his brother; he's just as big and strong.
3. Senator Harrison for Governor! Her splendid record in Congress shows she will be a fine Chief Executive for our state.
4. We made a mistake when we hired our coach. He wasn't good enough to make his college team.
5. My doctor gave me a prescription for some medicine that cured my sore throat overnight. Try some; you'll be fine in the morning.
6. Those two did such a fantastic job organizing the last dance that we should elect them to the student council.
7. I'll never be able to balance a budget. I'm terrible at algebra!
8. Why should I go to college? John Denver didn't, and look at him now!

9. Eat your dinner! Think of all the starving children in the world who'd love it.

10. John F. Kennedy and Martin Luther King were both assassinated. Anyone who takes a strong stand today on civil rights is just asking for the same end.

11. She's been playing the piano for eight years. She'll be a concert pianist before she's twenty.

12. I spent six hours on this paper; you have to give me an "A."

13. The insurance rates on male teenage drivers are very high; they are obviously reckless and irresponsible.

14. A bartending job should be required for psychologists, as bartenders listen to problems constantly.

15. If you can, you do it; if you can't, you teach it.

Chapter 13

Using the Library and Reference Materials

Knowing how to use the library resources quickly and efficiently is of great practical value not only for your work in English but for all your studies. You will find the library an indispensable ally as you do research in literature, history, science, and other subjects.

To make effective use of the library, however, you need to know (1) how books are classified and arranged, and (2) how to find them by using the card catalog.

You also need to know how to find and use the many kinds of reference materials the library contains. These include dictionaries, encyclopedias, almanacs, catalogs, atlases, biographical reference books, literary reference books, and magazines.

This chapter will give you the basic information you need to make the best use of the library.

Part 1

The Classification and Arrangement of Books

Finding any book you need requires a knowledge of how books are classified and how they are arranged on the shelves.

The Classification of Books

Fiction. Novels and anthologies of short stories are usually arranged in alphabetical order by author. When there are two or more books written by the same author, you would find them shelved alphabetically by title. For example, John Steinbeck's books would be found under S. His *East of Eden* and *The Grapes of Wrath* would be followed by *Of Mice and Men*.

Nonfiction. Most libraries—including high school libraries—use the Dewey Decimal System of classifying nonfiction books. This system is named for its originator, the American librarian, Melvil Dewey. There are ten major classifications in the Dewey Decimal System; all books fit into one of these classifications: The ten major classifications are these:

000–009	**General Works**	(encyclopedias, handbooks, almanacs, etc.)
100–199	**Philosophy**	(includes psychology, ethics, etc.)
200–299	**Religion**	(the Bible, theology, mythology)
300–399	**Social Science**	(sociology, economics, government, education, law, folklore)
400–499	**Language**	(languages, grammars, dictionaries)
500–599	**Science**	(mathematics, chemistry, physics, biology, etc.)

600–699	Useful Arts	(farming, cooking, sewing, nursing, engineering, radio, television, gardening, industries, inventions)
700–799	Fine Arts	(music, painting, drawing, acting, photography, games, sports, amusements)
800–899	Literature	(poetry, plays, essays)
900–999	History	(biography, travel, geography)

As you can see from the major categories of the Dewey Decimal System, each discipline has a classification number. For example, all books on the fine arts are classified between 700 and 799, and all literature books will be found between 800 and 899. The system becomes more detailed as each of these major groups is subdivided. The table below subdivides works in history as follows:

900–999 History

910 General geography and travel
920 General biography
930 Ancient history
940 European history
950 Asian history
960 African history
970 North American history
980 South American history
990 General history of other parts of the world

970 North American history

971 Canada
972 Middle America-Mexico
973 United States
974 Northeastern United States
975 Southeastern United States
976 South central United States
977 North central United States
978 Western United States
979 Great Basin and Pacific Slope regions of the United States

The numbers in a particular classification, combined with the letter of the author's last, name make up the **call number.** The call number helps you locate the book on the shelf once you have found it in the card catalog.

Arrangement of Books on the Shelves

You can see that books are arranged on the shelves numerically in order of classification. Most libraries prominently mark their shelves with the numbers indicating the books to be found in each particular section. Like fiction books, nonfiction books are arranged alphabetically by authors' last names.

Biographies are one of the most popular kinds of books in libraries. The Dewey Decimal System division for them is 920. However, large libraries will often place biographies in a separate section because of the large number of these books. In this case, they will have a "B" on the spine of the book and on the catalog card. If you are looking for a particular biography and are unable to locate the 920 division, ask the librarian for assistance.

Reference Books are located in the library's reference room or area. They are classified according to the Dewey Decimal System and often with the letter "R" or "Ref" above the classification number. Usually, a reference book may not be checked out of the library.

Exercise
The Classification and Arrangement of Books

Using the Dewey Decimal Classification summary on pages 244 and 245, assign the correct classification number to each of the following books:

1. *The Coming of the French Revolution,* by George Lefebvre
2. *Fun with Mathematics,* by Jerome Meyer

3. *Dictionary of Classical Mythology*, by J. F. Zimmerman
4. *The Theatre*, by Sheldon Cheney
5. *Garden Flowers in Color*, by Daniel Foley
6. *Words and Ways of American English*, by Thomas Pyles
7. *The Magic of Black Poetry*, comp. Raoul Abdul
8. *Television News*, by Irving Fang
9. *Psychology for Life Today*, by Charles Foster
10. *Invitation to Skiing*, by Fred Iselin
11. *Your Legal Rights as a Minor*, by Robert Loeb, Jr.
12. *Outdoor Photography*, by Erwin Bauer
13. *Life in a Medieval Castle*, by Joseph Gies
14. *Alternatives in Education*, by Vernon Smith
15. *The American Novel and Its Tradition*, by Richard Chase

Part 2

Using the Card Catalog

The **card catalog** will determine whether the library has the book you want and, if so, where you will find it. The card catalog is a cabinet of small drawers or file trays containing alphabetically arranged cards. Each card bears the title of a book and the classification or call number of the book. (Sample cards are found on pages 248 and 249.)

There are usually at least three cards for the same book in the card catalog. These are the *author card*, the *title card*, and at least one *subject card*. The convenience of having three different ways of finding a book is described here.

The Author Card. Perhaps you are writing a paper for your American history class. For a unit on First Ladies, your subject is Eleanor Roosevelt. Because you know that her son, Elliott Roosevelt, has written a book about his parents, you look up his name in the card catalog. The author card will look like the sample shown at the top of the next page.

973.9   **Roosevelt, Elliott, 1910-**
R

A rendezvous with destiny: the
Roosevelts of the White House/by
Elliott Roosevelt and James Brough.
New York: Putnam, c 1975.
446 p., 4 leaves of plates: illus.;
Includes index.

Author cards for all books by an author will be filed together
alphabetically according to title. Books *by* an author are followed
by books *about* an author.

The Title Card. If you know the title of a book but not the
author's name, the title card will help you locate the book.
Look in the card catalog for a card bearing the title at the top
of the card.

The place of the title card in the catalog is determined by the
first letter of the first word in the title. (*A, An,* and *The* do not
count as first words.)

973.9   **A rendezvous with destiny**
R
Roosevelt, Elliott, 1910-

A rendezvous with destiny: the
Roosevelts of the White House/by
Elliott Roosevelt and James Brough.
New York: Putnam, c 1975.
446 p., 4 leaves of plates: illus.;
Includes index.

The Subject Card. You may not have a specific book in mind, or you may simply suspect that there are many books about Mrs. Roosevelt. By looking' up Eleanor Roosevelt in the card catalog, you will find a subject card similar to this:

973.9   **ROOSEVELT, ELEANOR, 1884-1962**
R

     Roosevelt, Elliott, 1910-
        A rendezvous with destiny: the
     Roosevelts of the White House/by
     Elliott Roosevelt and James Brough.
     New York: Putnam, c 1975.
        446 p., 4 leaves of plates: illus.;
     Includes index.

Subject cards are most useful when you want information on a specific topic from a variety of sources. Cards for all books on a particular subject are cataloged together. The subject card may also indicate that a book has chapters on a single aspect of the topic you are interested in. The publication date on the card will help you find the most up-to-date book on your subject.

Information on Catalog Cards. The three types of catalog cards—author, title, subject—carry the same information. This information includes:

1. The call number.
2. The title, author, publisher, and date of publication.
3. The number of pages, and a notation on whether the book has illustrations, maps, table, or other features.

Cross Reference Cards. Occasionally, while researching a particular subject, you will find a card that reads *See* or *See also*. The "See" card refers you to another subject heading in the catalog which will give you the information you want.

The "See also" card refers you to other subjects closely related to the one you are interested in. This card may be helpful to you in making sure that your research on a particular topic is complete.

Compare the cross reference cards and see how they both can assist you in thorough research on a particular topic:

Photography — Darkroom technique

see

Photography — Processing

Photography — Processing

see also

Special photographic processing
Photography—Printing processes
Photography—Developing and developers

Guide Cards. Besides the catalog cards, you will find guide cards in the cabinet trays. The guide cards bear a tab that projects above the other cards; they will aid you in finding other catalog cards quickly. For example, in your search for materials on Jimmy

Carter, you will find them easily by means of alphabetically arranged guide cards like these:

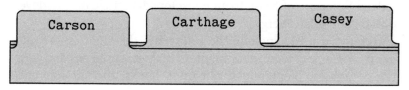

Exercise
Using the Card Catalog

Use the card catalog to find the author, title and call number of a book on the following subjects:

1. A play by Archibald MacLeish
2. A book on the science of genetics
3. A pictorial history of the American theatre
4. A book on the future of American politics
5. A novel by Thomas Hardy
6. A book on the conservation of natural resources
7. A book on American English
8. A book about F. Scott Fitzgerald
9. A book with badminton rules
10. A book on interior decoration
11. An introduction to filmmaking
12. A handbook of logic
13. A history of Indians in the Southwest
14. A book on public opinion polls
15. A book on prehistoric man

Part 3

Using Reference Materials

One of the best ways to obtain information on a particular topic is to consult a reference work. Libraries have either a reference section or a reference room. It is here that you will find just about everything you want, from a *Time* article on our federal Secretary of State to an encyclopedia article on the development of solar energy.

Reference works include the following: dictionaries; encyclopedias; pamphlets, handbooks, and catalogs; almanacs and yearbooks; atlases; biographical reference books; literary reference books; and magazines.

Reference works are tools and, like tools, should be used in definite ways. Most reference works have prefaces which describe how information is arranged, show sample entries, and explain the symbols and abbreviations used in the book. Before using any reference work for the first time, you would be wise to at least skim the preface.

The basic types of reference books are described in this section.

Dictionaries

The most widely used reference books in the library are the general dictionaries. General dictionaries fall into three major categories:

1. **Unabridged** dictionaries are dictionaries with over 250,000 entries.

2. **"College"** or **"desk"** dictionaries generally carry 130,000 to 150,000 entries.

3. **Concise** or **"pocket"** dictionaries are those with a smaller number of entries.

Unabridged Dictionaries. An unabridged dictionary may contain up to 500,000 words. It gives uncommon, as well as common meanings of many words, and explains in detail how they are used. The best known unabridged dictionaries are the following:

Webster's Third New International Dictionary
The Random House Dictionary of the English Language,
    Unabridged Edition

You will find at least one—if not both—of these in your school or community library.

College or Desk Dictionaries. A college or desk dictionary is a quick and convenient reference. It provides information you would normally need about definitions, spellings, pronunciations, and matters of usage. It usually contains a special section which gives biographical information about well-known people, and articles on such topics as pronunciation, spelling, and dialects.

Your school or local library probably carries several different college dictionaries. The best known are these:

> *The American Heritage Dictionary of the English Language*
> *The Macmillan Dictionary*
> *The Random House Dictionary of the English Language,*
>   *College Edition*
> *Thorndike-Barnhart Dictionary*
> *Webster's New Collegiate Dictionary*
> *Webster's New World Dictionary of the American Language*

Dictionaries about Language. Another group of dictionaries is available to you. Each of these deals with a specific aspect of our English language: synonyms and antonyms, rhymes, slang, Americanisms, etymology, and so forth.

As a young writer, you need to be concerned with precision in your writing. A help in finding the precise word you are looking for is a **thesaurus,** or dictionary of synonyms.

A thesaurus should be used only as a "memory-jogger", to help you find words that are already in your vocabulary. You are treading on dangerous ground if you select from a thesaurus a word you don't know in place of word you do know. From your study of Chapter 1, you know that most synonyms are not interchangable.

A list of reliable thesauruses follows:

> *Roget's International Thesaurus*
> *Roget's Thesaurus in Dictionary Form*
> *Roget's Thesaurus of English Words and Phrases*
> *Webster's Collegiate Thesaurus*
> *Webster's Dictionary of Synonyms*

Additional dictionaries dealing with our language are the following:

Abbreviations Dictionary: (Abbreviations, Acronyms,
    Contractions, Signs and Symbols Defined)
Acronyms, Initialisms, and Abbreviations Dictionary
Brewer's Dictionary of Phrase and Fable
A Dictionary of American Idioms
Dictionary of American Slang
Dictionary of Literary Terms
A Dictionary of Slang and Unconventional English
A Dictionary of Word and Phrase Origins (3 Volumes)
Harper Dictionary of Contemporary Usage
Mathews Dictionary of Americanisms
The Oxford Dictionary of English Etymology
Wood's Unabridged Rhyming Dictionary

Special-Purpose Dictionaries. Finally, there are special-purpose dictionaries that deal exclusively with music, medicine, foreign language, biography, and many other subjects. Check your library as to the availability of the many titles in print.

Encyclopedias

General Encyclopedias. An encyclopedia (from the Greek *enkyklios paideia*, which means "general education") is a collection of articles alphabetically arranged in volumes on nearly every conceivable subject. It is designed for quick reference, and provides you with general information on various fields or branches of learning.

Guide letters on the spine of each volume and guide words at the top of the pages assist you in finding information. It is best, however, to check the general index when looking for information. It may list several good sources. For up-to-date information on a topic, check the yearbook which many encyclopedias include.

Never use an encyclopedia as your only source. Use it only to obtain a general survey of your subject. The library is a storehouse of information; an encyclopedia should be used only as a door to that storehouse.

Most libraries include the following encyclopedias in their reference section:

The *Encyclopaedia Britannica* is unique in its organization. In dealing with the great amounts of knowledge known to humankind, the *Britannica* has broken down its encyclopedia into three parts: the *Propaedia* (pro meaning "prior to"), the *Micropaedia* (micro meaning "small") and the *Macropaedia* (macro meaning "big").

The *Propaedia,* or Outline of Knowledge and Guide to the *Britannica,* presents more than 15,000 different topics, arranged according to fields or areas of knowledge. For each topic in the Outline, there are references to the *Macropaedia* of three kinds: (1) whole articles, (2) sections of articles, (3) other references. These references make possible systematic study or reading on any subject in the encyclopedia.

The *Micropaedia,* consisting of 10 volumes, is a ready reference and index to the entire encyclopedia. As a ready reference, it is a short-entry encyclopedia. Its more than 100,000 entries, arranged in alphabetical order, give the most important and interesting facts about their subject. Often this is all you will want to know. But when a subject is also treated in depth in the *Macropaedia,* the *Micropaedia* becomes an index.

The *Macropaedia,* which contains knowledge in depth, is the main body of the *Britannica.* The *Macropaedia's* 19 volumes contain 4,207 long articles by world-renowned contributors on major subjects.

Encyclopedias on Specific Subjects. Encyclopedias on a wide variety of specific subjects fill library shelves. To give you some idea of the diversity of encyclopedias, here is a partial list:

ENCYCLOPEDIAS ON SPECIFIC SUBJECTS

ART

Encyclopedia of Modern Art
LaRousse Encyclopedia of Byzantine and Medieval Art
LaRousse Encyclopedia of Prehistoric and Ancient Art
LaRousse Encyclopedia of Renaissance and Baroque Art

HISTORY

An Encyclopedia of World History
Encyclopedia of American History

HOBBIES AND INTERESTS

Encyclopedia of Gardening
The Illustrated Encyclopedia of World Coins
The International Encyclopedia of Cooking

LITERATURE

The Concise Encyclopedia of English and American Poets
    and Poetry
The Concise Encyclopedia of Modern Drama
LaRousse Encyclopedia of Mythology
McGraw-Hill Encyclopedia of World Biography
    (12 volumes)
McGraw-Hill Encyclopedia of World Drama (4 volumes)

SCIENCE AND MATHEMATICS

Encyclopedia of Animal Care
The Encyclopedia of Chemistry
Grzimek's Animal Life Encyclopedia (13 volumes)
The Illustrated Encyclopedia of Aviation and Space
International Encyclopedia of Social Sciences (17 volumes)
Universal Encyclopedia of Mathematics

Pamphlets, Handbooks, and Catalogs

The Vertical File. Pamphlets, handbooks, booklets, and clippings on a variety of subjects are available in most libraries. These subjects include information about vocations, travel, census data, and program schedules. It is here you may find college catalogs, too. All of this information is kept in a set of file cabinets called the **vertical file.**

One of the most important ideas behind the vertical file is that the information in it is current. This file can be an invaluable source to you when writing a report on a contemporary topic, seeking current statistics, or looking up information on careers.

Information about Vocations, Colleges and Universities. The reference section of the library can be a starting point in seeking information about careers and about colleges. Again, depending on the size of your library, the availability of materials does vary. Here is a list of some resources you might use:

Encyclopedia of Careers and Vocations
Barron's Guide to the Two-Year Colleges
Barron's Profiles of American Colleges
Lovejoy's College Guide

The 300 section of your reference area will provide related material. Many libraries also have on reserve many college catalogs.

Almanacs and Yearbooks

Published annually, almanacs and yearbooks are useful sources of facts and statistics on current events, as well as on matters of historical record in government, economics, population, sports, and other fields:

Guinness Book of World Records
Information Please Almanac, Atlas and Yearbook
Statesman's Yearbook
Statistical Abstract of the United States
Women's Rights Almanac
World Almanac and Book of Facts

Atlases

We usually think of an atlas mainly as a book of maps, but it also contains interesting data on a number of subjects. The excellent *National Geographic Atlas of the World*, for example, lists some of the following topics in its table of contents: "Great Moments in Geography," "Global Statistics," and sections on population, temperature, oceans, and place names. Below is a list of other widely used atlases:

Atlas of World History
Atlas of World Wildlife
The Britannica Atlas
Collier's World Atlas and Gazetteer
Goode's World Atlas
Grosset World Atlas
The International Atlas from Rand McNally
The Times Atlas of the World
Webster's Atlas with Zip Code Directory

Biographical References

There are brief biographical notations in dictionaries and longer biographical articles in encyclopedias. Often, however, a better source is one of the specialized works listed below:

Current Biography. Biographies of current newsworthy individuals are published here monthly. Each issue is indexed. All copies are bound in an annual volume with a cumulated index of people in that particular volume as well as previous annual volumes. Also found at the end of the annual volumes are the names of the people in *Current Biography* according to their profession. Biographies of internationally known persons are found here, but Americans are well represented throughout this reference.

Dictionary of American Biography. This is the most famous and most reliable of all American biographical dictionaries.

Alphabetically arranged, this twenty-two-volume work carries articles on the lives and accomplishments of prominent deceased Americans. The work contains 14,870 biographies of Americans from the colonial days to 1940. The length of the articles varies from half-page sketches to chapter-length essays.

Dictionary of National Biography. This multi-volume dictionary is the most famous and the most reliable of British biographical dictionaries. Its accurate and concise information makes it a most valuable source.

The International Who's Who. Alphabetically listed, this source provides brief biographical sketches of prominent living people of all nations. This publication includes thousands of personalities and provides a valuable source for current biographies.

Webster's Biographical Dictionary. This is a source of biographical facts about noteworthy people, past and present. More than 40,000 individuals are listed alphabetically and pronunciation keys are given for each name.

Who's Who. Principally concerned with British personalities, this source provides a very brief description of the life and accomplishments of each individual included. You would probably need to refer to another source if you needed detailed information.

Who's Who in America. This source, alphabetically listed, provides biographical sketches of prominent living Americans who are known either for their positions or their accomplishments. Published every two years, this is a reference book which can guide you to other sources in seeking detailed information about a particular person.

Who's Who in America also has regional editions: *Who's Who in the Midwest, Who's Who in the South and Southwest,* and *Who's Who in the West.*

Who's Who in American Women. Unusual in its title, this book not only lists outstanding American women, but women of international acclaim.

Books about Authors. For biographical information about authors, and critical evaluations of their works, the following sources are especially useful:

American Authors: 1600-1900
British Authors Before 1800
British Authors of the Nineteenth Century
Contemporary Authors
Cyclopedia of World Authors
Twentieth Century Authors
Twentieth Century Authors: First Supplement
World Authors: 1950-1970

Literary Reference Books

The following are valuable reference books on the history of literature, on quotations and proverbs, for locating poems and stories, and for finding information about writers:

Bartlett's Familiar Quotations
Book Review Digest
Contemporary Poets
Cyclopedia of Literary Characters
Encyclopedia of World Drama
Granger's Index to Poetry and Recitations
Illustrated Encyclopedia of the Classical World
A Literary History of England
A Literary History of the United States
Mencken's A New Dictionary of Quotations
The Oxford Companion to American Literature
The Oxford Companion to Classical Literature
The Oxford Companion to English Literature
The Oxford Companion to the Theatre

From the above list, three widely used reference works are the following:

Bartlett's Familiar Quotations. This is one of the best known of the dictionaries of quotations. Its completeness and accuracy have made it notable for over a century.

Quotations are arranged chronologically by author in the main section of the book. A shorter section of passages from the Bible, Koran, and the Book of Common Prayer follow. To find the complete source of a quote, you should use the main index in the back of the book. Whether you know the entire quotation or simply have a general idea of its topic, you would be able to find it in the index.

For example, study this quotation by Carl Sandburg:

"The fog comes
on little cat feet.
It sits looking
over the harbor and city
on silent haunches
and then moves on."

You may find this quote in three places:

1. under Carl Sandburg entries in the main index of the book.
2. in the index under the first line of the quote.
3. under the subject of Fog.

Whatever your recollection or your need for a quotation on a particular subject, *Bartlett's* is an excellent source.

Book Review Digest. Arranged alphabetically by authors of the book reviewed, this digest gives short quotations from selected reviews from many popular American and English periodicals. If a work of fiction has had four or more reviews or a work of nonfiction has had two or more reviews, and if the book is hard-bound and has been published in the United States, it will appear in this digest. It is published monthly and cumulated annually.

You will find this to be a good source in finding both unfavorable and favorable reviews of particular books.

Granger's Index to Poetry and Recitations. This source includes an index of first lines as well as an index of authors to assist you in finding a poem if its title is unknown to you. By using this reference book, you will also be able to locate not only a quotation but an entire short work. For example, let us say you need to find an anthology or book containing the poem "Song of the Open Road" by Walt Whitman. You would look up this title in the *Index* and under the poem's title you will find listed a number of books containing this poem. The titles, however, are coded, and you will find the code explained in the front of the book.

Granger's Index to Poetry and Recitations is a standard, worthwhile source for any student of literature.

Magazines

The *Readers' Guide to Periodical Literature* lists the titles of articles, stories, and poems published during the preceding month in more than 100 leading magazines. It is issued twice a month from September through June and once a month in July and August. An entire year's issues are bound in one hardcover volume at the end of the year. Articles are listed alphabetically under *subject* and *author* (and *titles* when necessary). You will find the *Readers' Guide* invaluable when looking for articles on a subject for a composition.

The excerpt from the *Readers' Guide* on page 263 illustrates how articles are listed.

Exercises
Using Reference Materials

A. **Dictionaries and Encyclopedias.** Using the dictionaries and encyclopedias listed on pages 253-257, indicate the best source for answers to these questions. Include the page reference.

1. Find an article listing important events in France during the 18th Century.
2. Give a definition and examples of a limerick.
3. Who is Merlin?
4. What were the "Jim Crow" laws?
5. Who wrote the ballet "Slaughter on Tenth Avenue"?
6. Give two examples of twentieth century fables.
7. What is meant by the expression "French leave"?
8. What do the following abbreviations mean?
SHAPE   EKG   USAF   Mayday

Excerpt from the Readers' Guide

CARICATURES and cartoons
Facing it: Levine, Conrad. Steadman and Hirschfeld on each other. il Esquire 86:126-9 Ag '76

CARR, Allan
Gatsby of Benedict Canyon. por Time 108:52 Ag 30 '76 —— title of article

CARR, Susan
Search for American Indian seed. il Org Gard & Farm 23:85-6+ Ag '76

CARRIER, Herb
Auto-maintenance basics. il Pop Sci 208:88-90 Mr; 112-13 —— name of magazine
Ap; 106-7 My; 120-1 Je; 209:100-2+ Ag '76

CARTELS, International. See Trusts. Industrial—Industrial trusts.

CARTER, Jimmy
Around city hall. A. Logan. New Yorker 52:72-8 Ag 23 '76 —— volume number
Carter building policies would return to traditional Democratic stands. F. Swoboda and L. Walczak. Archit Rec 160:35 Ag '76 —— page reference
Carter dances on. Nat R 28:882 Ag 20 '76
Carter's road show. il por Time 108:23 Ag 23 '76
Coming out swinging. il pors Time 108:6-15 Ag 30 '76
Courting big business. Nat R 28:881 Ag 20 '76 —— date of magazine
Efficiency expert. E. Marshall. New Repub 175: 15-17 Ag 21 '76
Jimmy Carter: how you gonna get him back on the farm? J. J. Kirkpatrick. il Nat R 28:886-8+ Ag 20 '76
Man who sold Jimmy Carter. P. Smith. il por Duns R 108:32-3 —— illustrated article
Ag '76
Republicans start probing for Carter's weak spots. il por U.S. News 81:14-15 Ag 23 '76
Smiling damned villain; views of P. Stanford. Nat R 28:939 S 3 '76
Trooping to Plains. New Repub 175:5-7 Ag 21 '76

CARTHAN, Hattie
Brooklyn's tireless tree lady. J. Wandres. il pors Ret Liv 16:40-1+ Ag '76

CARTOGRAPHY —— subject entry
New look in maps brings out patterns of plate tectonics. A. Spilhaus. il Smithsonian 7:54-63 Ag '76

CASALINI, Mario —— author entry
Book exports to the United States: two views: Italian-language books. Pub W 210:70-2 Ag 16 '76

CASS, Heather Wilson
Architecture as human experience. il Archit Rec 160:78+ Ag '76

CASSETTES, Magnetic tape. See tape cartridges, cassettes, etc. —— "see" cross reference

CATHOLIC church

Music
See Church music

Rites and ceremonies
See also
Ordination —— "see also" cross reference

9. Compare the form of the Miltonic sonnet with the Shakespearean sonnet.

10. What are the techniques for reproducing color?

11. Find a copy of the Greek alphabet.

12. What was the original meaning of the word "johnnycake"?

13. What is the plot of Eugene O'Neill's play *Mourning Becomes Electra?*

14. When was the guillotine used?

15. Find an explanation of a dangling participle.

B. Almanacs, Yearbooks and Atlases. Using the almanacs, yearbooks and atlases listed in this chapter, indicate the best source for answers to these questions. Include the page reference.

1. How many Americans have won the Nobel Prize for Literature?

2. Where are the National Seashores?

3. What is the literacy rate in India?

4. How can you obtain a passport?

5. Where can you find illustrations of the different American Revolution flags?

6. Compare life-expectancy rates of men and women in the United States.

7. Find a copy of the Bill of Rights.

8. Who made the first orbital flight?

9. What are the provisions of the Campaign Finance Act?

10. Find a map showing the density of world population.

11. What are the four time zones in the United States?

12. How many miles long is the Mississippi River?

C. Biographical References. Using the biographical references listed in this chapter, give the best source for answers to these questions. Include the page reference where you found the information.

1. Find a list of the rulers of the British Empire.

2. When did Sir Edmund Hillary climb Mount Everest?

3. Was James Thurber's *My Life and Hard Times* autobiographical?

4. How did Alfred Eisenstadt achieve fame as a photographer?

5. What was the family background of Charlotte and Emily Brontë?

6. How do you pronounce the name of the French aviator and writer Antoine de Saint Exupéry?

7. Which of James Michener's writing does he think will survive?

8. What historical works is Carl Sandburg famous for?

9. What were Frederick Jackson Turner's views on the significance of the frontier in American history?

10. Why were Ogden Nash's writings so popular?

D. **Literary Reference Books.** Use the literary reference books listed in this chapter to find answers to the following questions. Write after each answer the name of the reference book you used.

1. From what source did Aldous Huxley take the title *Brave New World?*

2. In what American novel is Carol Kennicott a character?

3. How favorable were the reviews of Richard Wright's *Black Boy?*

4. What is the title of the poem that begins "Some say the world will end in fire"?

5. Who coined the phrase "the lost generation"?

6. What plays did the Irish dramatist, Sean O'Casey, write for the Abbey Theatre?

7. What is the setting of Stephen Vincent Benét's poem "John Brown's Body"?

8. Who were the nine muses?

9. Who was the famous founder and editor of *The New Yorker* magazine?

10. On what occasion did Sir Winston Churchill say "Never in the field of human conflict was so much owed by so many to so few"?

11. Find a poem on the subject of pride.

12. List the volumes of poetry written by Mark Van Doren.

E. **Readers' Guide to Periodical Literature.** Use the excerpt from *The Readers' Guide* on page 264 to answer the following questions:

1. Under what subject will you find articles on international cartels?

2. Which magazine articles have a picture of Jimmy Carter?

3. Give the volume and the pages of the *Time* article on "Gatsby of Benedict Canyon" by Allan Carr.

4. To which magazines do the abbreviations *New Repub, Ret Liv, Archit Rec, Nat R* refer?

5. How many issues of *Popular Science* have articles on auto-maintenance basics?

F. **Using Reference Materials for a Research Paper.** You are doing a research paper on John Steinbeck's place in American literature. Using the reference sources listed in this chapter, find the specific books which give the answers to these questions. Include the page references.

1. Reviews of *The Grapes of Wrath, Cannery Row, Of Mice and Men, The Pearl*.

2. Comprehensive biographical information.

3. A bibliography of his writings.

4. The text of his acceptance speech upon receiving the Nobel Prize for Literature.

5. His experiences as a war correspondent.

6. The sources of the titles of these novels: *The Grapes of Wrath, The Winter of Our Discontent*.

7. His novels which were made into movies.

8. The area in California which is the background for many of his stories.

9. The plot of his novel *Tortilla Flat*.

10. A list of the books by Steinbeck which are in your school library.

Handbook

A detailed Table of Contents of the Handbook appears in the front of this book.

How To Use the Handbook

This Handbook is your reference book. In it the concepts of grammar and usage are organized so that you can study them efficiently and refer to them quickly.

To use the Handbook well, you should first leaf through it to become familiar with its organization and contents. Note especially the following:

Organization of the Handbook

Grammar (Sections 1–4) Sections 1–4 provide a comprehensive treatment of English grammar. They give the rules and explanations for grammatical questions you want answered.

Usage (Sections 5–9) Sections 5–9 are a guide to English usage. When you are puzzled about which form of a word to use in your writing, turn to the appropriate part of these sections.

Forms and constructions marked STANDARD are accepted as standard usage—the kind of usage that is appropriate at all times and in all places. Forms and constructions marked NONSTANDARD are not accepted everywhere. While they may go unnoticed on the playground or in the locker room, in many other situations they mark the user as careless or untrained in the English language.

Capitalization (Section 10)

Punctuation (Sections 11–14)

Spelling (Sections 15–16)

Good Form (Sections 17–18)

Throughout the Handbook are many exercises that test your understanding of the concepts explained. These exercises are the first steps in putting what you learn here to practical use. The next steps are in your own writing and speaking.

1.0 The Classification of Words

The words in our language have been classified into eight large groups according to the jobs they perform in a sentence. These eight groups are called the eight *parts of speech*. Here are the eight parts of speech.

nouns	adjectives	conjunctions
pronouns	adverbs	interjections
verbs	prepositions	

In addition to the parts of speech, there are three kinds of words, formed from verbs, that do many different jobs. These words are called *verbals*. Verbals are all formed from verbs and have several of the characteristics of verbs. They are unlike verbs, however, in that no verbal can stand by itself as a complete verb. The verbals are the *infinitive*, the *participle*, and the *gerund*.

This section provides a comprehensive treatment of the parts of speech and the verbals.

1.1 The Noun

Certain words in the language are used as labels with which we identify people and things.

A noun is the name of a person, place, or thing.

Things named by nouns may be visible, such as *hats, buildings,* and *books.* Things may be items that we perceive with our other senses: *odors, sounds, tastes.* Other things are abstract and not observed through the five senses: *beliefs, ideas, wishes,* and so on.

PERSONS	PLACES	THINGS
Thomas Jefferson	Detroit	desk
architect	library	courage
salesperson	continent	morality

A **common noun** is the name of a whole group of persons, places, or things. It is a name that is common to the whole group: *coat, road, picture, newspaper.*

A **proper noun** is the name of an individual person, place, or thing.

A proper noun always begins with a capital letter.

COMMON NOUNS	PROPER NOUNS
singer	Beverly Sills
tunnel	Lincoln Tunnel
river	Hudson River
cemetery	Arlington National Cemetery
building	John Hancock Building

As the above list shows, a noun may consist of more than one word. Each word in a proper noun is capitalized.

Any word that can be immediately preceded by *the* is a noun: *the* river, *the* Snake River, *the* language. Many proper nouns but not all of them, can be preceded by *the:* *the* Black Hills, *the* San Diego Zoo, but not *the* Jimmy Carter or *the* Canada.

Exercise A: Find all the nouns in the following sentences.

1. Glass is made of melted sand mixed with soda and lime.

2. Grasshoppers and crickets "sing" by rubbing their legs together.

3. Frogs lay eggs which look like a mass of dark-centered tapioca.

4. The raccoon has a sharp nose, dainty feet, and a long, ringed tail.

5. Snakes move by a wavelike motion along the body.

6. Geckos are soft-skinned lizards which lay hard-shelled eggs.

7. Our thermostat keeps the heat at a constant temperature.

8. Dr. Alexander Fleming was an obscure researcher in a hospital when he discovered penicillin.

9. The anthropologist studies human beings—their make-up, their social customs, and the things they make.

10. The atmosphere is not a calm ocean of air but a tossing sea laced with swift currents.

Exercise B: Decide which of the following are common nouns and which are proper nouns. Write the proper nouns, beginning each with a capital letter.

1. town, philadelphia, woodhaven, state
2. eskimo, fur, walrus, bering sea
3. airport, midway airport, airplane, hangar
4. magazine, *newsweek*, newspaper, calendar
5. river, hudson river, harbor, bay of fundy
6. gulf, gulf of mexico, lake, lake erie
7. pupil, national honor society, teacher, scholarship
8. algebra, mathematics, french, chemistry
9. alabama, state, country, democracy
10. citizen, neighbor, mayor aldrich, governor

1.2 The Pronoun

Since it would be awkward and cumbersome to repeat the name of a person or thing every time we wish to refer to it, we use other words in place of names. These words are pronouns. They may be used in a sentence in any way that a noun is used.

A pronoun is a word used in place of a noun.

The noun for which the pronoun stands and to which it refers is its **antecedent.**

> *Sue* was satisfied with *her* grades. (*Sue* is antecedent of *her*.)
>
> The *guides* endangered *their* lives. (*guides* is antecedent of *their*.)
>
> Mr. Carter is the *counselor* with *whom* I discussed my plans for college. (*counselor* is antecedent of *whom*.)

Sometimes the antecedent of a pronoun appears in a preceding sentence.

> The *candidate* was asked about *foreign aid. She* said *it* was necessary for the security of the United States. (*She* refers to the antecedent *candidate; it* refers to *foreign aid*.)

Indefinite pronouns do not often refer to any specific noun. The indefinite pronoun itself may be the antecedent of a personal pronoun.

> The *fans* were discouraged. *Some* began to leave the stadium. (The antecedent of the indefinite pronoun *Some* is *fans*.)
>
> *Everyone* made *his* own costume. (The antecedent of *his* is the indefinite pronoun *Everyone*.)

There are six kinds of pronouns:

personal pronouns	demonstrative pronouns
compound personal pronouns	interrogative pronouns
indefinite pronouns	relative pronouns

Personal Pronouns

Pronouns used in place of persons' names are called **personal pronouns.** They permit us to identify the person speaking, the person spoken to, and the person spoken about. Personal pronouns are also used to refer to things.

FIRST PERSON (the person speaking)
I, me, my, mine, we, us, our, ours

SECOND PERSON (the person spoken to)
you, your, yours

THIRD PERSON (the person or thing spoken about)
he, she, it, they
his, hers, its, their, theirs
him, her, them

Personal pronouns change their form, or spelling, for different uses in sentences. This change of form is called the **case** of pronouns. There are three cases: *nominative, possessive,* and *objective.* Personal pronouns also change their form to show the difference between singular (one) and plural (more than one). This change of form is called the **number** of pronouns.

The following table shows the forms for the three *persons,* for the three *cases,* and for the *number* of all of the personal pronouns.

Personal Pronouns

Singular

	NOMINATIVE	POSSESSIVE	OBJECTIVE
First Person:	I	my, mine	me
Second Person:	you	your, yours	you
Third Person:	he, she, it	his, her, hers, its	him, her, it

Plural

	NOMINATIVE	POSSESSIVE	OBJECTIVE
First Person:	we	our, ours	us
Second Person:	you	your, yours	you
Third Person:	they	their, theirs	them

Third person pronouns that refer to male persons are in the **masculine gender.** Those that refer to female persons are in the **feminine gender.** Pronouns that refer to things are in the **neuter gender.**

Here are some important things to remember about pronouns:

The pronoun *it* is called a personal pronoun even though it refers to things more often than to persons.

Countries, ships, and airplanes are sometimes referred to by the feminine pronouns, *she, her, hers.* Animals may be referred to by *it* and *its* or by *he, his, she, her, hers,* depending on the sex of the animal.

The words *mine, yours, hers, ours,* and *theirs* are always used as pronouns. The words *my, your, its, our,* and *their* are always used as modifiers before nouns. They are **possessive pronouns.** *His* may be used either as a pronoun or as a modifier.

This transistor radio is *mine.* (pronoun)
Here is *my* license. (modifier)
That motorboat is *theirs.* (pronoun)
I agree that *his* is better. (pronoun)
We were proud of *his* record. (modifier)

Compound Personal Pronouns

A **compound personal pronoun** is formed by adding *-self* or *-selves* to certain of the personal pronouns, as follows:

FIRST PERSON: myself, ourselves
SECOND PERSON: yourself, yourselves
THIRD PERSON: himself, herself, itself, oneself, themselves

There are no other acceptable compound personal pronouns. Never say *hisself* or *theirselves*.

Compound personal pronouns are used *intensively* for emphasis or *reflexively* to refer to a preceding noun or pronoun.

The mayor *himself* inspected the slum buildings. (intensive)

Mary hurt *herself* when she fell. (reflexive)

Exercise A: In the following sentences find the personal pronouns. Find the antecedent of each pronoun.

1. Alice did her shopping. Then she went to a museum.
2. Bob and Jim had their lunch. Then they went skiing.
3. Claire has two careers, and she says they are compatible.
5. Her friends in Madison are giving Janet a shower.
5. Jim said, "I lost my umbrella on the bus."
6. Beth, have you made your decision yet?
7. The salesperson gave Betty his card, but she lost it.
8. Fred bought a sweater. As it didn't fit, he returned it.
9. After Sarah had sanded the chairs, she painted them.
10. Bob has a key, but he didn't bring it with him.

Exercise B: Supply the correct compound personal pronoun needed in each of these sentences. Find the antecedent for each compound personal pronoun.

1. Roy injured _____ on the band saw.
2. Darlene taught _____ to type.
3. You _____ should have delivered the message.
4. Sue hurt _____ by diving in shallow water.
5. The cheerleaders exhausted _____ .
6. By abusing his rivals, Ed defeated _____ in the election.
7. Lincoln _____ heard the woman's complaint.
8. They took the responsibility upon _____ .
9. Brace _____ for the next announcement.
10. I found _____ in a predicament.

Indefinite Pronouns

Some pronouns, such as *anyone* and *anything*, do not refer to a definite person or thing. They are called **indefinite pronouns.** Normally, indefinite pronouns do not have antecedents.

SINGULAR INDEFINITE PRONOUNS

another	anything	either	everything	no one
anybody	one	everyone	neither	someone
anyone	each	everybody	nobody	somebody

PLURAL INDEFINITE PRONOUNS

both   many   few   several

The pronouns *all, some, any* and *none* may be singular or plural, depending upon their meaning in the sentence.

All of the research *was* completed. (singular)
All of the supplies *were* donated. (plural)

Some of the butter *was* rancid. (singular)
Some of the officers *have* resigned. (plural)

None of the corn *has* been harvested. (singular)
None of the stories *were* published. (plural)

Has any of the publicity helped? (singular)
Have any of the risks been considered? (plural)

Demonstrative Pronouns

The words *this, that, these,* and *those* are used to point out, or demonstrate, which one or which ones are meant. Since they point to what is meant, they are called **demonstrative pronouns.** They always refer to a definite person or thing, but the words they refer to may come later.

This is the *poem* I wrote. (*poem* is the word referred to.)

On the ship were two Bengal *tigers. These* were headed for the St. Louis Zoo. (*tigers* is the word referred to by *These*.)

Note: The demonstrative pronouns *this, that, these,* and *those* may be used as adjectives: *this hat, those curtains.*

Interrogative Pronouns

The pronouns *who, whose, whom, which,* and *what* are used to ask questions. When used in this way, they are **interrogative pronouns.**

Who won the game?   *What* did he say?
Whom did she vote for?   *Which* should I choose?
Those skis are John's. *Whose* are these?

Relative Pronouns

The words *who, whose, whom, which,* and *that* are sometimes used to introduce an adjective clause. They relate the clause to some other word in the sentence. When used in this way, they are called **relative pronouns.**
A relative pronoun is used to introduce a relative clause. It also has a use within the relative clause. See Section 3.6.

Exercise: List the pronouns in these sentences. Tell what kind each pronoun is.

1. Are those hermit crabs? They don't look like whelks.
2. This is my bike. Is that yours?
3. Everyone took the test except him.
4. Not one of my classmates heard me.
5. You should have delivered the message yourself.
6. Few are better educated than he.
7. She asked me to give the book to the man who called for it.
8. I wish you had given them a more definite answer.
9. Her twin Sally looks older than she.
10. Everybody went out of his way to be nice to Rob.

1.3 The Verb

Every sentence must contain a word that tells what is happening. This word is the verb.

A verb is a word that tells of an action or state of being.

Grammatically, the verb is the most important word in the sentence. If you can find the verb and manage it properly, many of your grammar and usage problems will be solved.

Most verbs change their form (their sound or spelling) to show past time and present time. They are the only words to do so. This fact can help you decide which word in the sentence is the verb.

Summer jobs *were* very scarce this year. (past)
Summer jobs *are* very scarce this year. (present)

The rank and file *demanded* a voice in government. (past)
The rank and file *demand* a voice in government. (present)

Most verbs also change their form to show the difference between singular and plural in the third person.

Gulliver *meets* many people in his travels. (third person singular)
Travelers *meet* many interesting people. (third person plural)

Action Verbs

The action asserted by an action verb may be visible, physical action, or it may be invisible action.

Ken *dropped* the test tube. (visible)
The cars *collided*. (visible)
Alfred *shoveled* snow. (visible)
We *enjoyed* the comic effects. (not visible)
Eileen *decided* to wait. (not visible)
Her speech *impressed* me. (not visible)

Linking Verbs

A few verbs such as *be,* link the subject to a noun or adjective. Hence they are called **linking verbs.**

> Pat *became* the editor. Helen *seemed* confused.

The most common linking verb is *be* with its forms *am, are, is, was, were, been, being.*
Other linking verbs are *appear, become, seem, look, sound, grow, feel, smell, taste, remain, stay.*

> The substance *appeared* transparent. Ann *sounds* bored.
> Al *grew* mellower with age. He *looks* strong.
> No one *seems* satisfied. I *feel* contented.
> His father *became* angry. The grapes *taste* sour.
> The room *smells* musty.
> We *remained* standing throughout the performance.
> It *stayed* upright till the storm began.

Many linking verbs may also be used as action verbs.

> Jack *felt* a sharp blow. We *smelled* the hamburgers.
> The farmers *grow* wheat. José *tasted* the lobster.
> The city *sounded* the curfew.
> She *looked* under the bleachers.

Main Verbs and Auxiliaries

Many verbs consist of more than one word. They consist of a **main verb** and one or more **auxiliaries,** or helping verbs. The last word in the phrase is the main verb.

There are three verbs that can be used either as main verbs or as auxiliaries. Here are their forms.

DO	HAVE	BE		
do	has	is	was	be
does	have	am	were	been
did	had	are		being

AS MAIN VERB	AS AUXILIARY
He will *do* his duty.	I *do* need a new dress.
Have they a reason?	We *have* been chosen.
The rockets *were* powerful.	The crops *were* exported.

The most frequently used auxiliaries are the forms of *be* and *have*. The most common of the other auxiliaries are the following:

must	may	shall	could	would
might	can	will	should	

VERB	AUXILIARY	MAIN VERB
has had	has	had
had been	had	been
was doing	was	doing
had done	had	done
could have gone	could have	gone
might have been seen	might have been	seen
is being improved	is being	improved

Often the parts of a verb are separated by a modifier or modifiers that are not part of the verb.

He *was* unjustly *accused*.
Don *had* quietly *assumed* control.

Exercise A: Find the verb in each of these sentences. Include all the words that make up the verb. Do not include any word that separates an auxiliary from a main verb.

1. Several candidates are being considered for the job.
2. The thief may still be lurking in this house.
3. I could meet you at the Guggenheim Museum.
4. I have just read some facts about solar energy.
5. Dr. Ferrera will return from her vacation next week.
6. *Moby Dick* is now regarded as a classic.
7. Heather will probably be elected editor-in-chief.
8. Our old Buick has just been painted.

9. Is anyone using the Volkswagen?
10. New sources of fuel are being developed every year.
11. *Romeo and Juliet,* the story of the most famous of romances, will always be a favorite.
12. Everything was being readied for the President's inauguration.
13. We probably should have taken the train.
14. Termites have practically consumed the beams on our porch.
15. The mayor would undoubtedly have been defeated anyway.

Exercise B: Find each verb and tell whether it is an action verb or a linking verb.

1. Both Anita and Jerry are outstanding athletes.
2. Just leave your boots outside the door.
3. The child looked hungry.
4. The child looked hungrily at the cake.
5. The freshly baked bread smelled delicious.
6. The steak tasted delicious.
7. The audience grew tense with excitement.
8. Bob Summers, a cousin of mine, is a champion bowler.
9. The committee has been meeting at the home of the chairperson.
10. Water skiing seems relatively safe.
11. Even an eight-foot jump looks easy.
12. Riding on one ski was my undoing.
13. Her expression betrayed her lack of attention.
14. Laurie tasted the icing on the cupcake.
15. The cupcakes smelled tantalizing.

The Principal Parts

The principal parts of a verb are those from which all forms of the verb are made. They are (1) the *present infinitive* (usually called simply the *present*); (2) the *past*; and (3) the *past participle*.

A **regular verb** is one that forms its past and past participle by adding *-ed* or *-d* to the present.

PRESENT	PAST	PAST PARTICIPLE
need	need*ed*	need*ed*
bake	bake*d*	bake*d*
hear	hear*d*	hear*d*

An **irregular verb** is one that does not form its past and past participle by adding *-ed* or *-d* to the present. See Section 8.1 for usage of irregular verbs.

PRESENT	PAST	PAST PARTICIPLE
begin	began	begun
rise	rose	risen
lie	lay	lain

The **present participle** of a verb is formed by adding *-ing* to the present form: *eat—eating; save—saving; put—putting.*

The Progressive Forms

The **progressive forms** of the verb are used to show on-going action. They are formed by using the forms of *be* with the present participle:

They *are talking.*   Maria *has been driving.*
The clock *is working.*   The teacher *had been explaining.*
The actors *were rehearsing.*   I *must be dreaming.*
Joe *will be presiding.*   Louis *might have been sleeping.*

The Emphatic Forms

Special emphasis is given to a statement by using *do, does,* or *did* with the present form of the verb. These are examples of **emphatic forms.**

She *did stop* the car.
We *do want* world peace.
Mike *does play* a good game.

Transitive and Intransitive Verbs

A **transitive verb** carries over the action from the subject to the object of the verb. An **intransitive verb** expresses an action that is complete in itself; it does not carry action over to an object.

TRANSITIVE ·	INTRANSITIVE
Cindy *liked* the **novel.**	The game finally *started.*
The debaters *argued* the **point.**	The battle *ended.*
The country *faced* a **crisis.**	The experiment *succeeded.*
Everyone *expressed* **regret.**	The non-thinkers *conformed.*

Many verbs may be transitive in one sentence and intransitive in another.

INTRANSITIVE	TRANSITIVE
No one *moved.*	Chico *moved* the **car.**
Did they *pass?*	*Did* they *pass* the **law?**
The pilot *could* not *see.*	The pilot *could* not *see* the **runway.**

The Active and the Passive Voice

When the subject performs the action expressed in the verb, the verb is in the **active voice.** When the subject receives the action of the verb, the verb is in the **passive voice.** The passive voice is formed by using some form of *be* with the past participle of the verb.

ACTIVE: The voters *studied* the *issues* carefully.
PASSIVE: The issues *were studied* carefully by the voters.

ACTIVE: The increase in vandalism *angered* the *police.*
PASSIVE: The police *were angered* by the increase in vandalism.

A transitive verb can be put into the passive voice because it has an object that receives the action of the verb. The object of the active verb becomes the subject in the passive form.

In a sentence containing an intransitive verb, there is no word that receives the action of the verb. For this reason no intransitive verb can be put into the passive voice.

> The class *discussed* Swift's satire. (active)
> Swift's satire *was discussed* by the class. (passive)
> The alumni *built* a trophy room for the teams. (active)
> A trophy room for the teams *was built* by the
>   alumni. (passive)

Exercise A: Find the verb and tell whether it is active or passive.

1. Larger contributions are needed by the National Kidney Foundation.
2. Washington was alive with politicians and representatives of foreign governments.
3. In 1912, Arizona was admitted to the Union.
4. The trees were pruned by the owner of the nursery.
5. My sister's class elected her president.
6. A package of sunflower seeds will be mailed to you.
7. The great pyramid of Cheops covers thirteen acres.
8. The amendment was passed by a two-thirds vote.
9. That window has been broken by every storm.
10. Basketball was invented in 1891 by James A. Naismith, a Y.M.C.A. instructor.

Exercise B: Change the active verbs to passive and the passive verbs to active.

1. The first ball was thrown out by the mayor.
2. The driver of the red car hit the fire hydrant.
3. Dr. Ramsey operated on my father.
4. Lee was chosen by the group to represent them.
5. The ordinance was finally passed by the City Council.
6. The Sixth Regiment took the city.
7. The maid was dusting the pictures.
8. The photographs have been retouched by the engraver.
9. The parade was reviewed by the governor and the mayor.
10. The famished students quickly devoured the sandwiches.

Tense

Most verbs change their forms to tell present, past, and future time. **Tense** means "time." There are three simple tenses and three perfect tenses for each verb. They are formed as follows:

1. **Present tense.** The **present tense** is formed from the present or simple form of the verb.

The present forms of verbs usually tell of something that exists at the present moment.

> The swimmers *are* nearing the shore. (right now)
> The news *sounds* good. (at this moment)

The simple or present forms of verbs, however, are not always used to tell of actions that are going on at the moment. We do not say, "I listen." We are more likely to use the **progressive form** "I am listening" or the **emphatic form** "I do listen." An exception is the use of the present to describe on-going sports events:

> McAdoo *intercepts* the pass and New York *wins*.

The present forms of verbs are used to tell of repeated or regular and habitual action.

> They *go* to camp every summer.
> My father *parks* the car in front of the house.
> The band *rehearses* on Saturdays.

The present forms of verbs are also used to tell of something that is generally true at all times.

> He learned yesterday that water *is* hydrogen and oxygen.
> Water *freezes* at 32° Fahrenheit.

The **historical present tense** is used to tell of some action or condition in the past as though it were occurring in the present:

> The boy *enters* the hall silently, *approaches* the door, and carefully *turns* the knob.

2. **Past tense.** Past time is usually told by the past tense, which is the second principal part of the verb: We *talked, they ran, nobody stirred.* Continuing past action is shown by the **past progressive:** We *were having* a good time.

3. **Future tense.** Future time is shown by using *shall* or *will* with the present form of the verb: W*e shall arrive, you will hear, I will listen.* (For usage of *shall* and *will,* see Section 8.7.)

Future time may be shown by the present tense together with an adverb or phrase that tells time. Future time may also be shown by the use of a form to *be* with *going to* or *about to.*

> We *get* our polio shots *tomorrow.* (*tomorrow* is an adverb telling time.)
> Linda plays center field *from now on.* (*from now on* is an adverb phrase telling time.)
> The Parks Department *is going to* build new playgrounds.
> That book *is about to* fall to pieces.

4. **Present perfect tense.** The present perfect tense is formed by using *has* or *have* with the past participle (third principal part) of the verb. This tense is used to refer to some indefinite time in the past.

> Thousands of Americans *have viewed* the *Mona Lisa.*
> Walter *has* already *auditioned* for the show.

The present perfect is also used to show action that began in the past and continues into the present.

> She *has worked* here for thirty years. (She is still working here.)
> He *has been waiting* for a permit. (present perfect progressive)

5. **Past perfect tense.** The past perfect tense is formed by using *had* with the past participle (third principal part) of the verb. The past perfect tense tells of an action completed in the past before some other action.

EARLIER	LATER
I *had admired* her	before I *met* her.
He *had praised* revolution	until he *realized* its dangers.
We *had been planning* the trip	before Jim *lost* his job.

6. **Future perfect tense.** The future perfect tense is formed by using *will have* or *shall have* with the past participle of the verb (third principal part). This tense is used to tell of one time completed in the future *before* some other time in the future.

> Before the musical *closes*, it *will have played* five hundred performances.

> By the time Bill *arrives*, the race *will have started*.

Note: The first verb in the present tense indicates far future action. The second verb indicates future action *before* the action of the first verb.

Exercise: Find each verb and tell its tense.

1. Somebody finally heard our cries for help.
2. The rehearsal will start promptly at eight.
3. Has the bell rung yet?
4. Melinda will undoubtedly be the next class president.
5. Betsy is playing a Strauss waltz.
6. Whom did you see at the game?
7. Shall we watch a comedian or a play?
8. The Todds had already sold their house.
9. In May, Art will have been in the Navy two years.
10. By four o'clock the snow plows were clearing the roads.
11. Have you ever forgotten your homework?
12. The juniors arrange a class trip every year.
13. Donna has finally decided to become an engineer.
14. By that time, Bob will have spent two years in college.
15. Why weren't you at the meeting last night?

Conjugation of Need

Conjugation is a presentation of the various forms of a verb. Usually, verbs are conjugated in the order shown here.

Principal Parts: need, needed, needed   **Present Participle:** needing
Present Infinitive: to need   **Perfect Infinitive:** to have needed

Present Tense

FIRST PERSON:	I need	we need
SECOND PERSON:	you need	you need
THIRD PERSON:	he, she, it needs	they need

     PRESENT PROGRESSIVE: I am needing, you are needing, etc.
     PRESENT EMPHATIC: I do need, you do need, he does need, etc.

Past Tense

FIRST PERSON:	I needed	we needed
SECOND PERSON:	you needed	you needed
THIRD PERSON:	he, she, it needed	they needed

     PAST PROGRESSIVE: I was needing, you were needing, etc.
     PAST EMPHATIC: I did need, you did need, etc.

Future Tense

FIRST PERSON:	I shall (will) need	we shall (will) need
SECOND PERSON:	you will need	you will need
THIRD PERSON:	he, she, it will need	they will need

     FUTURE PROGRESSIVE. I shall be needing, you will be needing, etc.

Present Perfect Tense

FIRST PERSON:	I have needed	we have needed
SECOND PERSON:	you have needed	you have needed
THIRD PERSON:	he, she, it has needed	they have needed

PRESENT PERFECT PROGRESSIVE:	I have been needing, you have been needing, he has been needing, etc.

Past Perfect Tense

FIRST PERSON:	I had needed	we had needed
SECOND PERSON:	you had needed	you had needed
THIRD PERSON:	he, she, it had needed	they had needed

PAST PERFECT PROGRESSIVE:	I had been needing, you had been needing, he had been needing, etc.

Future Perfect Tense

FIRST PERSON:	I shall have needed	we shall have needed
SECOND PERSON:	you will have needed	you will have needed
THIRD PERSON:	he, she, it will have needed	they will have needed

FUTURE PERFECT PROGRESSIVE:	I shall have been needing, etc.

Mood

The mood of a verb shows the writer's attitude about the actuality of a happening. The **indicative mood,** which we use most of the time, indicates that we are talking or writing about a fact. That is, we are speaking of something that has happened, is happening, or definitely will happen.

The **subjunctive mood** is used to express only wishes, commands, and conditions that are doubtful or contrary to fact. The forms of the subjunctive mood are like those of the indicative mood except in the third person singular of the present tense where the *s* ending is omitted.

INDICATIVE:	He obeys the training rules.
SUBJUNCTIVE:	The coach demands that he *obey* the training rules.

The subjunctive form of the verb *be* is a special case. With this verb, the form in the present tense for all persons and numbers is *be.*

PRESENT TENSE: I recommended that they *be* suspended.
If this *be* treason, then I am guilty.

The past subjunctive form of the verb *to be* is *were.*

PAST TENSE: I wish I *were* a musician.
If the witness *were* honest, the accused
would be acquitted.
Do you wish he *were* your friend?

The **imperative mood** is used to express a command, a directive, or a request. The imperative mood has only one tense—the present—and only one person—the second.

Adjust your safety belts.
Read the directions carefully.
Please *clear* the aisles.

1.4   The Adjective

To express our point of view fully or to make our meaning clear and definite, we do not rely on nouns and verbs alone. We use other kinds of words to describe or limit or qualify the meaning. We call these words modifiers.

An adjective is a word that modifies a noun or pronoun.

Adjectives are used to tell *which one, what kind, how many,* or *how much* about nouns and pronouns.

WHICH ONE: this, that, these, those
WHAT KIND: large, sweet, dull, beautiful
HOW MANY: some, all, several, six, seven
HOW MUCH: little, much, plentiful

The Articles

The word *the* is called a **definite article** because it is usually, though not always, used to refer to a definite or specific thing or person.

The words *a* and *an* are called **indefinite articles** because they refer to no particular thing or person. *A* is used before words be-beginning with consonant sounds. *An* is used before words beginning with vowel sounds. The sound, not the spelling, makes the difference.

> I read *an* editorial on the subject.
> Tom gave *an* honest opinion about it.
> *An* honorary degree was conferred on President Carter.
> The council discussed *a* new expressway.

Proper Adjectives

A **proper adjective** is one formed from a proper noun. The proper adjective is always capitalized.

NOUN	ADJECTIVE	NOUN	ADJECTIVE
Italy	Italian	North	Northern
Germany	German	Democrats	Democratic
Africa	African	China	Chinese
Egypt	Egyptian	Hawaii	Hawaiian

Predicate Adjectives

An adjective is frequently separated from the noun or pro-noun it modifies by a linking verb.

> The cat seems *hungry*. (separated)

> The boys were *angry*. (separated)

An adjective in the predicate that modifies the subject is a predicate adjective.

Exercise: Find each adjective and tell which word it modifies. Ignore the articles.

1. The acoustics in the new auditorium are excellent.
2. He was frank with Congressional investigators but uncooperative with the press.
3. The first electric light burned for forty hours.
4. The northern part of Canada is a vast Arctic waste.
5. In a full orchestra there are four families of instruments.
6. Jellyfish are boneless animals with long, stringy tentacles.
7. Foreign sports cars are often a nuisance.
8. There were only twenty people in the huge auditorium.
9. The dance, colorful and sprightly, delighted the large audience.
10. Picasso is one of the major artists of modern times.
11. Some people have a strange antipathy for cats.
12. Aunt Carol was both musical and artistic.
13. There are several books on architecture on the second shelf.
14. The vehicular crossing at the bridge is dangerous.

Adjectives in Comparisons

Persons and things are compared as to various qualities. The comparison is made by use of two different forms of adjectives.

The **comparative** form of the adjective is formed in two ways:

1. All adjectives of one syllable and a few adjectives with two syllables add -er.

    Young—younger   tall—taller   funny—funnier

2. Most adjectives with two syllables and all adjectives with more than two syllables use *more* to form the comparative.

    harmful—more harmful   capable—more capable
    careful—more careful   efficient—more efficient

The **superlative** form of the adjective is formed by adding -est or by using *most*. Adjectives that form the comparative with -er form the superlative with -*est*. Those that form the comparative with *more* form the superlative with *most*.

COMPARATIVE	SUPERLATIVE
younger	youngest
funnier	funniest
more likely	most likely
more cautious	most cautious

Irregular Comparisons

We form the comparative and superlative of some adjectives by changing the words themselves.

	COMPARATIVE	SUPERLATIVE
good	better	best
well	better	best
bad	worse	worst
ill	worse	worst
little	less *or* lesser	least
much	more	most
many	more	most
far	farther *or* further	farthest *or* furthest

Exercise: Find the adjectives and tell whether they are in comparative form or superlative form.

1. I find biography more interesting than fiction.
2. Who is our most likely candidate?
3. Chris is the most ambitious person in the class.
4. Dogs have a keener sense of smell than cats.
5. New York is no longer the wealthiest city in the world.
6. The amoeba is the lowest of all animal forms.
7. Which person is older, Lynn or Randy?
8. The worst snowstorm in years has paralyzed Minneapolis.
9. Madlock's batting average is higher than Rose's.
10. Joyce is the person most qualified for the job.

1.5 The Adverb

Nouns and pronouns are modified by adjectives. Other parts of speech are modified by adverbs.

An adverb modifies a verb, an adjective, or another adverb.

MODIFYING A VERB: She voted *wisely*.

MODIFYING AN ADJECTIVE: Information is *readily* available.

MODIFYING AN ADVERB: He felt criticism *very* keenly.

Adverbs tell *where, when, how,* or *to what extent:*

WHERE: They lingered *outside*.
WHEN: The team left *early*.
HOW: The story ended *happily*.
TO WHAT EXTENT: The writing was *totally* illegible.

Many adverbs are formed by adding *-ly* to an adjective: *cautious—cautiously, quick—quickly, soft—softly, wise—wisely.* However, not all modifiers ending in *-ly* are adverbs. The following, for example, are adjectives: *lively, homely, friendly, lovely, kindly.*

Some words may be either adjectives or adverbs.

ADJECTIVE	ADVERB
a *hard* task	Study *hard*.
a *long* journey	Don't be *long*.
a *late* program	He arrived *late*.

Many adverbs do not end in *-ly*. The negatives *no, not,* and *never* are almost always adverbs. Many time-words, such as *now, ever, almost, soon,* are always adverbs.

Directive Adverbs

Adverbs that tell *where* (place or direction) about the verb are called **directive adverbs.** They normally follow the verb they modify.

They tiptoed *in*.	Stack the supplies *inside*.
The box slid *down*.	No one ventured *near*.
The elevator went *up*.	The workers walked *out*.

Many of these directive adverbs are combined with verbs to make idioms: *give out, give up, give in, give off*. An idiom is a group of words with a meaning different from the literal meanings of the words taken individually.

Position of Adverbs

A directive adverb normally follows the verb it modifies. An adverb modifying an adjective or another adverb usually comes immediately before the word it modifies. Other adverbs may be shifted from one place in the sentence to another.

DIRECTIVE: The ship sailed *away*.

ADVERB
MODIFYING MODIFIER: It was a *very* tense moment.

He left *rather* unexpectedly.

OTHER ADVERBS: *Quickly*, she opened the letter.

She *quickly* opened the letter.

She opened the letter *quickly*.

Adverbs in Comparisons

Like adjectives, adverbs are used in comparisons. The comparative and the superlative are formed as follows:

1. Adverbs of one syllable add *-er*.

Classes seemed to go *faster* today.
Draw the line *straighter*.

2. Most adverbs ending in *-ly* form the comparative with *more*.

He slammed the door *more violently* the second time.
When he heard a twig snap, he moved *more cautiously*.

3. The superlative form of the adverb is formed with *-est* or *most*. Adverbs that form the comparative with *-er* form the superlative with *-est*. Those using *more* for the comparative use *most* for the superlative.

COMPARATIVE	SUPERLATIVE
sooner	soonest
harder	hardest
more happily	most happily
more willingly	most willingly

Note: See Section 1.4 for irregular comparisons of adjectives. Some of the words listed there as adjectives may also be used as adverbs and are compared in the same way.

Exercise A: Find each adverb and tell which word or words it modifies.

1. You drive too fast for safety.
2. The supposedly unsinkable *Titanic* had actually sunk.
3. Suddenly a loud shot rang out.
4. The paint is not quite dry yet.
5. The story is only moderately interesting.
6. We rose early, breakfasted quickly, and drove to Memphis.
7. I have already made my decision.
8. Have you ever been deep-sea fishing before?
9. Unfortunately, I still could not find the key.
10. You will undoubtedly hear from her soon.
11. Hemingway's *A Farewell to Arms* was first published serially in *Scribner's* magazine.
12. The door will probably open if you press harder.
13. When will you repay the debt?
14. The food was too highly seasoned.
15. The weather satellite sent back clear pictures.

Exercise B: Find the adverbs and show what they tell about the word or words they modify.

1. The old man spoke slowly and deliberately.
2. You will have to look up the information again.
3. Yesterday my mother took us there in the car.
4. I did the job very hastily.
5. We arrived too late.
6. Finally he put the menu aside and glanced around.
7. Beverly Sills always sings this piece brilliantly.
8. The mail usually comes very late in the morning.
9. Messages on the CB radio were coming through clearly.
10. The little boy could hardly stay awake.

1.6 The Preposition

The words in an English sentence do not occur in haphazard order. They are arranged in precise patterns in order to convey meaning. The words that go together are joined or linked in a variety of ways. One means of linking words is the **preposition.**

There are seventeen one-syllable prepositions in English.* They are used to show the following relationships.

LOCATION: at, by, in, on, near
DIRECTION: to, from, down, off, through, out, past, up
ASSOCIATION: of, for, with, like

There are also certain two-syllable prepositions.

about	along	below	during
above	among	beneath	except
across	around	beside	inside
after	before	between	outside
against	behind	beyond	over
			under

* The word *but* may be used as a preposition with the meaning of *except*.

A number of prepositions have been formed by combining some of the one-syllable prepositions:

into	upon	without
onto	within	throughout

Compound prepositions have been formed by combining a modifier with a preposition or by grouping prepositions, as follows:

according to	out of	on account of	aside from
prior to	owing to	inside of	by means of
in front of	subsequent to	because of	as to

Objects of Prepositions

A preposition never appears alone. It is always used with a word or group of words that are called its **object**.

A preposition relates its object to some other word in the sentence.

The object of a preposition usually follows the preposition. The only exception occurs in a sentence or clause introduced by an interrogative pronoun or a relative pronoun.

> Light filtered *through* the damp subterranean *passage.*
> Light filtered *into* the damp subterranean *passage.*
> The motorcade moved slowly *through* the crowded *streets.*
> *Whom* did you offer the job *to?*
> Jack asked *whom* the telephone call was *for.*
> What *hotel* will they have the dance *in?*

The object of a preposition may be a single word or a group of words.

WORD:	The doctor hurried into the *house.*
WORD:	I went with *him* willingly.
WORD:	Upon *arriving,* Joan asked for an interview.
WORD GROUP:	After *testing the equipment,* I found it defective.

WORD GROUP:	Before *recommending the book,* read it carefully.
WORD GROUP:	Explain the problem to *whoever is in charge.*

Exercise: Find the prepositions. Tell the object of each one.

1. Everyone contributed to the success of the party.
2. There are several books with blue bindings on that shelf.
3. Heart disease is one of the chief causes of death.
4. Most accidents in mountain climbing happen to unescorted amateurs.
5. My first drive on the golf course sliced into the lake.
6. The armistice went into effect on November 11, 1918.
7. The grizzly bear gazed into my camera with all the composure of a professional model.
8. Traffic on Main Street was rerouted because of the accident.
9. The game was postponed on account of rain.
10. Whom are you going with?
11. Upon entering the earth's atmosphere, the meteor burned up.
12. Give the book to whoever wants it.

1.7   The Conjunction

Another kind of word used to tie the parts of a sentence together is the conjunction.

A conjunction is a word which connects words, phrases, or clauses.

There are three kinds of conjunctions: coordinating conjunctions, correlative conjunctions, and subordinating conjunctions.

Coordinating Conjunctions

There are three conjunctions used only to connect like sentence parts. They are called **coordinating conjunctions** because they tie together things of the same kind or order. These co-ordinating conjunctions are *and, but, or.*

> Her chief interests are backgammon *and* ceramics.
> (connects nouns)
>
> A camp counselor must be patient *and* resourceful.
> (connects adjectives)
>
> The marlin fought savagely *and* cunningly.
> (connects adverbs)
>
> Elton John got off the plane *and* into a limousine.
> (connects prepositional phrases)
>
> We could camp out *or* stay in motels. (connects predicates)
>
> The ship sank, *but* all the passengers were saved.
> (connects clauses)

For is used as a coordinating conjunction only between clauses. *Nor* is used as a coordinating conjunction only when it is preceded by another negative word.

> Voter apathy is dangerous, *for* it can undermine democracy.
> The old fellow has *no* education, *nor* is he eager to learn.
> The rookie *cannot* field, *nor* can he hit well.

Correlative Conjunctions

A few conjunctions are used in pairs: *not only . . . but (also)*; *either . . . or*; *neither . . . nor*; *both . . . and*; *whether . . . or.* Such conjunctions are called **correlative conjunctions.**

> Motocross racing requires *not only* skill *but* great daring
> as well.
> *Either* chemistry *or* physics is required.
> *Neither* the Picasso drawing *nor* the Dali painting pleases me.
> *Both* the organization *and* content of the composition
> were excellent.
> We must consider *whether* he will act responsibly
> *or* impulsively.

Subordinating Conjunctions

Words used to introduce adverb clauses are called **subordinating conjunctions.** These words not only introduce the subordinate clause but link it to the main clause. Their chief function is to make clear exactly what is the relation between the two clauses. The chief relations they show are *time, place, cause, result, exception, condition,* and *alternative.* The most common subordinating conjunctions are these:

after	as though	provided	till	whenever
although	because	since	unless	where
as	before	so that	until	wherever
as if	if	than	whatever	while
as long as	in order that	though	when	

Conjunctive Adverbs

Certain adverbs are used to join main clauses. When so used, they are called **conjunctive adverbs.** A conjunctive adverb is preceded by a semicolon and followed by a comma. The most common conjunctive adverbs are these:

accordingly	hence	nevertheless	therefore
consequently	however	otherwise	yet
furthermore	moreover	also	

Exercise A: Find the conjunctions and conjunctive adverbs. Tell what kind each joining word is.

1. We tried to hurry, but the crowd delayed us.
2. This is where we live.
3. He trembled as he spoke.
4. We put on our skates while we were waiting.
5. I felt as if I were drowning.
6. I usually order chicken or fish.
7. Act as if nothing were wrong.
8. I telephoned Sheila while I was in Cleveland.

9. I will not go unless she goes.
10. I took it just as it was.
11. They live where the weather is always warm.
12. Come to see us whenever you can.
13. The roads were partly flooded; nevertheless, we kept driving.
14. A paralyzing snowfall hit Chicago; consequently, all transportation was halted.
15. Korea has been called "The Land of the Morning Calm"; however, it has seen turbulent days.

Exercise B: Find the conjunctions. Show what words or word groups they join.

1. Either he or I must go.
2. He has a stern manner but a good heart.
3. I walked across the highway and along the tracks.
4. Sam tried to ask the librarian, but she was busy.
5. Elaine has written the report and has revised it.
6. William Jennings Bryan was often a candidate but never a President.
7. He knew when to talk and when to be silent.
8. The question was whether to stop here or to drive on to Atlanta.

1.8 The Interjection

An interjection is a word or group of words interjected, or thrown, into the sentence. It is usually followed by an exclamation point.

An interjection is a word or word group used to express surprise or other emotion. It has no grammatical relation to other words in the sentence.

Ouch! Oh! Ah! For heaven's sake! Hurrah! Great! Congratulations!

1.9 Words Used in Different Ways

Some words, such as *are, think, see,* are always verbs. The personal pronouns *I, me,* etc., are always personal pronouns. Many words, however, may be used in a sentence in different ways.

> The treaty was signed, *but* we still had
> misgivings. (conjunction)
> Everyone *but* the speaker noticed the incident. (preposition)
> Will you turn on the *light?* (noun)
> It needs a new *light* bulb. (adjective)

Noun or Adjective?

A word used to name a person, place, or thing is a noun. The same word may be used before another noun to tell "what kind." When so used, it is an adjective.

> The teacher viewed *history* as a story of the human quest
> for freedom. (noun)
> The *history* book was tattered and out of date. (adjective)
> The world's tallest building is in *Chicago.* (noun)
> The *Chicago* skyline has changed remarkably in the last
> ten years. (adjective)

Adjective or Pronoun?

A demonstrative pronoun—*this, that, these,* and *those*—may also be used as an adjective. If the word is used alone in place of a noun, it is a pronoun. If it is used before a noun to tell "which one," it is an adjective.

> *This* is a Polaroid camera. (pronoun)
> *These* are more practical shoes for you. (pronoun)

That experience is hard to forget. (adjective
 modifying *experience*)
Those aspects of the case are clear. (adjective
 modifying *aspects*)

In a similar way the words *what, which,* and *whose* may be used alone as pronouns or before nouns as adjectives.

What will your salary be? (pronoun)
What grade did you get? (adjective modifying *grade*)
Which is the best route to take? (pronoun)
Which play should I read? (adjective modifying *play*)
Whose did you want? (pronoun)
Whose skateboard is this? (adjective modifying *skateboard*)

The words *your, my, our, his, her, their* are forms of the personal pronouns used to show possession. Used in this way, they perform the job of adjectives. The words *mine, yours, hers, ours,* and *theirs* are always pronouns. The word *his* may be used either as a pronoun or an adjective. See Section 1.2.

That hat of *hers* is colorful. (pronoun)
The fingerprints are definitely *his*. (pronoun)
His autobiography is rich in anecdotes. (adjective use)

Adjective or Adverb?

Several words have the same form whether used as adjectives or adverbs. To tell whether a word is used as an adjective or as an adverb, determine what other word in the sentence it goes with, or modifies. This is a matter of sense, which you can get from the meaning. If it modifies a verb, it is used as an adverb. If it modifies a noun or pronoun, it is used as an adjective. If it tells *how, when, where,* or *how much,* it is an adverb. If it tells *what kind,* it is an adjective.

Jets travel *fast*. (adverb telling *how* about *travel*)
Drive in the *fast* lane. (adjective telling *what kind of lane*)

Adverb or Preposition?

A number of words may be used either as prepositions or as adverbs. If the word is followed by a noun or pronoun, it is probably a preposition. The noun or pronoun is its object. If the word in question is not followed by a noun or pronoun, it is probably an adverb. If the word can be moved to another position, it is an adverb.

> The coach sent *in* a substitute.
> The coach sent the substitute *in*.
>> (In both sentences *in* is an adverb. It can be moved without changing the meaning.)
> Everyone danced *at* the disco.
>> (*at* cannot be moved; it is a preposition.)
> The bulb finally burned *out*. (adverb)
> The cold drove the cattle *inside*. (adverb)
> *Whom* were you talking *to*? (*Whom* is the object of the preposition *to*.)

Exercise A: Determine how the italicized word is used in each sentence.

1. The orchestra warmed up *before* the concert.
2. Neither candidate had held public office *before*.
3. Look *before* you leap.
4. We were just having a *friendly* argument.
5. Sound thinking is *essential* to good writing.
6. The moderator kept the discussion on the *main* topic.
7. A water *main* has burst.
8. The people who *frequent* this place are actors.
9. The man from the nursery *pruned* the trees.
10. Roy is finding *college* algebra extremely difficult.
11. Whole-wheat bread contains greater *food* value than white.
12. The Acropolis *towers* over the city of Athens.
13. Can a hummingbird really fly so *fast*?
14. *Which* is your raincoat?
15. *Which* raincoat is yours?

Exercise B: Determine how the italicized word is used in each sentence.

1. The lightning had knocked *down* the flagpole.
2. We admired Mrs. Leonard's *rose* garden.
3. I *rose* at six this morning.
4. The crocodile sheds *no* tears.
5. Flames from the *oil* refinery illuminated the sky.
6. We took the *through* train to Chicago.
7. Larry's education was *haphazard.*
8. Expect progress, *but* don't expect miracles.
9. He had subsisted on nothing *but* berries and water.
10. The mayor said he would not *countenance* any such proposal in an election year.
11. The Senate was faced with a *procedural* deadlock.
12. He looks ridiculous as a *would-be* professor.
13. The party is looking for a *gubernatorial* candidate.
14. *This* Pontiac belongs to the Hatfields.
15. *This* is the car I was telling you about.

1.10   Verbals

There are a number of highly useful words in English that are difficult to classify. These are **infinitives, participles,** and **gerunds.** They are called **verbals** because all of them are formed from verbs.

1.11   The Infinitive

Usually, but not always, the infinitive is preceded by *to*, which is called the "sign of the infinitive." The kinds of infinitives are as follows:

> *Active Present:* to invite
> *Passive Present:* to be invited
> *Active Perfect:* to have invited
> *Passive Perfect:* to have been invited

The infinitive may appear without the word *to:*

> Let him *give* his opinion.
> Please *register* for the election.
> Helpless, I watched my hat *float* away.

The infinitive may be used as a noun. It may be subject or object of the verb, a predicate noun, or an appositive.

> *To explain* the phenomenon was impossible. (subject of *was*)
> The author wants *to write* a trilogy. (object of *wants*)
> The aim of the bill is *to reduce* taxes. (predicate noun)
> Leo's job, *to barbecue* the meat, took almost two
> hours. (appositive)

The infinitive may also be used as a modifier. Used as an adjective, it may modify nouns and pronouns.

> This is the book *to read.*   She is someone *to emulate.*

As an adverb, the infinitive may modify adverbs, adjectives, or verbs.

> Laughter is good *to hear.* (modifying the adjective *good*)
>
> Courtney tried too hard *to succeed.* (modifies the
> adverb *hard*)
>
> They dived *to get* pearls. (modifies the verb *dived*)

The Infinitive Phrase. An infinitive itself may have modifiers. It may also have a subject, an object, or a predicate word. An **infinitive phrase** consists of the infinitive together with its modifiers, its subject, object, or predicate word.

The infinitive may be modified by adverbs, phrases, or clauses. These modifiers are part of the infinitive phrase.

> *To think* logically is necessary in most situations.
> (*logically* modifies *To think.*)
>
> *To finish* in time, I cannot waste a minute.
> (The phrase *in time* modifies *To finish.*)

I decided *to go* home after I delivered the package.
(The clause *after I delivered the package* modifies *to go*.)

The infinitive may have a direct object, an indirect object, or a predicate word. These words, completing the meaning of the infinitive, are part of the infinitive phrase.

To get the best *results*, follow directions carefully.
(*results* is the direct object of *To get*.)
The board voted *to grant him* a posthumous *award*.
(*him* is the indirect object and *award* is the direct object of *to grant*.)
Pat's sister has decided *to be* a *biochemist*.
(*biochemist* is a predicate noun after *to be*.)
He intended the soft music *to be soothing*.
(*soothing* is a predicate adjective after *to be*.)

The infinitive may have a subject. The subject always follows the main verb and comes directly before the infinitive. Since it follows the main verb and is in the objective case, it is sometimes mistaken for an object of the main verb. The subject of the infinitive is part of the infinitive phrase. In the following examples, the entire phrase is direct object of the verb.

Both Dan and Ed invited *her to go to the party*.
The committee persuaded *us to sell the tickets*.
Frank urged *his father to reconsider the decision*.

Note: If the main verb is a linking verb (a form of *be, appear, seem,* etc.), the noun following it is a predicate noun. If a predicate noun is followed by an infinitive, the infinitive modifies the noun.

She is the person *to see*.   They are the team *to beat*.

Exercise A: Find the complete infinitive phrase in each sentence that follows.

1. The author attempts to simplify everything.
2. Which is the best course to follow?

3. Jess has finally decided to get a haircut.
4. To pilot a boat skillfully requires practice.
5. We could take a jet from Idlewild to save time.
6. Would you like to have lived in Caesar's time?
7. Everyone in the room heard you say it.
8. Ted's instructions were to whistle three times.
9. I am sorry to have interrupted your conversation.
10. The nurse came periodically to check Martha's condition.
11. The citizens voted for a pageant to be held on Washington's Birthday.
12. My advice to you is to buy new skates.
13. My friend Ellis is learning to make pottery.
14. To study some instrument is a tradition for everyone in our family.
15. Grover Cleveland was the only President to serve two nonconsecutive terms.

Exercise B: Decide how the infinitive phrase is used in each sentence.

1. Elizabeth tried to teach me calculus.
2. A good book to read makes an evening pleasant.
3. Laura's ambition is to skate in an ice show.
4. I'd prefer to leave from San Francisco International Airport.
5. Her present goal is to master tennis thoroughly.
6. Shelley was eager to call the meeting to order.
7. Mike's ambition is to become a geologist.
8. There are still hundreds of votes to be counted.
9. The tellers have gone to count the votes.
10. I have been teaching my brother to play chess.

1.12 The Gerund

The gerund is a verbal noun that ends in -ing. It is used in a sentence as a noun and in almost every way that a noun can be used.

Training for the Olympics is hard work. (subject of the verb)
Juanita enjoys *camping.* (object of the verb)
Before *applying,* check your qualifications. (object
of the preposition)

The Gerund Phrase. A gerund may be modified by adjectives
or adverbs. It may be completed by objects or predicate words. A
gerund phrase consists of the gerund together with its modifiers,
objects, or predicate words.

The gerund may be modified by single adjectives and adverbs
or by phrases and by clauses.

Rapid reading has become a national interest.
(*Rapid* is an adjective modifying *reading.*)
Anita tried *walking quickly* to avoid meeting Charles.
(*quickly* is an adverb modifying *walking.*)
Experimenting without adequate equipment is frustrating.
(*without adequate equipment* is a phrase
modifying *Experimenting.*)
Persevering after you have failed is a test of character.
(*after you have failed* is a clause modifying *Persevering.*)

Gerunds may be completed by objects or predicate words.
These words are part of the gerund phrase.

Being stage manager of a school play is hard work.
(*stage manager* is a predicate noun completing *Being.*)
Conceding him the *victory* was very difficult.
(*him* is the indirect object and *victory* is the direct
object of *Conceding.*)

Exercise: Find the complete gerund phrases in these sentences.

1. He left without asking my permission.
2. Hearing that music always makes me sad.
3. I am interested in reading *The Contender*
by Robert Lipsyte.
4. An important skill in oratory is knowing when to stop.

5. Before leaving the house, he locked all the windows.
6. Try singing the tenor part.
7. Eating pizza is a mania with Janice.
8. Shari is clever at imitating others.
9. The screaming of the seagulls came from that cove.
10. John is skillful at navigating in rough waters.
11. I have finally mastered the art of skimming a newspaper.
12. Let's practice swimming ten laps.
13. The islanders' chief occupations are weaving straw hats and raising cacao.
14. Cleaning up after a party is often harder work than getting ready for a party.
15. This is asking too much.

1.13 The Participle

There are several forms of the participle, all widely used.

PRESENT PARTICIPLE:	instructing
PAST PARTICIPLE:	instructed
PERFECT PARTICIPLE:	having instructed
PASSIVE PERFECT PARTICIPLE:	having been instructed

The present participle always ends in -*ing*. The past participle is the third principal part of the verb, and its endings are various. (See Section 1.3)

The participle is always used as an adjective to modify a noun or a pronoun. In the examples below, the arrow indicates the word modified by the participle.

Hesitating, Art questioned the wisdom of reporting the incident.

Surrounded, the guerrilla forces capitulated.

Having been forewarned, the pilot prepared for an emergency.

The Participial Phrase. A participle may be modified by single adverbs or by phrases and clauses. The participle may also be completed by objects or predicate words. A **participial phrase** consists of the participle together with its modifiers, objects, or predicate words.

When a participle is modified by an adverb, a phrase, or a clause, these modifiers are part of the participial phrase.

> *Listening attentively,* he heard the plane approaching.
> (*attentively* is an adverb modifying *Listening*.)

> *Driving without a license,* Jim got into trouble.
> (*without a license* is a phrase modifying *Driving*.)

> *Fiddling while Rome burned,* Nero assured himself of a place in history.
> (*while Rome burned* is a clause modifying *Fiddling*.)

When a participle is completed by objects or predicate words, these words are part of the participial phrase. In the examples below, the arrow indicates the word modified by the participial phrase.

> *Having found our way,* we continued the hike.
> (*way* is the direct object of *Having found*.)

> The children sat on the front steps, *looking forlorn.*
> (*forlorn* is a predicate adjective completing *looking*.)

> *Giving his horse a pep talk,* the jockey rode toward the starting gate.
> (*horse* is the indirect object and *pep talk* is the direct object of *Giving*)

Exercise: Find the complete participial phrase and show which word it modifies.

   1. Being an aviator, Dawn enjoyed *Wind, Sand and Stars.*

   2. She stood at the window, anticipating the arrival of the first guests.

   3. The player, having accepted a bribe, was expelled.

4. The letter, written hurriedly, contained many errors.
5. The street, crowded with cars, looked impassable.
6. Swinging his tennis racket, Don approached the court.
7. Built over a hundred years ago, the house is still sturdy.
8. Tracey is the player now passing the ball.
9. Struck by lightning, the barn caught fire.
10. Neatly dressed, the children set out for school.
11. The White House, first occupied by John Adams in 1800, has been enlarged several times in recent years.
12. Watering his zinnias, Fred noticed that holes were appearing in the leaves.
13. Puzzled about the cause, he wondered whether insects might be responsible.
14. Seeking advice at a seed store, he was told of a useful spray.
15. Responding to his care, the plants began to flourish.

2.0 The Parts of a Sentence

Single words in English are used widely to convey meaning. The words *stop, danger, poison,* for example, express full meaning to the reader. In general, however, meaning is expressed in English by groups of words acting together: *in the morning, playing tight end, Laura laughed.*

These groups of words are neither spoken nor written in haphazard order. In the English sentence there are fixed patterns into which words are placed to express meaning. These patterns are learned in childhood. They are learned because they are the chief means by which the child can express his feelings and get what he wants.

A knowledge of what these sentence patterns are and of how they work is essential for effective use of language in adult life.

2.1 The Sentence

Sentences are used to make statements and to ask questions. To be understood, they must express a complete thought, a complete idea, or a complete question. Now, a complete thought can be expressed by a word or a phrase:

Great!   Not at home   Grocery Store

On the other hand, words and phrases may *not* express a complete idea:

Having been nominated   The man in the three-piece suit

You know that these expressions are incomplete because they leave you asking *what? what about it? what happened?*

A group of words must express a complete thought or it is not a sentence. We begin studying the sentence with this partial definition:

A sentence is a group of words that expresses a complete thought.

INCOMPLETE	The player on the sidelines (What about her?)
COMPLETE	The player on the sidelines was injured.
INCOMPLETE	Jack Allen, a sophomore, (Did what?)
COMPLETE	Jack Allen, a sophomore, placed first in public speaking
INCOMPLETE	Building a boat (who did what?)
COMPLETE	Building a boat, he was happily occupied.

Exercise: Which of the following groups of words are sentences?

1. Easily the best dancer in the troupe
2. Sleek, high-stepping horses parading around the track
3. A book about the history of Chicago
4. Eugene O'Neill, possibly the greatest playwright of the century
5. Representing the United States in the Olympic Games
6. An expert performer on the parallel bars
7. An interesting article about exchange students
8. Two men on base and Ken Griffey at bat
9. Speleologists explore caves
10. Has the yearbook gone to press
11. The heron, a large water fowl with long, thin legs
12. The Appalachian Mountains, much older than the Alps
13. Lorainne Hansberry's A *Raisin in the Sun,* one of my favorite plays

14. The Red Cross important in peace time as well as in war
15. Administers help during floods and other
natural catastrophes

2.2 Kinds of Sentences

Sentences may be classified as to structure* or as to the purpose of the speaker or writer. There are four principal purposes served by sentences:

1. The **declarative sentence** is used to make a statement. The statement may be one of fact, wish, intent, or feeling.

> Plans for the Bicentennial were begun years before 1976.
> He wanted to read *Victory Over Myself* by Floyd Patterson.

2. The **imperative sentence** is used to state a command, request, or direction. The subject is always *You*. When the subject is not expressed, as is usually the case, it is "understood" to be *You*.

> (You) Follow the directions carefully.
> (You) Take Route 88 for nine miles.
> (You) Call the clinic sometime after six o'clock.

3. The **interrogative sentence** is used to ask a question. It is always followed by a question mark.

> Do you realize what you are saying?
> Who wrote *Billy Budd?*
> What is the temperature of the earth's interior?

4. An **exclamatory sentence** is used to express strong feeling. It is always followed by an exclamation point.

> What a game it was!   How happy we were!

---

* For classification of sentences by form or structure, see Section 3.0.

Exercise: What kind of sentence is each of the following?

1. Poe's life was short and tragic.
2. Go to the next corner and turn right.
3. How small these calculators are!
4. The first to come will receive souvenirs.
5. Do exactly as I tell you.
6. This is a book you would enjoy.
7. What events are included in the decathlon?
8. How tired we were!
9. Step this way, please.
10. The high school is visible from the highway?

2.3 Subject and Predicate

There are two parts in every complete sentence. (1) The **subject** is the person, thing, or idea about which something is said. (2) The **predicate** is the idea expressed about the subject.

Every sentence contains a subject and a predicate.
The subject of the sentence is the person or thing about which something is said.
The predicate tells something or asks something about the subject of the sentence.

The word *predicate* means "to proclaim, declare, preach, or affirm." The predicate of a sentence therefore "proclaims, declares, preaches, or affirms" something about the subject.

We may say that a sentence is a group of words that tells something (*predicate*) about a person or thing (*subject*). Our definition of a sentence may now be expanded:

A sentence is a group of words expressing a complete thought by means of a subject and a predicate.

SUBJECT	PREDICATE
Water	evaporates.
Water	evaporates quickly in the hot sun.

2.4 The Simple Predicate

In every predicate, however long, the most important word—the key word—is the **verb.** * In fact, the verb is the key word in the sentence. Sentences may be constructed without nouns, pronouns, or other parts of speech; but, without a verb, there can be no sentence.

The simple predicate of the sentence is the verb.

The verb may be a phrase consisting of more than one word: *have gone, might have gone, is running, had been running.* The words making up the verb may be interrupted by a modifier. Such a modifier is not part of the verb.

> *have* probably *gone*   *had* just *eaten*
> *was* never *questioned*   *had* almost *finished*

The simple predicate, which we shall hereafter call the *verb*, may be compound. The word *compound* means "having more than one part of the same kind." The parts of a compound verb are joined together by a conjunction (*and, or, neither-nor,* etc.).

> They **stood** up *and* **cheered** spontaneously.
> Judy **gathered, painted** *and* **shellacked** the tiny shells.
> The union members **may** either **accept** *or* **reject** the contract.

2.5 The Simple Subject

Every verb has a subject. It is the word or the words that answer *who? or what?* before the verb.

> The sled crashed.   Scientists use nuclear energy.
> *Verb:* crashed   *Verb:* use
> *What crashed?:* sled   *Who uses?:* scientists
> *Subject:* sled   *Subject:* scientists

---

* The **complete predicate** consists of the verb, its modifiers, and complements. The **complete subject** consists of the simple subject and its modifiers.

The **simple subject** is the subject of the verb. The subject of the verb may be a word, a phrase, or a clause.

> *To want peace* is the first requisite. (phrase as subject)
> *That food shortages will continue* seems certain.
>   (clause as subject)

The subject of a verb may be an entire phrase, but it is never one word within a phrase.

> **One** *of the glasses* was cracked.
>   (Only one was cracked. *One* is the subject. The word
>   *glasses* lies within the prepositional phrase and is object
>   of the preposition *of*.)
> **Fighting sharks** is not my idea of fun.
>   (The gerund phrase *Fighting sharks* is the subject of *is*.)
> **Marion,** *together with her cousins,* is at the lake.
>   (*Marion* is the subject of *is*; *cousins* is the object of the
>   preposition *together with*.)

The subject of the verb may be compound. The parts of a compound subject are normally joined by a conjunction.

> **Mood, rhythm,** *and* **harmony** are aspects of music.
> **Television** *and* **radio** are mass communication media.
> *Both* **meaning** *and* **form** should be considered in analyzing
>   a poem.

Exercise: Find the verb and its subject.

1. Our school will soon be celebrating its centennial.
2. Both Jan and Bob work on the fourth floor.
3. Newsstands and bookstores throughout the country
sell the book.
4. You can either come along or stay here.
5. Neither the young nor the old should have time to be bored.
6. Catching trout is my favorite sport.
7. The east wing of the high school building contains
the auditorium.
8. Putting good ideas into circulation is everybody's job.

9. The old Model-A Ford sputtered, wheezed, and finally came to a halt.

10. Stamp collectors, amateur musicians, and model engineers are happy people.

11. A drop of swamp water is alive with animals.

12. A professor of physics at the state university lives next door.

13. A fast camera speed produces slow-motion film.

14. The make-up crew was well supplied with cleansing tissue.

15. Dick fell and hurt his knee during last night's game.

2.6 Subjects in Unusual Positions

In most sentences the subject appears before the verb. This subject-verb order is the normal pattern of English sentences. In many sentences, however, this order is reversed.

Questions. In most questions the subject appears between the words making up the verb phrase.

VERB	SUBJECT	VERB
Did	he	forget?
Has	he	returned?
Will	she	understand?
Could	we	have gone?

In most questions beginning with interrogative words such as *where, when, why, how, how much,* the subject falls between the parts of the verb. In questions beginning with *who* or *what,* the verb may follow the subject in normal order:

Who won?   What fell?

Sentences Beginning *There* and *Here*. Many sentences begin with *There* or *Here* immediately followed by some form of *be: There is, There was, There will be, Here is, Here were,* and so on, In these sentences *Here* and *There* are introductory words used to get the sentence started. They are never the subject of the verb. In this kind of sentence, the subject follows the verb.

Here is the dictionary you asked for. (*dictionary* is
    the subject.)
There are complex issues involved. (*issues* is the subject.)
There will be a flower show this spring. (*show* is
    the subject.)

Note: Not all sentences beginning with *Here* and *There* follow the above pattern: *Here we can pitch our tent. Here he
comes. There he goes.* In these sentences, *Here* and *There* are
adverbs modifying the verb.

Sentences in Inverted Order. For emphasis or for variety of style,
the subject is sometimes placed after the verb.

Through the woods strolled a strange *figure.*
Toward the cliff ran the frightened *boy.*
From his mistakes emerged my *victory.*

Finding the Subject of the Verb. To find the subject of the verb
in any sentence, find the verb first. Then ask *who?* or *what?* before it. If the sentence is not in normal word order, change it to
normal order, and the subject will become clear.

INVERTED   Up from the grass flew a family of pheasants.
NORMAL   A family of pheasants flew up from the grass.

Exercise A: Find the verb and its subject.

1. There is an urgent need for library books.
2. Where is the school greenhouse located?
3. High into the air leaped the shortstop.
4. Here the embattled farmers stood.
5. Did Dorothy Hamill win an Olympic gold medal?
6. At 10 Downing Street lives the Prime Minister of England.
7. How do you make this dessert, Helen?
8. From all over the world came congratulatory telegrams.
9. There in front of us was an impassable ravine.
10. High above the valley moved a cable car.

Exercise B: Find the verb and its subject.

1. Directly behind me was the mayor.
2. Where are you going after the play?
3. Along the streets of Berne were tempting pastry shops.
4. Here are the books.
5. Straight between the goalie's legs shot the puck.
6. In the back of the theater were several dozen standees.
7. There have been several rumors about the President's plans.
8. Mingling with the crowd were several Secret Service agents.
9. Why have you done this to me?
10. Overhead, in triangular formation, roared the Air Force jets.

2.7 The Direct Object

In many sentences the action verb carries action over from the subject to some other word. It serves to tie these words together. The word to which the action is carried from the subject is the **direct object.**

Sometimes the direct object tells what receives the action of the verb. Sometimes it tells the result of the action.

RECEIVER OF ACTION The naturalist set a trap. (set what?)
RESULT OF ACTION The naturalist captured the bird (captured what?)

RECEIVER OF ACTION Art carved the ham. (carved what?)
RESULT OF ACTION Art enjoyed the ham. (enjoyed what?)

Action verbs that carry over the action from subject to object are called **transitive verbs.** Action verbs that are not followed by direct objects are called **intransitive.** Some verbs may be transitive in one sentence and intransitive in another.

The hikers *were eating.* (intransitive)
The hikers *were eating* the *mushrooms.* (transitive)

In some so-called action verbs, the action is not visible, nor otherwise evident. However, the verb does carry the thought from subject to object, tying them together.

> I *understand* your position. (understand what?)
> The stranger *appreciates* your help. (appreciates what?)
> Joanne *honored* my request. (honored what?)

The direct object is a word or group of words to which the verb carries over the action from the subject.

The direct object may be a word, a phrase, or a clause.

> Carlos wants *to prepare dinner.* (phrase)
> He tried *interpreting the poem.* (phrase)
> Wilma meant *what she said.* (clause)

The direct object may be compound.

> Winter campers need insulated *boots* and nylon *jackets.*
>   (need what?)
> I like *to play the piano* and *to compose for it.* (like what?)

A word that completes the meaning of the verb is called a **complement.** The direct object is one kind of complement.

Direct Object or Adverb? To find the direct object, ask *what?* after the verb. An adverb following an action verb tells *how, when, where,* or *how much* about the verb. A direct object tells *what* after the verb.

> The guerrillas crept *forward.* (where)
> Craig walked *stiffly* to the front of the room. (how)
> The elderly lady dropped the *letter* in the slot. (what)

2.8 The Indirect Object

The indirect object of the verb tells to or for whom, or to or for what, something is done.

> You promised *them* higher wages. (*to* them)
> Dad bought *me* a new AM/FM radio. (*for* me)

A verb has an indirect object only if it also has a direct object. Find the direct objects in the examples above.

The indirect object may be compound: I told *Jim* and *Carlos* the truth.

The words *to* and *for* are never placed before the indirect object. When followed by a noun or pronoun, *to* and *for* are prepositions. The noun or pronoun following the preposition is its object.

> Lend *Bert* your compass. (*Bert* is the indirect object.)
> Ed lent his compass *to Bert*. (*Bert* is the object of
>   the preposition.)

> The company offered *me* a job. (*me* is the indirect object.)
> The company offered a job *to me*. (*me* is the object of
>   the preposition.)

Exercise: Find both the direct and indirect objects.

1. I sent Alice a book about India.
2. My friend in Atlantic City sent me some salt-water taffy.
3. They allowed me five dollars for expenses.
4. I'll give you a lift to the station.
5. Pat wrote Ann Landers a question.
6. Will the store give you a refund for the sweater?
7. Jimmy Carter told them the story of his life.
8. We offered Ray cash for his jeep.
9. We promised to send her safari pictures.
10. Please sing us a song, Jean.
11. Mr. Briggs left his college a million dollars.
12. The coach gave us excellent training in hockey.

2.9 Predicate Words

The linking verb links its subject to a word in the predicate. The word in the predicate, so linked, is called a **predicate word**. The subject may be linked to a **predicate noun,** a **predicate pronoun,** or a **predicate adjective.**

Shakespeare is one of the world's greatest dramatists. (predicate noun)

The winner could have been you. (predicate pronoun)

The chemistry experiment seemed easy. (predicate adjective)

A word that completes the meaning of a verb is called a **complement.** Predicate words complete the meaning of linking verbs, and since they refer to the subject, they are called **subject complements.**

Diagraming. The simple sentence with an action verb is diagramed as follows:

Eskimos hunt.   Eskimos hunt walrus.

| Eskimos | hunt. | | Eskimos | hunt | walrus |

Eskimos hunt walrus skillfully.

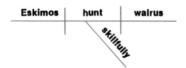

Note: The single-word modifier goes on a slant line below the word it modifies.

The simple sentence with a linking verb is diagramed as follows:

Dad looks grim.   Pam is president.

| Dad | looks \ grim | | Pam | is \ president |

Note: The line following the linking verb slants toward the subject.

The action verb with an indirect object is diagramed as follows:

The President awarded Wyeth the Freedom Medal.

Exercise A: Find the predicate words.

1. The President looked tired after his trip.
2. The juniors were quite successful in the drive.
3. These funnels are handy for pouring liquids.
4. The snow was deep in the driveway.
5. Bob will probably be an excellent rancher.
6. The Republicans' chances seemed promising.
7. Her wisdom became apparent.
8. Should this cream cheese taste so sour?
9. The Rocky Mountain bighorn is a wild sheep.
10. The best writer in our class is Barbara Brady.

Exercise B: Make five columns. Head them *Subject, Verb, Direct Object, Indirect Object,* and *Predicate Word.* Place those parts of the following sentences in the proper columns.

1. In the fog, the car hit a post.
2. He is a firm but fair disciplinarian.
3. Charles Dickens paid his first visit to the United States in 1842.
4. The pizza smelled tantalizing in the oven.
5. The attendant gave us a new ping-pong ball.
6. Barbara sent me a telegram from Detroit.
7. Dave's steer won a blue ribbon at the 4-H fair.
8. Many people regard autumn as their favorite season.

9. The pugilist dealt his opponent a savage blow.
10. Mr. Quinn paid me three dollars for cutting the grass.

2.10   Compound Parts of Sentences

Subjects, objects, and verbs may all be compound. That is, they may consist of more than one part *of the same kind.* The parts are joined by a conjunction.

COMPOUND SUBJECT	Old *cars* and rusted *parts* clutter the junkyard.
COMPOUND VERB	The sea *whirls* and *eddies.*
COMPOUND DIRECT OBJECT	Volcanoes eject *lava* and *rocks.*
COMPOUND INDIRECT OBJECT	The officer told *Tom* and *me* the news.
COMPOUND OBJECT OF PREPOSITION	We talked about our *careers* and our *hopes.*
COMPOUND PREDICATE WORD	He was *restless* and *fearful.*
COMPOUND PREDICATE	Clare *turned off the television set* and *began her homework.*

Diagraming. Compound sentence parts are diagramed as follows:

Ed and Judy (*compound subject*) stayed and worked (*compound verb*).

The director gave Joseph and Susan (*compound indirect object*) their scripts and costumes (*compound direct object*).

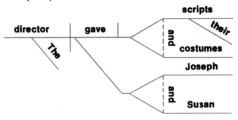

The opinions of the reporters and candidates (*compound object of preposition*) were diverse but pertinent (*compound predicate adjective*).

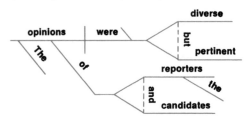

The class read the novel and evaluated the plot (*compound predicate*).

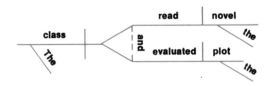

Exercise: Make five columns. Head them *Subject, Verb, Direct Object, Predicate Word,* and *Predicate.* Find the compound parts of the following sentences, and write these parts in the proper columns.

1. Down at the other end of the pool were Julie and Debby.
2. The lecturer discussed India and China.
3. A third-string halfback made the interception and scored the touchdown.
4. Our cheering section seemed listless and completely indifferent.
5. We were not only hungry but extremely tired.
6. Mitch tries but seldom succeeds.
7. Helping underdeveloped countries seems both charitable and practical.
8. Marilyn is a homemaker and a dietitian.
9. He loves golf but cannot make a living at it.
10. On the table are two batteries and a new bulb.
11. Joe took the snowshoes, skis, and skates from the closet.
12. Walking toward us were the mayor and his assistant.
13. Bach, Mozart, and Beethoven are Ann's favorite composers.
14. A helicopter rushed food and supplies to the stranded mountain climbers.
15. The book and the pamphlets will give you information about fields of specialization.

2.11   The Phrase

A phrase is a group of words without a subject and a verb, used as one part of speech.

A phrase is used as one part of speech. A **verb phrase** is two or more words used as a verb: *could go, might have gone.* A **noun phrase** is two or more words used as a noun: *Yosemite National Park, Ohio Turnpike.*

2.12   The Prepositional Phrase

The prepositional phrase consists of the preposition, its object, and modifiers of the object.

> Macbeth yielded to temptation *at his wife's persuasion.*
> *In our first football game,* Carl played first-string quarterback.

The object of a preposition is always a noun, a pronoun, or a group of words used as a noun.

> The cottage is *near* the ocean. (*ocean* is the object of *near.*)
> We lent our books *to* them. (*them* is the object of *to.*)
> Law is a career *for* which I am qualified. (*which* is the object of *for.*)
> By raising Mike's salary, Mr. Cook persuaded him to stay. (*raising Mike's salary* is a gerund phrase. It is the object of *By.*)
> The merchants promised the plaque *to* whoever won three times. (*whoever won three times* is a noun clause, the object of *to.*)

The prepositional phrase is a modifier. It is used either as an adjective or as an adverb. A prepositional phrase that modifies a noun or pronoun is an **adjective phrase;** that is, it is a phrase used as an adjective.

> Her car is the one *with the sun roof.* (*with the sun roof* modifies the pronoun *one.*)
> The sound *of music* filled the corridors. (*of music* modifies *sound.*)
> Distrust *among nations* threatens peace. (*among nations* modifies *distrust.*)

An adjective phrase always comes immediately after the noun or pronoun it modifies.

A prepositional phrase that modifies a verb, an adjective, or an adverb is an **adverb phrase.** That is, it is a phrase used as an adverb to tell *how, how much, when,* or *where* about the word it modifies.

> The letter was hidden *under some books.* (*under some books* tells *where* about the verb *was hidden.*)

The project was successful *beyond everyone's expectations.* (*beyond everyone's expectations* tells *how much* about the adjective *successful.*)

The baby cries early *in the morning* to awaken her parents. (*in the morning* tells *when* about the adverb *early.*)

When two or more prepositional phrases follow each other in succession, they may modify the same word, or one phrase may modify the object in the preceding phrase.

We ate *at a diner after the show.* (Both phrases modify *ate; at a diner* tells *where* and *after the show* tells *when* about the verb.)

Joan put the music *on the chair near the piano.* (*on the chair* modifies *put; near the piano* modifies *chair.* It tells *which* chair.)

They analyzed the symbolism *in a novel about court intrigue in sixteenth-century England.* (*in a novel* modifies the verb *analyzed; about court intrigue* modifies *novel; in sixteenth-century England* modifies *intrigue.*)

Diagraming. Prepositional phrases are diagramed as follows:

Dom ordered a copy *of the book.* (adjective phrase)

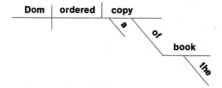

The season opens *early in the month.* (adverb phrase)

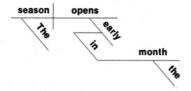

The ball went *over the fence.* (adverb phrase)

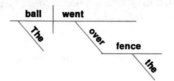

The stack *of books on the porch* got soaked. (adjective phrase)

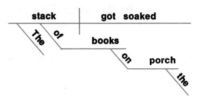

Exercise A: Write each prepositional phrase and the word or words it modifies.

1. There were newspaper clippings between the pages of the book.
2. I went to the counselor's office and asked advice about my courses.
3. The book with the green cover is mine.
4. Some forms of cancer have been checked by radioactive materials.
5. Unbridled power in the hands of one person is always dangerous.
6. The china on the shelf of the cupboard is very rare.
7. There was a feeling of unrest among the players.
8. All but one of these sentences is easy.
9. Cerebral palsy is high on the list of unsolved medical problems.
10. Each year, in our country, ten thousand children are born with injuries to the brain cells.

Exercise B: Write each prepositional phrase and the word or words it modifies.

1. Guatemala is located near Mexico.

2. Excavations at a prehistoric Mayan site began recently.
3. The excavations are in the Mayan jungle in Guatemala.
4. The area was occupied about 500 B.C.
5. Most of the pottery and other objects were made between 200 and 900 A.D.
6. The Mayas excelled in astronomy and in mathematics.
7. Their pyramids tower over a cluster of smaller mounds.
8. Excavating for relics in Guatemala must be very exciting.

2.13 The Infinitive Phrase*

Usually, but not always, the **infinitive phrase** begins with *to*. The phrase consists of *to*, the infinitive, its complements and its modifiers. If the infinitive has a subject, that is also part of the phrase.

> Tony likes *to read widely*. (The infinitive phrase is object of the verb *likes*.)
> Lee is able *to take dictation well*. (The infinitive phrase modifies the adjective *able*.)
> I watched *him dive*. (The infinitive phrase is object of *watched*. The infinitive is *dive* without the usual *to*. *Him* is subject of the infinitive.)
> Ponce de León was trying *to find the Fountain of Youth*. (The infinitive phrase is object of the verb *was trying*.)

Diagraming. The infinitive phrase is diagramed as follows:

Hal hoped to see a good play soon.

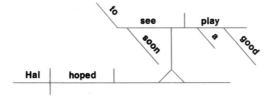

---

* See also Section 1.11.

To resolve the controversial issue was very difficult.

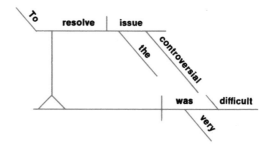

Exercise: Find the infinitive phrases in the sentences below.

1. The man wanted to cash a check.
2. We went to see the African exhibit at the museum.
3. She visited the library to find out about her ancestors.
4. The librarian displayed magazines to attract readers.
5. To work hard is to be happy.
6. I am happy to accept your invitation.
7. I have work to do.
8. It is too late to start now.
9. The doctor started to leave.
10. The team went to Clinton to debate on foreign relations.
11. I asked permission to work in the library.
12. The dramatic club has decided to present *Our Town*.
13. I wish I had time to spend on my carpentry project.
14. To be a good conversationalist is to be a good listener.
15. We saw Henry play.

2.14 The Participial Phrase*

The **participial phrase** usually begins with the participle. The phrase consists of the participle, its modifiers, and its comple-

* See also Section 1.13.

ments. The modifiers and complements may themselves be phrases and clauses.

> Mary reread the instructions, *trying to salvage the dress.*
> (The participial phrase modifies *Mary.* The infinitive phrase *to salvage the dress* is the object of the participle *trying.*)
>
> *Having heard the signal,* the runners pounced off the starting mark. (The participial phrase modifies *runners.*)
>
> *Stopped at the border,* the travelers had to show their visas. (The participial phrase modifies *travelers.*)
>
> *Explaining how the problem could be solved,* the teacher began to work it out. (The participial phrase modifies *teacher.* The noun clause *how the problem could be solved* is the object of *Explaining.*)

Diagraming. The participle and the participial phrase are diagramed as follows:

Chuckling quietly, the stranger walked away.

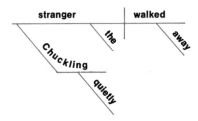

Quickly calculating the risk, he scaled the wall.

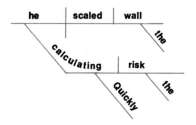

Exercise: Find the participial phrases. Tell the word each phrase modifies. Do not overlook phrases made from past participles and present participles.

1. Pushing hard, he managed to move the trunk an inch.
2. The boy wearing the red jacket is Larry.
3. Living in Chevy Chase, he was within easy reach of the Capital.
4. Guided by radar, the pilot kept in his lane.
5. Convinced of her client's innocence, the defense attorney worked harder than ever.
6. A film well liked by people of all ages is Disney's *Fantasia*.
7. Seen through a microscope, a drop of swamp water is alive with animals.
8. Every night we could hear the waves lapping on the beach.
9. Never having eaten spumoni before, I didn't know what to expect.
10. Having conquered the world's highest peak, Edmund Hillary was knighted by Queen Elizabeth.
11. Exhausted from the climb, the hikers lay down to rest.
12. Shut off from navigation, Africa had been difficult to explore.
13. Called "the man of the century," Albert Schweitzer has given unselfishly of himself to Africa.
14. Enriched by words from ancient and modern tongues, the English language is extraordinarily expressive.

2.15 The Gerund Phrase*

The **gerund phrase** consists of the gerund, which always ends in *-ing*, and the modifiers and complements of the gerund. The modifiers themselves may be phrases or clauses. The gerund phrase is always used as a noun.

> *Planning for a career* requires foresight. (The gerund phrase is the subject of the verb *requires*.)

* See also Section 1.12.

He finished *assembling the amplifier.* (The gerund phrase
is the object of the verb *finished.*)

By concentrating doggedly, he grasped the idea. (The
gerund phrase is the object of the preposition *By.*)

Studying all night when you have an exam is self-defeating.
(The gerund phrase is the subject of the verb *is.* The
adverb clause *when you have an exam* modifies
the gerund.)

Diagraming. The gerund and the gerund phrase are diagramed
as follows:

Sailing is great fun.

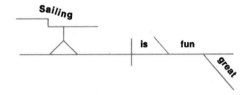

Careful checking revealed the mistake.

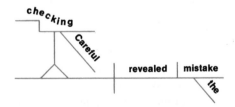

They began sorting the shells.

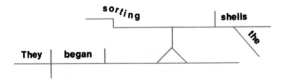

After returning from the swim, we feasted.

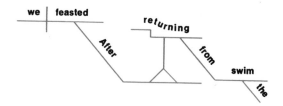

Exercise A: Find the gerund phrases. Tell how each is used.

1. Her father was delighted at Kate's winning the athletic scholarship.
2. Directing a play is a complex job.
3. The course requires the reading of many plays.
4. Working all summer at engineering gave Kathy an advantage.
5. He found excitement in using a powerful telescope.
6. Driving to the top of Mt. Palomar was a memorable experience.
7. I enjoyed watching the sunset at Palm Springs.
8. Competing as a speaker gave Charles confidence.
9. Knowing where to look for information saves time.
10. Rehearsing the play occupies Janet's time after school.
11. Before writing a composition, you should prepare an outline.
12. I enjoy walking my dog Pretzel.
13. Running a summer camp is a heavy responsibility.
14. Watching television can be both entertaining and educational.
15. The law forbids smoking in the theater.

Exercise B: Find the verbals.

1. Spectators admired the speedboat cutting through the water.
2. In college Beth decided to specialize in nuclear physics.
3. Reading science fiction consumed many hours of his time.
4. Having studied bookplates, Fran was able to design one for the school library.

5. By having been alert to a previous court decision, the lawyer won the case.

6. To cohere is to stick together.

7. We want to see the sunrise at Bryce Canyon.

8. By paying interest at 6½ percent, the bank increased its number of depositors.

9. This old house, defying wind and weather, has stood here for two hundred years.

10. For serving as coxswain in the crew races, Larry was given an oar.

2.16   The Appositive Phrase

An appositive is a word placed after another word to explain or identify it.

The novel, a mystery story, appealed to me.
Pat, an honor student, earned a gold pin.

The appositive always appears after the word it explains or identifies. It is always a noun or pronoun, and the word that it explains is also always a noun or pronoun.

An **appositive phrase** consists of the appositive and its modifiers, which themselves may be phrases or clauses.

The fair, *an annual event that attracts thousands,* opens next week. (The appositive phrase identifies *fair.* The adjective *annual* and the adjective clause *that attracts thousands* modify the appositive *event.*)

The principal presented the trophy, *a tall silver cup with handles.* (The italicized words are the appositive phrase, identifying *trophy.* The adjectives *tall* and *silver* modify the appositive *cup,* as does the adjective phrase *with handles.*)

Note: The compound personal pronoun used intensively is not regarded as an appositive. It is used for emphasis and does not explain or identify the word to which it refers: The speaker *himself* was not sure of the answer.

Diagraming. The appositive is diagramed as follows:

The author, a dynamic speaker, lectured about UFOs.

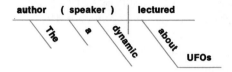

2.17   Diagraming the Simple Sentence

Meaning is conveyed in English by word-groups arranged in definite order in the sentence. Diagraming will help you see which words go together and how they are arranged.

The base of the simple sentence is composed of subject-verb-complement. These words are placed on the base line of the diagram. The indirect object is placed below the verb.

Subject	Action Verb	Direct Object

Indirect Object

The introductory word *There* or *Here* is placed above the base line. The subject of an imperative sentence, *you* (understood), is placed in parentheses. Note the slant line after the linking verb.

There

Subject	Linking Verb	Predicate Word

(You)	Verb	Direct Object

A single-word modifier is placed on a slant line below the word it modifies. An adverb modifying an adjective or adverb is placed as shown below.

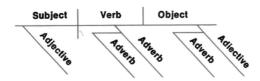

The prepositional phrase is attached to the word it modifies, as follows:

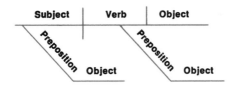

The participial phrase is shown as follows:

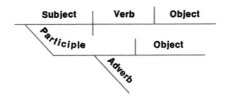

The gerund phrase is placed above the base line unless it is the object of a preposition.

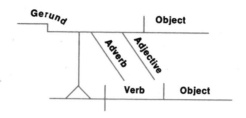

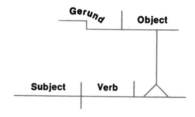

The infinitive phrase is shown in this way:

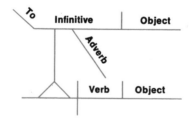

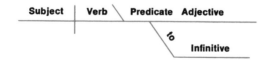

3.0 Sentence and Clause

We have seen (Section 2.2) that sentences can be classified according to the purpose of the speaker: *declarative, imperative, interrogative,* and *exclamatory.* This classification is helpful in problems of punctuation.

For help in writing better sentences, there is another, more useful classification. This is the classification by form. There are three basic forms of sentences: the *simple sentence,* the *compound sentence,* and the *complex sentence.* A fourth kind, the *compound-complex sentence* is a combination of other forms.

3.1 The Simple Sentence

A simple sentence contains only one subject and predicate. Both the subject and the predicate may be compound.

You will recall that *compound* means having two or more similar parts.

> COMPOUND SUBJECT   The *designer* of the car and the *consultant* worked together for many months. (The designer worked; the consultant worked.)

> COMPOUND VERB   The audience *cheered* and *applauded* the actor. (The audience cheered; the audience applauded.)

COMPOUND PREDICATE I *located the leak* and *called the plumber*. (I located; I called.)

COMPOUND SUBJECT AND PREDICATE Faculty *advisers* and student *officers* of the various organizations *discussed the problem* and *arrived at a solution*. (Advisers and officers discussed; advisers and officers arrived.)

All of the preceding sentences are simple sentences. In these sentences both parts of a compound subject go with the same verb. Or both parts of a compound verb have the same subject. In all of these sentences there is only one subject-verb connection.

For contrast, note that in the following sentence the first subject goes with the first verb while the second subject goes with the second verb. There are two subject-verb connections. This is not a simple sentence:

The *boys prepared* lunch; the *girls played* volleyball.

The Compound Predicate. The compound predicate is worth special attention because it is most useful in writing clear, smooth sentences.

The compound predicate consists of two verbs having the same subject. At least one of the verbs has a complement.

The earthquake *destroyed* the city and *left* thousands homeless.
Both of his children *studied* hard and *won scholarships*.

Exercise: Identify the compound parts in the following sentences. Look for compound subjects, compound verbs, and compound predicates.

1. The roses and the carnations were in the same vase.
2. For five hours I read and wrote.
3. The turtle lays eggs and never gives the next generation a backward glance.
4. The lake and the mountain behind it were covered with snow.

5. Killer whales hunt in packs and are the worst threat to other creatures of the sea.

6. Ostrich eggs are as big as grapefruit and weigh two to three pounds.

7. Decaying leaves and animal matter make the richest soil.

8. The anteater rips anthills open with its powerful claws and then removes the ants with its long tongue.

9. Koala bears always smell sweetly of eucalyptus and constantly wear an expression of hurt dignity.

10. All birds, reptiles, fishes, amphibians, and mammals have backbones and are called vertebrates.

3.2 The Compound Sentence

The compound sentence consists of two or more simple sentences put together.

The parts of a compound sentence are put together: (1) with a comma and a coordinating conjunction (*and, but, or, for, nor*); (2) with a semicolon.

> The plan seemed feasible, *but* I still felt unsure.
> The plane made a forced landing, *and* a crowd
>   gathered quickly.
> You can drive slowly and survive, *or* you can drive fast and
>   become a statistic.
> I understood his problem, *for* I had once faced it myself.
> Mary could not remember where she had left her music, *nor*
>   could her friends help her.
> I understood his problem; I had once faced it myself.
> José joined the drama club; Sheila preferred the
>   debating club.

Conjunctive adverbs (*then, however, moreover, hence, consequently,* etc.) are also used to join the parts of a compound sentence. The conjunctive adverb is preceded by a semicolon.

All the polls predicted a Dewey victory in 1948; *however,* Truman won.

Read the directions carefully; *then* begin the examination.

The majority voted against it; *therefore,* the picnic was canceled.

Diagraming. The compound sentence is diagramed on two parallel base lines as follows:

The car was nearly full, but we piled in.

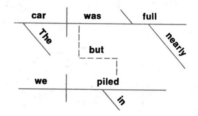

The announcer repeated the news; the tragedy completely unnerved us.

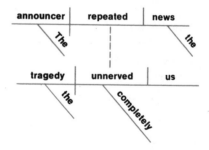

Compound Sentences and Compound Predicates. In the compound predicate every verb has the same subject. In the compound sentence, each verb has a different subject. This difference can be seen readily in diagrams.

SIMPLE SENTENCE WITH COMPOUND PREDICATE:

They accepted my story and published it.

COMPOUND SENTENCE:

They accepted my story, but the editor delayed publication.

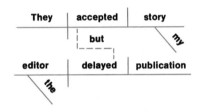

Exercise: Decide which of these sentences are compound and which are simple. In the simple sentences identify all compound predicates.

1. Laura learned German and got a job as an interpreter.
2. Canada covers almost half of North America and is as large as all Europe.
3. Jeff commutes, but Pete works here.
4. Lacrosse is fun, but it can be dangerous.
5. Peg and Jill played expertly and were praised by the coach.
6. Mike has played all positions on the team and is now a top-ranking player.
7. Skin diving is exciting, but it can be hazardous for beginners.
8. Thomas Jefferson founded the University of Virginia in 1819 and designed some of the buildings.
9. Poe wove a quality of music into his poems and became the father of the short story.

10. Your first problem is correct, but you have made an error in the second.

11. Pocahontas was the daughter of Powhatan, the most powerful chieftain in Virginia.

12. Shall we take a jet from JFK Airport to save time or shall we take a ship from New York?

13. The Irish potato is not a native of Ireland, nor has the Jerusalem artichoke any connection with Jerusalem.

14. Robert E. Lee not only won the devotion of his men but commanded the respect of his enemies.

15. In 1943 a cornfield in Mexico cracked open, and a new volcano, Paricutin, began to erupt.

3.3 The Clause

A clause is a group of words containing a verb and its subject.

According to this definition, a simple sentence is a clause. Indeed, the simple sentence is sometimes defined as consisting of one main clause. However, we shall find it simpler to use the word *clause* to name a *part* of a sentence.

Each part of a compound sentence has its own verb and subject. These parts of the compound sentence are therefore clauses.

Each clause in a compound sentence can be lifted out and written separately as a simple sentence.

A clause that can stand by itself as a sentence is a main clause.

We have defined a compound sentence as consisting of two or more simple sentences put together. We can now also define it is consisting of two main clauses.

A clause that cannot stand by itself as a sentence is a subordinate clause.

While you were talking . . . (What happened?)

Unless she improves her spelling . . . (What?)

If *you* *have* the strength . . . (Then what?)

Phrase or Clause? A clause has a subject and a verb. A phrase does not.

> I heard them *rehearsing for the concert.* (phrase)
>
> I heard them *when they were rehearsing for the concert.* (clause)
>
> Students *in the caucus* did admirable work. (phrase)
>
> Students *who were in the caucus* did admirable work. (clause)

Exercise: Are the italicized words in each sentence a phrase or a clause?

1. Jim scowls *when Jamie tells him his faults.*
2. *Because he worked nights,* he was sleepy in school.
3. The jury recessed *to eat their dinner.*
4. Interesting animals *found in South America* are the llama, the vicuña, and the tapir.
5. They substituted a contract *that was more remunerative.*
6. The giant panda is much more closely related to the raccoon than to the bear, *which it resembles.*
7. Jules Verne had an extremely vivid imagination *coupled with a rare scientific knowledge.*
8. The toboggan is six to eight feet long, and *a foot and a half wide.*
9. Indian hunters were the first *to build toboggans.*
10. *How migrating birds find their way* is a great mystery.

3.4 The Complex Sentence

The complex sentence consists of one main clause and one or more subordinate clauses.

In a complex sentence, the subordinate clause is always used as a noun or a modifier. If it is used as a modifier, the subordinate clause modifies a word in the main clause.

Although he knew the answer, he did not raise his hand.
(clause modifies *did raise*)

Read the paper *while you are waiting.* (clause
modifies *Read*)

This is the music *that I like.* (clause modifies *music*)

In each example above, the main clause can stand as a sentence by itself: *he did not raise his hand, Read the paper, This is the music.*

The subordinate clauses, however, cannot stand alone because their meaning is complete.

Although he knew the answer ... (what happened?)
while you are waiting ... (What is to be done?)
that I like ... (What is it?)

Complex sentences containing noun clauses are somewhat different. The noun clause may be used as a noun *within the main clause.* The noun clause, in other words, is part of the main clause.

That he voted for the Equal Rights Amendment is certain.
(Noun clause is subject of *is.*)

What you read influences your thinking. (Noun clause is
subject of *influences.*)

The teachers felt responsible *for what the students did.*
(Noun clause is object of the preposition *for.*)

No one understood *what she was saying.* (Noun clause is
object of *understood.*)

In these sentences, neither the main clause nor the noun clause can stand by itself. Nonetheless, a sentence containing one main clause and a noun clause is regarded as a complex sentence.

Exercise A: Indicate whether each of the following sentences is simple, compound, or complex.

1. The rear tire needed no air, but the front tire did.

2. The ball circled the rim of the basket and finally slipped in.

3. Unless Henry can obtain a scholarship, he may not go to college next fall.

4. Dad is unhappy about his golf score, which has not been improving lately.

5. On this tour, you can take a side trip to Disney World at no extra cost.

6. At the end of the season, the team was given a banquet and presented with trophies.

7. The campers said good-bye with regret; they would not meet again for a long time.

8. The motor sputtered and then stalled.

9. The motor sputtered before it stalled.

10. Did you know that the onion is a lily?

Exercise B: Find the subordinate clause in each sentence below.

1. Bill Cosby has a humor that wears well.

2. Bridal Veil Falls is at its best in late afternoon, when it forms beautiful rainbows.

3. South American monkeys have tails that are prehensile, or grasping.

4. James Madison is the person who drafted the Bill of Rights.

5. The candidate's mistakes in grammar show that he is too illiterate for the office.

6. The bald eagle looks bald only because it has white feathers on its head.

7. This is the meadow where I saw the deer.

8. The car he drives is an old Mercedes.

9. The trapdoor spider lives in a silk-lined room with a door that fits exactly.

10. We were in the train station when we heard the election results.

11. The Bronx Zoo, which is the largest in the world, covers nearly 300 acres.

12. *Macbeth* is the story of a man who suffered disaster through too much ambition.

3.5 The Compound-Complex Sentence

A compound-complex sentence consists of two or more main clauses and one or more subordinate clauses.

The main clauses are joined by a coordinating conjunction (preceded by a comma), a conjunctive adverb (preceded by a semicolon), or by a semicolon alone. The subordinate clause modifies a word in one of the main clauses or acts as a noun within one of them.

MAIN CLAUSE   MAIN CLAUSE   SUBORDINATE CLAUSE

Carol entered the meet, and she won the medal that was donated by her uncle.

MAIN CLAUSE   MAIN CLAUSE   SUBORDINATE CLAUSE

We missed the bus; however, we arrived home before the others did.

3.6 The Adjective Clause

The single-word adjective, the adjective phrase, and the adjective clause are used in the same way. They modify a noun or pronoun.

An adjective clause is a subordinate clause used to modify a noun or pronoun in the main clause.

Introductory Words. A majority of the adjective clauses in modern writing begin with an introductory word. There is a growing tendency, however, to use adjective clauses with no introductory word.

> That is the spot *where I fell.* (*Where* is an introductory word.)
> This is the time *when we must attack.* (*When* is an introductory word.)
> Legends *I read* told of his origin. (no introductory word)
> Legends *that I read* told of his origin. (*that* is an introductory word.)

It's a program *I enjoy.* (no introductory word)
It's a program *that I enjoy.* (*that* is an introductory word.)

In the first two examples above, the introductory words *where* and *when* are both used within the subordinate clause as modifiers of the verb: *fell* **where;** *attack* **when.**

Relative Pronouns. The pronouns *who, whose, whom, which,* and *that* are used to introduce adjective clauses. Used in this way they refer to a word in the main clause and are used in place of that word. That word is the antecedent of the pronoun. It is also the word modified by the adjective clause.

Tom Dooley was the doctor *who inspired him.*
(*doctor* is antecedent of *who* and is modified by
the adjective clause.)
She is a writer *whose works deserve acclaim.*
(*writer* is antecedent of *whose* and is modified by
the adjective clause.)
The trout season, *which opens in April,* is welcomed
by anglers.
(*season* is antecedent of *which* and is modified by
the adjective clause.)

An adjective clause introduced by a relative pronoun is sometimes called a relative clause.

The relative pronoun has two functions. It introduces the clause, and it is used as a sentence-part within the clause.

The explanation *that she gave* was lucid.
(*that* is the direct object of *gave.*)
That teacher is the one *whom I respect highly.*
(*whom* is the direct object of *respect.*)
The letter *to which you refer* has been lost.
(*which* is the object of the preposition *to.*)
My father is a man *who likes hard work.*
(*who* is the subject of *likes.*)

Diagraming. The adjective clause is joined to the word it modifies in the main clause. A dotted line leads from this word to the introductory word. Note that the relative pronoun is placed to show its use in the sentence.

The car that I borrowed belongs to Tammy.

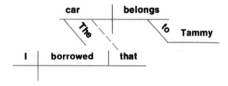

This is the building where my father works.

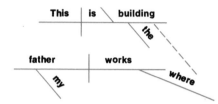

Exercise: Find each adjective clause and the word it modifies.

1. This is the room that I decorated.
2. Springs are fed by rain, which seeps through the soil.
3. I couldn't find the place where you bought the bulbs.
4. A sharp-edged tool was the first instrument that human beings needed.
5. Germany is the country where Beethoven was born.
6. I have seen the house in which Betsy Ross lived.
7. You can buy dwarf lemon trees that will grow in your room.
8. The dog that barks the loudest usually bites the least.
9. How can we choose a play that everyone will like?
10. His father, whom he introduced as a captain, was not wearing a uniform.
11. Her conviction that taxes need to be raised kept her from winning the election.
12. Surely the story you are telling me is not true.
13. All that glitters is not gold.
14. A diver who gets panicky may rise to the surface too rapidly.
15. He may get the "bends," which is a dangerous condition.

3.7 The Adverb Clause

The single-word adverb, the adverb phrase, and the adverb clause are all used in the same way. They are used to modify verbs, adjectives, and adverbs.

An adverb clause is a subordinate clause used to modify a verb, adjective, or adverb in the main clause.*

Adverb clauses tell *when, where, why, how, to what extent,* and *how much* about the word they modify.

ADVERB CLAUSES MODIFYING VERBS

We **put** the key *where we could locate it easily.*
(where)
When you go to New York, **see** the Guggenheim Museum. (when)
The candidate **canceled** his speech *because he had a cold.* (why)
The dog **looked** *as if he would attack us.* (how)

ADVERB CLAUSES MODIFYING ADJECTIVES

This test is as **hard** *as the first one was.* (to what extent)
The school days are **longer** *than they used to be.*

ADVERB CLAUSE MODIFYING AN ADVERB

The dog ran **quicker** *than the sheep did.* (how much)

Subordinating Conjunctions. Every adverb clause is introduced by a subordinating conjunction. The function of this word is to show how two clauses are related. By use of the subordinating conjunction, one clause is made to tell *how, when, where, to what extent,* or *how much* about another.

When a subordinating conjunction is placed before a clause, the clause can no longer stand alone.

---

* Some authorities suggest that an introductory adverb clause may modify an entire main clause rather than a single word in it.

The cheerleader is losing her voice. (complete)
If the cheerleader loses her voice . . . (incomplete)
Since the cheerleader is losing her voice . . . (incomplete)

A new building has been erected. (complete)
When a new building is erected . . . (incomplete)
Until a new building is erected . . . (incomplete)

A subordinating conjunction may be placed before either of two main clauses to tie it to the other. Which clause is subordinate depends upon the meaning the writer wants to express.

Although Mark Twain was a great humorist, he
  was pessimistic.
Although Mark Twain was pessimistic, he was a
  great humorist.
Because he was a victim of persecution, his fame grew.
Because his fame grew, he was a victim of persecution.

Subordinating conjunctions can be used to show a great variety of relationships between main ideas. The careful choice of conjunctions will enable you to express your ideas clearly and exactly.

TIME:	as, after, before, since, until, when, whenever, while
CAUSE OR REASON:	because, since
COMPARISON:	as, as much as, than
CONDITION:	if, although, though, unless, provided
PURPOSE:	so that, in order that

Note how the meaning changes with the change in conjunctions in these sentences.

Before the schedule was changed, I was upset.
Because the schedule was changed, I was upset.
Until the schedule was changed, I was upset.

Elliptical Clauses. The word *elliptical* come from *ellipsis*, which means "omission of a word." An **elliptical clause** is one from which words have been omitted.

While he was playing chess, he was contented.
While playing chess, he was contented.
When she is driving, she listens to the radio.
When driving, she listens to the radio.

Diagraming. The adverb clause is diagramed on a separate line:

When his friend whistled, he dashed outside.

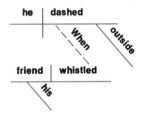

Exercise: Find each adverb clause and the word it modifies.

1. The parade was postponed because the floats
were not finished.
2. If we win this game, the trophy will be ours.
3. They arrived after you left.
4. When she saw the rain, she ran to close the windows.
5. Class begins promptly when the bell rings.
6. They will buy the house provided they can get a mortgage.
7. The kitten ate as if he had been without food for days.
8. The children followed the kitten wherever it went.
9. Park the car wherever you can find a place.
10. I drove off the road so that the trailer truck could pass.

3.8 The Noun Clause

A noun clause is a subordinate clause used as a noun.

The noun clause may be used as subject or direct object of the verb, as a predicate noun, as object of a preposition, or as an appositive.

I understand *what the law requires.* (direct object)

He was wondering about *where she had gone.* (object
of preposition)
The fact *that I am his son* made no difference. (appositive)
Whoever told you that was wrong. (subject)
The exciting part is *how Linda got the autograph.*
(predicate noun)

Introductory Words. As the examples above clearly show, noun
clauses may be introduced by some of the same words that introduce adverb clauses: *when, where.* Used with noun clauses, these
words are not regarded as subordinating conjunctions. They
are merely introductory words, used as adverbs within the noun
clause.

Similarly, noun clauses may be introduced by the same words
used to introduce relative clauses: *who, whose, whom, which,
that, when, where.* Used in noun clauses, these words are not regarded as relative pronouns, but they may serve as subjects or
objects within the noun clause.

Larry explained **where** *Ann was.* (noun clause as the
object of *explained*)
Luke went **where** *the fish were biting.* (adverb clause
modifying *went*)
Julia is the one **who** *broke the record.* (adjective clause
modifying *one*)
Who *won the election* is uncertain. (noun clause as the
subject of *is*)

Many noun clauses are written without any introductory word.
Every direct quotation preceded by words such as *he said, I
replied, Bob asked* is a noun clause within the introductory word.
Every indirect quotation is a noun clause preceded by the introductory word.

She said *that the road was treacherous.* (noun clause as
the object of *said*)
She said, *"The road was treacherous."* (noun clause as the
object of *said*)

Diagraming. The noun clause is diagramed as shown below. Note that the use of the noun clause determines its position in the diagram.

I think that you are improving.

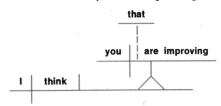

He gave his help to whoever was needy.

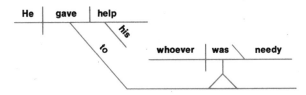

Exercise: Identify each noun clause. Tell how it is used in the sentence.

1. Lee asked what I was doing.
2. The fact that he had read about neutrons helped him.
3. What the players will do next is anyone's guess.
4. I inquired where she lived.
5. Please tell me why you did it.
6. I wonder who wrote the letter.
7. I know that you had hoped for a place on the program.
8. The fact that he attended the meeting is significant.
9. We gave book lists to whoever asked for them.
10. Please tell him what he wants to know.
11. That it is a beautiful work of art is plain to see.
12. The instructor told us that we were improving.
13. Whether the governor will invoke the new law is the big question.
14. What the future holds for us remains a challenging mystery.

3.9 The Sentence Redefined

We are now ready to complete the definition of a sentence that we started in Sections 2.1 and 2.3. We may begin by noting once again the differences between phrases, clauses, and sentences.

A **phrase** is a group of words used within a sentence as a single part of speech. A phrase may be used as a noun, a verb, an adjective, or an adverb. It does *not* contain a subject and verb.

A **clause** is a group of words which contains a subject and its verb. It may be used within the sentence as a noun, an adjective, or an adverb.

> PHRASE: Working on our project . . .
>
> CLAUSE: While *we were working* on our project . . .

A main clause can stand by itself as a sentence. A subordinate clause cannot stand by itself.

MAIN CLAUSE   MAIN CLAUSE

The camera was new, but the shutter did not work.

The camera was new. (*complete*)
The shutter did not work. (*complete*)

SUBORDINATE CLAUSE   MAIN CLAUSE

Although the camera was new, the shutter did not work.

The shutter did not work. (*complete*)
Although the camera was new . . . (*incomplete*)

Clauses and phrases are sentence parts. The sentence itself is not part of any other grammatical construction. (The paragraph is not a grammatical construction.) Our complete definition of a sentence then is in three parts:

A sentence is a group of words that

1. expresses a complete thought,
2. contains a subject and verb,
3. is not part of any other grammatical construction.

4.0 Complete Sentences

Uncompleted sentences are more often a problem in writing than in speaking. If you use an uncompleted sentence in speaking with someone face-to-face, he or she can interrupt and ask you what you mean. In writing, you usually do not have a second chance.

The sentence is the best means you have for getting your meaning across to someone else in writing. Through study and practice, you can learn to write effective and forceful sentences. To write effectively, however, you must learn to avoid two kinds of sentence errors: (1) the sentence fragment, and (2) the run-on sentence. Both of these errors cause confusion for the reader.

4.1 Fragments Resulting from Incomplete Thought

An uncompleted sentence is called a **sentence fragment.** It is only a part, or fragment, of a sentence.

You can think much faster than you can write. Many of your sentence errors, if you make them, happen because your mind has raced on ahead of your hand. You have started to write a second thought before you have finished writing the first. Or, perhaps in haste, you have left out a key word necessary for a complete sentence. Suppose you intended to say something like this:

> Ted and Miriam had a loud quarrel. After the quarrel, they wondered why they had been angry. They talked about their differences the next day.

In the hurry to get on with your writing, however, what you put down was something like this:

> Ted and Miriam had a loud quarrel. After they wondered why they had been angry. They talked about their differences the next day.

The second group of words is not a sentence. It causes confusion. The reader may suppose that you meant to say, "Ted and Miriam had a loud quarrel after they wondered why they had been angry."

Exercise A: Find the sentence fragments. Add the words needed to make each fragment a sentence.

1. As a child, I always made decisions slowly. Especially when choosing candy in the candy store.
2. My five cents for candy. Always seemed like five dollars.
3. The candy store had lots of candy on display. Most of it penny candy.
4. I always stood in front of the glassed-in shelves. Just looked and looked.
5. Some animals are nocturnal. For example, owls and bats.
6. How I used to practice for those lessons! And the concerts.
7. They tried every door in the house. But could not get in.
8. Dick advanced toward Sam. Holding a lemon pie.
9. The missing suitcase in the cupboard under the stairs.
10. Easton, where I was born. Just across the river from Phillipsburg.

Exercise B: Three of the following groups of words are sentences. The rest are fragments. Find the fragments and add words needed to make them sentences.

1. Heart disease, one of the chief causes of death
2. How the leopard managed to escape from its cage
3. *The Taming of the Shrew*, one of Shakespeare's wittier comedies
4. James Madison was one of the most scholarly of our presidents
5. The pink camellia, which was especially beautiful
6. If Martin weren't so unpredictable
7. The many billboards along the highway
8. The winding road, bordered by beautiful trees and the ocean
9. Carter Lake in Oregon rests in the cone of a dead volcano
10. Thomas Jefferson, our third President, was a very versatile man.

4.2 Fragments Resulting from Incorrect Punctuation

The first word of a sentence begins with a capital letter. The sentence is closed by a punctuation mark: *period, question mark,* or *exclamation mark.* A great many sentence fragments are written simply because the writer inserts a period and a capital letter too soon. This error is sometimes called a **period fault.**

FRAGMENT	*At the start of the second game.* It began to rain.
SENTENCE	At the start of the second game, it began to rain.
FRAGMENT	I read the paper. *While I was waiting for Dad.*
SENTENCE	I read the paper while I was waiting for Dad.
FRAGMENT	*Because the story was compelling.* He stayed up to finish it.
SENTENCE	Because the story was compelling, he stayed up to finish it.

Exercise: Find the fragments. Correct them by changing the punctuation or by adding the words needed to make a sentence.

1. At the market were Easter lilies and azaleas. Which were in pots.
2. I bought artificial flowers. Since they would require no care.
3. Pete enjoys science fiction. Because of his interest in science.
4. The car went off the road. When Ira fell asleep.
5. Joyce learned how to develop film. By assisting a photographer.
6. Elaine knows parliamentary law. As she runs student council meetings.
7. Bob's talk takes a different tone. When he is away from his boss.
8. Our magazine will have color plates. If enough students subscribe.
9. Stacey had a profitable summer. Taking care of bees.
10. Chris went into the garden. Where roses and irises were blooming.

4.3 Phrases as Fragments

You know that a phrase is a group of words that does not contain a verb and its subject. A phrase, therefore, cannot be a sentence by itself. It is a *part* of a sentence.

You are not likely to mistake a prepositional phrase for a complete sentence. If you write a long prepositional phrase or a series of phrases as a sentence, it is probably because you have punctuated incorrectly.

FRAGMENT	Bill studied advanced English. *In summer school.*
SENTENCE	Bill studied advanced English in summer school.

You are more likely to mistake a verbal phrase for a complete sentence. This error occurs because verbals look like verbs and function somewhat like verbs. Like verbs, they may be modified by adverbs. They can be followed by objects or predicate words.

They are not complete verbs, however, and they cannot be used as the main verb of a sentence.

The most troublesome verbals are those that end in *-ing*. All gerunds and present participles end in *-ing*. You will avoid many sentence errors if you will remember this fact:

No word ending in *-ing* can be a verb unless it is a one-syllable word like *sing, ring,* or *bring*.

If an *-ing* word is preceded by *is, are, was,* or some other form of *be*, the two words together are a verb.

PARTICIPLE	COMPLETE VERB
reading	is reading
holding	had been holding
breaking	were breaking

A long infinitive phrase may sometimes be mistaken for a complete sentence. Such a phrase sounds like a sentence since it often has everything that a sentence requires except a subject.

INCORRECT	This is my aim. To establish a trust fund .for you.
CORRECT	This is my aim. I plan to establish a trust fund for you.
INCORRECT	Dr. Kane was very eager. To encourage my interest in becoming a surgeon.
CORRECT	Dr. Kane was very eager to encourage my interest in becoming a surgeon.

An appositive phrase is sometimes written incorrectly as a complete sentence. Although it may seem like a sentence, it always lacks a verb.

FRAGMENT	This biography, *the only definitive account.*
SENTENCE	This biography is the only definitive account.
SENTENCE	This biography, the only definitive account, is a masterpiece.
FRAGMENT	My sax, *a new alto.*
SENTENCE	My sax, a new alto, was very expensive.

Exercise: Rewrite the groups of words beside each number below to make a complete sentence. You may need to add words in some instances.

1. The loon is a gray and brown bird. Very clumsy on the shore.
2. You can hold this microphone in your hand or mount it on a stand. Either way.
3. Buying a headphone and testing it instead of doing his homework.
4. I found it exciting. To see Rudolph Nureyev perform with a New York dance company.
5. Vesuvius, the most famous volcano in the world.
6. Greece is still an extremely poor country. A warehouse of rocks and ruins.
7. Barb Anderson, the photographer for the school newspaper.
8. He was in a great hurry. To get to Richmond by six o'clock.
9. Maple trees border the avenue. Bright orange and flaming red.
10. The speaker, a foreign correspondent for *The New York Times.*
11. Scientists hope to explore Venus. To determine whether life exists on that planet.
12. Kutztown is in the Pennsylvania Dutch country. The scene of an annual folk festival.
13. Fred's car was delivered today. Canary yellow and white.
14. Be there on Friday, March 12. At three o'clock.
15. The Declaration of Independence, one of the important documents in the struggle for human freedom.

4.4 Clauses as Fragments

A subordinate clause cannot stand alone as a sentence. See Section 3.3. A sentence may be changed into a subordinate clause by having a subordinating conjunction placed before it.

SENTENCE	I was trying to think of an excuse.
SUBORDINATE CLAUSE	*As* I was trying to think of an excuse . . .

Writers sometimes mistakenly place a period before or after a subordinate clause as though it were a sentence.

INCORRECT   When the landlord came. He broke up
our stickball game.
CORRECT   When the landlord came, he broke up
our stickball game.

INCORRECT   Angelo sold his car. Because it used too
much gas.
CORRECT   Angelo sold his car because it used too
much gas.

Exercise: Rewrite the word groups below to eliminate the fragments.

1. Few students borrow books from the school library. Although it has a wide selection.
2. We rushed to the scene at once. When we heard the news.
3. Jenny found time for chess, music, and debating. While she was editor of the school paper.
4. This is the old house. Where Uncle Jim was born.
5. The plane could not communicate with the airport. Because a storm was raging.
6. The two pieces of wood must be quickly clamped together. Before the glue dries.
7. The letter arrived in the morning mail. Just after Dad had left.
8. There was no fire-fighting company in Philadelphia. Until Ben Franklin formed one in 1746.

Review Exercise: In this exercise you will find examples of many kinds of fragments. Change them into sentences.

1. Leslie tried to buy glue. To mend the red glass dish.
2. They coasted down the hill. Thinking they could control the sled.
3. The game was over. The score 7–2 in our favor.
4. Talking about books on the sea. Joe made his listeners feel excitement and adventure.

5. The students presented Thornton Wilder's *Our Town*. After only three weeks' rehearsal.

6. Noel won an award in photography. At the art festival.

7. The table next to the wall. It should be moved.

8. The Orientals have had an exciting history. Going back thousands of years.

9. Dr. Power came for dinner last night. An excellent conversationalist.

10. I plan to buy a Flanders watch. Which will replace my Waltham.

4.5 Run-on Sentences

A **run-on sentence** is two or more sentences written as though they were one sentence. That is, the writer fails to use a period or other end mark at the end of each sentence.

RUN-ON	Years ago, driving was a pleasure there was less traffic.
CORRECT	Years ago, driving was a pleasure. There was less traffic.
RUN-ON	All waited excitedly then cheered the fiery launching.
CORRECT	All waited excitedly. They then cheered the fiery launching.

The most common run-on sentence error is the joining of two sentences by a comma. This error is called the **comma fault.**

COMMA FAULT	I decided not to go, it was too cold.
CORRECT	I decided not to go. It was too cold.
COMMA FAULT	The huge crane collapsed, it crushed a car below.
CORRECT	The huge crane collapsed. It crushed a car below.

In all of the foregoing examples, notice that the two sentences are closely related and that the second sentence begins with a personal pronoun: *it, he, she*. Watch for situations like these in your own writing and avoid the comma fault.

4.6 Avoiding the Run-on Sentence

There is no objection to joining two or more closely related statements into one sentence. In fact, it is often better to join them than to write them separately. There are three ways in which closely related sentences can be joined to make a compound sentence: (1) with a comma and a coordinating conjunction; (2) with a semicolon; (3) with a semicolon and a conjunctive adverb.

RUN-ON	Pat has two hobbies. He collects old coins, he saves match covers.
CORRECT	Pat has two hobbies. He collects old coins, and he saves match covers.
RUN-ON	Sandra did not choose her courses wisely, consequently her credits for college admission were inadequate.
CORRECT	Sandra did not choose her courses wisely; consequently, her credits for college admission were inadequate.
RUN-ON	We stayed up late watching the convention on television, then we could not get up in the morning.
CORRECT	We stayed up late watching the convention on television; then we could not get up in the morning.

Note: When a conjunctive adverb such as *consequently, however, moreover, therefore,* and *nevertheless* introduces a second main clause, it is preceded by a semicolon. Usually, it is followed by a comma.

Exercise A: Correct each of the following run-on sentences in one of these ways: (1) by using a period and a capital letter; (2) by using a semicolon; or (3) by using a comma and *and, but,* or *or.*

1. Only one paddle-wheel steamboat still operates on the Mississippi, she's the *Delta Queen.*

2. Something went wrong with the party, it just wasn't a success.

3. I overslept again, nobody woke me.

4. There must be a mistake, I didn't order any linoleum.

5. Don't be discouraged, Pete, try to look at the bright side.

6. Some of the guests sat on the patio, others sat on the grass.

7. I've been trying to close this suitcase, it's impossible.

8. I didn't finish the test, neither did Louise.

9. Mike tried to get up, he was simply unable to stand.

10. Laura and Lee were both being considered, Laura got the job.

11. The Peter Zenger case was a famous Colonial trial, it established freedom of the press.

12. First we went to Sequoia, then we visited King's Canyon.

13. Working on the farm hardened my muscles, it also softened my disposition.

14. Laughs drowned out the speaker, we could hardly hear him.

15. Hamilton wrote the Federalist Papers, he got help from Madison and Jay.

Exercise B: The first part of a sentence is given on each line below. Add a second main clause, beginning it with the word in parentheses at the end of the line. If the word is a conjunctive adverb, place a semicolon before it and a comma after it. If the word is a personal pronoun, use a semicolon or use a comma with a coordinating conjunction.

1. Some of the steak was burned (nevertheless)
2. Not only did they come for dinner (they)
3. That nail should be bent back (it)
4. I know Jacques Cousteau (in fact)
5. He was advised not to use colored stationery (he)
6. In high school she learned how to take notes (therefore)

7. I was amazed to learn that he played in a band (moreover)
8. The blizzard lasted all day (consequently)
9. Often people believe what they want to believe (they)
10. We had planned an all-day picnic (however)
11. No sign of the crew has been found (nevertheless)
12. The concert begins with an orchestral overture (then)

5.0 Agreement of Subject and Verb

In grammar the word *agreement* means "likeness." To make two words agree is to make them alike in some respect.

A common error in American speech is the failure to make subject and verb agree in number (*you was, we was, he don't*). Errors of agreement in speaking are sometimes difficult to avoid. In writing, however, these errors should be easier to avoid because the writer always has the time and the opportunity to revise his work before presenting it to a reader.

5.1 Subject-Verb Agreement in Number

There are two numbers in grammar: **singular** and **plural.** A word is singular in number if it refers to one person or thing. A word is plural if it refers to more than one person or thing.

Except for *be,* English verbs show a difference between singular and plural only in the third person and only in the present tense. The third person singular present form ends in *s.*

$$\left.\begin{matrix} \text{I} \\ \text{you} \\ \text{we} \\ \text{they} \end{matrix}\right\} \text{walk} \qquad \left.\begin{matrix} \text{he} \\ \text{she} \\ \text{it} \end{matrix}\right\} \text{walks}$$

The verb *be* presents several special problems in agreement. First, the second person pronoun *you* is always used with the plural form of the verb: *you are, you were.* Second, the difference between singular and plural is shown in the past tense as well as in the present tense.

SINGULAR	PLURAL	PRESENT TENSE	PAST TENSE
I *was*	we *were*	I *am*	we *were*
you *were*	you *were*	you *are*	you *were*
he, she, it *was*	they *were*	he, she, it *is*	they *were*

The most common errors with *be* are *you was, we was, they was.*

A singular verb is used with a singular subject.

A plural verb is used with a plural subject.

The subject determines whether the verb is singular or plural. The verb does not agree with any other part of the sentence.

> The theorem (singular) *is* clear.
> The theorems (plural) *are* clear.
>
> The coach (singular) *works* hard.
> The coaches (plural) *work* hard.

Note: A verb also agrees with its subject in *person*. When there are two or more subjects that differ in person, the verb agrees with the subject nearest to it.

> Neither Kent nor she *is* prepared.
> Either the Olsons or the Kellys *are* moving.

5.2 Plural Words Between Subject and Verb

The verb agrees only with its subject. Occasionally a word with a different number from that of the subject occurs between the subject and the verb. This word usually has no effect upon the number of the verb even though it is closer to the verb than the subject is.

> The *plane*, carrying fifty passengers, *is* landing.
>   (*plane* is the subject)
> *One* of the cars *needs* a battery.
>   (*One* is the subject.)
> The *candidates* for the Presidency *are* stumping the country.
>   (*candidates* is the subject.)
> The *uprisings* in small countries often *involve* violence.
>   (*uprisings* is the subject.)

The words *with, together with, along with, as well as* are prepositions. The objects of these prepositions have no effect upon the number of the verb.

> The trapped *miner*, together with the rescue squad, *is* safe.
>   (*miner* is the subject.)
> His facial *expression*, as well as his tone of voice,
>   *gives* him away.
>   (*expression* is the subject.)
> The *defendant*, with his lawyer, *enters* the courtroom.
>   (*defendant* is the subject.)

Exercise: Choose the right verb from those given in parentheses.

1. Our choir with its sixty voices (is, are) very popular.
2. A bunch of grapes often (makes, make) an attractive centerpiece for a dining table.
3. The bride, with her attendants, (is, are) coming down the aisle.
4. Jack, as well as Jean, (play, plays) in the All-State Orchestra.
5. The rugs in our house (have, has) been tacked down to prevent slipping.

6. One of the most daring feats (are, is) the fifty-foot dive into five feet of water.

7. They (were, was) relieved that I had decided to stay home.

8. The noise of so many typewriters (were, was) deafening.

9. The teacher, not the pupils, (was, were) doing most of the work.

10. Frank's knowledge of the Old Masters (are, is) remarkable.

11. Her choice of words (is, are) remarkable for a ten-year-old.

12. The code of ethics for our school (is, are) posted in the hall.

13. Nobody except members and their guests (are, is) allowed to attend the beach party.

14. Art, with some of his friends, (has, have) gone to band practice.

15. The bandleader, together with two arrangers, (is, are) preparing a Dixieland version of the tune.

5.3 Indefinite Pronouns

Some indefinite pronouns are always singular. Others are always plural. Some may be either singular or plural.

SINGULAR			PLURAL
each	everyone	anyone	several
either	everybody	someone	few
neither	no one	somebody	both
one	nobody		many

Each of the tests *is* challenging.
Neither of your parents *is* satisfied.
Everybody in the cast *was* applauded.
Several of the books *are* lost.
Few of the crowd *have* left.
Both of the contestants *were* congratulated.

SINGULAR OR PLURAL

some	all	most
none	any	

Some, all, most, none, and *any* are singular when they refer to a quantity. They are plural when they refer to a number of individual items.

> *Some* of the money *was* stolen. (quantity)
> *Some* of their answers *were* wrong. (number)
>
> *Most* of the sugar *is* gone. (quantity)
> *Most* of the survivors *were* dazed. (number)
>
> *All* of the food *was* donated. (quantity)
> *All* of the tools were expensive. (number)

None and *any* may be either singular or plural depending on whether the writer is referring to one thing or to several.

> None of the stories *was* true. (not one)
> None of the stories *were* true. (no stories)
>
> Any of these careers *is* rewarding. (any one)
> Any of these careers *are* rewarding. (any careers)

Exercise: Choose the right word from the two given.

1. Every one of the runners (was, were) given an award.
2. Most of the cabins in the camp (was, were) repainted.
3. Not one of my shipmates (were, was) able to swim.
4. Neither of these books (interests, interest) me.
5. One of the shyest of animals (are, is) the giraffe.
6. (Does, Do) either of you play a guitar?
7. Neither of the experiments (have, has) been completed.
8. Several of the roads (were, was) washed away by the flood.
9. None of the staff (was, were) at the meeting.
10. One of the best clarinetists (is, are) Benny Goodman.
11. Either of the motorboats (is, are) available.
12. Not one of the bulbs (were, was) working.
13. Everyone in the regiment (seem, seems) courageous in conversation.
14. Several of our best players (has, have) the flu.
15. Each of us (have, has) a perfect attendance record.

16. One of Arthur Miller's best plays (is, are) *The Crucible.*
17. Nobody in those communities (wants, want) a sales tax.
18. Anyone who wants to help collect funds (are, is) welcome.

5.4 Compound Subjects

Compound subjects joined by and are plural.*

Physical fitness and mental agility *are* necessary for athletes.

Singular words joined by or, nor, either-or, neither-nor to form a compound subject are singular.

Neither his sincerity nor his reliability *is* questioned.
Either their team or our team *has* a chance to win.
Ellen or Gordon *deserves* the scholarship.

When a singular word and a plural word are joined by or or nor to form a compound subject, the verb agrees with the subject that is nearer to it.

Neither the folk singers nor their agent *likes* the program.
   (*agent* is closer to the verb than *folk singers.*)
The management or the unions *are* making concessions.
Neither the actors nor the play *appeals* to anyone.

Exercise: Find the errors in subject-verb agreement in these sentences. Write the sentences correctly. Two of the sentences are correct.

1. The engine and one car was derailed.
2. Chuck or his brother are usually at the meetings.
3. Are your mother or your father going to the school play?
4. Neither the driver nor his passengers was expecting a bump.
5. The captain or the lieutenant is always on duty.
6. Neither the babies nor the baby sitter were happy.

* If the words making up the compound subject are habitually used together to refer to a single thing, the subject may be used with a singular verb: *bread and butter, macaroni and cheese,* etc.

7. Swimming and ice skating calls for good judgment.
8. Were either Josie or Emily there?
9. Either Joe or Henry are going to save a seat for you.
10. Neither illness nor financial loss seem to lessen her spirit.
11. Neither the Wilmington squad nor the Plainfield team were invited to the Holiday Tournament.
12. Either the meat or the potatoes are burning.
13. To travel and to write a novel is Judy's ambitions.
14. In the gymnasium is a basketball court and an indoor track.
15. Neither the Wayside Inn nor the House of the Seven Gables are in Boston.

5.5 Subject Following Verb

The most difficult agreement problem in speech arises when the subject follows the verb. The speaker must think ahead to the subject in order to decide whether the verb is to be singular or plural.

This problem arises in sentences beginning with *There* and *Here*. It also arises in questions beginning with *who, why, where, what, how.*

NONSTANDARD	Here's the tickets for the game.
STANDARD	Here *are* the tickets for the game.
NONSTANDARD	There's only two possible answers.
STANDARD	There *are* only two possible answers.
NONSTANDARD	Who's the officers in the debating club?
STANDARD	Who *are* the officers in the debating club?
NONSTANDARD	What's your reasons for refusing?
STANDARD	What *are* your reasons for refusing?
NONSTANDARD	Down the avenue *comes* the band and the color guard.
STANDARD	Down the avenue *come* the band and the color guard.

5.6 Predicate Words

The linking verb agrees with its subject, *not* with the predicate word.

| NONSTANDARD | New theories *is* not the answer. |
| STANDARD | New theories *are* not the answer. |

| NONSTANDARD | Joe's first love *are* sailboats. |
| STANDARD | Joe's first love *is* sailboats. |

| NONSTANDARD | Being accepted and registering *is* only the beginning. |
| STANDARD | Being accepted and registering *are* only the beginning. |

5.7 Don't and Doesn't

The word *does* and the contraction *doesn't* are used with singular nouns and with the pronouns *he, she,* and *it*. The word *do* and the contraction *don't* are used with plural nouns and with the pronouns *I, we, you,* and *they*.

DOES, DOESN'T	DO, DON'T
the boat does	the boats do
he doesn't	we don't
she doesn't	you don't
it doesn't	they don't

Exercise: Choose the right word from the two given in parentheses.

1. After the thaw (comes, come) the floods.
2. There (are, is) oranges in the refrigerator.
3. The fruit I like best (is, are) seedless grapes.
4. Why (don't, doesn't) he take the back road?
5. On the Fourth of July (comes, come) our annual picnic.
6. There (were, was) about fifty people present at the meeting.
7. (Where's, Where are) the instructions for assembling the folding chair?

8. Inside the cave (was, were) many stalactites.

9. For the person who wants to advance, (there's, there are) numerous evening courses.

10. There (were, was) four students from our school in the all-city orchestra.

11. On the bulletin board (was, were) a list of ten names.

12. (There's, There are) many things to consider in planning a garage sale.

13. My only regret (is, are) the days wasted.

14. A glass of lemonade and a comfortable chair on the back lawn (are, is) all I want.

15. There (seem, seems) to be a pile of letters in the box.

5.8 Collective Nouns

A collective noun names a group of people or things: *committee, flock, team, herd, crowd.*

When the writer refers to a group acting together as one unit, the collective noun is used with a singular verb. When the writer refers to the individuals in the group acting separately, one by one, the collective noun is used with a plural verb.

> The herd *heads* for the barn. (united action)
> The herd *were* running in all directions. (separate action)

> The team *was* the winner of the play-off. (united action)
> The team *were* voting for a captain. (separate action)

Once the writer decides whether the collective noun is a unit or a group of individuals, he must abide by his choice. Later in the same sentence he may not use a verb or pronoun of different number.

> NONSTANDARD The panel *has* (singular) submitted *their* (plural) findings.
> STANDARD The panel *has* submitted *its* findings.

5.9 Nouns Plural in Form

Some nouns are plural in form but are regarded as singular in meaning. That is, they end in *s* as most plural nouns do, but they do not stand for more than one thing: *news, mumps, measles*. Therefore, they are used with a singular verb.

There are many words ending in *-ics* that may be either singular or plural: *economics, athletics, civics, politics*. These words are singular when they are used to refer to a school subject, a science, or a general practice. When singular in meaning, they are not usually preceded by *the, his, some, all* and singular modifiers.

> Politics *is* a field for serious study. (singular)
> His politics *are* in no way suspect. (plural)
>
> Economics *appeals* to many college students. (singular)
> Our economics *are* endangered by right- and left-wing
>   extremists. (plural)
>
> Hysterics *are* sometimes halted by a slap in the face. (plural)
>
> News *is* a major attraction on television. (singular)
>
> Not all athletics *are* recommended for every student. (plural)

5.10 Titles and Groups of Words

The title of a book, play, story, film, musical composition, or other work of art is used with a singular verb. The name of a country is used with a singular verb. Such words, even though they may be plural in form, refer to a single thing.

> The Netherlands *has* a colorful history.
> *Leaves of Grass is* Walt Whitman's greatest achievement.
> The United States *is* a relatively young nation.
> *Amahl and the Night Visitors is* an opera in English.
> *The Potato-Eaters is* a famous painting by Van Gogh.

Any group of words referring to a single thing or thought is used with a singular verb.

> What our country needs *is* dedicated men and women.
> "Haste makes waste" *is* sound advice.

5.11 Words of Amount and Time

Words or phrases that express periods of time, fractions, weights, measurements, and amounts of money are usually regarded as singular.

> Two-thirds of the town's shelter needs *has* been supplied.
> Two yards of wire *is* enough to buy.
> Three dollars *seems* like a fortune to him.
> Fifty tons *is* the capacity of the freight train.
> Two hours *has* sometimes seemed like eternity.

If a prepositional phrase with a plural object falls between the subject and the verb, the verb is singular if its subject is considered as a single thing or thought. The verb is plural if its subject is felt to be plural.

> Ten pounds of potatoes *is* what we ordered.
>   (singular meaning)
> Ten crates of oranges *were* piled on the floor.
>   (plural meaning)

Exercise: Choose the right words from those given in the parentheses.

1. The man's ethics (were, was) questionable.
2. What our magazine needs (is, are) more contributors.
3. Mathematics (is, are) Ted's favorite subject.
4. What this theater needs (are, is) two new projectors.
5. Three fourths of our lawn (have, has) been reseeded.
6. About three-quarters of the oranges (was, were) moldy.

7. Over one-half of the employees in this town (commute, commutes).

8. The jury (were, was) arguing heatedly.

9. Two or three feet of twine (is, are) probably enough.

10. Five dollars (is, are) too much to pay for a parking place.

11. Measles (is, are) a contagious disease.

12. Three hundred miles (is, are) a good day's trip.

13. The team (are, is) getting into their new uniforms.

14. Politics (have, has) always been my father's main interest.

15. Two thousand pounds of paper (was, were) collected.

16. Ten weeks (are, is) the length of time required for the course.

17. *The Six Wives of Henry VIII* (was, were) shown on public television.

18. The Netherlands (has, have) just issued some interesting stamps.

19. Only one-half of the eligible voters (have, has) registered.

20. Ten cartons of canned goods (was, were) piled outside the store.

5.12   Relative Pronouns

A relative pronoun stands in place of its antecedent (the word to which it refers). If that antecedent is plural, the relative pronoun is plural. If the antecedent is singular, the relative pronoun is singular.

A relative pronoun agrees with its antecedent in number.

When a relative pronoun is used as subject of the verb in the relative clause, the number of the verb depends upon the number of the pronoun's antecedent.

These are the *researchers* (plural) who (plural) *are* testing our new products.

Chagall is the *artist* (singular) who (singular) *has* made a free-form mosaic in downtown Chicago.

Katie is one of those *members* who always *volunteer.*
(*members* always volunteer.)

He was the only *one* of the skin divers who *was* attacked
by a shark. (only *one* was attacked.)

The problem of agreement arises in the sentences above because there are two words, either of which *might* be the antecedent of the relative pronoun. Usually the meaning of the sentence shows which word *is* the antecedent.

Exercise: Choose the right word from those given in parentheses.

1. Debby is the only one of the contestants who (have, has) practiced.
2. This is one of the motorhomes that (is, are) fully equipped.
3. The eagle is one species which (nest, nests) in a high tree.
4. This is the first of several meetings that (is, are) to be held.
5. He is one of those teachers who (expect, expects) the best from each student.
6. We found one of the kittens that (were, was) lost.
7. Larry is one of those golfers who always (gets, get) a good score.
8. *The Canterbury Tales* is one of those books that (defy, defies) translation into modern English.
9. Of all the diseases that (attack, attacks) elderly persons, hardening of the arteries is the most common.
10. Peter is the only one of the boys who (has, have) a scholarship.

6.0 Pronoun Usage

In grammar, the term *inflection* has a special meaning. It means "a change in form to show how a word is used in a sentence." Prepositions, conjunctions, and interjections do not change their form. All other parts of speech do. Usually, the change in form is just a change in spelling:

NOUN:	boy	— boy's	— boys	— boys'
VERB:	walk	— walks	— walked	— walking
ADJECTIVE:	big	— bigger	— biggest	
ADVERB:	hard	— harder	— hardest	

Often, however, the change involves the use of a completely new word:

VERB:	go	— went	— gone
PRONOUN:	I	— me	— mine

Pronouns change their form in both ways. The changes in pronouns correspond to their use in sentences. These changes are called the **cases** of pronouns. The cases are the **nominative, possessive,** and **objective.**

You will recall that pronouns can be used in sentences in the following ways:

subject of the verb   object of a preposition
object of the verb   appositive
predicate pronoun   modifier

Nearly all pronouns change their form for different uses in the sentence. The indefinite pronouns have the least change. They change only when used as modifiers. As modifiers, they are in the possessive case:

POSSESSIVE

everyone — everyone's
nobody — nobody's
anyone — anyone's

The pronouns *this, that, these, those, which,* and *what* do not change their forms to indicate case. None of these has a possessive form.

The pronoun inflections are as follows:

NOMINATIVE	POSSESSIVE	OBJECTIVE
I	my, mine	me
we	our, ours	us
you	your, yours	you
he	his	him
she	her, hers	her
it	its	it
they	their, theirs	them
who	whose	whom
whoever	whosever	whomever

6.1 The Pronoun as Subject of a Verb

The nominative form of the pronoun is used as subject of a verb.

The problem of which pronoun form to use as subject arises

chiefly when the subject is compound. The compound subject may be made up of pronouns or of both nouns and pronouns.

To decide which pronoun form to use in a compound subject, *try each part of the subject by itself with the verb.*

> Dan and (I, me) bought the used car.
> (Dan bought; I bought, *not* me bought.)

> My parents and (they, them) are going to Florida.
> (My parents are going; they are going, *not* them are going.)

> Sally and (I, me) went fishing.
> (Sally went; I went, *not* me went.)

> We and (they, them) worked at the lodge.
> (We worked; they worked, *not* them worked).

The plural forms *we* and *they* sound awkward in many compounds. They can be avoided by recasting the sentence.

> AWKWARD   The referees and we have agreed.
> BETTER   We and the referees have agreed.
> AWKWARD   We and they prefer camping.
> BETTER   We all prefer camping.

6.2 The Predicate Pronoun

The verb *be* is a linking verb. It links the noun, pronoun, or adjective following it to the subject. A pronoun so linked is called a **predicate pronoun.**

The nominative pronoun form is used as a predicate pronoun.*

The problem of which form to use in a predicate pronoun occurs primarily after the verb *be*. The rule applies to all verb phrases built around forms of *be*: *could have been, can be, should be,* etc.

---

* Standard usage permits the exception in both speech and writing of *It is me.*

It was **I** who refused to go.
Could it have been **she** who won?
It must have been **they** who gave the signal.

Sometimes the nominative form sounds awkward. The awkwardness can be avoided by recasting the sentence.

AWKWARD   The co-editors are she and Toby.
BETTER   She and Toby are the co-editors.

AWKWARD   It was we who made the suggestion.
BETTER   We are the people who made the suggestion.

6.3   The Pronoun as Object of a Verb

The objective pronoun form is used as direct or indirect object.

The problem of which pronoun form to use as object of the verb arises chiefly when the object is compound. The compound object may consist of pronouns or of both nouns and pronouns.

To decide which pronoun form to use in a compound object, *try each part of the object by itself with the verb.*

Phil showed Tad and (I, me) how to complete
the experiment.
(showed Tad, showed me, *not* showed I)
The problem puzzled Yolande and (he, him).
(puzzled Yolande; puzzled him, *not* puzzled he)
Mrs. O'Leary told (they, them) and (we, us) about the
potato famine.
(told them, *not* told they; told us, *not* told we)
Do you want (she, her) and (I, me) to read the part?
(want her, *not* want she; want me, *not* want I)

Exercise A: Choose the right form from those given in parentheses.

1. The Ford Foundation gave (her, she) and her assistant
a grant.

2. I invited Barbara and (he, him) to the party.

3. Show Larry and (I, me) the map of Long Island.

4. The only returning staff members are Terry and (him, he).

5. (Her, She) and Tim will design the posters.

6. Are you implying that it was (him, he)?

7. If I were (she, her), I'd take a foreign language.

8. Wasn't it (he, him) who gave the nominating speech?

9. The workers rescued (him, he) and the other miners.

10. Lil and (he, him) have been studying the classical guitar.

11. The Rotary Club gave Wally and (I, me) partial scholarships.

12. The orthodontist examined Margaret and (he, him).

13. Mary and Carl are going to teach Dave and (I, me) to play racquetball.

14. What reason did (he, him) and the architect give?

15. Will you lend Marty and (I, me) your field glasses?

Exercise B: Choose the right form from those given in parentheses.

1. We saw Michelle and (he, him) at the Science Fair.

2. How many hamburgers did you and (he, him) eat?

3. If I were (her, she), I would apply for the job.

4. Why don't you meet Vinny and (me, I) on the first tee?

5. We suspect that it was (he, him) who played the practical joke.

6. They spotted (him, he) and his accomplice in the getaway car.

7. Will you help Bernie and (I, me) shovel the snow?

8. Neither the Gibsons nor (we, us) have been to Sea Island.

9. I couldn't believe that it was (them, they).

10. Wasn't it (she, her) who became a famous court reporter?

11. The tallest boys in the class are Sandy and (I, me).

12. It was either Eric or (he, him) who saw the eclipse.

13. Randy and (her, she) have been accepted at Gettysburg College.

14. The co-captains of the baseball team are Cliff and (him, he).

15. It was (they, them) who discovered the theft.

6.4   The Pronoun as Object of a Preposition

The objective pronoun form is used as object of a preposition.

The problem of which pronoun form to use as object of a preposition arises only when the object is compound. The compound object may consist of pronouns or of both nouns and pronouns.

To decide which pronoun to use in a compound object of a preposition, *try each part of the object by itself with the preposition.*

> The librarian is reserving a book for him and (I, me).
> (for him; for me, *not* for I)
> The news came as a surprise to Sheila and (we, us).
> (to Sheila; to us, *not* to we)
> I received letters from (they, them) and Nancy.
> (from them, *not* from they)

The preposition *between* causes especially noticeable errors in pronoun usage. Use only the objective pronoun forms after *between.*

> between you and him, *not* between you and he
> between him and me, *not* between he and I

6.5   The Pronoun Used with a Noun

In a construction such as *we girls* or *us boys,* the use of the noun determines the case form of the pronoun.

> We Republocrats are a united party.
> (*Republocrats* is the subject of *are;* the nominative
> pronoun is therefore required.)

> The lifeguard drove us surfers from the beach.
> (*surfers* is direct object of *drove;* the objective pronoun
> is therefore required.)

To decide which pronoun form to use in a construction such

as *we boys,* try the pronoun by itself with the verb or preposition.

> The warning was directed mainly to (we, us) boys.
> (to us, *not* to we)
> They allowed (we, us) amateur photographers to compete.
> (allowed us, *not* allowed we)
> (We, Us) flag bearers will lead the line of march.
> (We will lead, *not* Us will lead)

Exercise A: Choose the right form from those given in parentheses.

1. (We, Us) students in the Film Club elected officers.
2. Did you hear the news about (him, he) and his brother?
3. Between you and (I, me), I regret my hasty answer.
4. Why should there be a misunderstanding between Ed and (I, me)?
5. Nobody went to the bowling alley except Dennis and (I, me).
6. I wrote letters to Amelia and (he, him).
7. Mother has packed lunches for you and (me, I).
8. No one was there but Leonard and (he, him).
9. (We, Us) varsity players hope to get athletic scholarships.
10. The guidance counselor's reminders were intended for Diane and (me, I).
11. The snow sculptures were done by Meg, Tim, and (me, I).
12. None of (us, we) juniors was put on the team.
13. These plans must be kept a secret among (us, we) four.
14. Several of (us, we) sophomores were asked to serve refreshments.
15. The first passengers to board the plane were (us, we) four.

Exercise B: Choose the right form from those given in parentheses.

1. The coach praised (us, we) players for our teamwork.
2. Wait for Gus and (I, me) in the stationery store.
3. The gym was decorated by Pat, Sandra, and (I, me).
4. The prize money will be divided between you and (me, I).
5. Directly below Don and (I, me) sat the corps of cadets.

6. Who marches between you and (he, him) in the parade?
7. The florist talked to Peggy and (me, I) about the corsages.
8. Everyone has accepted the invitation except Grace and (me, I).
9. This matter concerns no one but you and (I, me).
10. To (us, we) substitutes, the regulars looked helpless.
11. A trust fund is being established for Kevin and (him, he).
12. The reprimand was intended for (us, we) girls.
13. There was not a scholarship winner among (us, we) applicants.
14. The screen version was written by the author and (he, him).
15. The police want (us, we) pedestrians to cross streets carefully.

6.6 Who and Whom in Questions

The pronouns *who* and *whom* are used as interrogative pronouns in questions. Within the question, the pronoun may be the subject of the verb, object of the verb, or object of a preposition.

In standard usage, the nominative form *who* is used as the subject of the verb. The objective form *whom* is used as the object of the verb or of a preposition. (In informal usage there is a growing tendency to use *who* at the beginning of a sentence, whether subject or object.)

The pronouns *whoever* and *whomever* follow the same rules as *who* and *whom*.

To decide which form to use, determine how the pronoun is used within the question.

To (who, whom) were you writing?
  (*whom* is correct as the object of the preposition *To.*)

(Who, Whom) gave you the information?
  (*Who* is correct as the subject of the verb *gave.*)

(Who, Whom) are you talking about?
  (*Whom* is correct as the object of the preposition *about.*)

(Who, Whom) was the teacher praising?
> (*Whom* is correct as the object of the verb *was praising.*)

(Who, Whom) found the missing child?
> (*Who* is correct as the subject of the verb *found.*)

Do not be misled by parenthetical expressions like *do you think, can you imagine, do you suppose, do you believe.* They do not determine the case of the interrogative pronoun.

Who do you think will win the championship?
> (*Who* is the subject of *will win.*)

Whom do you suppose he recommended?
> (*Whom* is the object of *recommended.*)

Who do you believe is the stronger leader?
> (*Who* is the subject of *is.*)

6.7 Who and Whom in Clauses

The pronouns *who* and *whom* may be used as relative pronouns to introduce adjective clauses or as introductory words in noun clauses. These pronouns also perform a job within the clause they introduce.

Whoever and *whomever* follow the same rules as *who* and *whom* when used as introductory words.

The use of the pronoun within the clause determines whether the nominative or objective form is used.

I did not see *whom Jed met.*
> (Noun clause; *whom* is the object of the verb *met* within the clause.)

(Our teachers are those *whom we should remember with gratitude.*
> (*whom* is the object of *should remember* within the clause.)

He is the President *who was not elected to office.*
   (*who* is the subject of the verb *was elected* within
   the clause.)

I wonder *who received the Nobel Prize.*
   (Noun clause; *who* is the subject of the verb *received*
   within the clause.)

He is the person *to whom you should write.*
   (*whom* is the object of the preposition *to* within
   the clause.)

Whoever writes the best essay will win a trip to Spain.
   (*Whoever* is the subject of the verb *writes* within the
   noun clause.)

Victory comes to *whoever stands for high principles.*
   (The noun clause is the object of the preposition *to*;
   whoever is the subject of the verb *stands* within
   the clause.)

It is important to cooperate with *whomever you elect.*
   (The noun clause is the object of the preposition *with*;
   whomever is the object of the verb *elect* within the clause.)

Exercise: Choose the right form from those given in parentheses.

   1. (Whom, Who) do you think will get the leading part?
   2. (Who, Whom) are those people touring the building?
   3. Robert Redford is the actor to (whom, who) she
was referring.
   4. (Whom, Who) are they sending to meet the train?
   5. Ms. Voss is the person from (whom, who) you must
get permission.
   6. (Who, Whom) do you believe is telling the truth?
   7. (Whoever, Whomever) applies must fill out an
application blank.
   8. (Who, Whom) do you suppose gave him the key
to the room?

9. He is a person (who, whom) I trust implicitly.
10. (Whom, Who) did you say was elected vice-president?
11. The lecturer varied his talk depending on (whom, who) was in the audience.
12. We must support (whomever, whoever) is elected.
13. The case will come up before (whomever, whoever) is presiding at this session.
14. I'll vote for (whoever, whomever) has the proper qualifications.
15. You may go with (whoever, whomever) you choose.
16. Give the message to (whomever, whoever) answers the telephone.
17. There is the boy about (who, whom) you were asking.
18. (Whom, Who) does the new baby look like?

6.8 Pronouns in Comparisons

Sometimes a comparison is made by using a clause that begins with *than* or *as*.

> Marie is more musical *than Lillian is.*
> I have as much will power *as anyone else has.*
> George trusts you more *than he trusts her.*

Sometimes the final clause in the comparison is left incomplete.

> Marie is more musical than Lillian (is).
> I have as much will power as anyone else (has).

To decide which pronoun form to use in an incomplete comparison, complete the comparison.

> Harry earned more credits than (I, me).
> (Harry earned more credits than *I earned.*)
> The noise scared Phyllis more than (I, me).
> (The noise scared Phyllis more than *it scared me.*)

6.9 Possessive Case with Gerunds

The possessive form of the pronoun is used when the pronoun immediately precedes a gerund.

All gerunds end in *-ing*, and they are all formed from verbs. The present participle also ends in *-ing*, and it, too, is formed from a verb. If the *-ing* word is used as a modifier, it is a participle. If it is used as a noun, it is a gerund.

The possessive form of the pronoun is used before a gerund. The nominative and objective forms are used before a participle.

I saw *him browsing* in the library.
   (*browsing* is a participle modifying *him*.)

The teacher discouraged *her daydreaming*.
   (*daydreaming* is a gerund, the object of the
   verb *discouraged*.)

His driving was terrifying to others.
   (*driving* is a gerund, the subject of the verb *was*.)

We watched *him driving* down the street.
   (*driving* is a participle modifying *him*.)

6.10 The Pronoun with Infinitives

The objective form of the pronoun is used as the subject, object, or predicate pronoun of an infinitive.

The clerk asked *me to complete* the form. (*me* is the subject
   of *to complete*.)

Ray urged *him to keep* the training rules. (*him* is the subject
   of *to keep*.)

They took *him* to be *me*. (*him* is the subject of *to be*, and
   me is the predicate pronoun following *to be*.)

His boss decided *to reward him*. (*him* is object of *to reward*.)

We expected the winner *to be her*.
   (*her* is the predicate pronoun following *to be*.)

6.11 The Pronoun as an Appositive

The form of a pronoun used as an appositive is determined by the use of the noun to which it is in apposition.

> Your representatives, *Hugh* and *I*, need your help.
> (*Hugh* and *I* are in apposition to *representatives*, which is the subject of *need*. Therefore, the nominative form of the pronoun is required.)

> For both of us, *Pam* and *me*, the victory was sweet.
> (*Pam* and *me* are in apposition to *us*, which is the object of the preposition *for*. Therefore, the objective form of the pronoun is required.)

> Uncle Gino offered the newcomers, *Sophia* and *him*, good jobs.
> (*Sophia* and *him* are in apposition to *newcomers*, which is the indirect object of *offered*. Therefore, the objective form of the pronoun is required.)

To determine which form of the pronoun to use in apposition, try the appositive by itself with the verb or preposition.

> The victims, Jerry and (her, she), were riding in the back seat.
> (Jerry and she were riding; *not* Jerry and her were riding.)

> The awards were given to the juniors, Willy and (she, her).
> (The awards were given to her, *not* to she.)

6.12 Compound Personal Pronouns

Compound personal pronouns are used only when their antecedents appear in the same sentence.

> STANDARD Jean bruised herself when she fell.
> STANDARD It is said that history often repeats itself.

NONSTANDARD	The decision is up to yourself.
STANDARD	The decision is up to you.
NONSTANDARD	The presents were for ourselves.
STANDARD	The presents were for us.

Exercise: Choose the standard form from those given in parentheses.

1. Dan and (myself, I) are in charge of the barbecue.
2. Mark is taller than (he, him).
3. Few girls are better dancers than (she, her).
4. Irene or (I, myself) will be glad to introduce you.
5. The baby sitter must have thought Linda to be (me, I).
6. My twin Jane is a few minutes older than (me, I).
7. (Our, Us) missing the bus caused considerable confusion.
8. Mr. Horn didn't like (our, us) playing catch on his front lawn.
9. I taught Mike and (she, her) how to ski.
10. We worried about (their, them) driving home in the storm.
11. The measuring stick proved that I was taller than (she, her).
12. Ginny and (I, me, myself) designed and built a rock garden.
13. Another girl and (myself, I) served as co-chairpersons.
14. The final decision must be made by you and (I, me).
15. The losers, Gerald and (she, her), were good sports.
16. We praised the losers, Gerald and (she, her).
17. Anyone as young as (her, she) cannot be admitted.
18. The prize was awarded jointly to Steve and (me, myself).
19. No one can make the decision but (him, himself).
20. Mr. Moss seemed even more frightened than (we, us).

6.13 Pronouns and Antecedents

A pronoun agrees with its antecedent in number, gender, and person.

Agreement in Number. If the antecedent of a pronoun is singular, a singular pronoun is required. If the antecedent is plural, a plural pronoun is required.

The indefinite pronouns that are singular in meaning cause the greatest difficulty. The following are referred to by singular pronouns.

anybody	either	neither	somebody
anyone	everybody	nobody	someone
each	everyone	one	

Each of the waiters wore *his* uniform.
Someone has not claimed *his* tickets.
Everyone indicated *his* preference.

Note: The general rule does not always apply to *everyone* and *everybody*. In certain sentences these words must be referred to by plural pronouns to make good sense.

POOR   *Everyone* stood when *he* saluted the flag.
BETTER *Everyone* stood when *they* saluted the flag.

POOR   *Everybody* cheered when *he* saw the President.
BETTER *Everybody* cheered when *they* saw the President.

In the sentences above, the verbs are all in the past tense. Verbs in the past tense do not change form to show singular and plural. If the verbs were in the present tense, the singular verb would be required and the singular personal pronouns (he, his) would also be required.

Everyone stands when *he* salutes the flag.
Everybody cheers when *he* sees the President.

Two or more singular antecedents joined by <u>or</u> or <u>nor</u> are referred to by a singular pronoun.

Either Joni or Rita will bring *her* guitar.
Neither Sal nor Ed has paid *his* fees.

Collective nouns may be referred to by either a singular or plural pronoun, depending upon the meaning intended.

The committee *has* announced *its* plans.
The committee *have* offered *their* services.

The indefinite pronouns <u>all</u>, <u>some</u>, <u>any</u>, and <u>none</u> may be referred to by either a singular or plural pronoun, depending upon the meaning intended.

Some of the workers *have* lost *their* jobs.

Some of the cider *has* lost *its* tang.

All the networks *are* holding over *their* best shows.

Note: In all of the foregoing examples, the collective nouns and indefinite pronouns are used as subjects. The number of the verb and the number of the pronoun referring to them must be the same.

NONSTANDARD	Some of the jury *are* giving *its* opinions.
STANDARD	Some of the jury *are* giving *their* opinions.
NONSTANDARD	None of the debaters *was* convincing *their* audience.
STANDARD	None of the debaters *were* convincing *their* audience.
STANDARD	None of the debaters *was* convincing *his* audience.

Agreement in Gender. Masculine gender is indicated by *he, his, him*. Feminine gender is indicated by *she, her, hers*. Neuter gender is indicated by *it* and *its*. These pronouns must be the same in gender as the word to which they refer.

The dog tried to slip out of *its* collar. (neuter)
The investigator submitted *his* report. (masculine)
The realtor was proud of *her* persuasive powers. (feminine)

When a singular pronoun must refer to both feminine and masculine antecedents, the phrase "his or her" is acceptable. It is, in fact, preferred by some people who wish to avoid what they consider to be sexist language.

STANDARD No parent wants to deny *his* child an education.

STANDARD   No parent wants to deny *his or her* child
an education.

Agreement in Person. A personal pronoun must be in the same person as its antecedent. The words *one, everyone,* and *everybody* are in the third person. They are referred to by *he, his, him, she, her, hers.*

NONSTANDARD   *One* should consider *your* hobbies an
investment for *you.*

STANDARD   *One* should consider *his* hobbies an
investment for *him.*

NONSTANDARD   *I* am convinced that the noise affects
your work.

STANDARD   *I* am convinced that the noise affects
my work.

Exercise: Find and correct the errors in agreement in these sentences. Make sure that both verb and pronoun are correct.

1. Neither Lori nor Bernadette have been in a play before.
2. One should try to profit by your mistakes.
3. Each of the caricatures were cleverly drawn.
4. No one likes to feel that they are being left out.
5. Has everyone made their contribution to the Red Cross?
6. Every citizen should exercise their right to vote.
7. Each of them hope to win an "Oscar."
8. I find that cooking is easy if you follow the directions.
9. Each of the thirty pupils raised their hand.
10. No one should try to be their own lawyer.
11. Everyone with a scientific mind should develop their potential.
12. Every player must provide their own shoes.
13. Has everyone done their homework?
14. If one doesn't know the road, you are apt to miss the cutoff.
15. We discovered that you couldn't hear a thing in the back row.

6.14   Indefinite Reference

To avoid any confusion for the reader, every personal pronoun should refer clearly to a definite antecedent.

INDEFINITE	A statement was issued, but *they* refused to comment on its significance.
BETTER	A statement was issued, but Pentagon officials refused to comment on its significance.
INDEFINITE	*It* says in the paper that Kennedy will run for the Senate.
BETTER	The *Times* announced that Kennedy will run for the senate.
INDEFINITE	I want to be a doctor because *it* is rewarding.
BETTER	I want to be a doctor because helping the sick is rewarding.
INDEFINITE	Be sure to see Rome if *they* include it in the itinerary.
BETTER	Be sure to see Rome if the agency includes it in the itinerary.

The pronoun *you* is sometimes used when it is not meant to refer to the person spoken to. The effect is usually confusing.

INDEFINITE	History shows that *you* must respect the dignity of the individual if *you* want *your* nation to survive.
BETTER	History shows that a nation's survival depends upon respect for the dignity of the individual.
INDEFINITE	In every contest *you* have specific rules to follow.
BETTER	In every contest there are specific rules to follow.

Exercise: Revise the sentences below to remove all indefinite references of pronouns.

1. It says on the radio that a hurricane is coming this way.
2. As soon as the President appeared, they played "Hail to the Chief."

3. In this exercise it says we are to eliminate indefinite references.

4. In the armed services they train you for a special skill.

5. At our school they don't have a golf team.

6. In pioneer days you had to make the trip on horseback.

7. It said on the base of the monument that the soldier is unknown.

8. In the pocket calculators, it takes little power to operate them.

9. In the "Help Wanted" section they tell you accountants are needed.

10. Gary wants to be a farmer because it keeps you close to the land.

6.15   Ambiguous Reference

The word *ambiguous* means "having two or more possible meanings." The reference of a pronoun is ambiguous if the pronoun may refer to more than one word. This situation arises whenever a noun or pronoun falls between the pronoun and its true antecedent.

AMBIGUOUS   Take the cap off the bottle and give *it* to me.
BETTER   After you take off the cap, give the bottle to me.

AMBIGUOUS   The Red Sox and Yanks were scoreless until *their* pitcher tired.
BETTER   The Red Sox and Yanks were scoreless until the Yankees' pitcher tired.

AMBIGUOUS   Mary told Kim that *she* was going to be a great movie star.
BETTER   Mary told Kim, "I am going to be a great movie star."

AMBIGUOUS   Bob told Harry that *his* dog was found.
BETTER   Bob told Harry, "Your dog was found."

Exercise: Revise the sentences below to remove all ambiguous pronoun references.

1. Before putting the car in the garage, Dad cleaned it out.
2. When the reporter interviewed the consumer expert, she was unfriendly.
3. Replace the gears on both engines and lubricate them.
4. Eleanor asked Kay if her cousin had arrived.
5. Mary gave Andrea a math problem she could not solve.
6. We took the screens from the windows and ran the hose over them.
7. Mike told his father that he had been worrying too much.
8. Nancy told Karen that her painting received the award.
9. Take the gloves off your hands and wash them.
10. Mrs. Olson told Ms. Maki that the account was hers.

6.16 Vague Reference

The words *this, which, that,* and *it* are sometimes used to refer to a preceding idea or chain of ideas. The reader is confused by this vague reference.

VAGUE	The organ accompaniment was very loud. *This* made the singer's voice almost inaudible.
BETTER	The singers's voice was almost inaudible because the organ accompaniment was very loud.
VAGUE	Computers are being used to help farmers get data on crop qualities and selling prices. *This* helps them to know which of their operations are profitable.
BETTER	The use of computers to get data on crop qualities and selling prices is helping farmers to know which of their operations are profitable.
VAGUE	Long summer vacations become boring for city high school students who are unemployed and cannot afford trips, *which* is one of the major causes of juvenile delinquency.

BETTER	One of the major causes of juvenile delinquency is the boredom of city high school students who are unemployed and cannot afford trips.
VAGUE	The weather was humid, and not a leaf was stirring on the few trees in the neighborhood. *It* made everyone irritable.
BETTER	Everyone was irritable because the weather was humid and not a leaf was stirring on the few trees in the neighborhood.

Exercise: Revise the sentences below to remove all vague references of pronouns.

1. They sailed constantly. It was their favorite pastime.
2. The mayor promised to pave the road out our way. It sounded good to us.
3. Tanya reads widely and enjoys it very much.
4. Don bought a 1970 Plymouth, which was a mistake.
5. We sat through the movie twice, which made us very late for supper.
6. We bought a house in Arizona. It was more than we had expected to pay.
7. Skilled labor is expensive, which makes Mr. Betts afraid to expand his business.
8. The school orchestra played each piece very well, and everyone liked it.
9. Trigonometry is a hard subject. This makes students take snap courses.
10. We took a left turn, which was a mistake.

Review Exercise: Revise the sentences below to remove vague, indefinite, or ambiguous reference of pronouns.

1. Linda and Lauri took turns playing her guitar.
2. At camp they expect you to eat in the lodge.
3. Jim told his brother that he was in the musical.
4. The permanent-press shirt looked smooth, which pleased me.
5. Mix the gravel with the cement when it is wet.

6. Mr. Cross walks haltingly, which makes him seem old.

7. We arrived at the theater early, which meant we had time to read the program.

8. They tell us that the fiords of Norway are majestic.

9. Poison ivy and poison oak can ruin your vacation, and it is a shame that everyone isn't immune to it.

10. Special tablets can give you immunity, and that is clinically safe.

11. Clare told her mother that she looked stunning in teal blue.

12. Our timetable was outdated, which made us miss the train.

13. They say that you should try barbecued fish fillets.

14. Spelunkers like to explore Southern caves, which has been done since the fourteenth century by American Indians in Kentucky.

15. Crossword puzzles increase our knowledge of words, for this is the way we became familiar with unusual words.

7.0 Adjective and Adverb Usage

Certain adverbs are formed by adding *-ly* to adjectives, as *sweet—sweetly*. The problem then is whether to use the modifier with or without the *-ly* ending after a verb.

7.1 Adverbs with Action Verbs

When a modifier comes just before an action verb, it is always an adverb, and no problem arises. When the modifier follows the action verb, there is a temptation to use an adjective rather than an adverb.

The problem is made more difficult by the fact that many adverbs have two forms, one with and the other without the *-ly* ending.

Shut the door *tight*.   Drive *slow*.   Don't play so *loud*.

All of the words used above as adverbs are also used as adjectives: a *loud* noise, a *slow* stream, a *sharp* knife, and so on.

Most of the words that may be either adjectives or adverbs are words of one syllable. Adjectives of two or more syllables almost never have the same form for the adverb.

> The *angry* mob shouted defiantly. (adjective)
> He swung the bag *angrily*. (adverb)
>
> *Careful* inquiries were made. (adjective)
> We proceeded *carefully*. (adverb)

After an action verb use the -ly form of the modifier if the modifier has two or more syllables.

7.2 Adjectives with Linking Verbs

Linking verbs are usually followed by adjectives rather than adverbs. The adjective is a predicate adjective and modifies the subject.

There is no problem with modifiers following the form of *be*, the most common linking verb. Most of the other linking verbs, however, may also be used as action verbs. As action verbs, they may be followed by adverbs.

> The ship *appeared suddenly* out of the fog.
>   (*appeared* is an action verb modified by an adverb.)
>
> The parents *appeared worried*.
>   (*appeared* is a linking verb followed by a
>   predicate adjective.)
>
> He *looked suspiciously* at my driver's license.
>   (*looked* is an action verb modified by an adverb.)
>
> Sean *looked ridiculous*.
>   (*looked* is a linking verb followed by a
>   predicate adjective.)

The following verbs are linking verbs. Most of them may also be used as action verbs.

look	appear	smell	stay	grow	seem
sound	feel	taste	remain	become	

To decide whether a verb is used to link or to show action, try substituting a form of *be*. If the sentence still makes sense, the verb is a linking verb.

> The salesperson *seemed* (confident, confidently).
> (*The salesperson seemed confidently* does not make sense. *The salesperson was confident* makes sense; *seemed* is a linking verb here.)

> The salesperson *looked* (inquiring, inquiringly) at the customer.
> (*was* does not make sense with either modifier; *looked* is an action verb here.)

Exercise A: Choose the standard form from those given in parentheses.

1. *Watership Down* is a (real, really) interesting novel.
2. Matt plays too (rough, roughly) with the little children.
3. I worked (steadily, steady) for five hours.
4. The children looked (envious, enviously) at her brother's cotton candy.
5. The hikers grew (uneasy, uneasily) as nightfall approached.
6. Be sure to measure the ingredients very (careful, carefully).
7. The cherry pie smelled (delicious, deliciously) in the oven.
8. His voice sounded (harshly, harsh) on the telephone.
9. This year Bill's marks have improved (considerable, considerably).
10. Laura looks (beautiful, beautifully) with long hair.

Exercise B: Decide whether the italicized modifier is standard or nonstandard. If it is nonstandard, substitute the standard form.

1. Ted has been feeling *strange* all afternoon.
2. The lemonade tasted *sour*.
3. The whole story sounds *peculiar*.

4. Be sure to put the paint on *even.*
5. Pick the baby up as *gentle* as you can.
6. This hot chocolate tastes too *sweet.*
7. I couldn't hear the signals *clear* enough.
8. The children remained *silent* throughout the concert.
9. Bruce cleared the hurdle *easy.*
10. Mr. Hale sounds *abrupt* when he meets people.

7.3 This—These; That—Those

This and *that* modify singular words. *These* and *those* modify plural words. The words *kind, sort,* and *type* require a singular modifier.

NONSTANDARD   *These* kind sold immediately.
STANDARD   *This* kind sold immediately.

NONSTANDARD   *These sort* of games are tiring.
STANDARD   *This sort* of game is tiring.

7.4 Them—Those

Those may be either a pronoun or an adjective. *Them* is always a pronoun and never an adjective.

NONSTANDARD   Did you enjoy *them* stories?
STANDARD   Did you enjoy *those* stories? (adjective)

7.5 Bad—Badly

In standard usage, *bad* is always used after linking verbs.

He felt bad. (*not* he felt badly)
He looked bad.
The water tastes bad.
The news sounds bad.

7.6 Good—Well

Good is used only as an adjective to modify nouns and pronouns.

Well is an adjective when it means "in good health, of good appearance, or satisfactory." Well is used as an adverb to modify an action verb when it means that the action was performed properly or expertly.

> The patient looks *well* today. (adjective)
> The scarf looks *well* with that suit. (adjective)
> The lawn mower is working *well* now. (adverb)

7.7 Fewer—Less

Fewer is used to describe things tht can be counted. Less refers to quantity or degree.

> Careful driving results in *fewer* accidents.
> Use *less* heat for that dish.
> I have *less* respect for him now.

Exercise: Decide whether the italicized words are standard or nonstandard usage. Substitute a standard form for each nonstandard one.

1. Jeff feels *good* about winning the essay contest.
2. I did *well* in the history test.
3. The injured skier needed help *bad*.
4. If you check your answers, you will have *less* errors.
5. I don't like *that* sort of shoe.
6. *These* kind is much more practical.
7. This recipe requires *less* milk and *less* eggs.
8. Did you eat *well* at camp?
9. I'd like to have one of *them* CB radios.
10. That tie looks *well* with your jacket.
11. I don't play chess very *good*.

12. Nowadays there are *fewer* circuses than there used to be.
13. *Those* kinds of remarks never help.
14. *Those* kind of camera is very expensive.
15. Where did you get *them* kittens?
16. Our car runs *well* since we had the engine overhauled.
17. *These* kind of exercise is easy to do.
18. *Them* foreign cars are economical to operate.

7.8 Comparative and Superlative

The comparative form is used to compare two things; the superlative is used in comparing more than two.

STANDARD	We tried both lobsters and fried clams, but we liked lobsters better. (*not* best)
STANDARD	Of her five major subjects, Penny likes history best. (*not* better)
STANDARD	I could have gone by plane or by ship, but I decided that flying was more exciting. (*not* most)

7.9 The Double Comparison

The comparative form of a modifier is made either by adding -er or by using *more*. It is nonstandard to use both.

The superlative form of a modifier is made either by adding -est or by using *most*. It is nonstandard to use both.

NONSTANDARD	We had a much more easier time with that test.
STANDARD	We had an easier time with that test.
NONSTANDARD	Speak in a more softer tone.
STANDARD	Speak in a softer tone.
NONSTANDARD	It was the most funniest movie I ever saw.
STANDARD	It was the funniest movie I ever saw.

7.10 Illogical Comparisons

The word *other*, or the word *else*, is required in comparisons of an individual member with the rest of the group.

ILLOGICAL Our school won more scholarships than any school in the city. (Our school is also in the city.)

CLEAR Our school won more scholarships than any *other* school in the city.

ILLOGICAL Angela is as bright as anyone on the debating team.

CLEAR Angela is as bright as anyone *else* on the debating team.

The words *than* or *as* are required in a compound comparison.

ILLOGICAL The begonia is as healthy if not healthier than the cactus.

CLEAR BUT AWKWARD The begonia is as healthy as, if not healthier than the cactus.

BETTER The begonia is as healthy as the cactus, if not healthier.

ILLOGICAL This cake is as good if not better than the one I baked for the County Fair.

CLEAR This cake is as good *as*, if not better than the one I baked for the County Fair.

ILLOGICAL We had as many opportunities to score if not more than our opponents.

CLEAR We had as many opportunities to score *as*, if not more than our opponents.

Both parts of a comparison must be stated completely if there is any chance of its being misunderstood.

CONFUSING I admire her more than Joan.

CLEAR I admire her more than Joan *does*.

CLEAR I admire her more than *I admire* Joan.

CONFUSING	Central defeated Southern worse than Northeast.
CLEAR	Central defeated Southern worse than Northeast *did*.
CLEAR	Central defeated Southern worse than it *defeated* Northeast.
ILLOGICAL	The training of a nurse is longer than a technician.
CLEAR	The training of a nurse is longer than *that* of a technician.
BETTER	A nurse's training is longer than a technician's *is*.

Exercise: Revise the following sentences to make the comparisons clear.

1. You should try to make your explanation more clearer.
2. Vicki beat me in tennis worse than Chuck.
3. Who is the oldest, you or Frank?
4. Mrs. Frisbee likes picnics more than her husband.
5. This model is probably as expensive if not more expensive than that one.
6. Of the two candidates, Toni seems the most likely to win.
7. This dessert is more tastier.
8. I like Susan better than Charlotte.
9. W. Somerset Maugham's *Of Human Bondage* is as good or better than any of his other books.
10. It was the most saddest movie I had ever seen.
11. Which of the two hats do you think is the most appropriate?
12. Of the two exercises, the second is easiest.
13. I like professional hockey better than Harry.
14. The United States is bigger than any country in the Americas.
15. Which of these two trees do you think is most healthy?
16. Strawberries are much more cheaper this week than last.
17. Diamonds are harder than any substance.

7.11   The Double Negative

A double negative occurs when a negative word is added to a statement that is already negative. The double negative is nonstandard usage.

NONSTANDARD   'He didn't ask me nothing.
STANDARD   He didn't ask me anything.

NONSTANDARD   Clerks don't have no homework.
STANDARD   Clerks don't have any homework.

Hardly or *barely*, used with a negative word, is nonstandard.

NONSTANDARD   There wasn't hardly any rain in May.
STANDARD   There was hardly any rain in May.

NONSTANDARD   The award didn't scarcely cover his expenses.
STANDARD   The award scarcely covered his expenses.

Exercise: These sentences cover all of the problems of adjective and adverb usage in this section. Choose the standard form from those in parentheses.

1. Marlene (can, can't) hardly keep up with her work.
2. You (will, won't) get hardly any bad effects from this medicine.
3. The inland route is longer, but it is (safer, more safer).
4. I (can't, can) scarcely believe that such a terrible thing has happened.
5. Please talk as (quiet, quietly) as possible.
6. You'll stay in good condition if you exercise (regular, regularly).
7. We haven't had (any, no) warm weather since August.
8. Do you feel (confident, confidently) about today's game?
9. He (didn't have, had) hardly any money with him.
10. The river has risen (considerable, considerably) during the night.
11. Little Timmy (could, couldn't) scarcely keep his eyes open.

12. Are (them, those) portable typewriters heavy?
13. The hole should be a little (wider, more wider).
14. Instant oatmeal tastes surprisingly (well, good).
15. He ran down the hill as (quick, quickly) as he could.
16. This coat material feels (rough, roughly).
17. Would you like to hear a (really, real) interesting story?
18. Of the boys in the glee club, Ben has the (better, best) voice.

8.0   Verb Usage

Most of the several thousand English verbs cause no problems of usage at all. They are **regular verbs.** That is, the past tense is formed by adding *-ed* or *-d* to the present, and the past participle is the same as the past tense form:

PRESENT	PAST	PAST PARTICIPLE
appear	appear*ed*	appear*ed*
listen	listen*ed*	listen*ed*
use	use*d*	use*d*

There are about sixty commonly used verbs, however, whose past forms do not follow this pattern. They are **irregular verbs.** The most commonly used verbs, *be* and *have,* not only form the past tenses irregularly but change from person to person in the present tense: *I am, you are, he is, I have, he has.*

8.1   The Past Forms

The main problem with irregular verbs is the choice between the past form and the past participle form. These are two of the **principal parts** of every verb. (See Section 1.3.) All forms of any verb are made from the principal parts. Since they are always given in the same order in dictionaries and reference books, learning them in that order will make usage choices easier.

The past tense form is used alone. The past participle form is used with forms of *be* or *have.*

> The hunter *shot* the bear. (past)
> The stores *were* all *closed*. (past participle with form of *be*)
> My father *had* already *written*. (past participle with form of *have*)

There are five groups of irregular verbs.

Group 1. The easiest of the irregular verbs are those that have the same form in all principal parts.

PRESENT	PAST	PAST PARTICIPLE
burst	burst	burst
cost	cost	cost
hit	hit	hit
hurt	hurt	hurt
put	put	put
set	set	set

Group 2. A second group that causes little difficulty is composed of verbs that have the same form for the past and the past participle.

PRESENT	PAST	PAST PARTICIPLE
bring	brought	brought
catch	caught	caught
dive	dived *or* dove*	dived
fight	fought	fought
flee	fled	fled
fling	flung	flung
get	got	got *or* gotten
lead	led	led
lend	lent	lent

* Where two forms are given, both are standard usage, but the first is more common.

PRESENT	PAST	PAST PARTICIPLE
lose	lost	lost
say	said	said
shine	shone	shone
sit	sat	sat
sting	stung	stung
swing	swung	swung

Exercise A: In the sentences below, the present form of the verb is given in parentheses. Substitute either past or past participle, whichever the sentence requires.

1. The mayor was (sting) by the unexpected criticism.
2. Charles Evans Hughes (lose) the Presidency by only 23 electoral votes.
3. Upon raising the curtain, the audience (burst) into applause.
4. Unexpected frosts have (cost) fruit growers millions of dollars.
5. No one was (hurt) in the collision.
6. The epidemic has already (spread) to neighboring towns.
7. The election of 1860 (bring) Lincoln to the White House.
8. The villagers (flee) before the rising waters.
9. The shortstop (catch) the ball and tagged the runner.
10. The hurricane had (fling) street signs to the pavement.
11. Bernstein (lead) the orchestra in an all-Beethoven program.
12. The bank (lend) Dad some money to redecorate the house.
13. The old farmer made hay while his son (shine) on the gridiron.
14. The large urban vote (swing) the election.
15. Tony (bring) me an Italian newspaper.

Exercise B: Choose the standard form from those in parentheses.

1. Ronnie blew up the balloon until it (bust, busted, burst).
2. Paul has already (caught, catched) the legal limit of trout.
3. Alex (lent, lended) me his power saw.
4. The speedboat (swang, swung) around the buoy.
5. Dad has (losed, lost) his automobile insurance policy.

6. The cadets (flung, flang) their caps into the air.
7. The hornet (stang, stung) Eleanor on the elbow.
8. Rescuers (led, leaded) the dazed miners out of the shaft.
9. Aunt Marion (brang, brought) back slides of her trip.
10. The sun has not (shined, shone) for over a week.
11. The campers (fleed, fled) as the river began to rise.
12. Our trip (cost, costed) more than we had anticipated.

Group 3. Another group of irregular verbs adds **n** or **en** to the past form to make the past participle.

PRESENT	PAST	PAST PARTICIPLE
bear	bore	borne*
beat	beat	beaten
bite	bit	bitten
break	broke	broken
choose	chose	chosen
freeze	froze	frozen
speak	spoke	spoken
steal	stole	stolen
swear	swore	sworn
tear	tore	torn
wear	wore	worn

Exercise A: Choose the standard form from those in parentheses.

1. Somebody has (broke, broken) Stevie's toy pickup truck.
2. Jamie's dump truck was (broke, broken) also.
3. The company (beared, bore) all of the expenses of his trip.
4. Has the team (chose, chosen) its captain yet?
5. The Supreme Court justices (wore, weared) their black robes.
6. The eggs were (beat, beaten) separately to make a fluffy omelet.
7. Meat that has been thawed should not be (froze, frozen) again.

* Note that *borne* retains the final *e*.

8. I could have (sweared, swore, sworn) that there were two people in that car.

9. Have you (broken, broke) your appointment with the dentist?

10. Allen has (chose, chosen) *The Bermuda Triangle* for his report.

11. The patient (bore, beared) traces of deep suffering.

12. Uncle Ben wishes he had (chose, chosen) a different profession.

13. Several diamond rings have been (store, stolen) from Ms. Van Hoot's apartment.

14. I have just (tore, torn) my new overcoat on a nail.

15. The witness was promptly (swore, sworn) in.

16. The insect repellent kept us from being (bit, bitten) by mosquitoes.

17. Sue has hardly (spoke, spoken) to me since my arrival.

18. We have (beat, beaten) Dover only once in the last ten years.

19. Marsha (teared, tore) the letter up and threw it in the fire.

20. Have you ever (spoke, spoken) in assembly?

Exercise B: The present form of the verb is given. Substitute past or past participle, which ever the sentence requires.

1. Thousands panicked when the stock market (break).

2. What book have you (choose) for your report?

3. You should have (wear) your woolen mittens.

4. Phil has (steal) more bases than any other player on the team.

5. Carol has (break) the school record for the high jump.

6. The Red Sox have finally (beat) the Yankees.

7. The rock (tear) a hole in the bottom of the canoe.

8. The Seminoles (swear) to avenge the death of their chief.

9. The milk on the porch has (freeze) solid.

10. The carpet on the stairs was (wear) out.

11. The committee has not yet (choose) a date for the dinner.

12. The candidate (speak) earnestly and persuasively.

13. The campers were badly (bite) by mosquitoes.

14. Leslie was (beat) badly in the quarter-finals.
15. The doctor thinks Andy's wrist is (break).
16. Have you ever (speak) in public?
17. The steak in the refrigerator was (freeze) solid.
18. Even our greatest President (bear) constant criticism.
19. Our mail carrier has never been (bite) by a dog.
20. We have already (beat) Springfield once this year.

Group 4. Another group of irregular verbs is alike in changing the middle vowel from **i** in the present, to **a** in the past, and to **u** in the past participle. Memorize these seven verbs as a unit. They are the only verbs to follow this pattern.

PRESENT	PAST	PAST PARTICIPLE
begin	began	begun
drink	drank	drunk
ring	rang	rung
sing	sang	sung
sink	sank *or* sunk	sunk
spring	sprang *or* sprung	sprung
swim	swam	swum

Exercise: The present form is given in parentheses. Substitute the past or past participle, whichever the sentence requires.

1. I (ring) for the nurse.
2. I (drink) the cocoa even though it was stone cold.
3. Andrew Carnegie (begin) his career as a bobbin boy in a factory.
4. She had (sing) at La Scala before coming to the Metropolitan.
5. The fisherman (sink) a line through the hole in the ice.
6. They turned back when their rowboat (spring) a leak.
7. We (drink) cool spring water while camping in Colorado.
8. When Claire arrived, the examination had already (begin).
9. Have you ever (drink) papaya juice?
10. All over the yard, dandelions had (spring) up.
11. The *Graf Spee* was (sink) by her own crew.

12. The telephone (ring) once and then stopped.

13. The role of Carmen has been (sing) by many famous opera stars.

14. Skin divers (swim) down to inspect the sunken ship.

15. The *Edmond Fitzgerald* (sink) in the tumultuous waters of Lake Superior.

16. When Johnson missed the field goal, our hearts (sink).

17. The men (spring) out of their bunks when the captain entered.

18. We must have (drink) a whole case of Pepsi.

19. At the three-quarter mark, the Navy crew had (begin) to tire.

20. Cheryl (swim) in the 50-yard free-style event.

21. Cheers (ring) out when the Penn quarterback fumbled the ball.

22. Have you ever (drink) goat's milk?

23. While the crowd held its breath, Jack Nicklaus (sink) the putt.

24. A mouse had taken the cheese and (spring) the trap.

25. The players (drink) a toast to the winning pitcher.

Group 5. Another group of irregular verbs is alike in making the past participle from the present form rather than from the past form.

PRESENT	PAST	PAST PARTICIPLE
blow	blew	blown
come	came	come
do	did	done
draw	drew	drawn
drive	drove	driven
eat	ate	eaten
fall	fell	fallen
give	gave	given
go	went	gone
grow	grew	grown
know	knew	known
ride	rode	ridden

PRESENT	PAST	PAST PARTICIPLE
rise	rose	risen
run	ran	run
see	saw	seen
shake	shook	shaken
slay	slew	slain
take	took	taken
throw	threw	thrown
write	wrote	written

Exercise A: Choose the standard form from those in parentheses.

1. Most of the icicles have (fell, fallen) to the ground.
2. Alan has (gone, went) to the basement for the brace and bit.
3. You should have (gave, given) the matter more thought.
4. I had never (ate, eaten) fried clams before.
5. The officials have always (run, ran) this town efficiently.
6. I (seen, saw) an unusual television play last night.
7. This letter must have been (wrote, written) on a moving bus.
8. Many celebrities had (came, come) for the opening night performance.
9. The catcher (throwed, threw) the ball into center field.
10. The wind had (shook, shaken) all the apples from the tree.
11. The class has (took, taken) their lunch with them.
12. I wonder who has (took, taken) my scarf.
13. The wind (blew, blowed) down several trees last night.
14. This year all the birthdays in our family have (fell, fallen) on weekends.
15. The teller was badly (shook, shaken) by the attempted robbery.
16. Sally must have (knowed, known) where we were going.
17. The President must have (shook, shaken) hands with a thousand people.
18. Who (did, done) the illustrations for this book?
19. Stocks have (rose, risen) for the tenth consecutive day.
20. Have you ever (ridden, rode) in a helicopter?

Exercise B: The present form is given in parentheses. Substitute the past or past participle, whichever the sentence requires.

1. I (see) the new high school yesterday.
2. The soldiers stood at attention while taps was (blow).
3. Amy and Fran have (drive) across the continent in six days.
4. I (do) the sanding job in two hours.
5. Mr. Cross (give) me his entire coin collection.
6. We have (grow) our own vegetables for years.
7. The judge (throw) the case out of court.
8. Betty (shake) the mop vigorously.
9. The next census will be (take) in 1980.
10. The price of butter has (rise) sharply.
11. Have you ever (eat) Philadelphia scrapple?
12. The new Broadway musical (draw) capacity audiences.
13. Charlie has (write) a letter to *The Chicago Tribune*.
14. A stranger (come) up to us and asked for directions.
15. I should have (known) the stores would be closed.
16. Angrily the catcher (throw) his mask to the ground.
17. Bart would have (go) if he had had a coat and tie.
18. The salesperson (do) his best to sell Dad some insurance.
19. Cindy lectured while Chuck (run) the projector.
20. The tide has already (rise) two feet.

Exercise C: The present form is given. Substitute the past or past participle as the sentence may require.

1. The Yale goal post was (take) down by the happy Harvard rooters.
2. You must have (know) I was coming.
3. These orchids were (grow) in Hawaii.
4. The pitcher quickly (throw) the ball to first base.
5. Mrs. Wharton has (go) to northern Michigan for the summer.
6. A heavy blanket of snow had (fall) during the night.
7. I had never (eat) fried shrimp before.
8. It had (take) all morning to pack the car for the trip.
9. The ink had (run) down the length of the paper.

10. The mayor was (shake) by the news of his defeat.
11. Have you (ride) in Fred's new Chevette?
12. The referee (blow) the whistle when I stepped out of bounds.
13. I (do) the best job I could with that old lawn mower.
14. Over 100,000 people (come) to see the game.
15. Six fire engines were (draw) up in a neat row.
16. One of the guards was (slay) in the prison riot.
17. The firemen scrambled when the siren (blow).
18. Who (draw) this sketch?
19. Some of the girls have (go) to the Museum of Natural History.
20. In five minutes she had (draw) a sketch of Ann's profile.

8.2 Problem Pairs of Verbs

Three pairs of verbs are often confused because the meanings of each pair are closely related. They are related, but they are not identical. To use these verbs correctly, it is important to keep their meanings distinct.

Lie and lay. The verb *lay* means "to put or place something." The verb *lie* has many meanings, all of them having in common the idea of "being in a horizontal position, or to remain, or to be situated."*

Lie is always an intransitive verb. It never has an object. *Lay* is a transitive verb. It almost always has an object. The principal part of these verbs are as follows:

PRESENT	PAST	PAST PARTICIPLE
lay	laid	laid
lie	lay	lain

* There is a homonym meaning "to tell an untruth." The principal parts of this verb are *lie, lied, lied*.

Sit and set. The verb *sit* usually means "to rest with the legs bent and the back upright," but there are many other related meanings. The verb *set* means "to put or place something."

Sit is an intransitive verb; it never has an object. *Set* is a transitive verb; it almost always has an object. The principal parts of the verbs are as follows:

PRESENT	PAST	PAST PARTICIPLE
sit	sat	sat
set	set	set

Rise and raise. The verb *rise* means "to go to a higher position." The verb *raise* means "to lift to a higher position."

Rise is intransitive; it never has an object. *Raise* is transitive; it almost always has an object. Things *rise* by themselves; they are *raised* by something else. The principal parts of these verbs are as follows:

PRESENT	PAST	PAST PARTICIPLE
rise	rose	risen
raise	raised	raised

Note: It is very difficult to make any general statements about English usage that will hold without exception. There are exceptions to the statements given above about the three pairs of verbs:

> The sun *sets* early in the winter. (intransitive)
> The mixture will *set* in an hour. (intransitive)
> *Sit* the patient in the chair. (transitive)
> The hens are *laying* well. (intransitive)

Exercise A: Choose the standard form from those in parentheses.

1. New London (lies, lays) midway between New York and Boston.
2. Stan told the dog to (lie, lay) down.

3. The deserted bus was (lying, laying) in the ditch.

4. The foreign ministers (lay, laid) the groundwork for the summit conference.

5. Charlie is (lying, laying) in the hammock.

6. The motion was (laid, lain) on the table.

7. The book that I (laid, lay) on the table has disappeared.

8. Your wallet is (lying, laying) on the floor.

9. Margaret (lay, laid) the silverware on the table.

10. Grandmother has gone upstairs to (lie, lay) down.

11. The pup is (laying, lying) the bone under the table.

12. The pup is (laying, lying) under the table.

13. Have the foundations been (laid, lain) for the new school?

14. I was (laying, lying) down when the Russells came.

15. The group (lay, laid) their plan before the City Council.

16. My purse had (laid, lain) in the breezeway all night.

17. The injured worker (lay, laid) unconscious on the ground for several minutes.

18. At the foot of Mt. Vesuvius (lies, lays) Naples.

Exercise B: Choose the standard form from those in parentheses.

1. Peggy (raised, rose) quickly and answered the door.

2. The curtain was (rising, raising) as we reached our seats.

3. What time did the sun (raise, rise) this morning?

4. The elderly man (raised, rose) from his chair with difficulty.

5. The nurse (rose, raised) the patient's pillow.

6. Has the water (raised, risen) at all since last night?

7. The sun had not yet (risen, raised) above the horizon.

8. Gales of laughter (raised, rose) from the audience.

9. I am glad that these questions have been (raised, risen).

10. The supermarket will (rise, raise) the price of dairy products next week.

11. Commuter fares have (risen, raised) substantially in recent years.

12. Will everyone in favor please (rise, raise)?

13. Will everyone in favor please (rise, raise) his or her hand?

14. A heavy cloud of black smoke was (rising, raising) from the oil refinery.
15. The officers saluted as the flag was (raised, risen).
16. Our spirits (raised, rose) when our team tied the score.
17. The price of lumber has (raised, risen) sharply again.
18. Everyone (raised, rose) when the team trotted onto the field.
19. The rent cannot be (rose, raised) more than five percent.
20. Brenda's cake failed to (rise, raise).

Exercise C: Choose the standard form from those given in parentheses.

1. (Sit, Set) in the armchair if you wish.
2. I'll (set, sit) the tray on your lap.
3. Come and (sit, set) by the fire.
4. Please (set, sit) this vase on the desk.
5. We have (set, sat) in the sun for over an hour.
6. Just (sat, set) your glass on the trap.
7. May I (set, sit) this wet umbrella in the kitchen?
8. From where I was (setting, sitting), it looked like a touchdown.
9. Bert was too nervous to (sit, set) still.
10. Barbara (sat, set) the lantern inside the tent.
11. The actress was (sitting, setting) her deck chair in the sun.
12. The actress was (sitting, setting) in the sun.
13. Everyone (sat, set) quietly during Marie's talk.
14. Just (set, sit) the trunk in the hall.
15. How long have these cartons of milk been (setting, sitting) on the step?

8.3 Distinguishing Two Actions in the Past

In telling of things that have happened in the past, it is sometimes necessary to tell of one thing that happened before another.

The past perfect tense is used to tell about the earlier of two past happenings.

	EARLIER	LATER
STANDARD	I *had swum* to the shore before the storm broke.	

	LATER	EARLIER
STANDARD	I understood that you *had eaten* earlier.	

NONSTANDARD I told the printer last week that I *have canceled* the order.

STANDARD I told the printer last week that I *had canceled* the order.

NONSTANDARD The paper stated that the candidate already *conceded.*

STANDARD The paper stated that the candidate *had* already *conceded.*

8.4 The Tense of Infinitives

The perfect infinitive (see Section 1.11) is used to show an action earlier than that of the main verb. The present infinitive is used to show action at the same time as that of the main verb, or later.

I am sorry *to have offended* you. (earlier time)
I was sorry *to have offended* you. (The perfect infinitive shows the earlier of the two past times.)
We are happy *to welcome* you. (same time)
We were happy *to welcome* you. (same time)
Mom plans *to leave tonight.* (later time)

The present infinitive is used if the main verb contains the word have.

NONSTANDARD She would have preferred *to have gone* alone.
STANDARD She would have preferred *to go* alone.
(same time)

STANDARD	She would prefer (now) *to have gone* alone. (earlier)
NONSTANDARD	Joel intended *to have invited* you. (the intention preceded the inviting.)
STANDARD	Joel had intended *to invite* you.
STANDARD	Joel intended *to invite* you.

8.5 The Split Infinitive

When a modifier appears between *to* and the verb in an infinitive phrase, the infinitive is said to be split. It is wise to avoid splitting the infinitive. Usually, the modifier can be placed before or after. There are some sentences, however, in which a split infinitive is the only means of avoiding clumsy expression.

NEEDLESSLY SPLIT	Miguel was urged to immediately register.
IMPROVED	Miguel was urged to register immediately.
NEEDLESSLY SPLIT	They agreed to voluntarily participate.
IMPROVED	They voluntarily agreed to participate.
AWKWARD	The plan is intended substantially to increase sales.
PERMISSIBLE	The plan is intended to substantially increase sales.

8.6 The Tense of Participles

The present participle and the past participle show an action or state of being at the same time as that of the main verb.

Being new to the organization, I hesitate to offer suggestions.
   (Present participle; same time as main verb)

Shaken by the experience, he went home immediately.
   (Past participle; same time as main verb)

Knowing her way around San Francisco, Jill always has a
good time there.
(Present participle; same time as main verb)

The perfect participle shows an action or state of being earlier than that of the main verb.

STANDARD   *Having helped* in the rescue, Tim received
a citation.
(The helping occurred before
the receiving.)

STANDARD   *Having explored* the cave, the scientists
returned to camp.
(The exploration took place before
they returned.)

NONSTANDARD   *Approving* the program, we set up
research centers.

STANDARD   *Having approved* the program, we set up
research centers.

NONSTANDARD   *Buying* a ticket, Jack went into the stadium.

STANDARD   *Having bought* a ticket, Jack went into
the stadium.

NONSTANDARD   *Reaching* the wall, he climbed it and jumped
to safety.

STANDARD   *Having* reached the wall, he climbed it and
jumped to safety.

Exercise: Change the nonstandard usage to standard usage in the
following sentences.

1. Dad is hoping to some day build a garage.
2. I felt I answered the questions correctly.
3. I'm not going to ever make that mistake again.
4. Lisa would have been delighted to have won a door prize.
5. Missing the first act, Mary did not enjoy the play.
6. The play started before we entered the theater.
7. We served ice cream that we made ourselves.
8. The band would have preferred to have toured only six weeks.

9. We were warned to carefully obey the camp rules.

10. Some of the students admitted that they were misled by the glib sales talk.

11. I would have liked to have seen the expression on his face.

12. Making the best of the ingredients, Pat turned out a good meal.

13. I hoped to have finished the job last night.

14. Gail is determined to somehow get to Europe.

15. Completing his quota of calls, the canvasser went home.

16. I was thrilled that the magazine decided to publish my story.

17. The club members voted on all the questions they discussed at the meeting.

18. Saving the little girl from the fire, the Irish Setter was given a steak dinner.

8.7 Shall and Will

Earlier practice, which some people still insist upon, is as follows:

Future time is shown in the first person by *shall* with the verb. Future time is shown in the second and third person by *will* with the verb.

Emphasis or determination about future action is shown in the first person by *will* and by *shall* in the second and third persons.

	FUTURE TIME	EMPHASIS
FIRST PERSON:	We shall tell you.	We will win the game.
SECOND PERSON:	You will see the pictures.	You shall win the game.
THIRD PERSON:	They will cooperate.	They shall not leave the house.

Today, however, the usage of *shall* and *will* is undergoing rapid change. In speech, the general custom is to use the contractions *I'll, he'll, you'll,* which suit either *shall* or *will.* In good writing today, the tendency is to use *will* for all three persons.

8.8 The Subjunctive

The subjunctive form of the verb is used to express (1) a statement contrary to fact; (2) a request or command; (3) a wish, hope, or prayer.

> *If you were here now,* would you be happy?
>   (contrary to fact)
> The customer demanded *that the store refund his money.* (command)
> The blessing of God *descend* upon you. (prayer)

The subjunctive forms of the verb *be* are as follows: *be* with all persons in the present tense except for clauses contrary to fact, which take *were.*

> If this *be* a dream, let me sleep.
> If he *were* dependable, I would not worry.

For all other verbs, the only difference between regular forms and the subjunctive is that the *s* is dropped in the third person singular.

> The teacher suggested that he *buy* more books.
> The manager requested that no one *leave* the theater.

The words <u>would have</u> are not used in a clause beginning with <u>if</u> or <u>even though</u>.

> NONSTANDARD   If he *would have* apologized, I would have
>   overlooked it.
> STANDARD   If he *had* apologized, I would have
>   overlooked it.
>
> NONSTANDARD   If you *would have* gone, you would have
>   seen the Pope.
> STANDARD   If you *had* gone, you would have seen
>   the Pope.

Exercise: Find the nonstandard usage in each of the following sentences. Supply the standard form.

1. I suggest that Carrie brings the tape recorder.
2. If I was you, Gary, I would apply for a scholarship.
3. If the snow would have stopped, we would have walked to the village.
4. I move that the meeting is adjourned.
5. The principal ordered that the crosswalks near the school are policed.
6. Rob kept wishing he was working in the research division.
7. If I would have known about the dinner, I would have planned to come earlier.
8. If Judy was here, we could begin the meeting.
9. The lawyer demands that her client is given his freedom.
10. If I was a millionaire, I wouldn't want a better house than the one I now live in.
11. The fire department requests that these doors are kept closed.
12. If you would have kept your eyes on the road, this would not have happened.
13. We would be there by now if we would have taken the plane.
14. I know what I would do if I was coach.
15. The management asks that each person without a ticket lines up on the left.

9.0 The Right Word

The preceding pages of this Handbook have been concerned with problems of usage. They have presented choices of words and constructions that are accepted as **standard usage**—the kind of usage that is appropriate at all times and in all places.

Some forms and constructions have been marked **nonstandard usage.** While these may go unchallenged or unnoticed on the playground or in the locker room, they are nonstandard because they are not acceptable everywhere. In many situations they mark the user as careless or untrained in the English language.

American English is not composed of just *standard* and *nonstandard* usages. Every good dictionary makes other distinctions such as *colloquial, slang, dialectal, archaic, poetic*. These labels limit the areas in which a word or expression is accepted. Thus, some words are acceptable in poetry but nowhere else. Slang expressions are acceptable only in everyday speech, not in writing.

A special note should be made of the term **colloquial.** Colloquial language is the informal language of everyday speech and writing. You would not expect to find it in a government document or in a formal speech, but there is no objection to colloquial usage in school, in business, or in ordinary everyday situations.

The glossary that follows lists alphabetically (a) usage items not covered in the preceding pages, and (b) words commonly confused as to meaning.

This glossary is too short to cover all the problems and questions that may arise. It is intended only as a first resort; if it fails, consult a good dictionary.

Distinctions of Meanings and Items of Usage

accept, except   To *accept* is to agree to something or to receive something willingly. *To except* is to exclude or omit. As a preposition, *except* means "but" or "excluding."

> Carol *accepted* the offer at once.
> We will *except* the seniors who are going to college. (verb)
> Everyone *except* the driver was laughing. (preposition)

advice, advise   You *advise* someone. What you give that person is *advice*.

affect, effect   *Affect* is a verb meaning either to influence or to pretend. *Effect* as a verb means to accomplish or to produce as a result. As a noun, *effect* means result.

agree to, with, on   You agree *to* something such as a plan of action. You agree *with* someone else. Or, something such as spinach does not agree *with* you. You agree with others *on* a course of action.

allusion, illusion, delusion   An *allusion* is a reference to something. An *illusion* is a false idea or a faulty interpretation of the facts. A *delusion* is a belief in something that is contrary to fact.

> The newspaper story made an *allusion* to our poor
>   football record.
> Betty had the *illusion* that her work was satisfactory.
> Hitler suffered from the *delusion* that he could make
>   no mistakes.

anywheres, nowheres, somewheres   The final *s* is nonstandard. The words are *anywhere, nowhere, somewhere.*

alumna, alumnus   An *alumna* is a female graduate; the plural is *alumnae.* An *alumnus* is a male graduate; the plural is *alumni.*

all right   The misspelling *alright* is nonstandard usage. The two words are separate.

all the   Clumsy and nonstandard in such expressions as "all the longer," "all the farther," and so on.

> NONSTANDARD   Is that all the louder you can yell?
> STANDARD   Can't you yell any louder than that?

altogether, all together   *Altogether* means entirely or on the whole. *All together* means that all parts of a group are considered.

> The report of the accident is *altogether* wrong. (entirely)
> The crew pulled on the rope *all together.*

among, between   *Between* expresses the joining or separation of *two* people or things. *Among* refers to a group of three or more.

> NONSTANDARD   Let's divide the money between the
>   three of us.
> STANDARD   Let's divide the money among the
>   three of us.

amount, number   *Amount* is used to indicate a total sum of things. It is usually used to refer to items that cannot be counted. *Number* is used to refer to items that can be counted.

> The *amount* of food consumed is amazing. (*food* cannot
>   be counted.)
> The *number* of hamburgers consumed is amazing.
>   (*hamburgers* can be counted.)

angry at, with   You are angry *with* a person and angry *at* a thing.

apt, likely, liable   These three words have in common the meaning of *probable*. However, they cannot be substituted for each other at random. With respect to probability, *apt* means "naturally inclined to." *Likely* means "something that can reasonably be expected." *Liable* means "subject to something, usually something unpleasant."

> Most people are *apt* to worry when the airplane suddenly drops in a downdraft.
> It is *likely* to rain before nightfall.
> If you speed on this road, you are *liable* to be arrested.

bad, badly   See Section 7.5.

being   This completely acceptable present participle is most safely used as part of a main verb. Used as a modifier it creates extremely awkward sentences. *Being as* and *being that* are not satisfactory substitutes for *since* or *because*.

> AWKWARD   Being on the jury, she could not talk about the case.
> BETTER   Since she was on the jury, she could not talk about the case.

> NONSTANDARD   Being that he is the boss, we do what he says.
> STANDARD   Because he is the boss, we do what he says.

beside, besides   *Beside* means at the side of. *Besides* means in addition to.

> Larry's dog rode *beside* him in the front seat.
> There are other rewards *besides* the money.

between each   *Between* is not followed by a singular noun.

> NONSTANDARD   Between each bite, he sipped his cocoa.
> STANDARD   Between *bites*, he sipped his cocoa.

> NONSTANDARD   Between every page, Jack inserted a paper.
> STANDARD   Between *all the pages*, Jack inserted papers.

borrow, lend   *Borrow* and *lend* are verbs. You *borrow from* someone. You *lend* to someone.

NONSTANDARD   Will you *borrow* me your atlas?
STANDARD   Will you *lend* me your atlas?
STANDARD   May I *borrow* your atlas?

bring, take   *Bring* means motion toward someone or some place; *take* means motion away from someone or some place.

I will take this book to school. (*away* from here)
He will bring us some milk. (*toward* us)
Mark will take me home. (*away* from here)

but that, but what   The word *but* has a negative meaning. If it is preceded by another negative, it creates a double negative situation.

NONSTANDARD   I have *no* doubt *but that* Terri will win.
STANDARD   I have *no* doubt that Terri will win.

NONSTANDARD   There is not a chance *but what* Marty was hurt.
STANDARD   There is not a chance that Marty was hurt.

continual, continuous   *Continual* means occurring repeatedly or at intervals over a long period. *Continuous* means extending without interruption in space or time.

There were *continual* sounds of hammering.
There is a *continuous* stretch of desert across North Africa.

compliment, complement   A *compliment* is a remark spoken in praise. A *complement* is something needed to complete a whole.

can, may   *Can* means able or having the power to do something. *May* is used to ask or to grant permission. It also expresses the probability of something happening.

Can you solve the first problem? (ability)
May we go to the library? (permission)
It *may* snow tomorrow. (probability)

Could is the past tense of *can*; *might* is the past tense of *may*.

differ from, with   One thing or person differs *from* another in characteristics. You differ *with* someone when you disagree with him.

different from   In most situations *different from* is better usage than *different than*. However, there are some situations in which *than* must be used to avoid awkward expression.

> Gil's book is different *from* ours.
> The school is much different *than* it used to be.

emigrate, immigrate   To *emigrate* is to leave one's homeland. To *immigrate* is to enter a country for the purpose of settling there. An *emigrant* is one who is on his way from a former home. An *immigrant* is one who has arrived in a new country.

etc.   The abbreviation *et cetera,* meaning "and so forth," or "and others." The abbreviation is avoided in most writing. If it is used, it must not be preceded by *and,* because the *et* means "and."

fewer, less   See Section 7.7.

formally, formerly   *Formally* means in a formal manner. *Formerly* means previously.

> He was *formerly* Ambassador to India.
> We have never been introduced *formally.*

good, well   See Section 7.6.

had of, off of   The *of* is both unnecessary and undesirable.

> NONSTANDARD   I wish you had of come.
> STANDARD   I wish you had come.

> NONSTANDARD   Dick jumped off of the stage.
> STANDARD   Dick jumped off the stage.

hanged, hung Criminals are *hanged*. Things are *hung* on walls, hooks, or elsewhere.

>The mob *hanged* the horse thief.
>The doctor's diplomas *hung* on his office wall.

in, into *In* means inside something. *Into* tells of motion from the outside to the inside of something.

NONSTANDARD	The books fell in the mud.
STANDARD	The books fell into the mud.
NONSTANDARD	Jane ran in the house.
STANDARD	Jane ran into the house.

imply, infer A speaker or writer suggests or *implies* something. The reader, listener, or observer comes to a conclusion or *infers* something on the basis of what he sees and hears.

>The speaker *implied* that we are lazy.
>I *infer* that you disagree with the speaker.

ingenious, ingenuous *Ingenious* means clever and resourceful. *Ingenuous* means frank and honest.

kind, sort, type See Section 7.3.

kind of a, sort of a The *a* is unnecessary.

NONSTANDARD	What kind of a car did you buy?
STANDARD	What kind of car did you buy?

lay, lie See Section 8.2.

leave, let *Leave* means to go away from. *Let* means permit. The principal parts are *leave, left, left*, and *let, let, let*.

NONSTANDARD	Please *leave* the boy go on with his story.
STANDARD	Please *let* the boy go on with his story.
NONSTANDARD	We should have *left* Sue go.
STANDARD	We should have *let* Sue go.
STANDARD	*Leave* me alone with my work. (Depart.)
STANDARD	*Let* me alone. (Don't interfere.)

like, as, as if   While the use of *like* as a conjunction is common in speaking, its use as a conjunction is not fully established in writing. *Like* is better used as a preposition.

NOT ACCEPTED   I feel *like* Sally does about swimming.
BETTER   I feel *as* Sally does about swimming.

NOT ACCEPTED   Jeff acted *like* he had already heard the story.
BETTER   Jeff acted *as if* he had already heard the story.

majority   This word can be used only with items that can be counted. It is incorrectly used in speaking of time or distance.

NONSTANDARD   The *majority* of the milk did not sour.
STANDARD   *Most* of the milk did not sour.

NONSTANDARD   The *majority* of the time was spent in sleeping.
STANDARD   *Most* of the time was spent in sleeping.

NONSTANDARD   The *majority* of the decoration is amateurish.
STANDARD   *Most* of the decoration is amateurish.

of   When *could have, might have, must have,* and similar phrases are spoken, they usually come out as contractions: *could've, might've, must've,* and so on. Because the contracted form *'ve* sounds like *of,* some persons write mistakenly *could of, might of, must of.*

NONSTANDARD   Someone *might of* seen you.
STANDARD   Someone *might have* seen you.

percent, percentage   *Percent* is correctly used only when preceded by a number. When there is no preceding number, *percentage* is correct.

About 70 *percent* of the pictures turned out well.
A large *percentage* of our students go to college.

raise, rise   See Section 8.2.

seldom ever   The *ever* is unnecessary. You can say instead *seldom, very seldom,* or *hardly ever.*

> AWKWARD   We *seldom ever* saw the owner of the house.
> BETTER   We *very seldom* saw the owner of the house.

so   There is a good deal of objection to this completely acceptable conjunction on the grounds that it is overused. If you overuse it, try some other connective. *So* as a conjunction usually indicates result. The clause it introduces states the result; the main clause states the cause. You can eliminate the *so* entirely by changing the main clause to a subordinate clause introduced by *since* or *because.*

> CAUSE   RESULT
>
> The house was dark, *so* we turned around and came home.
>
> CAUSE   RESULT
>
> Since the house was dark, we turned around and came home.

So is correctly used in place of *so that* to indicate result.

> Judy did her homework on Friday night so that she could go
>   out Saturday night.
>
> Judy did her homework on Friday night so she could go
>   out Saturday night.

So should never be used for emphasis unless it is followed by a clause beginning with *that.*

> NONSTANDARD   He was so busy.
> STANDARD   He was so busy that he could not go.

way, ways   *Ways* is misused when it refers to distance.

> NONSTANDARD   We went a little *ways* into the forest.
> STANDARD   We went a little *way* into the forest.

10.0 Capitalization

10.1 A.D., B.C., I, O

Capitalize the abbreviations _A.D._ and _B.C._, the pronoun _I_, and the interjection _O_.

The abbreviations B.C. and A.D. occur only with the number of a year: 1001 B.C., A.D., 1492. The interjection O occurs in poetry, in the Bible, or in prayers or petitions: O Lord, O King, O Master.

O is quite different from the explosive interjection _oh_, which is capitalized only at the beginning of a sentence.

10.2 First Words

Capitalize the first word of a sentence, a direct quotation, and a line of poetry.

1. What brought the man to our hideout?
2. "I have come," he said, "to repay a debt."

3. Whenever Richard Cory went down town,
   We people on the pavement looked at him:
   He was a gentleman from sole to crown,
   Clean favored, and imperially slim.*

---

* From _Richard Cory_ by E. A. Robinson, quoted by permission of the Macmillan Company.

Note: The second example is a divided quotation.

The second part of a divided quotation does not begin with a capital letter unless it starts a new sentence. See Section 14.2.

10.3   Proper Nouns and Adjectives

A **common noun** is the name of a whole group of persons, places or things. A **proper noun** is the name of an individual person, place, or thing. A **proper adjective** is an adjective formed from a proper noun.

COMMON NOUN	PROPER NOUN	PROPER ADJECTIVE
country	England	English
state	Texas	Texan
city	Paris	Parisian

Proper nouns and adjectives occur in many compound words. Capitalize only the parts of these words that are capitalized when they stand alone. Do not capitalize prefixes such as *pro-, un-, anti-* attached to proper nouns and adjectives.

un-American   pro-French   Spanish-speaking people

Proper nouns occur in great variety. The following rules with their illustrations will help you solve the capitalization problems that proper nouns present.

10.4   Geographical Names

In a geographical name, capitalize the first letter of each word except articles and prepositions.

The article *the* appearing before a geographical name is not part of the geographical name and is therefore not capitalized.

CONTINENTS: Australia, Africa, Europe

BODIES OF WATER: the Atlantic Ocean, San Francisco

Bay, the Mississippi River, the Great Lakes, the Strait of Magellan, the Firth of Forth, Cape Cod, New Hampton Roads

LAND FORMS: the Gobi Desert, the Rocky Mountains, the High Plains, Crystal Cave, Mount Hood, Shenandoah Valley

POLITICAL UNITS: the United States of America, the Republic of Texas, the Commonwealth of Massachusetts, the Province of Quebec, St. Louis County, Newcastle Township, the City of Detroit, Stratford-on-Avon, the Fields of Dan, the Department of Health, Education, and Welfare

PUBLIC AREAS: Glacier National Park, Mammoth Cave, Big Hole Battlefield, Fort Laramie, Joshua Tree Monument

ROADS AND HIGHWAYS: Fifth Avenue, New Jersey Turnpike, U.S. Highway 1, Twelfth Street, London Road, Thrity-fourth Street, Michigan Boulevard

10.5   Common Nouns in Names

A common noun that is part of a name is capitalized. A common noun used to define or refer to a proper noun is not capitalized.

PART OF THE NAME	REFERENCE OR DEFINITION
New York State	the state of Minnesota*
New York City	the city of Buffalo
the Western Plains	plains in the West
Hudson Valley	the valley of the Hudson

* In official documents, words like *city, state,* and *county* are capitalized when they are part of the name of a political unit: *the County of Westchester, the State of Mississippi, the City of Los Angeles.*

10.6 Words Modified by Proper Adjectives

The word modified by a proper adjective is not capitalized unless adjective and noun together are a geographical name.

the Indian Ocean	the Indian nation
the Swiss Alps	a Swiss watch
the English Channel	the English language
the Irish Sea	Irish songs

Exercise: Copy the following sentences, supplying necessary capitals.

1. A chief crop of hawaii is pineapples.
2. The british frigate struck her colors and bowed to the american ship.
3. Yellowstone national park is in the state of wyoming.
4. Thousands of people of irish descent marched down fifth avenue in the st. patrick's day parade.
5. At the mouth of the mississippi lies the city of new orleans.
6. Have you visited mt. rushmore in the black hills?
7. Saul was made the first king of the hebrew nation in 1095 b.c.
8. About one-third of the canadian people are french-speaking.
9. The mason-dixon line was the southern boundary of pennsylvania.
10. The canadians were neither pro-russian nor pro-american in the hockey play-offs.
11. The st. lawrence seaway links the atlantic ocean and the great lakes.
12. The shenandoah river in virginia flows into the potomac.
13. Malone is a town in new york state near the canadian border.
14. Not far from pike's peak lies the city of colorado springs.
15. The st. lawrence seaway is the largest waterway built since the panama canal.
16. The american continents were named for an italian sailor, amerigo vespucci.
17. In the gobi desert of asia, nomadic mongols live in felt tents.

18. After the spaniards had conquered the aztec capital, they rebuilt the city and called it mexico city.

10.7   Directions and Sections

Capitalize names of sections of the country but not of directions of the compass.

> The South is now heavily industrialized.
> The climate attracts settlers to the West.
> To the north lies Kalamazoo.
> We are going south this winter.
> Los Angeles is east of Reno, Nevada.
> You will find mountains to the west of here.
> The wind is from the southwest.

Capitalize proper adjectives derived from names of sections of the country. Do not capitalize adjectives derived from words indicating direction.

a westerly breeze	a Midwestern university
a northbound flight	a Southern state

Exercise: Copy the following sentences, supplying the necessary capitals.

1. Anne has applied to three colleges in the midwest.
2. The Appalachian Mountains extend down the eastern side of North America.
3. It is doubtful that the cold front now in the middle west will reach the eastern states.
4. Read the timetable upward for eastbound trains.
5. Lars went to a vocational school in the southwest.
6. After touring the near east, we flew south to Cape Town.
7. The nearest ranger station is a mile south of here.
8. The street on the west side of our school is Mills Street.
9. Our doctor was born and raised in the south.
10. Stratford-on-Avon is a small town eighty miles northwest of London, England.

11. The middle east is well represented at the United Nations.

12. Are the Watsons going south for the winter?

13. The path of the hurricane changed from a northwesterly to a northeasterly direction.

14. Do midwestern teams really play better football than eastern teams?

15. The Joshua tree wages its life battle in the scorching aridity of the southwest.

16. The north central states are one of our country's chief farming, mining, and manufacturing areas.

10.8 Languages, Races, Nationalities, and Religions

Capitalize the names of languages, races, nationalities, and religions and the adjectives formed from them.

the Caucasian race	Buddhism	Jew
the Spanish language	Catholic	Brazilian
Mexican history	Protestant	Dutch

10.9 Organizations and Institutions

Capitalize important words in the names of organizations, buildings, firms, schools, churches, and other institutions. Do not capitalize *and* or prepositions. Capitalize an article (*a, an,* or *the*) only if it appears as the first word in a name.

Chicago Symphony Orchestra	Evanston Township High School
University of Alabama	Standard Gas, Incorporated
St. Luke's Hospital	Library of Congress
Book-of-the-Month Club	Chicago and Northwestern Railroad

Note: In brand names, the common noun is not capitalized: *a Volkswagen bus; Indian River grapefruit; Crest toothpaste.*

Exercise: Copy the following sentences, supplying necessary capitals.

1. Have you tried kreemo instant cocoa?
2. There is a sale on california oranges at tony's market.
3. Copies of all new books go to the library of congress.
4. Ship the books to morris hills regional high school.
5. Mrs. Hovis works for the department of agriculture in a laboratory at beltsville, maryland.
6. Mr. quinn is an officer of the parent-teacher association.
7. The new york public library has an exhibit of japanese woodcuts.
8. The guest speaker is a physicist who used to work for the national aeronautics and space administration.
9. Professor saville of oberlin college addressed the league of women voters.
10. The rockefeller institute for medical research is located on york avenue.
11. A graduate of oberlin college, Elise is going to business school.
12. You can get hunt's tomato sauce at bell and hoffman's store.
13. The masterwork chorus will give a concert in the morristown high school auditorium.
14. Have you seen mr. case's new pontiac sunbird?
15. We bought our perfecto power mower at the kane hardware store.
16. The ajax printing company is in the first national bank building.
17. Wisconsin will play northwestern in dyche stadium.
18. The american petroleum company sponsors the program.

10.10 Titles of Persons

Capitalize words that show rank, office, or profession, when they are used with a person's name.

Doctor Walsh	Aunt Mary	Father Flynn

Lieutenant Flagg	Rabbi Jacobs	Judge Wright
Chief Joseph	Controller Bucklin	Dean Smith

The titles of high officials are capitalized even when they are used without the official's name.

the President of the United States	the Governor
the Secretary of State	the Pope
the Prime Minister	the Bishop

The prefix *ex-* and the suffix *-elect* are not capitalized when attached to titles: *ex-President Nixon*, the *Senator-elect*.

10.11 Family Relationships

Capitalize the name of a family relationship when it is used with a person's name.

Aunt Ruth   Uncle Bill   Grandma Moses

When words like *mother, father, dad,* and *mom* are used alone in place of a particular person's name, they are capitalized. When modified by a possessive pronoun, as in *your mother,* they are not capitalized. When these and other words of family relationship do not stand for a particular person, they are not capitalized.

My Uncle Phil will be here tomorrow.
We have a letter from Cousin Sue.
Bob asked Dad for the car yesterday.
I saw your father at the airport.
Does Alice have a sister?

10.12 Titles of Books and Works of Art

Capitalize the first word and every important word in the titles of books, stories, articles, poems, films, works of art, and musical compositions.

The only words considered not important are conjunctions, articles (*a, an,* and *the*), and prepositions containing fewer than five letters. But even these are capitalized when used as the first word in a title.

Under Milkwood	*"The Sounds of Silence"*
Go Tell It on the	*Out of the Silent Planet*
Mountain	*One Flew over the*
The Mona Lisa	*Cuckoo's Nest*

Exercise: Copy each word that requires a capital in these sentences.

1. Is dad going to drive judge fuller to the airport?
2. My sister played "tales from the vienna woods" and "voices of spring."
3. Have dad and mom met lieutenant wickham?
4. I think aunt dorothy or my mother will drive.
5. At the banquet the governor praised the secretary of state and the vice-president.
6. My favorite overture is beethoven's "egmont."
7. The chief speaker at the meeting will be fire chief schwenker.
8. Joe asked uncle george to lend him *rockets, missiles, and space travel.*
9. Alec's father drove us out to see grandmother stone, who is dad's grandmother.
10. I have read "to a skylark" in shelley's *complete poems.*
11. The mayor introduced senator pooley as the next president of the united states.
12. I would like you to meet colonel triggs, who is senator-elect.
13. The matter is to be taken up with dean wood tomorrow.
14. The secretary of state is flying to meet the president-elect.
15. Assistant attorney-general robertson may be the next chief justice of the supreme court.

10.13 The Deity

Capitalize all words referring to the Deity, the Holy Family, and to religious scriptures.

God	the Almighty	the Gospel
the Father	the Lord	the Torah
the Son	Jehovah	the Talmud
the Holy Ghost	Allah	the Koran
the Virgin Mary	the Bible	

Capitalize personal pronouns but not relative pronouns that refer to the Deity.

May God make His light to shine down upon you.
Praise God from whom all blessings flow.

10.14 Days, Months, Holidays

Capitalize the names of days of the week, of months, and of holidays. Do not capitalize the names of the seasons.

Monday	the Fourth of July	autumn
January	Washington's Birthday	Veterans Day

10.15 Historical Names

Capitalize the names of historical events, documents, and periods.

Declaration of Independence	the Middle Ages
Battle of the Bulge	the Jacksonian Period

Exercise A: Copy the words that require capitals in these sentences.

1. Margaret's favorite period in our history is the age of jackson.
2. The boston tea party took place in 1773.

3. The second continental congress lasted for five years.

4. The first shots of the american revolution were fired in the battle of lexington.

5. Columbus day is now celebrated on the monday closest to october 12.

6. The victorian era is usually thought of as an age of gentleness and propriety.

7. The period in which shelley, keats, and byron wrote is known as the romantic age.

8. We celebrated new year's eve at fred murphy's house.

9. The united states senate rejected the treaty of versailles.

10. Chief sitting bull defeated general custer in the battle of little big horn.

Exercise B: The following exercise reviews all the uses of capitals in this chapter. Copy the words that need capital letters.

1. My uncle's hobbies are music, archery, golf, english literature, and american history.

2. I think millet's best painting is "man with the hoe."

3. The language of the brazilian people is portuguese.

4. Mom served us french toast with vermont maple syrup.

5. In 1890, the battle of wounded knee was the last major conflict between indians and u.s. troops.

6. The president of the builders club called the meeting to order.

7. Why did the young indian woman save captain john smith's life?

8. On the first friday in april, the american legion will hold its annual convention in detroit.

9. Seldom is there a balance of power between republicans and democrats in the united states senate.

10. The poem "the charge of the light brigade" tells of a heroic event in the crimean war.

11.0 End Marks and Commas

11.1 Periods at the Close of Sentences

Place a period at the close of every declarative sentence and of most imperative sentences.

A period is also used at the close of groups of words that are used as sentences even though they are not complete sentences.

> Please hand me the broom.
> Oh, no. We were not near the fire.

11.2 Periods in Abbreviations

Place a period after every part of an abbreviation.

E. A. Robinson	Edwin Arlington Robinson
A.D.	Anno Domini
U. S. A.	United States of America
Washington, D. C.	Washington, District of Columbia

Since the 1930's it has become the custom not to use periods in abbreviations of certain government agencies and of international organizations.

ICC	Interstate Commerce Commission
FHA	Federal Housing Authority

FBI	Federal Bureau of Investigation
UN	United Nations
HEW	Department of Health, Education, and Welfare

11.3   Exclamation Points

Place an exclamation point after an exclamatory sentence and after an exclamation set off from a sentence.

Great! We can't lose now.   Wow! I don't believe it!
What a pass!   We want Jackson!
Hold that line!   Wilson for Senator!

11.4   Question Marks

Place a question mark after an interrogative sentence or after a question that is not a complete sentence.

The word order in questions is sometimes the same as in declarative sentences. In speech, the speaker raises his voice at the end of the sentence to show that it is a question. In writing, the question mark performs the same function.

Have they changed premiers?   They have changed premiers?
Do you call this a composition?   This is a composition?
The date? January 21.   The date is January 21?

Exercise: Copy these sentences, using end marks and punctuation as required for sentences and abbreviations. Use question marks only for sentences in normal interrogative form.

1. Just hand me that pair of pliers
2. What a close call that was
3. You could have taken a later flight, couldn't you
4. You can reach me at 208 So King St, Mt Arlington, N J
5. Down, Rover The very idea of your jumping up like that
6. Please send the package C O D to Nashville, Tenn

7. "Shall I get you a screwdriver?" Paul asked
8. Howard received his B S degree from N Y U
9. Has Charlie a driver's license
10. The principal asked whether Charlie has a driver's license

Uses of the Comma

11.5   Introductory Words

Introductory words such as _yes_, _no_, _well_, _why_, and _oh_ are followed by a comma.

Oh, no, not another detour.
Well, there we were, drifting with the current.
Why, nobody in his right mind would do that.

Adverbs such as *besides, however, anyhow, nonetheless* at the beginning of a sentence are followed by a comma.

11.6   Introductory Phrases and Clauses

A participal phrase at the beginning of a sentence is followed by a comma.

A long adverbial clause at the beginning of a sentence is followed by a comma.

A succession of prepositional phrases at the beginning of a sentence is followed by a comma.

Watching the trail, we saw the wagon train approach.
(participial phrase)

On the ledge at the top of the tower, the princess brushed her long blond tresses. (succession of prepositional phrases)

When the prince arrived, he scratched his bald head and looked up at the tower. (adverbial clause)

11.7   Transposed Words and Phrases

Words and phrases moved to the beginning of a sentence from their normal position are usually set off by a comma.

He naturally checked the address in the directory.
(normal order)
Naturally, he checked the address in the directory.
(transposed order)
It was obviously a case of mistaken identity. (normal order)
Obviously, it was a case of mistaken identity.
(transposed order)
You need a guide book to get the most out of the fair.
(normal order)
To get the most out of the fair, you need a guide book.

Exercise: Copy the following sentences, inserting commas where necessary. Two of the sentences are correct.

1. When the lightning struck our terrier pup dashed under the dining room table.

2. Driving on Dad began to sing.

3. For the best view sit here.

4. If I had moved an inch the boat would have turned over.

5. Well you do seem a little heavier.

6. If your answers are incorrect change them.

7. When Ben has finished the house will look like new.

8. Down at the bottom of the valley people were walking about.

9. Now we know your secret!

10. While the fire was burning Otto had to keep getting more and more firewood.

11. Yes I thought Arlene's speech was the best.

12. From the stage people looked as if they were enjoying the show immensely.

13. Why every picture in my roll of film was spoiled!

14. Speaking in public was a skill he had exhibited since grade-school days.

15. While Roger watched Ellen played two sets of tennis with Mom.

11.8 Appositives

An appositive is set off from the rest of the sentence by commas.

Mrs. Clark, *an authority on Dutch elm disease*, thinks our tree can be saved.
The collector, *Mr. Lisle*, bought the chair at an auction.

11.9 Words of Direct Address

Words of direct address are set off by commas.

Ray, did you buy a season ticket?
My fellow citizens, I ask you to vote—not for me alone—but for a greater America.

11.10 Parenthetical Expressions

Words and phrases used to explain or qualify a statement are called **parenthetical expressions.** These same words and phrases may also be used as basic parts of the sentence. It is only when they are parenthetical that they are set off by commas.

I understand that her theory is sound.
Her theory, *I understand*, is sound.
Of course Mort knows where it is.
Mort, *of course*, knows where it is.

Parenthetical expressions are set off by commas.

Some expressions often used parenthetically are:

of course	as a matter of fact	for example
in fact	I believe (hope, think)	on the other hand
indeed		

Conjunctive adverbs (see Section 1.7) used parenthetically within the sentence are set off by commas: *therefore, moreover, nevertheless, however, consequently,* and so on.

You realize, *therefore,* that you run a risk.
The coat, *moreover,* does not fit properly. ·
The carnival, *however,* was a tremendous success.

Occasionally, words like *however, therefore,* and *consequently* are used to modify a word in the sentence. As modifiers they are an essential part of the meaning of a sentence. Since they are essential they are not set off by commas.

My friends insisted that I could not succeed. I was *therefore* determined not to give up.
The procedure for screening security risks was *consequently* changed.
My father cannot stop smoking *however* hard he tries.

11.11 Dates, Addresses, Geographical Names

In dates and addresses of more than one part, set off every part after the first from the rest of the sentence.

We visited the baseball museum in Cooperstown. (one part)

In Cooperstown, New York, we visited the museum.
(two parts, the second set off by commas)

The package arrived on June 6. (one part)

Wisconsin entered the Union on May 29, 1848.
(two parts with a comma after the first)

The letter was addressed to 280 East End Avenue, Pleasantville, Ohio 43148, as you requested.
(three parts, the second and third set off by commas)

Note: The day of the month and the month are one item. The name of the state and the house number are one item. The name of the state and the zip code are one item.

June 6   240 East Thirty-first Street   Illinois 60610

Exercise: Copy these sentences, inserting the necessary commas.

1. Write to me at 110 North Spooner Street Madison Wisconsin 53705.

2. Would you consider July 4 1776 a more important date than March 4 1789?

3. The affair on the whole came off very successfully.

4. Both athletes and actors it is said are highly superstitious.

5. You bad dog you have chewed my slipper.

6. Ladies and gentlemen of the jury I wish to present Exhibit A.

7. That was as I shall explain the narrowest escape of my life.

8. Hans after all is a foreign exchange student and needs time to adjust.

9. Lucky the beagle next door barks twice when the bell rings.

10. If you move the picture to the right Nancy it will look better.

11. Julia Ward Howe writer of *The Battle Hymn of the Republic* was a prominent worker for world peace.

12. His hearty laugh a high-pitched cackle could be heard above the audience.

13. Let me remind you fellow juniors that we simply must sell more tickets for the dance.

14. If you really want to watch this program Lynn stop reading.

15. George Washington retired from the army at Annapolis Maryland on December 23 1783.

16. The record states that he was born on February 2 1944 at 1091 San Pasqual Street Pasadena California.

17. Send your contributions to Mr. Frank Quinn 1851 West 107th Street Chicago Illinois 60643.

18. I shall be at the Beach Hotel 11 South Kentucky Avenue Atlantic City New Jersey.

11.12 Nonrestrictive Modifiers

A clause that identifies or points out the person or thing it modifies is a **restrictive clause.** It is essential to the meaning of the sentence. It cannot be dropped out without confusing the meaning or making the meaning incomplete.

> The biography *that I mean* is the new one about
> Conan Doyle.
> (The clause tells *which* biography.)
>
> Young people need heroes *whom they can admire*
> *and imitate.*
> (The clause describes essential characteristics of
> the heroes.)
>
> The person *who has a pleasant disposition* attracts friends.
> (Without the clause the sentence has no
> specific meaning.)

Restrictive clauses are not set off from the rest of the sentence by commas.

A **nonrestrictive clause** does not contain information essential to the meaning of the sentence. It presents merely added information. It can be dropped without confusing the meaning of the sentence.

> The speed limit, *which is rigidly enforced,* helps decrease
> traffic accidents.
> Teachers, *who spend themselves in educating young people,*
> are rarely remembered when their students attain
> success as adults.

Nonrestrictive clauses are set off by commas from the rest of the sentence.

Participial phrases that identify or point out the thing or person they modify are restrictive.

> The jet *making a forced landing* has mechanical trouble.
> (Without the phrase, the sentence loses its specific
> meaning.)
> The bird *perched on the tree outside the window* awakened
> me with its chirping. (The phrase identifies the bird.)

Nonrestrictive participial phrases merely add meaning. They are not essential and can be dropped without making the sentence meaning incomplete.

Looking back, we could see the undulating hills.
The boys, approaching the clearing, saw the campers preparing supper.

Nonrestrictive participial phrases are set off from the rest of the sentence by commas. Restrictive phrases are not set off by commas.

Exercise: Number your paper 1–18. Decide whether the adjective clause or the participial phrase is restrictive or nonrestrictive. After each number write *restrictive* or *nonrestrictive*. Copy and insert commas in the sentences in which commas are needed.

1. The train which goes to Philadelphia is on Track 3.
2. Ms. Moss who teaches industrial arts has just bought a station wagon.
3. Robyn who is a jockey must keep her weight down.
4. Harold Leach is the boy wearing the green sweater.
5. My ice skates which had been packed in a carton were lost in moving to our new home.
6. Buy the paper which is least expensive.
7. The little girl smiling shyly is my sister.
8. The plane which left Honolulu at noon carried two hundred passengers.
9. Enclosed is forty dollars which is the amount you asked for.
10. This bank established by my grandfather many years ago has grown into a thriving institution.
11. Vacation seemed unreal coming after months of anticipation.
12. My mother's cheese cake of which I eat more than my share is our family favorite.
13. The person receiving the package must sign for it.
14. Michele who is my closest friend would not even talk to me.
15. Boys who are over six feet tall have an advantage in basketball.
16. Cora's application handed in two weeks ago has not been acted on as yet.

17. Carolyn who was the first speaker introduced the subject.
18. The girl who was the first speaker is Carolyn Davis.

11.13 Compound Sentences

Place a comma before the conjunction that joins two main clauses in a compound sentence.

You must get your work done on time, *or* you will be fired.
Thomas More hoped to die peacefully, *but* one day he
     became certain that he would die at the executioner's hand.
Suddenly the thunder rolled, *and* the picnickers scattered.
I could not remember the title of the book, *nor* could I
     remember the author.

When the clauses are quite short, the comma may be omitted.

He invited me to dinner but I could not go.
I ate shrimp and Jim had clams.

11.14 Series

A **series** is a group of three or more items of the same kind.

SERIES OF NOUNS: *Typewriters, calculators,* and *dictaphones* were ordered for the business education rooms.

SERIES OF VERBS: The human rights committee *met, discussed* specific proposals, and *adopted* a new constitution.

SERIES OF ADJECTIVES: Blamed for the loss of the game, Paul felt *embarrassed, bewildered,* and *lonely.*

SERIES OF PHRASES: He piled the luggage *on the counters, in the corners,* and *outside the doors of the waiting room.*

Commas are used to separate the parts of a series.

No comma is required after the last item in a series. When the last two items of a series are joined by *and* or *or*, the comma is sometimes omitted. To avoid all possibility of misunderstanding, it is wise to use a comma before the conjunction.

Do not use a comma if all parts of the series are joined by *and*, *or*, or *nor*.

> The electric fan whirred and buzzed and oscillated.
> A book or a newspaper or a magazine will satisfy me.

11.15 Coordinate Adjectives

Commas are placed between coordinate adjectives that modify the same noun.

> The soaring, majestic spire seemed to reach for the sky.
> The flashing, blinding, zigzag lightning terrified us.

To determine whether adjectives are coordinate, try placing an *and* between them. If it sounds natural, they are coordinate, and a comma is needed.

PROBLEM	The soft soothing music relaxed him.
NATURAL	The soft *and* soothing music relaxed him.
SOLUTION	The soft, soothing music relaxed him.

PROBLEM	The tempting delicious aroma made our mouths water.
NATURAL	The tempting *and* delicious aroma made our mouths water.
SOLUTION	The tempting, delicious aroma made our mouths water.

PROBLEM	The small gray car uses less gasoline.
NOT NATURAL	The small *and* gray car uses less gasoline.
SOLUTION	The small gray car uses less gasoline.

In general, it is safe to omit the comma before numbers and adjectives of size, shape, and age.

CORRECT   The little round jug
CORRECT   A fat old dachshund
CORRECT   Four local bands

Exercise: Copy these sentences, placing commas where they are needed.

1. The members of the forensics team are sophomores juniors and seniors.
2. The house is modern but the furniture is old-fashioned.
3. Please get a pound of butter a loaf of bread and a melon.
4. The rain was gentle warm and spring-like.
5. I like vanilla but maple walnut is my favorite.
6. She was a sprightly old woman.
7. We packed some sandwiches and fruit and then we rode our bikes to the fairgrounds.
8. For breakfast we had ham and eggs toast and jam and coffee.
9. Notice your own mistakes or someone else will.
10. The old dilapidated backless book was finally discarded.
11. Our homemaking teacher taught us to bake huckleberry raisin and pumpkin pies.
12. I gave up my social life studied hard and managed to pass the examination.
13. The salesperson showed me a tape recorder but it was too expensive.
14. I never saw anyone as inquisitive as persistent and as baffling as Grandpa Larsen.
15. I did not see the hole in the ice nor did I hear the warning cries.
16. That I was weak tired and sick to my stomach made no difference to the boss.
17. It was one of those warm muggy days in early September.
18. Daniel Boone served well in the American Revolution but we remember even better his courage on the Wilderness Trail.

11.16 Clarity

Use a comma to separate words or phrases that might be mistakenly joined in reading.

There are three common situations in which words may be mistakenly read together. The first occurs when the conjunctions *but* and *for* are mistaken for prepositions.

CONFUSING	No one spoke but Christie looked hopefully at the doctor.
CLEAR	No one spoke, but Christie looked hopefully at the doctor.
CONFUSING	George wrote to the factory for a part was missing.
CLEAR	George wrote to the factory, for a part was missing.

A second source of confusion is a noun following a verbal phrase.

CONFUSING	Before attacking the soldiers checked supply lines.
CLEAR	Before attacking, the soldiers checked supply lines.
CONFUSING	To understand a student must grasp basic principles.
CLEAR	To understand, a student must grasp basic principles.
CONFUSING	After eating the survivors had renewed strength.
CLEAR	After eating, the survivors had renewed strength.

A third source of confusion is the word that may be either adverb, preposition, or conjunction at the beginning of the sentence.

CONFUSING	With Joseph Andrew pitched the tent.
CLEAR	With Joseph, Andrew pitched the tent.

CONFUSING   Below the rocks were sharp and treacherous.

CLEAR   Below, the rocks were sharp and treacherous.

11.17 Words Omitted

Use a comma when words are omitted from parallel word groups.

Pat sewed the seams, and Joan, the hem.
I prefer languages; my brother, science.
The riper, the tastier.

Exercise: Copy these sentences, placing commas where necessary to avoid confusion.

1. Inside the fire was burning brightly.
2. The day before he had scarcely spoken.
3. Jeff had to hurry for the clock was wrong.
4. In her Mother has unlimited confidence.
5. Having ordered Jill studied the faces of the other diners.
6. Joe has read four novels by Charles Dickens; Martha three.
7. Donna is going to the University of Iowa; Stan to the Air Force Academy.
8. To Alice Elizabeth sent a handsome gift.
9. *Abraham Lincoln* was written by John Drinkwater; *Abe Lincoln in Illinois* by Robert E. Sherwood.
10. Tom's occupation is carpentry; his hobby fixing old clocks.

12.0 The Semicolon, the Colon, the Dash, and Parentheses

12.1 Semicolons Between Main Clauses

A semicolon is placed between the main clauses of a compound sentence when they are not joined by a conjunction.

The clauses of a compound sentence are closely related in thought. That is the reason for joining them into one sentence rather than writing them as separate sentences.

In some sentences the semicolon is more effective in joining main clauses than one of the conjunctions. This is especially true when *and* or *but* add little meaning to the joined clauses.

> You may approve of the measure, *but* we do not.
> You may approve of the measure; we do not.
> Mr. Ames discussed the nature of time, *and* he introduced many new ideas to us.
> Mr. Ames discussed the nature of time; he introduced many new ideas to us.

12.2 Semicolons and Conjunctive Adverbs

A semicolon is used between clauses joined by conjunctive adverbs or by phrases like *for example, in fact, for instance.*

The problem of absences has become acute; in fact, it is
first on the agenda for faculty consideration.

Three people had asked me to that movie; however, I had
promised Hubert that I would play Monopoly with him
that night.

Sir Walter Scott was only a silent partner in the bankrupt
firm; nevertheless, he assumed responsibility for
paying the debts.

Jill has a genius for leadership as well as many other talents;
for example, she can play three musical instruments.

Note that the conjunctive adverb or phrase is followed by a
comma in the examples above.

12.3 Semicolons Between Word Groups Containing Commas

A sentence containing a great many commas is difficult to
read. If commas precede the conjunction between main clauses,
another comma at this point would lose its value as a guide to
the reader.

A semicolon is used between main clauses joined by a conjunction if the clause before the conjunction contains commas.

The train stops at Davis, Foster, and Central Streets;
but it does not run at all after midnight.

The camp counselors planned games, races, and a variety
show; and everyone agreed that the program was successful.

A semicolon is used between a series of phrases if they contain commas.

My ambition is to be a lawyer; Noreen's, a photojournalist;
and Jack's, the owner of a chain of stores.

At the carnival Rick won a radio; Sandi, a cassette tape
recorder; and Rita, a huge panda bear.

The tickets for Thursday evening cost $3.50; Friday and
Saturday evenings, $5.00; and Sunday afternoon, $4.50.

Exercise: Two of the following sentences need no semicolons. For the other sentences, indicate the point at which a semicolon should replace a comma.

1. If you enjoy hunting and fishing, go to Maine, but if you enjoy crowds and excitement, go to Atlantic City.
2. Linda sang and danced in the school musical, and she won the archery tournament.
3. Inside the old house, it was dark, outside, the air was cool and fragrant.
4. In some ways I like geometry, in other ways I don't.
5. Stop in for your papers on Monday or Tuesday, otherwise, you may have to wait a whole week.
6. Mom would not change her mind and let us go, however, she agreed to our having company for dinner.
7. Thoreau was unlike many of his contemporaries, he would not compromise with his convictions.
8. Juanita is as excited as a child when it snows, she never saw a snowstorm until she was twenty.
9. On the night before, Bert went to bed early, consequently, he was at his best for the examination.
10. The following officers were elected: Elaine Berek, president, Jane Carrolton, vice-president, George Goodson, secretary.
11. Gritting his teeth, he steeled himself for the jab, but when the nurse injected the vaccine, he scarcely felt it.
12. On his short-wave set, Ed has received stations in Pusan, Korea, Anchorage, Alaska, Edmonton, Canada, and Shannon, Ireland.
13. Diane enjoyed the pictures of the Olympic Games, she was a newsphotographer and a track star herself.
14. Every morning he set out to sea, and every evening he returned with a boatload of fish.

12.4   Colons To Introduce Lists

The colon is used to throw the reader's attention forward to what follows. It is in some respects like an equal sign, saying that what follows is the explanation or equivalent of what has gone before.

A colon is used to introduce a list of items.

Usually, a colon is required when a list is preceded by the words *the following* or *as follows.* A colon is not used before a series of modifiers or complements immediately following the verb.

> We camped out at the following places: Lake Tahoe, Nevada; Jackson's Hole, Wyoming; and Yellowstone National Park. (list)
>
> His virtues are patience, wisdom, and understanding of human motives. (series of complements)
>
> The distinguishing features of the hog-nosed skunk are a hog-like snout, a broad white band across the back, and short, coarse fur. (series of complements)
>
> Information is available in encyclopedias, in atlases, and in dictionaries. (series of modifiers)

12.5   Colons with Formal Quotations

A colon is used to introduce a formal quotation.

> The president opened the meeting with these words: "We are beginning a period of expansion in which all of you will play a key role. Many of you will have added responsibilities; others will have entirely new responsibilities."

12.6   Colons Before Explanatory Statements

A colon is used between two sentences when the second explains the first. The second sentence begins with a capital letter.

> Now I understand what caused his downfall: His failure to admit his guilt and make a public apology turned away those who might have shown him mercy.
>
> I think I know the cause: I ate six chocolate eclairs.

12.7　Other Uses of the Colon

A colon is used (1) after the formal salutation of a letter, (2) between hour and minute figures of clock time, (3) in Biblical references, (4) between the title and subtitle of a book, (5) between numbers referring to volume and pages of books and magazines.

> Dear Sir or Madam: Genesis 2:4–7
> Dear Ms. Sims: *The Wide World: A High*
> 6:15 A.M. *School Geography*
> Volume II: pages 65–72

12.8　The Dash To Show Break in Thought

A dash is used to show an abrupt break in thought.

In dialogue, the break in thought is often caused by uncertainty or hesitancy as in the first example below.

> The trouble is—I suppose he knows it himself—he just
> can't get along with people.
> We are to meet at Mary's for the surprise—oh, here she comes.
> I am firmly convinced—but what weight do my opinions carry?

12.9　The Dash with Interrupters

A dash is used to set off a long explanatory statement that interrupts the thought.

> Robert Frost—who had to gain his first recognition abroad—
> is now considered by many to be America's most
> distinguished poet.
> There was a feeling of curious anticipation—a feeling shared
> throughout the world—when Communist China first
> invited the President of the United States to visit Peking.

12.10 The Dash Before a Summary

The dash is used after a series to indicate a summarizing statement.

> Old prints, faded manuscripts, the yellowed pages of books long out of print—these were his special delights.
>
> Simplicity of operation, low cost, assembly-line production—these were the factors that Henry Ford introduced to revolutionize the manufacture of automobiles and make them available to the masses.

Exercise: Copy the following sentences, inserting semicolons, colons, and dashes where necessary.

1. The plant shop sold only the following varieties English ivy, Swedish ivy, and grape ivy.

2. Alice telephoned to ask that on my way home I buy the following whole wheat bread, Swiss cheese, and dill pickles.

3. Jack promised to come at 5 30, but he was not even there by 6 15.

4. The title of the book is *Past to Present A World History*.

5. The newsboy apologized for his poor service he had been afraid of the dog.

6. Let me explain how I oh, here comes George!

7. My schedule this year includes the following subjects English III, French III, Algebra II, Physics II, and Physical Education III.

8. Eliza would not want a kitten for a pet she has a canary.

9. We can summarize Emerson's philosophy in these words "Trust thyself; every heart vibrates to that iron string."

10. Tom Saunders was a model student he made all A's; he was a talented football player; he worked constantly for the good of the school.

11. "He he didn't refuse you, did he?" asked Uncle Jack.

12. We went down the embankment in a hurry slid down, in fact.

13. I know how the accident happened by the way Jake stopped in a few minutes ago and left a message for you.

14. Do we can we send fourteen-year-olds out on the gridiron to be mauled and maimed?

15. Robert Holt shall we call him class clown was in the main hall "directing traffic."

16. In the general atmosphere of gaiety the dance was the high point of the holiday festivities Fred soon lost his feeling of homesickness.

17. Well, here we are face to face with a difficult and new problem difficult and new, that is, in the sense that we are strange to it.

18. The campus was beautifully planted with pin oaks, flowering trees, and a great variety of perennials all gifts of former graduating classes.

19. To arrive promptly, to concentrate on his work, to organize these were the things he found difficult.

20. Judge Potter she is a friend of my mother's helped me get a summer job.

12.11 Parentheses To Enclose Supplementary or Explanatory Words

Commas, dashes, or parentheses are used to set off words that are supplementary or explanatory. Commas are used when the material set off is fairly close to the main thought of the sentence. Dashes are used to set off material more loosely connected, and parentheses are used to set off material so loosely related to the main thought that it might be made a separate sentence.

There are few occasions in high school writing when parentheses are needed. The safest course for the student is to use commas, or even dashes, to set off parenthetical matter. If the material is so distantly related as to require parentheses, the passage might better be rewritten to place the parenthetical material in a separate sentence.

COMMAS ADEQUATE: Mark's best point, *which he saved for the end,* was that every group needs leadership.

DASHES REQUIRED:	Modern science no longer deals directly with the visible world—that is, it deals directly only with ions, atoms, electrons, and other particles that are too small to be seen.
PARENTHESES APPROPRIATE:	She speaks French and Arabic (her family has lived in France and the Middle East), but English is her first language.
PARENTHESES AVOIDED:	She speaks French and Arabic, since her family has lived in France and the Middle East, but English is her first language.

12.12 Punctuation Within Parentheses

Commas, semicolons, and periods are placed outside the closing parenthesis. The question mark and exclamation point are placed inside if the parenthetical material is itself a question or exclamation; otherwise, outside.

The performance begins promptly at 8:30 (no seating after the curtain).

Donna has four brothers; Alice, two (counting her stepbrother); Ann, three.

Everyone hoped that Jim would at least offer (as if he ever offered!) to help in the emergency.

I was not interested (why should I be?) in his plans.

12.13 Brackets

Brackets are used to enclose corrections or material inserted by a writer who is quoting someone else's material.

"On the 4th [5th] of March, Hayes took office." (correction)
The letter read: "We have him [Jordahl] at our mercy."
    (explanatory word inserted by the writer)

13.0 The Apostrophe

The apostrophe is used with nouns to show possession or ownership: *Mr. Carr's station wagon, Bob's boat, the doctor's coat.* The apostrophe is also used to show the following:

CLOSE RELATIONSHIP:	Jane's friend, someone's mother
SOURCE OR ORIGIN:	Ed's speech, Betty's idea
IDENTIFYING CHARACTERISTICS:	the man's expression, Bob's tone of voice, Terry's temper

13.1 The Possessive of Singular Nouns

The possessive form of a singular noun is usually made by adding an apostrophe and *s* ('s) to the noun.

boy + 's = boy's	city + 's = city's
Charles + 's = Charles's	Ross + 's = Ross's

When a singular noun of more than one syllable ends in *s*, the possessive *may* be formed by adding only the apostrophe.

waitress + ' = waitress'	witness + ' = witness'
Phyllis + ' = Phyllis'	Jesus + ' = Jesus'

13.2 The Possessive of Plural Nouns

If a plural noun does not end in s, add both apostrophe and s ('s) to form the possessive.

men + 's = men's   children + 's = children's
alumni + 's = alumni's   women + 's = women's

If a plural noun ends in s, add only the apostrophe to form the possessive.

horses + ' = horses'   waiters + ' = waiters'
actors + ' = actors'   editors + ' = editors'

Exercise: Number 1–20 on your paper. Write *correct* for each sentence in which the possessive form is correct. If the form is incorrect, write it correctly.

1. "The Children's Hour" is one of Longfellows best-known poems.
2. The witness' testimony greatly impressed the jury.
3. Jess's make-up was like an actress's.
4. Brooks's store is having a sale on mens' shoes.
5. Charles's father was invited to sit at the captains' table.
6. Our Olympic team did well in women's downhill skiing.
7. The Joneses dog barked all night.
8. The hostess' conversation put her guests at ease.
9. The jewels in the duchess' tiara were diamonds and emeralds.
10. Dad attended the alumnis' annual dinner.
11. Robert Burns's poems are beloved by the Scots.
12. Moses' Ten Commandments are also known as the Decalogue.
13. One canary birds' song could be heard over the mens' voices.
14. The Francis farm sits on a knoll between two oak trees.
15. Have you read Henry James's *Washington Square?*
16. Marcus' sister goes to a girl's preparatory school.
17. The heiress's estate was administered by her lawyers.
18. For Bess's birthday her mother gave her a handbag.
19. Both editor's arguments influenced the author's decision.
20. Squirrel's tails are not bushy in the springtime.

13.3   The Possessive of Compound Nouns

A **compound noun** is a noun composed of more than one word. Some compound nouns are written with hyphens between the parts.

Only the last part of a hyphenated noun shows possession.

mother-in-law + 's = mother-in-law's
editor-in-chief + 's = editor-in-chief's

Nouns such as *the Queen of England, the President of the United States, the Secretary of State* form the possessive by adding an apostrophe and *s* to the last word only: the *Secretary of State's name.* However, this awkward construction can be avoided by using an *of* phrase.

the jewels of the Queen of England
the address of the President of the United States
the name of the Secretary of State

13.4   Joint Ownership

When the names of two or more persons are used to show joint ownership, only the name of the last person mentioned is given the possessive form. Add an apostrophe or an apostrophe and *s* in accord with the spelling of that name.

Bob and Tom's family
fathers and sons' banquet
author and critic's correspondence

The rule applies also to firm names and to names of organizations.

Clarke and Taylor's sale
Brown, Jackson and Company's building
The League of Women Voters' pamphlet
Johnson and Andrews' advertisement

13.5   Separate Ownership or Possession

If the names of two or more persons are used to show separate ownership, each name is given the possessive form.

> Adams' and Jefferson's careers
> Webster's and Clay's orations

This construction may become awkward. It can be avoided by using an *of* phrase.

> the careers of Adams and Jefferson
> the orations of Webster and Clay
> the signatures of buyer and seller

13.6   Possessive of Indefinite Pronouns

Use an apostrophe and *s* to form the possessive of indefinite pronouns.

> someone + 's = someone's   nobody + 's = nobody's
> another + 's = another's   anyone + 's = anyone's

The apostrophe and *s* are added to the last word in forms like *someone else, anybody else, no one else:*

> no one else's   anybody else's

The apostrophe is not used to form the possessive of personal pronouns.

> NONSTANDARD   their's, your's, her's, our's, it's
> STANDARD   theirs, yours, hers, ours, its

13.7   Expressions of Time and Amount

When used as adjectives, words expressing time and amount are given the possessive form.

> a day's wages   ten minutes' walk

an hour's time	three days' wages
a month's delay	two hours' time
a week's vacation	four months' delay
a dollar's worth	two decades' history

Exercise: Copy the italicized words, changing them to show ownership or possession correctly.

1. Carrie's *sister-in-law* party was a great success.
2. The weather is *nobody* fault.
3. *Jane and Tim* cousin spent the week end with them.
4. The red scarf is *your's*; the blue one is *her's*.
5. Herb said, "It's a good fifteen *minutes* walk to the bus stop."
6. The *attorney-general* office is on the tenth floor.
7. The *Senator from Maine* motion was being considered.
8. The *accountant* and *taxpayer* signatures were on the tax return.
9. The *West Side Savings Bank* window was broken.
10. The workers struck for a two *week* vacation with pay.
11. I took *someone else* umbrella by mistake.
12. The *Marquess of Queensberry* rules are a code for the boxing ring.
13. The committee heard the *Secretary of Commerce* report.
14. There was a gala opening of *Clayton and Hart* store today.
15. The *catcher* throw cut-off the base runner.
16. The Quick Cleaners clean a suit in three *hours* time.
17. If that remark were *anybody else* except yours, I would get mad.
18. *Adams and Jefferson* letters are of great historical interest.
19. The *Governor of Ohio* address was the main speech at the dinner.
20. Those skis are *their's*; these are *our's*.

13.8 Apostrophes To Show Omissions

An apostrophe is used to show the omission of letters or figures.

the gold rush of '49   *1849*

the class of '79	*1979*
o'clock	*of the clock*
doesn't	*does not*

13.9 Plurals of Letters, Words, Numbers, and Signs

An apostrophe is used to show the plurals of letters, words, numbers, and signs used as words.

How many *s's* are there in Mississippi?
Beware of using too many *and's* in your themes.
His *7's* look like *9's*.
Make sure that your *+'s* look different from your *—'s*.

Note: The plurals of letters, numbers, signs, and words used as words are always italicized in print. In manuscript and type-script they may be underlined or placed in quotation marks. (See Section 14.7.)

Exercise A: Copy the following sentences, inserting an apostrophe (and *s*) where needed. This exercise reviews all the uses of apostrophes.

1. Shes the best basketball player on the team.
2. Havent you asked for a weeks vacation?
3. I can never distinguish your *is* from your *es*.
4. After ten days delay, the publisher answered my letter.
5. Mother belongs to two womens political groups.
6. Alice's conversation has too many *ands* and *buts*.
7. White and Judsons store has just installed escalators.
8. In the spring of 76 we visited Washingtons home at Mt. Vernon.
9. We discovered we had bought fifty dollars worth of groceries.
10. My brother-in-laws telephone number is unlisted.
11. Venus orbit is between Mercurys and the earths.

12. Is that jacket hers? It looks suspiciously like her sisters.
13. Columbus sailors threatened to throw him overboard.
14. A meeting was held in the editor-in-chiefs office.
15. Graces parents are planning to take a three months cruise.
16. We bought a record of one of Strauss waltzes.
17. Dahl and Gross store is having a fashion show today.
18. The bus leaves Harringtons Corner at six o'clock.
19. The Brooks dog goes over to Jim and Babs house every day.
20. No one else singing could compare with hers.

Exercise B: Write the possessive singular and the possessive plural of each of the following words:

1. day	6. salesperson	11. mouse
2. city	7. sister	12. woman
3. class	8. son-in-law	13. county
4. children	9. country	14. Jones
5. baby	10. lady	15. deer

Exercise C: The following sentences contain errors in the use of apostrophes. Copy the sentences, correcting all errors.

1. Margaret's and Don's mother, after two year's work in a bookstore, decided to start her own business.
2. Rutherford B. Hayes term of office was in the late 1800s.
3. Nancy said she hadnt read any of Keats poems.
4. Joan begins all her sentences with *sos*.
5. My sister spent the weekend at her mother's-in-law home.
6. Wasnt the five-oclock bus late tonight?
7. Bess' cake won a prize at the food fair.
8. Theres your jacket; Ive mended the sleeve.
9. Nobody elses violin was out of tune except Charles'.
10. Green's and Company store was closing just as I arrived.
11. I couldnt read Phils' writing because his *es* and *is* look alike and he never crosses his *ts*.

12. Which came first, Adams or Jeffersons' administration?
13. The dogs hairs were all over the visitors suit.
14. Dad didn't see anything funny in Louis and Steves jokes.
15. All the employees at Steven's and Clark's department store get two week's vacation.

14.0 Quotations

14.1 Quotation Marks Are Used To Enclose a Direct Quotation

In a direct quotation, the words of the speaker are directly quoted exactly as he spoke them.

> Montaigne said, "The greatest thing in the world is to know how to be yourself."
> "The horse," Jim said, "is rearing again."

An indirect quotation reports the meaning expressed by the speaker but does not give his exact words.

> INDIRECT The television announcer warned that a hurricane was approaching.
> DIRECT "A hurricane is approaching," the television announcer warned.

Quotation marks are not used with an indirect quotation.

14.2   Punctuation of Direct Quotations

Punctuation and capitals are used as follows in direct quotations:

1. **In dialogue, the first word of the quotation is capitalized.**
The material quoted from another writer may begin in the middle of a sentence. If so, the first word is not capitalized.

> Washington considered religion "an indispensable support" of government.

2. **The speaker's words are set off from the rest of the sentence.**
Note the placement of commas in these examples:

> The reviewer stated, "Doctorow's novel is a masterpiece."
> "Doctorow's novel is a masterpiece," the reviewer stated.

When the end of the quotation is also the end of the sentence, the period falls inside the quotation marks.

3. **If the quoted words are a question or an exclamation, the question mark or the exclamation point falls inside the quotation marks.**

In this situation no comma is needed.

> "How do you like your courses?" Sue asked.
> "Don't touch that!" he shouted.

4. **If the entire sentence is a question or an exclamation, the exclamation point or question mark falls outside the quotation marks.**

> Wasn't their campaign slogan "Tippecanoe and Tyler too"?
> I deny my opponent's charge that I am "avoiding the issues"!

5. **The colon and the semicolon at the close of a quotation fall outside the quotation marks.**

> The governor told his constituents that the following were on his list as "must legislation": a tax cut, aid to education and subsidy for city transit.
> Read A. E. Van Vogt's "The Enchanted Village"; then compare it with Stanley G. Weinbaum's "Parasite Planet."

6. Both parts of a divided quotation are enclosed in quotation marks. The first word of the second part is not capitalized unless it begins a new sentence

"It was a great shock," Harry said, "to hear of his illness."

"I recommend not telling the patient," the doctor said. "You may alarm him and aggravate his suffering."

7. In dialogue, a new paragraph and a new set of quotation marks show a change in speaker.

"Why do you want to drop out of school?" the counselor asked.

"I've been in school for ten years," Tony said. "I want to get out and earn some money."

"If you check the job market for unskilled workers," the counselor replied, "I bet you'll have as much chance to get a good job as you would to bat clean-up spot for the Yankees."

14.3   Quotations Within Quotations

Single quotation marks are used to enclose a quotation within a quotation.

Gary reported, "When somebody told Churchill not to end sentences with a preposition, Sir Winston replied, 'That is the kind of nonsense up with which I will not put.' "

Sheila asked, "Was it Roosevelt who said, 'The only thing we have to fear is fear itself'?"

14.4   Long Quotations

A quotation may be several paragraphs in length.

In long quotations, begin each paragraph with quotation marks. Place quotation marks at the end of the last paragraph only.

Exercise: Copy the following sentences, adding the necessary punctuation marks and capital letters.

1. Did you bring all the necessary documents asked the lawyer

2. The prosecuting attorney insisted that the witness answer the question

3. Return all books by Friday said the librarian or there will be a fine

4. If the groundhog sees his shadow on February 2 said Bonnie there are supposed to be six more weeks of winter

5. Why don't you take your vacation in winter she asked there are many Southern cruises

6. Just think said the comedian when Mozart was my age he'd been dead for two years

7. I was speeding the driver admitted but I am sure I did not pass a red light

8. When we get enough signatures she said we will hand the petition to the governor

9. I wish I could attend this school said Steve I like the gymnasium

10. Boonesboro Jack reported is the name of the first American settlement west of the Appalachians

11. Did she say yes or yes if your father agrees

12. Bill reported that Dick had declared flatly there are no trout in this stream

14.5   Setting Off Titles

The title of a book, magazine, newspaper, long pamphlet, or bulletin is usually italicized in print. In your own writing, you indicate the italics by underlining.

To distinguish the title of a *part* of a book, magazine, or newspaper, quotation marks are used.

Use quotation marks to enclose the titles of chapters and other parts of books and to enclose the titles of stories, poems, essays, articles, and short musical compositions.

> In *Literature of America* I read Shirley Jackson's story
> "The Lottery."
> Isaac Asimov's "Anatomy of a Martian" first appeared in
> *Esquire* Magazine.

14.6   Words Used in Special Ways

Words used in special ways or special senses are enclosed in quotation marks.

A writer may want to show that he is using a word as some-one else has used it. The writer can make clear that he himself does not accept this use of the word by enclosing it in quotation marks.

Slang words and phrases are also enclosed in quotation marks to indicate that the writer does not accept them as standard usage.

> The bank teller was immediately called "on the carpet" for
> a shortage in his accounts.
> Social workers now call poor people "the
> socially disadvantaged."
> My brother was once in the habit of called everything "far
> out"; the month before that, everything had been "groovy."
> The economists talked about making a study of
> "human resources."
> One reviewer actually wrote that her performance was the
> "definitive Lady Macbeth"!

Note: When a comma or period immediately follows the quoted word, it falls *inside* the quotation marks. The semicolon falls *outside* the quotation marks. See the third example above. If the quoted word appears at the end of a question or exclamation, the question mark or exclamation point falls *outside* the quotation marks. See the last example above.

14.7   Words Used as Words

A word referred to as a word is italicized in print. In writing, the word is underlined.

In general, avoid using the word *physiognomy* for *face*.
I dislike the words *oriented* and *orientation*.

When a word and its definition appear in the same sentence, the word is italicized and the definition is placed in quotation marks.

The word *perspicuity* means "clearness of expression."

Exercise: Copy the following sentences. Insert quotation marks where necessary. Indicate italics by underlining.

1. Mary said that she was reading Stephen Leacock's essay My Financial Career.

2. John asked her if that essay is included in Literary Lapses.

3. We asked the candidate what he meant by law and order.

4. Letters to the Editor in the May issue of Time is particularly entertaining.

5. Did the report say continuously or continually?

6. You will enjoy the chapter called The Long Snowfall in Rachel Carson's interesting volume The Sea Around Us.

7. We will have our first air-raid drill this morning, the voice from the loudspeaker announced.

8. The school I attended last year called them safety drills.

9. Have you read Shelley's poem To a Skylark?

10. The word impasto means painting in which the paint is laid on thickly.

11. She once wrote appitamy for epitome.

12. Clare Boothe Luce once called confused thinking about international affairs globaloney.

15.0 Spelling

If you have trouble with spelling, you may be consoled by the fact that other students for generations back have also had trouble. If you are interested in improving your spelling, you may be encouraged to know that many generations of poor spellers before you have learned to spell.

There is no simple way to teach you to spell. There is no easy way to learn. If you are concerned about the problem, however, there are several helpful suggestions:

1. **Proofread all your writing.** Even the ablest scholar may write "their" for "there" or "here" for "hear" in a first draft. Many apparent errors are not spelling errors at all. They are mistakes caused by carelessness and too much haste.

2. **Learn to look at the letters in a word.** Most of us have learned to read by recognizing whole words or parts of words. Spelling errors are errors in the letters that compose a word. You will find it helpful to break a word into its parts to see and to memorize the spelling of each part.

3. **Keep a list of your spelling errors.** The point is that you can spell correctly most of the words you use. Your errors fall within a narrow range. If you will concentrate on this range—provided by your list—you may show quick improvement.

4. **Practice on your own spelling problem.** There is no reason why you cannot totally eliminate spelling errors *if you want to.* One recommended procedure is to use a card pack. Print your problem words on cards in large letters. Take a card from the pack. Look at every letter and let the order of the letters sink into your mind. Pronounce each part of the word separately. Turn the card over. Write the word on a piece of paper. Turn the card over again and compare what you have written with the correct spelling.

5. **Memorize and apply the few rules of spelling given below.** Be sure you understand the rules, or your memory work will be wasted. Practice using the rules so that their use becomes automatic and you can write *bragging, reference, occurrence,* and so on, quickly.

Exercise: Divide these words into syllables. Do not be concerned as to whether they conform to the dictionary division. Just make sure that every word part has a vowel sound.

1. occurrence	7. humorous	13. italicize
2. accidentally	8. specifically	14. miniature
3. accommodate	9. necessary	15. extraordinary
4. incredible	10. disappearance	16. secretarial
5. miscellaneous	11. mimeograph	17. athletic
6. maintenance	12. immediately	18. privilege

15.1 The Final Silent e

When a suffix beginning with a vowel is added to a word ending in a silent e, the e is usually dropped.

believe + ing = believing	architecture + al = architectural
invite + ation = invitation	admire + able = admirable
ice + y = icy	fame + ous = famous
create + ive = creative	imagine + ary = imaginary

When the final silent e is preceded by c or g, the e is usually retained before a suffix beginning with a or o.

> courage +ous = courageous   peace + able = peaceable
> notice + able = noticeable

When a suffix beginning with a consonant is added to a word ending in a silent e, the e is usually retained.

> state + ment = statement   safe + ty = safety
> same + ness = sameness

The following words are exceptions: *truly, argument, judgment, wholly, awful.*

15.2   Words Ending in y

When a suffix is added to a word ending in y preceded by a consonant, the y is usually changed to i.

There are two exceptions: (1) When -ing is added, the y does not change. (2) Some one-syllable words do not change the y: *dryness; shyness.*

> merry + ment = merriment   sixty + eth = sixtieth
> city + es = cities   hazy + ness = haziness
> hurry + ed = hurried   carry + ing = carrying

When a suffix is added to a word ending in y preceded by a vowel, the y usually does not change.

> delay + ing = delaying   employ + er = employer
> enjoy + ed = enjoyed
>
> EXCEPTIONS: day + ly = daily, gay + ly = gaily.

Exercise A: Find the misspelled words in these sentences and spell them correctly.

1. The arrival of the fameous actress caused quite a stir.

2. Bill's argument was truely ridiculous.

3. The administrateion may soon be forced to take disciplineary action.

4. The icey air was exhilarateing.

5. Their efforts toward a peacable settlement were both createive and couragous.

6. The sofa bed, the heavyest item, was immoveable.

7. The guideance counselor is in his office dayly.

8. Dan's lazyness is outragous.

9. His motives are not wholely admireable.

10. Believing that the inviteation was meant for him, Joe accepted.

11. Some of Frank Lloyd Wright's architectureal achievements are truely exciteing.

12. The Americans easyly overran the Spanish fortifycations.

13. The merryment lasted until an incrediblely late hour.

14. We are planning a surprise celebrateion for my grandparents' fiftyeth anniversary.

15. We enjoyed drifting lazyly down the stream.

16. Mark staggered clumsyly with the two heavyest suitcases.

17. The defendant's hazyness in recalling certain details was noticeable.

18. Tolkien's characters, though imagineary, are thoroughly believeable.

Exercise B: Add the suffixes as shown and write the new word.

1. mystery + ous	11. worry + ing	21. move + ment
2. relay + ing	12. carry + ed	22. change + able
3. body + ly	13. enjoy + able	23. change + ing
4. frenzy + ed	14. create + ive	24. hurry + ing
5. appraise + ed	15. copy + ing	25. debate + able
6. waste + ful	16. educate + ion	26. hasty + ly
7. amaze + ing	17. assemble + age	27. merry + ly
8. insure + ance	18. wide + ly	28. ease + ly
9. grease + y	19. constitute + ion	29. day + ly
10. situate + ion	20. like + able	30. argue + ment

15.3   The Suffixes -ness and -ly

When the suffix -ly is added to a word ending in l, both l's are retained. When -ness is added to a word ending in n, both n's are retained.

gradual + ly = gradually   even + ness = evenness
actual + ly = actually   thin + ness = thinness

15.4   The Addition of Prefixes

When a prefix is added to a word, the spelling of the word remains the same.

dis + appear = disappear   dis + similar = dissimilar
mis + spell = misspell   re + commend = recommend
im + mobilize = immobilize   trans + ship = transship
il + legal = illegal   re + enter = re-enter

15.5   Words with the "Seed" Sound

Only one English word ends in *sede: supersede.*

Three words end in *ceed: exceed, proceed, succeed.*

All other words ending in the sound of *seed* are spelled *cede: secede, accede, recede, concede, precede.*

Exercise A: Correct the spelling errors in these sentences.

1. This faded old map is virtually ilegible.
2. Kansas is being penalized fifteen yards for ilegal proceedure.
3. The eveness of the two teams made the game unusualy exciting.
4. A re-examination of our foreign policy was considered unecessary.
5. The meeting is usualy preceeded by a pot luck supper.
6. Breaking a leg normaly imobilizes a person for months.

7. The captain's sterness caused disatisfaction among his crew.

8. Rays from iradiated cobalt or gold have successfully attacked cancerous tissue.

9. The SEC investigates iregularities in the stock market.

10. Scientists dissagree as to whether the nose cone actualy re-entered the atmosphere.

11. This exceptionaly brilliant youngster should be unusualy successful.

12. The officer answered civily that driving without a license was ilegal.

13. Nuclear-powered ships will eventualy supercede conventionaly powered types.

14. The prosecuting attorney dissagreed that the evidence was irelevant.

Exercise B: Add the suffixes and prefixes as indicated. Write the new word.

1. thin + ness	6. co + operate	11. confidential + ly
2. mis + stake	7. incidental + ly	12. re + examine
3. ir + relevant	8. im + mobilize	13. ir + radiate
4. im + moderate	9. uneven + ness	14. cordial + ly
5. dis + satisfied	10. im + moral	15. dis + solution

15.6   Words with ie and ei

When the sound is long e (ē), the word is spelled ie except after c.

i before e

relieve	priest	chief
believe	shield	yield
piece	brief	niece

except after c

receive	ceiling	deceit
perceive	conceive	receipt

Exceptions: either, neither, financier, weird, species, seize, leisure. You can remember these word by combining them into such a sentence as: *Neither financier seized either weird species of leisure.*

Exercise A: Correct the spelling errors in these sentences.

1. My neice is here for a breif visit.
2. In her liesure time, she often yeilds to mischeif.
3. I am releived that I have found the reciept.
4. Across the feild raced the Labrador retreiver.
5. I beleive this is a rare speceis of butterfly.
6. The Vikings siezed the initiative on the first play and never yeilded it.
7. Can you peice together these wierd happenings?
8. The releif pitcher did not yeild a single hit.
9. The financeir had decieved his best freind.
10. A wierd shreik peirced the stillness of the night.
11. The cheif of police cornered the theif at the end of a peir.
12. The power that Hitler weilded was almost inconcievable.
13. Neither driver would yeild the right of way.
14. This crossbeam should releive the wieght on the cieling.
15. C. M. Bowra's book *The Greek Experience* sums up the whole acheivement of Greek civilization.

Exercise B: Copy the words below, filling the blank spaces with *ie* or *ei*.

1. perc__ve
2. n__ther
3. c__ling
4. rec__pt
5. repr__ve
6. f__rce
7. n__ce
8. sh__ld
9. s__ze
10. p__ce
11. gr__vance
12. hyg__ne
13. p__r
14. spec__s
15. l__sure

15.7 Doubling the Final Consonant

Words of one syllable, ending in one consonant preceded by one vowel, double the final consonant before adding a suffix beginning with a vowel.

1. Words of one syllable ending in one consonant:

> heat   sleep   near   foot

The rule does not apply to these one-syllable words because two vowels precede the final consonant.

2. Words of one syllable ending in one consonant preceded by one vowel:

> big   brag   slug   fat

These words are the kind to which the rule applies.

These words double the final consonant if the suffix begins with a vowel.

> fat + er = fatter   slug + er = slugger
> big + est = biggest   plan + ing = planning

3. The final consonant is doubled in words of more than one syllable:
When they end in one consonant preceded by one vowel.
When they are accented on the last syllable.

> re·fer′   o·mit′   con·cur′

The same syllable is accented in the new word formed by adding the suffix:

> o·mit′ + ed = o·mit′ted
> re·fer′ + ed = re·fer′red
> con·cur′ + ence = con·cur′rence

If the newly formed word is accented on a different syllable, the final consonant is not doubled.

re·fer′ + ence = ref′er·ence
pre·fer′ + ence = pref′er·ence
con·fer′ + ence = con′fer·ence

Exercise A: Copy these words, indicating with an accent mark (′) where each word is accented.

1. control	7. allot	13. defer
2. excel	8. impel	14. benefit
3. limit	9. travel	15. admit
4. resist	10. distill	16. differ
5. omit	11. forget	17. infer
6. regret	12. murmur	18. propel

Exercise B: Add the ending indicated, and write the new word.

1. control + ing	11. put + ing	21. admit + ance
2. bat + ed	12. get + ing	22. let + ing
3. compel + ed	13. plan + ing	23. pad + ed
4. bed + ing	14. prefer + ed	24. murmur + ing
5. differ + ence	15. sit + ing	25. repel + ed
6. limit + ed	16. remit + ance	26. omit + ed
7. commit + ed	17. transfer + ing	27. commit + ed
8. book + ed	18. nod + ing	28. ton + age
9. fur + y	19. begin + ing	29. allot + ed
10. disappear + ed	20. expel + ed	30. defer + ed

16.0 The Plurals of Nouns

16.1 Regular Formation of Plurals

The plural of most nouns is formed by adding s.

employee + s = employees   door + s = doors
sense + s = senses   badge + s = badges

16.2 Plurals Formed with es

The plural of nouns ending in s, sh, ch, x, and z is formed by adding -es.

fox + es = foxes   church + es = churches
sash + es = sashes   class + es = classes

16.3 Plurals of Nouns Ending in y

When a noun ends in y preceded by a consonant, the plural is formed by changing the y to i and adding es.

city   citi + es = cities
beauty   beauti + es = beauties
company   compani + es = companies
worry   worri + es = worries

When a noun ends in y preceded by a vowel, a plural is formed by adding s.

play + s = plays   holiday + s = holidays
galley + s = galleys   alloy + s = alloys
delay + s = delays   valley + s = valleys

16.4   Plural of Nouns Ending in o

The plural of nouns ending in o, preceded by a vowel, is formed by adding s.

studio + s = studios   radio + s = radios
rodeo + s = rodeos   ratio + s = ratios
folio + s = folios   duo + s = duos

The plural of most nouns ending in o, preceded by a consonant, is formed by adding s, but for some nouns of this class the plural is formed by adding es.

piano + s = pianos   auto + s = autos
solo + s = solos   alto + s = altos
credo + s = credos

tomato + es = tomatoes   echo + es = echoes
potato + es = potatoes   hero + es = heroes

There are some words ending in -o with a preceding consonant that may form the plural with either s or es: *motto, mango, mosquito.* The safest thing to do is to memorize the few words that add -es and to consult the dictionary when in doubt about others.

16.5   Plural of Nouns Ending in f or ff

The plural of most nouns ending in f or ff is formed regularly by adding s.

waif + s = waifs   proof + s = proofs

chief + s = chiefs   gulf + s = gulfs
staff + s = staffs   sheriff + s = sheriffs

The plural of some nouns ending in <u>f</u> or <u>fe</u> is formed by changing the <u>f</u> or <u>fe</u> to <u>ve</u> and adding <u>s</u>.

leaf—leaves	knife—knives	life—lives
wife—wives	loaf—loaves	elf—elves
wolf—wolves	sheaf—sheaves	thief—thieves

Since most of these words with irregular plurals are in common use, careful listening may help you to spell them correctly. If you are doubtful about spelling, however, look up the singular form of the word in a dictionary. If the plural of a word is irregularly formed, the plural will be given immediately after the singular.

16.6   Nouns with Irregular Plurals

The plural of some nouns is formed by a change of spelling.

foot—feet	goose—geese
man—men	mouse—mice
woman—women	ox—oxen
child—children	basis—bases
datum—data	phenomenon—phenomena
index—indices *or* indexes	hypothesis—hypotheses

The plural and singular forms are the same for a few nouns.

sheep	crops	Chinese
deer	cattle	Portuguese

16.7   The Plural of Names

The plural of a name is formed by adding <u>s</u> or <u>es</u>.

George Wolf—the Wolfs   Joyce Williams—the Williamses
John Perry—the Perrys   Henry Jones—the Joneses

16.8 The Plural of Compound Nouns

When a compound noun is written without a hyphen, the plural is formed at the end of the word.

handful + s = handfuls   teaspoonful + s = teaspoonfuls
cupful + s = cupfuls   doghouse + s = doghouses

When a compound noun is made up of a noun plus a modifier, the plural is added to the noun.

brothers-in-law (the phrase *in law* is a modifier.)
commanders-in-chief (the phrase *in chief* is a modifier.)
attorneys-general (*general* modifies *attorneys*.)
notaries public (*public* modifies *notaries*.)
hangers-on (*on* modifies *hangers*.)
bills of sale (the phrase *of sale* modifies *bills*.)

The following are exceptions: *smashups, standbys, lean-tos.*

Exercise A: Form the plural of each of the following words.

1. gash	11. corps	21. phenomenon
2. life	12. cattle	22. sheriff
3. valley	13. staff	23. smashup
4. belief	14. church	24. teaspoonful
5. worry	15. grief	25. hanger-on
6. laboratory	16. wife	26. bill of sale
7. cupful	17. potato	27. notary public
8. holiday	18. handful	28. commander-in-chief
9. gulf	19. hypothesis	29. chief of police
10. loaf	20. basis	30. mother-in-law

Exercise B: Find the errors in plural forms in the following sentences.

1. The northern lights are an unusual phenomena.
2. There are several boxs of matches in the cupboard.
3. Passer-bys admired the photoes.

4. For home economics we bought oranges, potatos, and tomatos.

5. Our allys needed our help against their enemys.

6. The picnickers used dull knifes to cut the loafs of bread.

7. The childrens brought handsful of sand from the beach.

8. I have two brother-in-laws living in Milwaukee.

9. Use two cupsful of flour and two tablespoonsful of sugar.

10. None of the studioes is large enough for two grand pianoes.

11. There are too many autoes in our city.

12. Two sopranoes will sing solos.

13. The watchmens were neglecting their dutys.

14. The thiefs covered their faces with handkerchieves.

15. We saw over a dozen deers in the woods and in the vallies.

16. The wolfs have been attacking the sheeps.

17. Both of my brother-in-laws are fishermans.

18. There are still a few wild turkies in these valleys.

19. We are going on a picnic with the Thomas's and the Barry's.

20. Over one-fourth of all the people on earth are Chineses.

21. You must expect delayes in postal service during the holidays.

22. The opposing commander-in-chiefs met with their staffs.

23. The scientists advanced different hypothesises.

24. Shall we plant lily-of-the-valleys in our window boxs?

25. There are too many autoes on our highways.

17.0 The Forms of Letters

In general, there are two classes of letters: (1) *friendly letters*, and (2) *business letters*. Any letter written for business purposes is a business letter; all other letters—love letters, apologies, invitations, letters written home, etc., are called friendly letters.

The terms *friendly* and *business* are simply means of designating different forms. They do not refer to the tone in which the letter is written. A business letter may be extremely cordial and friendly. A friendly letter may be most businesslike. A friendly letter may, actually, be cold and unfriendly in tone.

There are two aspects to the forms of letters. The first pertains to the "letter picture," that is, to the arrangement of the content on the page. The second pertains to punctuation, forms of address, and other aspects of content.

17.1 The Friendly Letter

1. It is generally considered that a handwritten letter is more friendly, thoughtful, and considerate than a typed letter. None-

theless, friendly letters may be typewritten if the circumstances make typing appropriate.

2. Handwritten letters are written on personal stationery, which comes in assorted sizes and colors. Scented papers and papers of unusual color are not considered to be in good taste.

If a friendly letter is typed, plain white typing paper 8½″ by 11″ is appropriate.

3. While there is some choice as to the size, shape, and color of correspondence paper, there is no choice as to the writing instrument. Pen and ink are required; pencil is not appropriate.

The Picture of the Friendly Letter

Indented Style

Heading

201 Walton Lane
Toledo, Ohio 43619
May 3, 1977

Dear Joe,   Salutation

Body

Complimentary close   Sincerely yours,

Signature   Jack

Block Style

201 *Walton Lane*
Heading   *Toledo, Ohio* 43619
May 3, 1977

Dear Joe,   **Salutation**

_____

_____
_____
_____   **Body**
_____
_____

Complimentary close   *Sincerely yours,*
Signature   *Jack*

Style of the Friendly Letter

1. **The Heading.** The heading consists of the writer's address and the date. It is better not to use any abbreviations, but if you abbreviate one item such as Street (St.) or Avenue (Ave.), use abbreviations throughout. Always include the date.

No commas appear at the ends of lines. Commas appear only between the city and state and between the day and the year. Note that the state and zip code are not separated by a comma.

2. **The Salutation.** The salutation begins with the word *Dear* which is capitalized. The word *Dear* is not used with a person's last name alone. The salutation, for example, is *Dear Mr. Jones,* not *Dear Jones.*

The salutation of a friendly letter is followed by a comma.

3. **The Body.** The first paragraph begins with a paragraph indention. Each later paragraph begins with the same indention.

The left margin is even, on a vertical line below the first letter of *Dear*—. The right margin should be kept as even as possible. It is better to let a line run short than to hyphenate a word at the end of a line.

4. **The Close.** The close of a friendly letter varies with the situation. The only inappropriate close is *Very truly yours*, which is suitable only in business letters. The close may be *Yours, Love, With love, Sincerely, Cordially, Affectionately*, etc.

The first letter of the first word in the close is capitalized. No other capitals are used. The close is followed by a comma.

The Envelope

The picture of the envelope follows that of the letter itself. If the letter uses the indented style, for example, the envelope uses it too. The writer's address is placed in the upper left corner as a convenience to postal authorities.

Indented Style

James L. Cawder
1421 Northwood Drive
Pleasantville, New York 10570

Ms. Anne Byers
1401 Seminole Road
Wilmette, Illinois 60091

17.2   The Business Letter

The Picture of the Business Letter

Block Form

Heading	6 Evergreen Terrace Maplewood, New Jersey 07040 February 6, 1977
Costa Brothers 142 Millburn Avenue Camden, New Jersey 08107	Inside address
Dear Sir or Madam :	Salutation

_____

_____

_____

_____ Body

_____

_____

_____

Complimentary close	Sincerely yours,
Signature	Kelly O'Shea

Modified Block Form

Heading

6 Evergreen Terrace
Maplewood, New Jersey 07040
February 6, 1977

Costa Brothers
142 Millburn Avenue   Inside address
Camden, New Jersey 08107

Dear Sir or Madam :   Salutation

_____

_____
_____
_____ Body

_____
_____
_____

Complimentary close   Sincerely yours,
Signature   Kelly O'Shea

In both typed and handwritten business letters, it is desirable to keep the right margin even. The left margin must be kept even. In both forms of business letters, a full line space is left between paragraphs.

1. **The Heading.** The heading of a business letter follows the form of that in the friendly letter except that it is always in block form without indented lines. The letterheads of business firms always have the address printed on them. The heading, then, consists only of the date.

2. **The Inside Address.** The inside address is the address of the person or organization to whom the letter is written. If the writer wants the letter to go to a particular person in the organization, he may use either of two forms:

Ms. J. B. Bennett, Vice-President The Powers Company
The Powers Company 421 Main Street
421 Main Street Madison, Wisconsin 53703
Madison, Wisconsin 53703 *Attention:* Ms. J. B. Bennett,
          Vice-President

3. **The Salutation.** The salutation of a letter addressed to a business firm or to an organization is *Dear Sir or Madam.* The salutation of a letter addressed to an individual is *Dear ——.* If the writer knows intimately the person to whom he is writing, he may use that person's first name: *Dear Henry.*

The salutation of a business letter is always followed by a colon.

4. **The Close.** The close of a business letter is usually one of the following:

    Very truly yours, Yours truly,
    Yours very truly, Sincerely yours,
    Yours sincerely,

Only the first letter of the first word in the close is capitalized. The close is followed by a comma.

5. **The Signature.** In all typed business letters, the writer's name is typed below the close. The writer then signs his name above the typed name. The reason for typing the name is that many signatures are difficult to read.

The Envelope

Ms. Jane Allen
9 Satter Road
Red Oak, Iowa 51566

Payne and Company
1402 Massachusetts Avenue
Boston, Massachusetts 02138

Attention:
Personnel Manager

The writer's name and address appear in the upper left corner. The punctuation is the same as that of the heading. The first line of the address is placed just above the lower half of the envelope.

18.0 Good Manuscript Form

It is well established that readers will grade a paper higher if it is neat and legible than if it is messy in appearance and hard to read. Good manuscript form assures a good reading for what you have to say. Many high schools and colleges have regular forms that students are expected to follow. Others require manuscripts to follow the form described below.

18.1   Legible Writing

Few schools require that student papers be typewritten. A typed paper, however, is easier to read than one written by hand.

If a paper is written by hand, it should be written with pen and a dark blue or black ink. An ink of any other color is not acceptable. Letters should be formed so that there is no doubt as to what they are: *a*'s and *o*'s should be distinctly different; *u*'s and *i*'s should be distinct; if *i*'s are dotted, there can be no chance of their being mistaken for *e*'s.

18.2 Margins and Spacing

Leave a margin of an inch at the top, the bottom, and the right side of each page. The left margin should be slightly wider. If a paper is typed, the left-hand margin must be carefully maintained. The right-hand margin should be approximately the same, and it should be as even as possible without an excess of hyphens to show the break in a word. It is a good rule not to permit more than two successive lines to end with a hyphen.

All typed copy should be prepared with a double space between lines. Usually five letter spaces are provided for each paragraph indentation. One space separates each word; two spaces follow the end punctution of a sentence. If material must be deleted, it can be struck out by x's or capital M's.

18.3 Proper Labeling

Your teacher will give you instructions on the heading for your papers. Follow these instructions exactly. Usually, you will be expected to place your name at the upper right-hand corner of the first page. On a line below your name, you will place the name or number of the course, and on a third line, you will place the date.

Number each page beginning with page two. (Do not number the first page.) The number may be placed in the upper right-hand corner. To guard against loss or misplacement, you may place your name under the page number.

18.4 Placement of the Title

The title of a paper appears only on the first page. Place the title two lines below the last line of your heading, and center it. Allow two lines between the title and the first line of your copy.

Capitalize the first word and all important words in the title. See Section 10.12. If you are typing, do not capitalize every letter but only the initial letters. Do not underline the title; do not place it in quotation marks unless it is a quotation from some other source.

If a paper is longer than three or four pages, your teacher may ask you to supply a title page. This is a separate page containing the heading in the upper right-hand corner and the title centered on the page.

18.5 Preparation of Final Copy

No one can write a paper exactly as he or she wants it the first time. After you have written your first draft, read it over carefully. Revise and correct it. After you have completed your revision, make a final copy. Then read over this copy.

You may find that you have left out words, or you may find errors. You can insert words neatly by writing above the line where they should appear and by using a caret ($\wedge$) to show their position. You can make corrections neatly by drawing a line through a word and writing the correction above it. If more than two or three corrections per page are necessary, recopy the page.

18.6 Numbers in Writing

Numbers that can be expressed in fewer than four words are usually spelled out; longer numbers are written in figures.

They made a profit of *thirty-one thousand* dollars.
The new school plant cost *two million* dollars.
The only seat for the show was one for *five and a half* dollars.
Ms. Blackall wrote a check for $5,450 for a new car.

A number beginning a sentence is spelled out.

Twelve students from our school won scholarships.
Forty-six students saw *Othello* at the Playhouse in the Park.

18.7 Figures in Writing

Figures are used to express dates, street and room numbers, telephone numbers, page numbers, decimals, and percentages.

President Kennedy was assassinated on November 22, 1963.
The number of Al's room in the hospital is 537.
Send the letter to 5127 North Banner Street.
Joanne's new telephone number is 786–1905.
The test will cover the material on pages 27 through 68.
My temperature was only 98.1 degrees.
Only 20 percent of the students voted against the dance.

Note: Commas are used to separate the figures in sums of money or expressions of large quantities. They are not used in dates, serial numbers, page numbers, addresses, or telephone numbers:

INCORRECT	Thoreau's *Walden* was first published in 1,854.
CORRECT	Thoreau's *Walden* was first published in 1854.
CORRECT	The fare for the tour was $1,150.50.
CORRECT	The world's population increases by 100,000 a day.

Exercise: Copy these sentences, correcting any errors in the writing of figures. Three of the sentences are correct as they stand.

1. The Library of Congress has almost 400 miles of bookshelves.
2. The library contains nearly 16,000,000 books.
3. The population of Los Angeles is now over 3,000,000.
4. The cost of the house is $47,650.
5. Our telephone number here is 251–7,050.
6. The auditorium has a capacity of 700 people.

7. 5 of the students in my class want to go to Oberlin.

8. About sixty percent of our high school graduates go to college.

9. Taking the 1980 census requires the services of over one hundred thousand people.

10. Questionnaires were mailed to all 60,000,000 households in America.

11. The first census was taken in seventeen hundred and ninety.

12. My new address is three hundred twenty York Boulevard.

13. Over eight hundred people attended the lecture.

14. Helen's room number at the hospital is three twenty-eight.

15. The highest temperature ever recorded in this country is 134 degrees.

18.8 Abbreviations in Writing

Abbreviations may be used for most titles before and after proper names, for names of government agencies, and in dates.

BEFORE PROPER NAMES:	Dr., Mr., Mrs., Ms., Messrs., Rev., Hon., Gov., Capt.
AFTER PROPER NAMES:	Jr., Sr., D.D., Ph.D.
GOVERNMENT AGENCIES:	FBI, FCC, AEC
DATES AND TIME:	A.D., B.C., A.M., P.M.

There are no periods after abbreviations of government agencies.

The abbreviations of titles are acceptable only when used as part of a name. It is not acceptable to write *The secy. of the club is a dr.* The titles *Honorable* and *Reverend* are not abbreviated when preceded by *the: The Honorable John Ross.* They appear with the person's full name, not just the last name. Abbreviations are not appropriate for the President and Vice-President of the United States.

In ordinary writing, abbreviations are not acceptable for names of countries and states, months and days of the week, nor for words that are part of addresses or firm names.

UNACCEPTABLE	A new cultural center was built in N. Y.
BETTER	A new cultural center was built in New York.
UNACCEPTABLE	Forty-six thousand U.S. troops died in battle in Vietnam.
BETTER	Forty-six thousand United States troops died in battle in Vietnam.
UNACCEPTABLE	Bart works for the Spalding Adv. Co.
BETTER	Bart works for the Spalding Advertising Company.
UNACCEPTABLE	School will reopen on Mon., Sept. 3.
BETTER	School will reopen on Monday, September 3.

In ordinary writing, abbreviations are not acceptable for the following: names of school courses, *page, chapter, Christmas,* and words standing for measurements such as *bu., in., hr., min., sec.*

Exercise: Correct the errors in abbreviation in the following sentences.

1. The Clarke Chem. Co. is a mfr. of pharmaceutical products.
2. Mr. Hollis and Chas. Dutton attended a convention in Evanston, Ill.
3. You have an appointment with Dr. Walsh on Thurs. at 3 P. M.
4. The vice-pres. presides in the absence of the pres.
5. Mom and Dad's checking account is at the 1st Nat'l Bank.
6. Isn't your father a vice-pres. of his co.?
7. My sister has to read ten chaps. a wk. in her phil. course.
8. Look at the chart on the second p. of Chap. 9.
9. What day of the wk. does Xmas fall on?
10. Aunt Sylvia is treas. of the Forbes Mfg. Co.
11. Rev. John Barry will speak at the Norton H.S. graduation ceremony.
12. The 747 flew from Los Angeles, Cal. to New York in 5 hr. and 30 min.

18.9 Italics for Titles

The word *italics* is a printer's term. It refers to a kind of type. When a writer wants the printer to set a word in italic type, he underlines it in his manuscript.

Titles of complete books and plays, of newspapers, magazines, works of art, and long musical compositions are printed in italics. The names of ships, trains, and airplanes are also printed in italics.

PRINTED FORM — The orchestra is rehearsing Handel's *Messiah*.

MANUSCRIPT FORM — The orchestra is rehearsing Handel's <u>Messiah</u>.

PRINTED FORM — A *Man for All Seasons* is a provocative play about St. Thomas More.

MANUSCRIPT FORM — A <u>Man for All Seasons</u> is a provocative play about St. Thomas More.

PRINTED FORM — Look in the *New York Times* for the President's arrival in *Air Force One*.

MANUSCRIPT FORM — Look in the <u>New York Times</u> for the President's arrival in <u>Air Force One</u>.

18.10 Italics for Foreign Words and Phrases

Many foreign words have become so widely used that they are now part of the English language: *chauffeur, cul-de-sac, entrepreneur*. These naturalized words are printed in regular type. Foreign words and phrases that have not become naturalized in our language are printed in italics: *cum laude, bon vivant, mirabile dictu*.

The only way to be sure whether a word or phrase of foreign origin should be printed in italics (underlined in manuscript) is to consult the dictionary.

18.11 Italics for Words, Letters, or Figures

Italics are used for words, letters, or figures referred to as such.

In printed works, words, letters, or figures referred to as such are in italics. In writing, they are underlined.

PRINTED FORM	The *to* should have been written *too*.
MANUSCRIPT FORM	The to should have been written too.
PRINTED FORM	In Australia, the long *a* is pronounced as long *i*.
MANUSCRIPT FORM	In Australia, the long a is pronounced as long i.

18.12 Italics for Emphasis

Italics (underlining) are used to give special emphasis to words or phrases.

The tendency in modern writing is to avoid the use of italics for emphasis. One reason is that italic type is considered harder to read than regular (roman) type, particularly if there is a great deal of it. Another reason is that modern writers are developing a direct, straightforward style which gives emphasis to important words without use of printing devices.

In high school writing, use italics for emphasis only to make meaning clear.

> The writer *implies* a suggested meaning; the reader *infers* it.
> The opposite of pure science is *not* impure science, but *applied* science.

18.13 Correction Symbols and Revision

Both in high school and in college your teacher will make marginal notes on your themes and reports before returning them to you. These notes will indicate errors or awkward passages that require rewriting. The correction of errors will make you alert to their recurrence in your later writing. Practice in rephrasing an awkward sentence will give you greater skill in turning out careful, clear writing that means what you want it to mean.

Many schools and colleges have their own system of indicating writing faults briefly. If your school has such a system of abbreviations, it will be made available to you. Your teachers may prefer to use the symbols listed below. These are symbols used by professional copyreaders who work for publishers. The manuscript bearing the marks is returned to the author, no matter how experienced or professional he may be, for correction and revision before the manuscript is set in type.

ab   *Abbreviation.* Either the abbreviation is not appropriate or the abbreviation is wrong. Consult a dictionary.

agr   *Agreement.* You have made an error in agreement of subject and verb or of pronoun and antecedent. Consult Sections 5.1 and 6.13 in your Handbook.

awk   *Awkward.* The sentence is clumsy. Rewrite it.

cap   *Capital letters.* You have omitted necessary capitals. Consult Section 10 in your Handbook.

cf   *Comma fault.* You have joined two sentences together with a comma. Change the punctuation.

dang   *Dangling construction.* You have written a verbal phrase in such a way that it does not tie up to another word in the sentence. Rewrite the sentence.

frag   *Sentence fragment.* You have placed a period after a group of words that is not a sentence. Join the fragment to an existing sentence or add words to complete the thought.

ital   *Italics.* You have omitted italics that are needed.

k   *Awkward.* See *awk* above.

lc *Lower case.* You have mistakenly used a capital letter where a small letter is required.

ms *Manuscript form.* You have not followed the proper manuscript form. Consult Section 18 in your Handbook.

no ¶ *No paragraph.* You have started a new paragraph too soon. Join these sentences to the preceding paragraph.

¶ *Paragraph.* Begin a new paragraph at this point.

nc *Not clear.* Your meaning is not clear. Rewrite the passage to say what you mean.

om *Omission.* You have left out words that are needed for clarity or smoothness of style.

p *Punctuation.* You have made an error in punctuation. Consult Sections 11, 12, 13, or 14 in your Handbook for sentences like the one you have improperly punctuated.

ref *Reference.* There is an error or a weakness in the reference of pronoun to antecedent. Consult Section 6 in your Handbook.

rep *Repetition.* You have repeated a word too often, or you have repeated something you wrote in preceding sentences.

shift *Shift.* You have shifted point of view or tense needlessly.

sp *Spelling.* You have misspelled a word. Consult a dictionary.

t *Tense.* You have used the wrong tense form. Consult Section 8 in your Handbook.

tr *Transpose.* You have misplaced a modifier; consult Chapter 10. Or, your meaning would be clearer if a sentence or passage were placed at another point.

wd *Wrong word.* You have confused homonyms, or you have used a word that does not fit the meaning, or you have used a slang word inappropriately. Consult Section 9 in your Handbook, or a dictionary.

Index

Index

Red numbers refer to pages in the Handbook
(the second half of this book).

Sources of Quoted Material

Page 17: William Collins + World Publishing Company, for entry from *Webster's New World Dictionary of the American Language,* Students Edition; copyright © 1976 by William Collins + World Publishing Company, Inc. Page 93: Harold Matson Company, Inc., for selection from *The Terrible Teens* by Herman Wouk; copyright 1957 by Herman Wouk. Page 94: Curtis Brown, Ltd., for selection from *This Hill, This Valley* by Hal Borland; copyright © 1957 by Hal Borland. Page 96, paragraph 1: Harcourt Brace Jovanovich, Inc., for selection from "Fair and Circus Days" from *Prairie-Town Boy* by Carl Sandburg; copyright © 1952, 1953, by Carl Sandburg. Page 97, paragraph 4: E. P. Dutton & Company, Inc., for selection from *Geronimo: His Own Story,* edited by S. M. Barrett; Introduction and notes copyright © 1970 by Frederick W. Turner, III. Page 97, paragraph 5: Broude & Hochberg, for selection from "My Well Balanced Life on a Wooden Leg" by Al Capp, reprinted by permission of Julie Cairol. Page 98, paragraph 8: Curtis Brown, Ltd., for selection from *This Hill, This Valley* by Hal Borland; copyright © 1957 by Hal Borland. Page 100, paragraph 1: Harold Ober Associates Inc., for selection from *Science Has Spoiled My Supper* by Philip Wylie; copyright © 1954 by The Atlantic Monthly Press. Page 101, paragraph 3: Random House, Inc., for selection from "Lola," from *The Dogs Bark: Public People and Private Places,* by Truman Capote. Page 101, paragraph 4: Harper & Row, Publishers, Inc., for selection from "Where's Everybody?", from *The Challenge of the Spaceship* by Arthur C. Clarke, copyright 1957 Arthur C. Clarke. Page 102, paragraph 6: Farrar, Straus & Giroux, Inc., for selection from *Everything That Rises Must Converge* by Flannery O'Connor; copyright by the Estate of Mary Flannery. Page 103: Houghton Mifflin Company, for selection from *A Time to Speak* by Archibald MacLeish, copyright © 1941 by Houghton Mifflin Company. Page 104, paragraph 1: *Fortune,* for selection from "How To Be an Employee" by Peter F. Drucker, *Fortune* Magazine, May 1952. Page 104, paragraph 2: Saturday Review, for selection from "Credo" by Frank W. Abrams, *Saturday Review,* January 23, 1954. Page 105, paragraph 4: Farrar, Straus & Giroux, Inc., for selection from "The Washwoman" from *A Day of Pleasure* by Isaac Bashevis Singer, copyright © 1962, 1963, 1964, 1966, 1969 by Isaac Bashevis Singer. Page 105, paragraph 5: The Viking Press Inc., for selection from "A Yo-yo Going Down, a Mad Squirrel Coming Up" by Frank Conroy from *Stop Time* by Frank Conroy; copyright © 1967 by Frank Conroy. Page 105, paragraph 6: Mrs. James Thurber, for selection from "Doc Marlowe" in *Let Your Mind Alone;* copyright © 1937; copyright © 1965 by Helen W. Thurber and Rosemary Thurber Sauers. Originally appeared in *The New Yorker.* Page 106, paragraph 7: Harper & Row, Publishers, Inc., for selection from "Seeing" from *Pilgrim at Tinker Creek* by Annie Dillard; copyright 1974 by Annie Dillard. Page 106, paragraph 8: Curtis Brown, Ltd. for selection from *This Hill, This Valley* by Hal Borland; copyright © 1957 by Hal Borland. Page 107: Harper & Row, Publishers, for selection from *Life on the Mississippi* by Mark Twain. Page 108, paragraph 3: Doubleday & Company, Inc., for selelction from *The Winged Horse* by Joseph Auslander and Frank Ernest Hill, from *The Winged Horse Anthology* by Joseph Auslander; copyright 1927, 1929 by Joseph P. Auslander. Page 109: Curtis Brown Ltd., for selection from *The Fan Club* by Rona Maynard. Page 111, paragraph 2: Oxford University Press, Inc., for selection from *The Sea Around Us* by Rachel L. Carson; copyright © 1950, 1951, 1961 by Rachel L. Carson. Page 113: McGraw-Hill Ryerson Ltd., Toronto, for selection from "Boys and Girls" from *Dance of the Happy Shades* by Alice Munro. Page 114: The Viking Press Inc., for selection from "A Yo-yo Going Down, A Mad Squirrel Coming Up," from *Stop Time* by Frank Conroy, copyright 1967 by Frank Conroy. Page 115: Harcourt, Brace Jovanovich, for selection from "The Artificial Nigger" by Flannery O'Connor; copyright © 1955 by Flannery O'Connor, reprinted from her volume *A Good Man Is Hard To Find and Other Stories.* Page 116, paragraph 2: Random House, Inc., for selection from *All about Cats* by Carl Burger; copyright 1966 by Carl Burger. Page 116, paragraph 3: J. B. Lippincott Company, for selection from "Jungle and Desert," *Latin American Cultures,* edited by Paul Thomas Welty. Page 120: American Heritage Publishing Co., Inc., for a selection from *The World Trade Center: Does Mega-architecture Work?* by Thomas Meehan, from HORIZON (Fall 1976); copyright © 1976 American Heritage Publishing Co., Inc. Page 121: Macmillan Publishing Co., Inc., for selection from "Harriet Tubman" in *Women Who Shaped History* by Henrietta Buckmaster; copyright © 1966 by Macmillan Publishing Co., Inc. Page 125, paragraph 5: Charles Scribner's

Correction Symbols

ab	abbreviation
agr	agreement
awk	awkward
cap	capital letters
cf	comma fault
dang	dangling construction
frag	sentence fragment
ital	italics
k	awkward
lc	lower case
ms	manuscript form
no ¶	no paragraph
¶	paragraph
nc	not clear
om	omission
p	punctuation
par	parallelism
ref	reference
rep	repetition
shift	shift
sp	spelling
t	tense
tr	transpose
wd	wrong word

For a detailed explanation of these correction symbols, see Handbook **Section 18.13.**

Handbook

The page numbers for the Handbook (the second half of this book) appear in red.